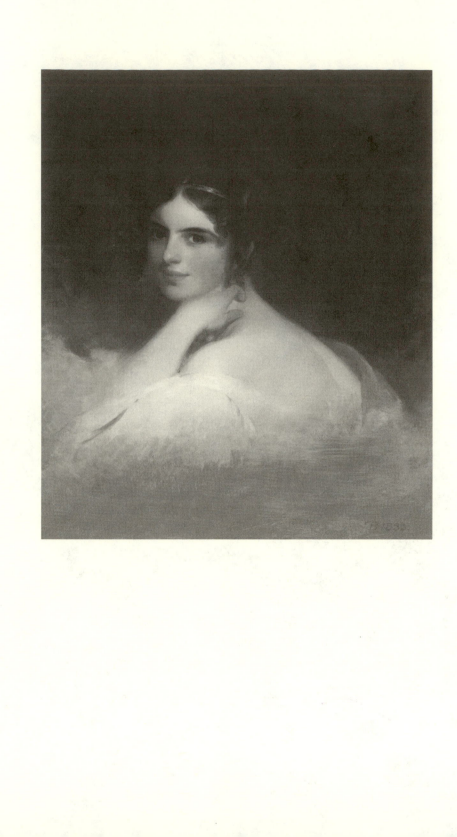

Fanny Kemble

A Performed Life

DEIRDRE DAVID

*for Bruce and London,
best of friends,
With much affection,
Deirdre, July 2007*

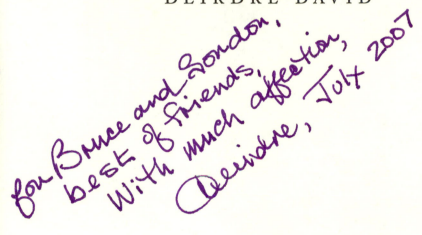

PENN

UNIVERSITY OF PENNSYLVANIA PRESS

PHILADELPHIA

Published by
University of Pennsylvania Press
Philadelphia, Pennsylvania 19104-4112

Printed in the United States of America on acid-free paper
10 9 8 7 6 5 4 3 2 1

LIBRARY OF CONGRESS CATALOGING-IN-PUBLICATION DATA

David, Deirdre.
Fanny Kemble: a performed life / Deirdre David.
p. cm.
Includes bibliographical references and index.
ISBN-13: 978-0-8122-4023-8 (alk. paper)
ISBN-10: 0-8122-4023-5 (alk. paper)
1. Kemble, Fanny, 1809–1893.
2. Actors—Great Britain—Biography. I. Title.
PN2598.K4 D38 2007   2007017365

Frontispiece: *Frances Anne Kemble as Beatrice*, 1833, by Thomas Sully.
Courtesy of the Pennsylvania Academy of the Fine Arts, Philadelphia.
Bequest of Henry C. Carey (the Carey Collection).

For Barry Qualls
"What larks!"

Contents

Illustrations

Prologue

Before the Curtain

A prouder nature never fronted the long humiliation of life.
—Henry James, "Frances Anne Kemble,"
Temple Bar, April 1893

On October 5, 1829, the audience at Covent Garden Theatre eagerly awaited the acting debut of Frances Anne Kemble (known always as Fanny).[1] The packed house had enjoyed the overture to *The Magic Flute*, and now the noisy crowd in the pit polished off its meat pies and the better-behaved people in the boxes adjusted their shawls and stopped scrutinizing their neighbors. The play was *Romeo and Juliet* and much was promised: a funeral procession in Act V with a solemn dirge, Fanny's vivacious mother as Lady Capulet, her darkly handsome father as Mercutio, and the first stage appearance of the newest member of the Kemble acting dynasty to enter the profession.

Theatrical nepotism was a Kemble trademark and audiences had been seeing them perform together for over fifty years. Fanny's grandfather, Roger Kemble, perhaps an actors' hairdresser but certainly a strolling player before his marriage in 1753 to Sarah Ward, the daughter of a manager of a Birmingham acting company, was an actor-manager on the West Country circuit. Sarah, a woman of remarkable physical stamina, gave birth to twelve children between 1755 and 1777, in most cases performing right up to the moment of her confinements. Her Lady Macbeth was said by Charles Young (1777–1856), a well-known Shakespearean actor and friend of the Kemble family, to have been the greatest he had ever witnessed: as a young man, he saw her act in a barn, and he declared much later in life that the performance was never surpassed, even by her famous daughter, Sarah Siddons.[2]

In the late eighteenth and early nineteenth centuries, the Kembles seemed to be everywhere in the theater world; as actors or managers (sometimes both), they constituted one of the great dynasties of the British stage, their fame similar to that enjoyed by such charismatic twentieth-century theater families as the Redgraves.[3] Fanny's uncle John Philip Kemble dominated in London, enthralling Covent Garden audiences with his majestic performances of Coriolanus and Macbeth, and entertaining them with extravagant productions that featured elaborate, historically accurate costumes and vast crowd scenes (for the triumphal ovation scene in *Coriolanus,* for instance, he mustered 164 people onstage).[4] The same audiences worshiped Fanny's aunt Sarah Siddons, who moved them to tears and terror with her mesmerizing performance in tragic roles, and Fanny's father, Charles Kemble, after a rocky start, gained prominence at the age of eighteen as a sensitive and romantic leading man. Another uncle, Stephen Kemble, managed theaters in Sunderland, South Shields, and Newcastle, and until his death in 1815, Fanny's cousin Henry Siddons had controlling interests in the principal theaters in Dundee and Edinburgh. Fanny's aunt Elizabeth Kemble Whitlock, laboring in the shadow of her sister Sarah, toured extensively in America at the end of the eighteenth century, and another aunt, Ann Julia, worked sporadically as an itinerant actress in the provinces.[5]

Born in 1809, Fanny was the second child of Charles Kemble and Marie-Thérèse de Camp, a winsome comic actress who was the daughter of a French musician and a woman about whom we know little beyond the fact that she was also French. In 1776, shortly after the birth of Marie-Thérèse, George Louis de Camp brought the family to London, where he found employment as a flautist in several theater orchestras, and where the talented Marie-Thérèse made her dancing debut at Drury Lane at the age of six. By the time she married Charles Kemble (in 1806), she had become a lively figure on the London stage, admired for her petite yet voluptuous figure, her dramatic singing voice, and her saucy comic acting. Fanny Kemble, then, was a child of the theater. She grew up in a heady atmosphere of theater gossip and ambitious nursery theatricals, encouraged as a child to perform by acting aunts and uncles and educated as a teenager at French schools in languages, music, and dancing. Yet at the moment of her theatrical debut in October 1829, her entry into the family business, she was unable to step onstage. Terrified by the weight of the Kemble heritage and the brevity of her three weeks' training for the occasion, she had to be pushed from the wings to answer Lady Capulet's call for Juliet. It was only after her love of Shakespeare's verse conquered her dread of failure that her melodious voice and unexpected command of early nineteenth-century theatrical technique convinced the audience she was a true Kemble.[6]

What the audience saw was a short and somewhat sturdy nineteen-year-old girl with luxuriant dark hair, enormous thick-fringed dark eyes, a large nose, and a rather spotty complexion. The dark coloring and the prominent features came from her father and the compact body and blotched skin she owed to her mother, who had, with the best intention, deliberately infected sixteen-year-old Fanny with smallpox as protection against catching it from her younger sister, Adelaide. Gaslight and makeup helped disguise the pitted complexion, however, and the audience on this October evening was mainly interested in how closely Fanny resembled her Aunt Siddons. The Kemble coloring was there and the flaming dark eyes were definitely Sarah's, as was the deep-pitched, resonant voice, but Fanny's short-waisted body and large hands and feet did not compare well with the statuesque suppleness of her aunt. In her memoirs (begun when she was in her sixties), Fanny ruefully confesses a feeling that she had been, all her life, "a very plain likeness" of her "very handsome family."[7] Where Sarah Siddons's face had been elegant and regular, hers, she felt, was snub and uneven, and the person she believed she most resembled was her grandmother, Mrs. Roger Kemble. But in October 1829, Fanny's charismatic stage presence overshadowed the physical irregularities and she was a tremendous hit. Her picture appeared in shop windows almost immediately, young men started sporting Fanny Kemble neck scarves, and her glamorous celebrity provided a tonic for the enfeebled Covent Garden box office, which was why she had gone onstage in the first place.

This narrative of reluctant fame is told by Fanny Kemble herself in a number of places in her autobiographical writings, which she began with *Record of a Girlhood*, published in 1879 when she was seventy, elaborated in *Records of Later Life* (1882), and completed in *Further Records* (1891), two years before her death. This narrative also figures in the *Journal* she published in 1835, which relates in often acerbic fashion the triumphs and travails of the acting tour of major American cities that she undertook with her father from 1832 to 1834. Moreover, it is a story to which she returns in letters to her friends and which she evokes with some frequency in her essays on acting, on performing, and on reading Shakespeare. Wherever the narrative appears, it remains one of reluctant transformation from accomplished and bookish girl to glamorous star, of moral disdain for the theater and preference for intellectual work. Shaping her narrative with considerable dramatic skill, Fanny Kemble comes onstage, as it were, revealing to the reader how fully she was formed by the theatrical culture in which she had been steeped from early childhood.

One critic has noted that in the nineteenth century the self-presentation of a public woman in autobiography was "no less a performance than anything she undertakes on stage," and I have found this to be particularly apt in telling Kemble's story.[8] Whether prancing in the garden at the age of eight for the entertainment of the Kemble neighbors, assuming her stately place to read Shakespeare to adoring transatlantic audiences, or crafting poems, plays, and memoirs, Kemble was a consummate performer. As her biographer, I have, in a sense, been her audience and I have witnessed her both literally and metaphorically onstage. To be sure, like all of Kemble's biographers, I have studied the published texts, the extant letters, the observations of contemporaries, and the reviews of her professional appearances, but I have done so less as a detective bent on discovery of the "truth" behind a performance than as a cultural critic intent on seeing how the performance itself has been put together.

In some ways, too, I have adopted an approach to understanding the life of a public figure that was advocated by Kemble herself. While in America in August 1832, she wrote in her *Journal*, "we must not look for the real feelings of writers in their works . . . what they give us, and what we take for heart feeling, is head weaving . . . bearing the same resemblance to reality that a picture does; that is—like feeling, but not feeling—like sadness, but not sadness, like what it appears, but not indeed the very thing."[9] For a biographer, "the very thing" remains, obviously, the constructed result of interpretation, and in what follows I have inevitably favored certain interpretive perspectives over others. However, when I have ventured, say, into psychological, feminist, or material explanation of Kemble's behavior, it has been through an interpretive prism that she herself identifies and elaborates. As I shall explain in a moment, my reading of her life has been grounded in her *own* interpretations of her temperament, her familial inheritance, and her behavior. If I have been present in this biography, it is not in the sense that the biographer invents herself as a character in the life of the subject, but rather as a feminist critic alert to my subject's resistance to prescribed nineteenth-century codes for women's lives.

The interpretations by Fanny Kemble's contemporaries of her "appearances" in their lives confirm that she was very often onstage, even when off. The American novelist Catharine Sedgwick, for example, was so dazzled by Kemble's social charisma that she worried about her own enslaved attention: Kemble was "an enchantress not to be resisted."[10] That Kemble was wittily conscious of her own dramatic presence in the lives of friends and acquaintances is revealed in a story told by S. Weir Mitchell, the Philadelphia physician who specialized in women's neurasthenic disorders. Visiting Kemble at York Farm, a cottage just outside the city where she was living when in her sixties, and finding her unable to provide dinner since she had been let down by the butcher, he made to leave: "No, do not go yet," she said. "Never again will you have these chances to talk with a woman who has sat at dinner alongside of Byron, who has heard Tom Moore sing, and who calls Tennyson, Alfred."[11] An actress on and off the stage, Kemble knew that in her own way she embodied nineteenth-century cultural history, recognized that she had been part of the show, and had almost always played to an audience.

Anyone who writes about Fanny Kemble must acknowledge that what *she* wrote about *herself* was, for the most part, written a long time after the events described. The three volumes of her memoirs were assembled over a twelve-year period, begun when she was in her mid-sixties and completed when she was in her late seventies. The memoirs are based almost entirely on a notably voluminous correspondence conducted over a period of fifty years between Kemble and her dearest friend, an Anglo-Irish woman named Harriet St. Leger; when Leger was close to death (in 1878), she returned to Kemble all the letters she had received from her. After editing and assembling the letters for her memoirs, Kemble destroyed them all. As published, they constitute a rich record of transatlantic society as seen through the eyes of an intelligent woman, and their seductive vitality has led some of Kemble's biographers to ground their interpretations of her life in an unexamined acceptance of the memoirs as though they were the "facts" of the story.[12] For me, however, the complex textual nature of the letters has provided compelling evidence of the "fact" that Kemble wanted to perform her life in her memoirs as she had aimed to perform it in actuality. She edited the letters, arranged them so that they formed a dramatic narrative, and interpolated commentary that is both about the events described in the letters and about her own feelings at the time she is, in actuality, editing them.

Kemble was undoubtedly strongly influenced by the conventions of theatrical autobiography as described by a critic who traces the emergence of this genre at the end of the eighteenth century. For him, these theatrical autobiographies are notable for well-rehearsed anecdotes; they are "episodic, chatty, and, of course, self-aggrandizing. Their defining character, and often their charm, depends upon the self-serving performance of the autobiographer, a masquerade moved from stage to page."[13] Kemble's primary literary model, for this same critic, is not the drama but the novel. Without question, familiar motifs of the nineteenth-century novel are found in Kemble's writings—one thinks of a powerful family and spirited heroine, difficult marriage and betrayal, delineation of domestic manners and public politics, and a social preoccupation with money—but it is the manner in which she *presents* these tropes that reveals her style as influenced more by dramatic than novelistic conventions. Indeed, she considered herself hopeless at novel writing (her sentences she dismisses as "the comicallest things in the world" by virtue of the end forgetting the beginning and the whole appearing as a "perfect labyrinth of parenthesis within parenthesis"),[14] and in her narratives of family, fame, and emotional struggle, she sets scenes, paints pictures, and moves herself and her supporting actors on and off the page.

The writing Kemble liked doing best was thick with allusions to Shakespeare's characters and studded often with quotations from *The Tempest* (her favorite of all his plays). In her memoirs, the setting of a significant scene in her life is often exactly that, a *scene,* as we see vividly, for example, in the descriptions of herself at her writing table on her husband's Georgia rice and cotton plantations during 1838–39. She creates a painting in which the placement of the furniture, the lighting, and the movement of the "actors"—the slaves of her husband, Pierce Butler, in this case—are carefully arranged. In a skillfully managed tableau, she sits writing about the slaves watching her writing about them. By both presenting her life in her autobiographical writing as riven by conflict and difficulty *and* simultaneously revealing the means by which she managed that conflict (a self-aware adoption of the role of "writer" and the tight arrangement of the material), we glimpse her extraordinary and heroic story.[15]

I have found this life extraordinary by virtue of the variety and density of her transatlantic experience, and heroic by virtue of Kemble's principled refusal to compromise her abolitionist politics when married to a slave owner and by her spirited rejection of the role of obedient wife that he struggled to impose upon her. She also battled valiantly throughout her life with an emotional illness we would now probably term clinical depression (an illness she, and her friends, attributed to her inheritance of Marie-Thérèse Kemble's volatile temperament). Again and again, Kemble tells us that when she tottered onstage in 1829, trembling and reluctant, she loathed the profession that was the lifeblood of her family: although the second generation of Kembles prided itself, with some justification, on its refined difference from the louche strolling player, the theater remained for Kemble a dangerous place, cheap in its provision of spectacular sensation and seductive in its gratification of an actor's need for audience acclaim. She had seen her Aunt Siddons restless and bored after retirement, sunk into depression at six o'clock in the evening when, rather than going to Covent Garden, she was forced to sit at home and drink tea. Until she went on the stage, Kemble spent her days reading Byron, Shelley, and Jane Austen, writing poems and drafting plays, and dreaming of success as a published author. It was only her parents' insistence that a young Kemble could restore the family finances devastated by the cost of running Covent Garden Theatre that persuaded her to put down her books and step onstage. She also thought it would be a brief deferment of her literary ambitions, but, as things turned out, in the first phase of her career she worked for five years in the profession she never ceased to despise, coining money for the Kemble family and, during those years, writing a best-selling book about America, two plays, and an impressive amount of verse.

When touring America in the early 1830s she made a disastrous marriage to Pierce Butler, a wealthy Philadelphian whose fortune was derived from his family's vast Georgia plantations. The marriage ended in sensational divorce fifteen years later. Returning to England, Kemble fashioned a new career as a brilliantly successful reader of Shakespeare's plays and as the author of her memoirs, several travel narratives and collections of poems, a short novel, and miscellaneous essays on the theater. She always shied from public identification with women's causes, but her public insistence on the right of women to forge careers, keep their own earnings, and speak their political minds, together with her private refusal to obey, in all things, her husband's wishes, make her a valiant Victorian heroine.[16]

Kemble's story is peopled with an amazing cast of characters culled from a transatlantic elite. As a dazzling young actress, she galloped in Hyde Park with famous politicians, chatted in splendid country houses with distinguished Victorian writers, and rode beside George Stephenson on the inaugural railway journey from Liverpool to Manchester. Her glamour bewitched William Thackeray, and her acting sent shivers down the spine of Walt Whitman. She sailed along the Rhine with Franz Liszt, and Henry Wadsworth Longfellow fell at her feet and composed a sonnet in celebration of her Shakespeare readings. She spent the last twenty years of her life invigorating social life on both sides of the Atlantic with her splendid talk and forthright political views, often in the company of the young Henry James, who absolutely adored her. When she died, for him it was like the end of a reign or the fall of an empire.

But not everyone was as devoted as James. Many dismissed Kemble as arrogant, spoiled, and intolerant. Harriet Martineau thought her "a finely-gifted creature, wasted and tortured by want of discipline, principle, and self-knowledge"; Anne Thackeray Ritchie recorded Fanny's reputation as "the most disagreeable old woman" many had encountered; and Henry Kemble, Fanny's nephew, confessed that much as he admired and loved his aunt, she had always "alarmed him," even to her last days.[17] Her manner was often comically intimidating: Samuel Rogers, the wealthy nineteenth-century patron and friend of writers and artists, recounts a story of Kemble shopping in New York and being touched upon the arm by the manager of the store, whereupon she cried, "Villain, unhand me!" Rogers adds that the young man's hair "turned white that night."[18] Whether this actually happened is far less interesting, of course, than what it says about Kemble's reputation for theatrical behavior.

In 1863, *Cornhill* magazine published an essay by Fanny Kemble in which she explains her ideas about stagecraft and explores the differences, as she saw them, between the "dramatic" and the "theatrical." Creating an explicit alignment of the former with her mother and the latter with her father, she elaborates her belief

that as an actress she had inherited from her mother "a vivid and versatile organization" of the intuition and passion that is the very stuff of acting; this is the essential material of performance, the spark of her mother's vitality onstage, and what
gave life to her own Juliet in October 1829. From her father, Kemble declares, she
had inherited the theatrical technique that had been developed over two generations. The dramatic faculty, she asserts, lies in "the power of apprehension quicker
than the disintegrating process of critical analysis."[19] If her aunt Siddons, she goes
on to say, had possessed "the order of mind capable of conceiving and producing
a philosophical analysis of any of the wonderful poetical creations which she so
wonderfully embodied, she would surely never have been able to embody them as
she did."[20]

If it was the Kemble women who brought life to the dramatic text, it was the
Kemble men who did the work of "philosophical analysis" in the family. When John
Philip Kemble died, his obituary in *Fraser's* magazine lauded his cultivated interests
in classical sculpture and philology and reported that the Kemble house was "at all
times the resort of persons of distinction in art and literature."[21] Quite consciously,
Fanny Kemble favored the dispassionate "theatrical" style she associated with her
father and resisted the volcanic "dramatic" mode she associated with her mother.
Enfolded from her childhood in a culture of performance, she transformed the
crafting and assumption of theatrical masks into her modus vivendi.[22]

Throughout the book I have aimed to show that Kemble's appropriation and
rewriting of the assigned roles of Kemble daughter and Butler wife represent a
valiant feminist defiance of patriarchal prescriptions for women. But to see her as
a helpless victim of her family or of Victorian gender politics would be to dishonor
her brave defiance of difficulty: she refused to be sacrificed to the vanity of the
Kembles; she valiantly defied the race and gender politics of her profligate husband;
and she turned up her nose at condescending Victorian literary culture.[23] Courageous independence is a defining mark of her existence. Without question, she was
emotionally maneuvered onto the stage by her parents, but she used this experience to her own purposes; certainly, she was manipulated by her husband, but her
struggle to leave him made her tougher and even more resilient; and although she
was often insufficiently appreciated in her own time as an astute observer of Anglo-
American culture and politics, this was no brake on her prolific writing.

In his 1878 review of the first volume of her memoirs, *Record of a Girlhood*, Henry James calls Fanny Kemble "doubly remarkable": he relishes her performance as
penetrating social observer *and* as participant in the cultural and political world
she describes. Intuitively understanding that she was both a dramatic and a theatrical figure, James pronounces her "superb" for her fusion of an "extraordinarily
brilliant career" as an actress and a vivid intellectual interest in "books, in ques-

tions, in public matters, in art and nature and philosophy."[24] Actress, intellectual, poet, travel writer, abolitionist, idiosyncratic feminist, and mesmerizing reader of Shakespeare: James loved what he called this "abundance of being," Fanny's vivid occupation of the moment. This book pays tribute to that bright abundance.

❧

One rimy November morning, when I was just beginning my research, I was seated in the cozy library of the Garrick Club in Covent Garden. On my way up the stairs, I had passed a rich pageant of portraits of English actors, including the spectacular life-size oil painting that hangs in the dining room of Fanny Kemble's Uncle John and Aunt Sarah in full and magnificent costume as Lord and Lady Macbeth. In front of me was a large book, an 1832 Clarendon Press edition of Shakespeare's plays, and it was that book that had brought me to the Garrick. Kemble had used it in her Shakespeare readings, as had her father before her. In order to compress a play into two hours, Charles had bracketed various parts of the text, in pencil, and I was about to figure out which parts had been read and which not. When I opened the book, the first thing I saw was a rather lovely ex libris plate inscribed with the name of John Gielgud, and then, right at that moment, behind me I heard the deep, resonant, and unmistakable voice of a very well-known English actor. It was Sir Donald Sinden, president of the Garrick, who had come up to say good morning to the librarians. Here I was, turning the pages of a book that had been owned by Charles and Fanny Kemble and John Gielgud, and now, in this very room, was an English actor whom I had seen many times in films and on television and, most memorably, as Othello in the 1980s on the London stage.

Kindly fellow that he is, Sir Donald came over to where I was sitting and asked what I was working on, and when I told him I was about to determine which parts, say, of *The Tempest* Charles and Fanny might have read, and which not, he announced he would take a look. He not only took a look but read aloud some of Prospero's speeches in Act I, and I imagined, for a moment, how Fanny Kemble would have relished this whole wonderful scene: a scene of performance set in the rich comfort of the Garrick Club library, its centerpiece the book of Shakespeare's plays that Charles Kemble and she had carried around with them for their readings, inscribed now with the name of one of England's finest Shakespearean actors, and being read from, now, by another fine English actor. For me, Fanny Kemble's extraordinary presence was there in the Garrick, and her memorable performance as a vibrant nineteenth-century woman lingered long after the curtain fell on my writing and I had left the theater of her life.

Fanny
Kemble

The Green-Room

Life then was new,
The senses easily pleased; the lustres, lights,
The carving and the gilding, paint and glare,
And all the mean upholstery of the place,
Wanted not animation in my sight.
> —William Wordsworth, *The Prelude*, 7:440–45

What a set of barren asses are actors!

> —John Keats

The Kembles

Newman Street, where Fanny Kemble was born on November 27, 1809, runs north from Oxford Street, close to the Tottenham Court Road end of what is now London's busiest and gaudiest shopping thoroughfare. In 1809, Oxford Street was called the Oxford Road, and it was the principal route west out of London. None of the great emporia that were built in the nineteenth century to satisfy the shopping needs of England's bustling and burgeoning middle class was in existence, and Newman Street itself was a terraced enclave of boardinghouses, replaced now by a rather nondescript parade of advertising agencies, printing companies, and sandwich shops. The street remains, however, a fifteen-minute walk from Covent Garden, and at the time of Fanny's birth Charles Kemble found it pleasantly convenient; after rehearsals, he liked to stroll home—through Soho and up to the

Oxford Road, a romantic figure with his splendid bearing, patrician nose, and smoldering eyes.

Kemble has "nothing to say" about Newman Street in her memoirs, which is fair enough since she was carried off as an infant to the leafiness of West London, where her mother, less attached than her husband to the Theatre and to the Covent Garden neighborhood, was happy to grow vegetables, put tasty meals on the table (she was a superb cook), and breathe some decent air. A few years after Fanny's birth, the Kembles settled in a stuccoed villa in Westbourne Green, near the Paddington Canal, which was next door to the home of Fanny's aunt Sarah Siddons, retired from the stage, in ill health, and glad to have company. By 1814, the family had moved further west, to a house near Paddington Church, in whose churchyard one can see a statue of Sarah Siddons placed close to her grave (she died in 1831).

Fanny Kemble may have chosen to remain silent about Newman Street since it was in a rather dodgy area from whose louche associations she had long distanced herself. It is to Newman Street that Esther Summerson in Dickens's *Bleak House* (1853) goes in search of Prince Turveydrop's Dancing Academy, a seedy establishment located in a "dingy house" in which also resides a drawing master, a coal merchant, and a lithographic artist.[1] At the time of Fanny's birth, her uncle John Philip and her Aunt Siddons, the children of vagabond actors, were as famous for their refinement as for their performances, and there was nothing "dingy" about their houses, their reputations, or their manners: Leigh Hunt, poet, essayist, and friend of Shelley and Keats, lauded John and Sarah's combination of intelligence and "high breeding" that led them to be received "everywhere among the truly best circles."[2] There was "such a natural patent of gentility" about John Philip Kemble, declared the Irish novelist Sydney Owenson, Lady Morgan (1776–1859), "that the highest nobility of the land gave way to it."[3] Similarly, Charles Kemble and his wife (after her marriage known simply as Thérèse) were regarded by those "best circles" as unspotted by the Bohemian atmosphere in which they lived and worked. Although they moved back to central London in 1827 to a small townhouse at 16 St. James Street with a view of Green Park so that Fanny's brother Henry might attend Westminster School, Fanny's parents ensured that their own cultured social life and the education of their sons and daughters as gentlemen and ladies kept them in good society. Good society was delighted to have them: Hunt, along with many others, considered all the Kembles "a remarkable race, dignified and elegant in manners, with intellectual tendencies, and in point of aspect very like what has been called 'God Almighty's nobility.'"[4] By the time of Fanny's birth, they had come a long way from the time that Sarah Kemble offered her Lady Macbeth in a barn in Worcester.

Soho had also changed dramatically by 1809. It branched out in a network of narrow streets from Covent Garden, beginning in the mid-1600s, and by 1809 the coffeehouses and taverns attracted artists, musicians, and writers. Joshua Reynolds lived in Great Newport Street, as did Hogarth and George Cruikshank; on Gerrard Street, home to John Dryden, Samuel Johnson frequented the Turk's Head tavern, where he and Reynolds founded the Literary Club in 1764. In pursuit of pleasure less respectable than discussing literary gossip, Johnson's biographer, James Boswell, loved to patrol the Soho streets in search of a "handsome actress of Covent Garden Theatre" to whom he had taken a fancy. Boswell also liked to linger near a brothel in Southampton Street where he had first "experienced the melting and transporting rites of Love,"[5] probably the Key, where prostitutes performed their sexual theater not too many minutes away from Covent Garden. Always enamored of Soho, between 1812 and 1813 Charles Kemble lodged in Covent Garden Chambers; by 1821 he was at 35 Gerrard Street (once the home of Lord Lyttleton, an eighteenth-century author, rake, Whig, and friend of Pope and Fielding); he then bought and sold a house at 5 Soho Square, and made his final Soho home at 29 Soho Square.

Well into the nineteenth century the area around Covent Garden remained notorious as a magnet for "the dregs of Soho and their paramours,"[6] and in Victorian novels disreputable characters often live in Soho, the most notorious of whom is William Thackeray's resourceful Becky Sharp in *Vanity Fair* (1848). The daughter of an impoverished painter and an "opera-girl" (a euphemism for a dancer of relaxed morals), Becky develops her brilliant talent for dissembling while growing up in Soho; her witty mimicry, Thackeray writes, formed "the delight of Newman Street, and Gerrard Street, and the artists' quarter," as she entertained her father's gin-drinking male friends.[7] It was from such racy scenes, set by Thackeray at a historical moment not too long after Fanny's birth on that same street, that the Kemble family disassociated itself, determined to remove from its name all taint of the green-room, that raffish backstage space reserved for actors where Becky would have been right at home.

For the Kembles, and for early nineteenth-century popular culture in general, just as Soho represented a tawdry world of dissolute poets and irresponsible artists, the green-room signaled actors and actresses lolling around in various states of undress awaiting their call to the stage. So called because the carpet and the covering of the divans were, and always had been, green, the room in most large theaters had several full-length mirrors in which the actors could review themselves before going onstage. The memoirs of one nineteenth-century actor, George Vandenhoff, evoke the Covent Garden green-room as a "most agreeable lounging-place, a divan adorned with beauties, where one could pass a pleasant hour in the society of charming women and men of gentlemanly manners."[8] Boswell relates that in the late 1750s Samuel Johnson used to frequent the green-room and "seemed to take delight in dissipating his gloom, by mixing in the sprightly chit-chat of the motley circle then to be found there," but he vowed, finally, to "deny himself this amusement, from considerations of rigid virtue," declaring to David Garrick that he would come no more behind the scenes, "for the silk stockings and white bosoms of your actresses excite my amorous propensities."[9] Fanny Kemble neither frequented the green-room nor admired *Vanity Fair*. When she became an actress, she was enveloped in a shawl and hustled directly between the stage and her dressing room, lest someone catch a glimpse of her "white bosom" and associate her with the lounging "beauties" chatting with a "motley circle." Although she never ceased to love William Thackeray, who had been at school with her brother John Mitchell, she did not "rejoice" in the company of the characters in *Vanity Fair*, even if she was prepared to admit that their "selfishnesses, and meannesses, and dirtinesses, and pettinesses" were admirably portrayed.[10]

After his marriage in 1753 to Sarah Ward, Fanny's grandfather Roger Kemble lived on the borderline between vagabond touring and domestic respectability. Clearly well suited to one another, they reconciled their different religious backgrounds by bringing up their sons as Catholics and their daughters as Protestants (Roger was the Catholic, and Sarah the Protestant), a decision that in the case of their son Charles seems to have had little lasting effect: he married Marie-Thérèse in an Anglican church and their children were raised as Protestants. Traveling between Hereford, Worcester, and adjacent towns, Roger and Sarah Kemble revised the supposed moral laxity of acting companies that toured the provincial circuits by creating a family life of notable repute.[11] Their son John Philip was sent to France for education in the Catholic priesthood but he quickly returned to England, determined to become an actor. When he became famous at Covent Garden, many were mesmerized by his stern Roman looks and elaborate, declamatory style, but others were alienated by his artificiality. One critic said he was "guided by everything but nature" and that he used upliftings of the brow and elaborate turns of the head for expression of feeling.[12] Joseph Donohue notes, however, that the contents of John Philip Kemble's library, inventoried after his death, show that "his approach to a role was an extraordinarily informed, conscious, and systematic one." Treatises on rhetoric, books on classical sculpture, and manuals on acting confirm that Kemble was strongly interested in a unity of style in production; Donohue argues, "However much he found it necessary to satisfy unruly audiences' demands for spectacle, his activities as man of the theater demonstrated his sense of the subtler unity to be found by correlating visual effects with the equally apprehensible qualities manifested by his subjective approach to character."[13]

We serve a KING whom we LOVE—a GOD whom we ADORE.
Pizarro.

Fig. 1. "We Serve a King Whom We Love—a God Whom We Adore." John Philip Kemble as Rolla in *Pizarro*, by Robert Dighton, 1799. © National Portrait Gallery, London.

Leigh Hunt was Kemble's most vociferous critic. Although he conceded admiration for the cultural ambition of the Kemble family, he dismissed John Philip's much-lauded learning: for Hunt, it was merely a vaunted smattering of knowledge, bits and pieces picked up from old books, pretentious posturing of a piece with his very peculiar onstage pronunciations ("perfidious" became "perfijjus," "odious" became "ojjus" and so on). His legendary power was "all studied acquirement."[14] But as Jonathan Bate observes, John Philip was ripe for debunking: with his plummy

Fig. 2. *Sarah Siddons as the "Tragic Muse,"* by Francis Haward, after Sir Joshua Reynolds, 1787. © National Portrait Gallery, London.

voice, intellectual pretensions, and studied grace, he was a favorite of cartoonists.[15] A trifle more generous when it came to Sarah Siddons, who at eighteen married a not terribly talented actor named Henry Siddons and became the most revered tragic actress of the age, Hunt still waspishly dismisses her as a somewhat "masculine beauty," too much the mistress of "the lofty, the queenly, and of appalling tragic effect."[16] Both John Philip and Sarah belonged to what was sometimes ridiculed as the "teapot school" of acting, a label derived from the fashion for actors to place one hand on the hip, the other extended and moving in curved lines, with a gradual descent to the side. This physical style was accompanied by a "teapot" tendency to trill in a treble voice, to deliver lines as if playing the flute. James Boaden, the biographer of both John Philip Kemble and Sarah Siddons, says that Kemble declaimed soliloquies "in the higher tones of his voice, and lost the cast of thought that the galleries might catch the words he uttered."[17]

Fanny's father, Charles, was Hunt's favorite Kemble by far: his handsome face, splendid figure, and sensitive delivery made him a perfect, romantic Shakespearean gentleman, both on and off the stage.[18] The youngest son in the Kemble family, he was born at Brecon in South Wales on November 25, 1775, and at the age of thirteen sent to be educated at the English College in Douai, France. Like his brother, he had no desire to become a priest (which had been Roger Kemble's hope for at least one of his sons), and when he returned to London a few years later, he began appearing in provincial acting companies. His first London performance was in April 1794 at the age of eighteen, performing Malcolm to his brother John's Macbeth and his sister Sarah's Lady Macbeth. The critics judged him "awkward in action, weak in voice, and ungraceful in deportment," and to have no future in the profession, although they gave him credit for his good intentions. Undeterred, he improved and eventually earned praise for becoming one of the "most graceful and refined of actors."[19] Although he lacked the passion and intensity of his Drury Lane rival, Edmund Kean (Othello, one of Kean's great triumphs, was beyond him), he excelled in bringing out the nuances of less vigorous characters, and until his death in 1854 he was a hardworking actor-manager. He performed many parts, managed a theater always on the verge of bankruptcy, deftly negotiated contracts with temperamental actors, and toured the provinces, a dispiriting trial for most London actors since they had to cope with inept regional companies, stay in dismal boardinghouses, and often play to lackluster audiences.

It was as Romeo that he first exhibited his talent for "theatrical love," as Leigh Hunt terms it, and in this role he was by far "the first performer on the stage."[20] The critic for the *Spectator*, however, found Romeo's taking of the poison somewhat vulgarly imagined in Kemble's interpretation: "However cold may have seemed his heart, his stomach evinces an acute sensibility . . . [he] testifies as clamorous an indisposition to quit the world, and, in mellow sounds, as loud a distaste for the means, as that animal so tenaciously attached to the joys of life, the luxurious pig."[21] As he got older he switched to Mercutio, which he played to his daughter's Juliet in October 1829, and according to one critic he brought to the role a suave nobility, flexible voice, and graceful manner.[22] He also excelled as Faulconbridge in *King John*, for which, with the assistance of his close friend and colleague the prolific dramatist James Robinson Planché (1796–1880), he mounted a spectacular

Fig. 3. *Charles Kemble*, by Henry Perronet Briggs, 1830s. © National Portrait Gallery, London.

production at Covent Garden in 1823 replete with historically accurate and very expensive costumes. The playbill for this production promises that "The Characters will be dressed in the precise HABIT OF THE PERIOD, The Whole of the Dresses and Decorations being executed from indisputable authorities, such as Monumental Effigies, Seals, illuminated mss., etc."[23] His Cassio, in later life, was also much admired, especially by Hunt, although Queen Victoria, in 1836, thought the changes in Charles Kemble (at the age of sixty-one) "very great." After seeing a performance of Joanna Baillie's *The Separation*, she wrote in her diary, "Kemble whines so much and drawls the words in such a slow peculiar manner; his actions too (to me) are overdone and affected, and his voice is not pleasant to me; he makes terrible faces also which spoils his countenance and he looks very old and does not carry himself well."[24]

Charles Kemble's embodiment of all that was contrary to images in popular culture of actors as vulgar, uneducated, and morally suspect is signaled by the fact that when Fanny first appeared at Covent Garden, one critic was so enthusiastic about the latest Kemble star that he included her father in his tribute, praising Charles as "elegant without affectation; learned without pedantry; witty without rancour; humourous without vulgarity."[25] Almost certainly out of gratitude to her father as well as a desire to fashion herself in his refined image, Fanny Kemble aimed to be elegant, although some thought her almost comically affected; she was learned and too forthright to go in for pedantry, although impatient with those less quick and clever than herself; her wit was legendary, and it was not merely because of her theatrical celebrity that she was a sought-after dinner guest. Her astringent talk could rejuvenate the most exhausted politician or bored army officer, and her musical accomplishments (thanks to Thérèse's rigorous training) made her a desirable presence in London's smartest drawing rooms. But however much Kemble might have resembled her father with her social poise, clever talk, and artistic interests, and however much she cherished him as a beau ideal of the acting profession, she knew herself to be strongly stamped with a painful legacy from her mother. Throughout her life, Kemble suffered from bouts of deep depression, which she, and many who knew her well, traced to her mother's manic-depressive illness—or, as Kemble called it, her mother's "intensely nervous organization."

A talented prodigy, Thérèse Kemble eventually became a member of the Drury Lane company, playing Desdemona, Portia, and a saucy Macheath in *The Beggar's Opera*. Admired as an excellent dancer, a charming singer, and a deft comic actress, she had a beautiful figure, fine dark eyes, and lively expressive features, and attracted many beaus. Her appeal for Charles Kemble, however, puzzled at least one of his friends, Jane Porter, who recorded in her diary, "I can see no point of her character or manners, that can unite with the softness, and dignity of Kemble's. She is lively, free, commanding, and self-assured. . . . This person, tho' well shaped and of fine contour, is coarse and unfinished."[26] Despite the opposition of John Philip Kemble (like his father, Roger, he did not want any of the Kembles to marry actors), Marie-Thérèse and Charles were married in one of Nicholas Hawksmoor's most beautiful eighteenth-century churches, St. George's in Bloomsbury, on July 3, 1806. That John Philip Kemble might have had less noble reasons for opposing his brother's marriage is suggested in Thérèse's obituary in the *Illustrated London News*.

"We believe that the private conduct of Miss De Camp, though she had many ardent admirers, and splendid offers of provisions, was always irreproachable," states the obituary, pointing slyly to the conventional image of actresses accepting

Fig. 4. *Maria Theresa Kemble*, by Alfred Edward Chalon, 1804. © National Portrait Gallery, London.

"offers of provisions" from wealthy admirers. More praise is heaped on Thérèse's virtue as the writer reminds his readers of the theatrical commotion occasioned "by the imprudence of John Philip Kemble, who, after having made some repelled advances to Miss De Camp, broke into her dressing room, and would have proceeded to violence, had she not been rescued by, we believe, Charles Kemble."[27] It would seem that Thérèse barely averted rape by her soon-to-be brother-in-law by being "a perfect mistress of the business of the scene," and the obituary concludes by saying that her fondness for "management" onstage was carried "into all her domestic arrangements." No evidence exists that this incident actually took place, and it can easily be attributed to green-room gossip; however, it is undeniable that Thérèse Kemble was a domestic terror and that her gift for "management" became obsessive and self-destructive.

Her insistence on perfection made her a fine cook, a meticulous housekeeper, a vigorous gardener, and a patient fisherman. But her family was constantly bewildered by the emotional fluctuations that led to frequent household moves and rearrangements of the furniture. The calming anchor of the household was Thérèse's sister, Kemble's beloved aunt Adelaide (known to everyone as Dall), who supervised the care of the four children (Fanny and her brother John Mitchell were joined by Adelaide and Henry), placated their mother's rages, and devoted herself to the family. Between 1812 and 1815, Charles toured frequently in Dublin, Edinburgh, Glasgow, and a few major English provincial cities, in addition to accepting the occasional offer to act on the Continent. Thérèse traveled with him on occasion, which made Dall the most stable female figure in Fanny's early childhood, for Jacky Bratton a figure whose life "offers a rare glimpse of the theatrical family woman making the strictly backstage contribution to the family business."[28] Thérèse was at her most serene when staying at a small family cottage in Weybridge, Surrey, where she fished in the River Wye at the end of the garden, tended her flowers, and made a lot of jams and jellies, as contented as she could ever be. Charles was happy to stay in Soho.

At her most admirable, Thérèse was fiercely ambitious for her children, and she did not favor her sons over her daughters. For the time, Fanny and Adelaide were well educated; bilingual from an early age by virtue of their mother's native French, they were subjected to strict regimens of training in music, dancing, deportment, horsemanship, and elegant manners. Fanny did well in all of these, except when her mother was watching. Although Adelaide was the better singer and later became a successful opera star, Fanny had a fine alto voice and sang and played the piano with graceful verve. She was also an excellent and enthusiastic dancer. At the age of sixteen or so, her deportment was not all it should have been, but her mother had it corrected with regular drilling from an army sergeant; Fanny claimed that until she was an old woman she never slouched. Like her mother, she was also a superb horsewoman, at least until she became too arthritic and too large to get on a horse. If at the age of five her father's bedtime readings of *Paradise Lost* created the love of language seen in her performances and in her writing, then as a young girl her mother's drilling in the social graces formed the poise that beguiled Anglo-American society. But Thérèse Kemble's training exacted a hard price. Fanny recalled that of the four children, she and John were the only ones in the family endowed with enough self-esteem, with a sufficiently "elastic conceit" as she put it, to resist, if not escape, the force of their mother's will. When she was a mother herself, unhappily married and less "elastic" than she had been as a girl, Fanny often thought that her own erratic behavior, so reminiscent of her mother's unpredictability, was caused by her turbulent childhood and an inescapable inheritance of depression.

As painfully as she documents in her memoirs the damaging influence of her mother's mercurial temperament on her children, Kemble also treasured (and recorded) the gift of her vital personality. Although Thérèse Kemble possessed nothing "in such perfection" as the talent of the Kembles, she had, says Fanny, a superb instinct for artistic criticism, a lively perceptiveness, and a brilliant vividness in her speech: "Had she possessed half the advantages of education which she and my father laboured to bestow upon us, she would, I think, have been one of the most remarkable persons of her time."[29] Paradoxically, what Kemble loved most about her mother was that dramatic flair and unmediated outpouring of feeling that was most dangerous for her, and this is what drew her self-protectively to the polished theatricality of her father. Onstage and off, Thérèse's speech was unguarded and spontaneous, in contrast to Charles's calculated emphases and inflections. Unhappily for Kemble, Thérèse's instinct for artistic criticism expressed itself in uncontrollable impatience with her daughter's skill as a pianist and singer, which Kemble interpreted as an "intrepid sincerity of nature" that made her mother's strictures "sometimes more accurate than acceptable."[30] However much Kemble tried to excuse her mother's irritability as the mark of high artistic standards, she was never able to sing in front of her without becoming frightened, hoarse, and off-key.

Covent Garden

On Newman Street in Soho, then, Fanny Kemble was born into a family that often disparaged the profession that sustained it, even while it welcomed the applause that greeted its appearances before the public. John Philip's haughty manners and idiosyncratic pronunciations, Sarah's imperious bearing, Charles's dreamy distaste for business, and Thérèse's removal to the countryside all signify, in one way or another, a fear of taint from the raffish side of theater life. But the Kembles, however haughty their manners, gracious their hospitality, and refined their tastes, knew they were part of a world that offered pantomimes as well as Shakespeare, that spawned a democratic jostling of all social classes in the warmth and glamor of the theater. Gaudily dressed prostitutes trafficked in the galleries as demurely gowned middle-class girls flirted in the boxes; actresses were protected by bankers and politicians, and one of them, Dora Jordan, even enjoyed impeccable domesticity with a prince.[31]

This double world of high and low theatrical cultures, of an electrifying Shylock acted by Edmund Kean at Drury Lane and a Jamaican bandit acted, against

THEATRICAL   PLEASURES . P^t 2.

Contending for a Seat.

Fig. 5. "Contending for a Seat," Drury Lane Theatre, 1821. This cartoon displays the ill-behaved nature of theater audiences at the time Fanny Kemble made her debut in 1829. V&A Images/Theatre Museum.

all expectations, by Charles Kemble in a pantomime titled *Obi, or Three-Fingered Jack* at Covent Garden on July 2, 1800, was not, however, always profitable. From its beginning, Fanny Kemble's life was shaped by her parents' need to fatten a scrawny box office. Popular entertainments brought people into the provincial and London theaters. One could see performing dogs, rowdy pantomimes, and productions like that mounted at Covent Garden in 1811 of *Blue Beard*, complete with an entire circus troupe, spectacular costumes, and jousting on horseback. Child prodigies were

MASTER BETTY, the YOUNG ROSCIUS,
in the character of ACHMET in BARBAROSSA.
---if thou darst Now view me!

Fig. 6. "Master Betty" (William Henry West), the sensational child actor who appeared at Covent Garden Theatre in 1804. V&A Images/Theatre Museum.

also a good draw, the most renowned of whom was William Betty, known everywhere as Master Betty, a thirteen-year-old Irish boy who astounded Belfast and Dublin audiences with his versatile turns as Romeo, Hamlet, and Prince Arthur, and who went on to amaze London in 1804 with his performances as Richard III and Macbeth. His first appearance at Covent Garden drew enormous crowds who filled the piazza and clamored for admission. Understandably, John Philip Kemble, then manager of the Theatre, was not enthusiastic about yielding his authority as England's supreme tragedian to a pretty boy, but he also understood the need to make money, even if it meant pandering to the public's lust for novelty.[32] Covent Garden's huge stage demanded expensive scenery, and a few weeks of *Master Betty* enabled some spectacular backdrops for Shakespeare's *King John*.

As the story of *Master Betty's* phenomenal success at Covent Garden suggests—he was presented to the royal family and the House of Commons suspended a sitting so that Members of Parliament could see his Hamlet—audiences wanted excitement and variety. In fact, they demanded innovation, pageantry, and patriotic spectacles, something to lighten things up after the wrenching experience, say, of watching Sarah Siddons's sepulchral Lady Macbeth do her sleepwalking scene. For example, Astley's Amphitheatre mounted shows such as the 1801 production of *The British Glory in Egypt*, with "REAL CAVALRY and INFANTRY," and in 1824 offered *The Battle of Waterloo*, replete with cavalry advances, bugle calls, and cannon fire. Eager to tap into this taste for patriotic pageant, Covent Garden enlivened its Christmas pantomime in 1827 with backdrop scenery based on recent British victories over Turkish and Egyptian fleets.[33] When a terrified Fanny Kemble was pushed onstage as Juliet in 1829, she entered a theater world that readily offered a colorful variety of entertainment.

When being amused by performing dogs, pantomimes, and patriotic panoramas, audiences responded very differently, of course, from the way they behaved when witnessing the tragic acting of Sarah Siddons. Siddons's performance in Thomas Southern's *Isabella, or The Fatal Marriage* (a play based on the Aphra Behn novel) caused men to weep, women to fall into hysterics, and the theater itself to shake with transports of applause: "her beautiful face and form, the exquisite tones of her voice, [and] her deep tenderness" were said to have created an excitement and enthusiasm "almost terrible in their intensity."[34] When her career was established, Fanny followed her aunt in this role, playing to a crowded house with great success, although she claimed always to dislike both the play and the part extremely and pronounced herself relieved to return to the "glorious poetry and the bright throbbing *reality* of Juliet."[35] When acting Juliet, she faced audiences of a different makeup from those that flocked to Covent Garden's jollier offerings, audiences who sometimes dispensed with the Shakespeare altogether and arrived for the pantomime or farce that always followed the main attraction. When she was thirty-nine, Kemble recalled that the raucous pantomimes of her childhood were the opposite from a rather decorous entertainment she had just seen with her friends Henry and Charles Greville: "I remember when, during the run of a pantomime, the galleries presented a scene of scandalous riot and confusion; bottles were handed about, men sat in their shirt-sleeves, and the shouting shrieking, bawling squalling, and roaring were such as to convert the performance . . . into mere dumb show."[36] In addition, early nineteenth-century audiences were often drawn more by the shadowy entertainments offered in the darkened galleries or secluded boxes than by what was promised on the playbill. After a visit to Covent Garden to see one of its audience-pleasing popular productions, Walter Scott reported, in strong tones of disgust, that half the people came to prosecute their debaucheries "so openly that it would degrade a bagnio," and the rest arrived to snooze off their beefsteaks and port wine.[37]

The history of Covent Garden Theatre begins, in essence, with the establishment by Charles II after the Restoration of two London theaters and his suppression of all other playhouses. The king issued patents to the two new acting companies—one, for the King's at Drury Lane, and the other, for the Duke's at Dorset Garden—and in the early eighteenth century, the Covent Garden Theatre and a new acting company took over the patent from the Dorset Garden. In 1792 the right to produce English legitimate drama (tragedy, comedy, and farce) in London was granted exclusively to Drury Lane and Covent Garden. Minor theaters were limited to an illegitimate repertoire, and it was not until the Theatres Regulation Act of 1843 that minor theaters were permitted to stage drama.[38] The rise of Covent Garden Theatre itself was accompanied by the beginning of a significant social shift in the history of the London theater. By the Georgian era, the London audience had become more democratic and the theater managers less reliant on royal and aristocratic patronage. Audiences also gained considerable power in the way they could make or break a play, celebrate or ridicule an actor, or precipitate an acting company into financial ruin.

Although the patents granted by Charles II were not revoked until 1843, by the end of the eighteenth century the London theater had become commercial theater, hospitable to an ascendant wealthy middle class busy solidifying its political and cultural power. In 1770, a journalist declared that "the playhouse in London is for all classes of the nation. The peer of the realm, the gentleman, the merchant, the citizen, the clergyman, the tradesman and their wives equally resort thither to take places, and the crowd is great."[39] By the early nineteenth century, these crowds came to Covent Garden to enjoy a long evening that demanded considerable investment by the management, who garnered healthy profits, to be sure, but who also ran the risk of serious financial loss. Moreover, owner-managers had to stem the financial hemorrhaging caused by disasters such as fires and audiences who rioted at the imposition of an increase in ticket prices. In the early 1800s a fire, a costly rebuilding, and an ill-advised increase in prices dealt a deadly financial blow to the Kemble family fortunes.

The famous "Old Price Riots" of 1809 drove John Philip Kemble out of the theater business. In June 1817, he retired from the stage and moved to Switzerland, beset by gout, tired of acting, and pessimistic about ever making money at Covent Garden in the wake of the infamous protests against raised ticket prices. His original purchase of a one-sixth share in the theater had cost him £22,000 (by today's calculations, approximately £1 million); for managing the theater, he had received £200 a year (now, approximately £9,400); and for acting there he had earned thirty seven pounds and sixteen shillings per week for three performances (£1,700).[40] By contemporary measures, he was hardly ill paid (it is staggering, for instance, that he could cobble together the initial outlay of a million pounds to purchase his one-sixth share in Covent Garden), but the carnivalesque riots in 1809 destroyed his financial security. As a one-sixth shareholder in the Covent Garden partnership, and as the leading tragedian in its acting company, John Kemble had a major say in the rebuilding of the theater after it was completely destroyed by a tremendous fire in 1808. On September 12 he was playing in Sheridan's drama *Pizarro*, in which he was called on to fire a gun, and it is generally believed that a piece of smoldering wadding from the piece burst into flames in the middle of the night. In the conflagration, twenty-two people were killed, Sarah Siddons lost her entire theatrical wardrobe, John Kemble lost almost all the private savings he had sunk into the now gutted theater, and many valuable dramatic and music manuscripts were destroyed. The damage was estimated at £100,000 (now, about £5.25 million), of which only one half was covered by insurance.

After John Philip Kemble raised money to rebuild Covent Garden through the sale of one hundred fifty-two shares at £500 each (now, roughly £27,000), he realized, as Tracy Davis points out in her economic analysis of the situation, that he and the other proprietors had mortgaged the patent of Covent Garden to these shareholders, and that there remained a distressing discrepancy between the share capital and the total cost of rebuilding. After the new theater was finished, there seemed no alternative but to raise the ticket prices.[41]

The stone-laying ceremony for the new Covent Garden Theatre on December 31, 1808, rivaled anything its manager had put onstage. To the playing of military bands and a twenty-one-gun salute, the Prince of Wales, dressed as Grand Master of the Freemasons, paraded down a green-carpeted platform with a silver trowel and spread the cement: John Kemble, at his most sternly majestic, also dressed in Masonic uniform, looked on, accompanied by Sarah Siddons, her black gown magnificently adorned with black ostrich feathers. The exterior of the theater was modeled on the Temple of Minerva on the Acropolis, and on the marble and porphyry walls were bas relief portraits of John and Sarah. An enlarged auditorium had seating for three thousand people, an indication that the Kembles had come a long way from the audience in the Worcester barn that witnessed Sarah Kemble's Lady Macbeth. John Kemble had designed the new Covent Garden with the third circle dedicated entirely to lucrative private boxes, a canny strategy, he thought, that would cover some of the rebuilding costs. But the ticket buyers thought otherwise. At the rival Drury Lane Theatre, private boxes were distributed throughout the house. In Kemble's new arrangement for Covent Garden, those who could not afford private boxes were driven either up to the remote galleries or down into the pit. In addition, to pay for this exclusive and, some charged, morally suspect arrangement (anterooms, after all, encouraged the debauchery and snoozing decried by Walter Scott), John Kemble increased the price of box seats from six to seven shillings and the pit from three shillings and sixpence to four shillings.[42] The newly built theater opened on September 18, 1809, with a production of *Macbeth* starring John Kemble and Sarah Siddons. Charles Kemble was playing Malcolm, and Thérèse Kemble was nearing the end of her pregnancy with Fanny.

As soon as John Kemble and Sarah Siddons came onstage, those in the pit put their hats on and turned their backs to the actors. The fact that Siddons was a blaze of jewels in a dazzling dress fashioned after the bridal garb of Mary Queen of Scots signaled that the new prices were paying for ostentatious costumes; John Philip also came in for ridicule from *The Times* on October 4, 1809, when he appeared extravagantly costumed as Cardinal Wolsey in *Henry VIII*: "Imagine that Cardinal Wolsey must of necessity, to give effect to the character, have a pocket-handkerchief of the finest cambric trimmed with lace at four, five, or six guineas a yard!!!"[43] Catcalls drowned out Kemble and Siddons as they spoke their opening lines in *Macbeth,* and the turmoil continued throughout the play. In the coming weeks the audience held up banners, wore badges in their hats, waved placards during the performance, and choreographed an outdoor protest, an "Old Price" dance that wound its way through the Covent Garden streets.

After three months of demonstrations (during which time Fanny Kemble was born on Newman Street) that featured people dressed up in red and white nightcaps, barristers' wigs, military hats, and large false noses (a mockery of John Kemble's most prominent feature), and others in full costume as butchers, Welshmen, and washerwomen, a formal peace treaty was drawn up.[44] The demonstrations had reached their lowest point when men sported medals inscribed with a picture of Kemble and the words, "This is the Jew that Shakespeare drew" (a sentiment that pointed to his large and supposedly Semitic nose and to the perceived Shylock-like nature of his financial plans for the theater),[45] and grew violent when gangs went to the houses of John Kemble and Sarah Siddons and threw stones at their windows. According to the final agreement, private boxes were to be reduced in number, the old pit was to be restored, and the new prices should remain. Performances could resume without interruption, but the settlement left Kemble and his five partners still saddled with the debt incurred in rebuilding the theater and with no prospect of increased revenues.

When a fatigued John Kemble retreated to Switzerland eight years after the Old Price Riots, he held on to his one-sixth share, but in November 1820, certain that he would return neither to acting nor to theater management, he transferred his investment by deed of gift to his brother Charles. On receipt of this questionable inheritance after John's death in Switzerland in February 1823, Charles found himself having to deal with the principal stockholder of the other five, Henry Harris, who from 1817 to 1820 had badly mismanaged things with too much gaudy spectacle and gilded melodrama and not enough Shakespeare and Sheridan. The challenge for every actor-manager, of course, was to fashion a mix that would appeal to the various social classes now crowding into the London theaters. Successful theater management entailed presenting tragedy, comedy, farce, ballet, and pantomime in engaging combinations so that everyone was happy; if the right mix was achieved, the two big London theaters could fight off competition from smaller, unlicensed playhouses, which despite their illegality managed to do well until they were shut down by the government. Unsuccessful in devising an appealing mix and encumbered by the debts incurred by the 1808 fire, the 1809 rebuilding, and subsequent riots, Charles Kemble quickly saw the Covent Garden run even more heavily into the red. Sued by Harris for mismanagement, he also found himself embroiled in seven years of Chancery litigation. When Fanny Kemble made her debut in 1829, Covent Garden was barely averaging £200 a night (now about £30,000): her smashing success led to a doubling of the box-office receipts. But this was not the life that her parents had envisioned for their daughter.

Fanny at Blackheath

Given the interwoven histories of the Kemble family and the Covent Garden Theatre, one governed by social ambition and financial worry and the other characterized by spectacular performances and backstage seediness, it is not surprising that Charles and Thérèse Kemble tried to keep their children out of the greenroom. They educated them as insurance against professional uncertainty and social demotion. From the age of ten until she was sixteen, Kemble was educated in accord with the standards set by the social group with whom her parents associated—the cultured upper middle class—but as a child, she was termed disobedient, willful, and unmanageable by all her nurses and teachers. Nobody seemed to know how to direct her amazing energy, and all were fazed by the good humor with which she accepted her punishments.

One of Kemble's earliest memories is of being taken at the age of six to a warm and sunny house in Blackheath, a part of southeast London far from Soho's vulgar bustle. It was a girls' school kept by two Italian sisters named Grimani, and Kemble was taken there often when she was little to visit her aunt Victoire de Camp, sister of Thérèse and Dall and an assistant governess at the establishment. Intrigued by Kemble's intelligence, the Grimani sisters spoiled and petted her, and as a middle-aged woman, she vividly remembered the blissful visits. Set in lush grounds, the house possessed a beautiful, south-facing drawing room; sunny and silent, it was "at once gay and solemn" to her imagination and to her senses, a temple dedicated to all things serene, bright, and lovely. Precious china jars filled with potpourri stood in each of three big windows, and in a reverential gesture, Kemble says she loved to place her six-year-old nose on a level with the wide necks of the jars, savoring their mellow, fragrant contents. The room had heavy velvet crimson curtains and a deep crimson carpet in which her feet seemed to be buried, "as in woodland moss." When Kemble was pronounced "very good," Bellina Grimani, her face like one of Giorgione's pictures and her voice "low, distinct, enchanting," would relate the story of the one large picture that adorned the room. At Kemble's "importunate beseeching," she would tell it over and over again, and the highly strung child who was the terror of the nursery remained silent, holding Bellina Grimani's hand, listening with an upturned face, her enormous brown eyes filling with tears of wonder and pity at the tale of Prospero and Miranda. At the center of the picture, in the midst of a stormy sea, there was a weltering bark, and in it sat a man "in the full flower of vigorous manhood," one hand covering his eyes and the other resting on the curls of a girl aged about three. Remembering all this—or, rather, reconstructing it—close to fifty years after the event (in her notes on *The Tempest*), Kemble wrote that there was something about the face and figure of Prospero that reminded her of her father.[46]

In her sensuous reconstruction of the scene, Kemble invests the moment with a characteristic theatricality. She leads us away from the crowded London streets, through the leafy southeastern suburbs, and to a world beyond the "encroaching tide" of hideous suburban villas that is creating yet "more London." She paints the rambling, rural house with its well-kept grounds, she makes us sense the silent, warm, richly carpeted drawing room, and we are moved by the touching spectacle of a six-year-old child in tears before a painting. The scene dramatizes the wonders of Shakespeare's stories and the brilliance of his verse; it presents the delight of deep carpets, warm sunlight, and golden rooms perfumed with potpourri; and it enacts the joy of language itself, as Kemble celebrates it in Bellina Grimani's telling of the tale and in her own evocation of the moment. It also stages an imaginative revelation of feelings whose pain was barely diminished at the time she was shaping the Blackheath scene in her memory.

Always, she confesses, she had a simple and unaffected longing to acquiesce to her father's wishes: first as an unmanageable little girl sent away to school; then as a tomboyish bluestocking forced to become an actress; and, finally, as a glittering celebrity, maneuvered into going to America in 1832 to try to make more money for the Covent Garden Theatre and for her family. But placating and gratifying her father's vanity and desires (her tantrums disturbed his cool composure; her success created family security) left her feeling exiled from family, friends, and nation. In all these disruptions, Dall was her comfort. At five, Kemble cried bitterly at being taken from her and sent to school; at nineteen, she quivered in her arms before being pushed onstage and into the theatrical profession; and the distress of going to America, which loomed as a cultural wasteland, was ameliorated somewhat by the fact that Dall was going with her. In the Blackheath scene she creates for her reader, we see her both as dutiful Miranda and as magical Prospero: the bewildered daughter exiled from home and the father who is imaginative master of the theatrical spectacle. Absent from this spectacle, of course, as indeed she is in *The Tempest* (except as Caliban's demonic parent, Sycorax), is the figure of the mother: Thérèse Kemble enters this psychological drama only in displaced fashion—as the idealized Bellina Grimani, patient with the beseeching child, bewitching as she tells the story of the picture that is the principal prop in Kemble's theatricalized memory, charming in her calm occupation of the lovely room. In light of Kemble's fidelity to the "theatrical" father and rejection of the "dramatic" mother, it is ironic that her strongest emotional attachments throughout her life were to women. In her memory, seeking always the perfect mother, she treasured Bellina Grimani as a revered surrogate.

Kemble memorialized Dall, her first idealized mother figure, as cheerful, self-forgetful, unprepossessing, and "the good angel" of the Kemble household. But much as she loved her aunt, Fanny constantly disobeyed her. A notoriously naughty child who, in her own self-deprecating words, displayed an "audacious contempt for all authority," she neither cried, sulked, nor repented of her crimes. She was bored with her lessons, uninterested in girls' games, and wary of dolls. In her memoirs, she says that she neither loved nor liked dolls for she had a nervous dislike of the "smiling simulacra that girls are all supposed to love with a species of prophetic maternal instinct,"[47] an admission that suggests a likely rejection in her child's consciousness of motherhood as she saw it enacted in her family. Always in need of an audience for her dramatic posturing—Dall was appreciative but she had seen it all before, and Adelaide was a dull baby—she would devise ways to turn punishment into performance as a means of attracting attention. On one occasion, forced to wear a fool's cap far too big for her and instructed to hide her disgrace from all beholders, she pranced defiantly down the carriage drive (at this time the Kembles were in Bayswater), first to attract the attention of the postman and next to climb up a high stagelike bank so that she could make a "public exhibition" of herself to people passing by. The postman applauded, and children and nannies on their way to Kensington Gardens thought she put on a splendid show, but her family was less impressed: sentenced to bread and water, she theatrically declaimed that she was now like "those poor dear French prisoners that everybody pities so."[48]

This was in late 1814, toward the close of the Napoleonic Wars, with the Battle of Waterloo a few months away and the Continent about to be reopened to the traveling British. Charles Kemble was acting at the Theatre (still under the management of his brother), and Thérèse Kemble was busy with baby Adelaide, who proved far more manageable than Fanny. Unable to deal with a child whose fiery temperament uncomfortably resembled her own, Thérèse called in her sister-in-law Sarah Siddons to reprimand Fanny, hoping that the tragic voice said to have curdled the blood of a shop assistant when Siddons asked the price of some calico would frighten Kemble into obedience as effectively as it terrorized London audiences. But Fanny, sitting on her Aunt Siddons's knee and playing with her necklace, merely laughed. Thérèse and Charles then turned to another aunt, and their difficult daughter was dispatched to a fashionable school for young ladies in Camden Place, Bath, run by Charles's sister and her husband, Frances and Francis Twiss. Before her marriage to a scholarly lawyer, Frances Kemble had been an actress; her three daughters were learned in Latin and mathematics and the pupils studied the social graces, screen painting, and music. Fanny Kemble returned to London after a year, the principal legacy of living with her learned and industrious cousins a precocious talent for punning.

In her memoirs, Kemble declares that when she was sent to school in Boulogne after two years back in London with her family it was because her father was eager to give her "every advantage," which was probably the case since the Kembles had high aspirations for their children. But Fanny appeared, by far, the most audaciously intelligent and undisciplined of all the grandchildren of Roger and Sarah Kemble, and it is easy to imagine that if she had been a child rather than a grandchild of the founders of the dynasty, her energy and zeal for performance would have presented less of a problem. Despite the desire for none of their children to be actors, Roger and Sarah would have put her on the stage, or at least had her declaiming in a barn. As it was, in 1817 neither Thérèse nor Dall could cope with her and she was packed off to the care of Madame Faudier in Boulogne, "a rather sallow and grim, but still vivacious" woman. Kemble took lessons in French literature, music, dancing, and Italian, and she loved it all, but she soon repeated her London misadventures. Locked in a garret for some misdeed or other, and again in search of an audience, she climbed out onto the roof, performed a dangerous and riveting dance on the slates, and became an object of terrified fascination to onlookers on the street below. After a year that left her with only one "agreeable impression" of going to school in France—wandering along the sandy dunes of Boulogne and clambering on the rocks in search of rabbits—she garnered more prizes than any other pupil. Since she was the youngest girl in the school, this was a remarkable tribute to her intelligence.

When Kemble was brought back to London, her French impeccable (it stayed that way throughout her life) and her intellect fired by the study of French classical literature, she sometimes stayed at the Soho flat on Gerrard Street where Charles Kemble now lived during the week and where Thérèse occasionally gave acting lessons to young ladies; the rest of the time she lived in one of the several suburban houses occupied by the Kemble family over the next few years. Chronically restless and bothered by the London fog, the ceaseless uproar of the horses, and the racy Soho streets Charles liked to grace with his stylish presence, Thérèse kept them on the move. She loved the pretty front and back gardens of West London, the green spaciousness of Kensington Gardens, and the opportunity to decorate every fresh house with the secondhand furniture she found at local sales. But no house was ever quite right. What Kemble termed her "rage" for moving the furniture strongly discomfited her children, and they never knew when they might find the rooms "a perfect chaos of disorder," their mother crimson and disheveled from shoving chairs around as she breathlessly organized a new combination.[49]

Recognizing in her memoirs her early fondness for role-playing, Kemble recalls that by the age of twelve she had become "a tragically desperate young person." Her brother John, now fourteen, was away at Dr. Malkin's School in Bury St. Edmunds (Malkin's son, Arthur, became a regular correspondent of Kemble's when they were both in the their middle years), and she missed the thrill of rehearsing and performing the plays she and John would devise for an audience of her parents' theatrical friends. The tedium was relieved a little by visits to Astley's Amphitheatre (home of spectacular entertainments for all ages), where she saw shows such as "Meg Murdoch, or the Mountain Hag" and "Hyppolita, Queen of the Amazons," the latter especially impressive since it featured Hyppolita mounted on a live snow-white charger. Desperate for some dramatic action in her tedious young life, she tried that reliable attention-getting strategy of running away from home. Trudging along the Bayswater Road, she got almost as far as Marble Arch, where she assured a bemused old needlewoman that she intended to apply for engagement at one of the London theaters, where, she confidently assured her, "nobody with talent need ever want for bread."[50] Retrieved by a frantic Dall, she was sentenced to a week's bread and water and daily confinement in the toolshed, where she amused and consoled herself by singing French songs whenever she heard footsteps on the gravel walk near her prison. However severely she was punished, she remained provocative, restless, and disobedient.

Resorting once more to the remedy of French schooling, Kemble's parents sent her to Paris, to an academy run by an old acquaintance of John Philip Kemble's family, Mrs. Rowden, whose undiminished infatuation with John was registered in a portrait of him in full "teapot" mode as Coriolanus that hung in her drawing room. The school was in the rue d'Angoulême, just off the Champs-Elysées, and Mrs. Rowden counted among her former pupils Mary Russell Mitford, the prolific poet, playwright, and intimate correspondent of many nineteenth-century literary figures, most notably Elizabeth Barrett Browning. It was now 1821, and Fanny remained at Mrs. Rowden's for four years without returning to England and so spent a crucial period of her adolescent life separated from everyone in her family except her father.

During these years Kemble absorbed the foundation of her serious education and developed into a charming girl. Already fluent in French and allowed to roam the city with the other pupils, she delighted in the cafés, the crowds of English tourists flocking to Paris after the final defeat of Bonaparte, the picture galleries in the Jardin de Luxembourg where she gazed at paintings by David, and her favorite promenade in the Parc Monceau, freshly converted from being private property of the Orleans family into a whole new quartier of Louis Napoleon's Paris. Mrs. Rowden was a stern schoolmistress and the curriculum was demanding: hours of Latin grammar, serious work in Italian literature, memorization of difficult passages in Racine and Corneille, and, to complete the transformation of gangly English girls into polished young ladies, music and dancing lessons taught by a trio of twinkly eyed masters. It was also at Mrs. Rowden's that Kemble's career as a writer began to blossom. Each Sunday the pupils were given the task of composing a sermon based on a particular passage from the Bible (the fiercely "Methodistical" Mrs. Rowden took them to three services), and Kemble recalls in her memoirs that a good-sized volume might have been made out of her own efforts. Her love of writing was so great that she not only composed long, erudite sermons for herself but completed the assignment for girls less interested in language and less fortunate in not having a father who had read Milton to them when they were six years old.

Kemble spent her holidays with a petit bourgeois family as *un enfant de la maison,* but her "real holidays," as she called them, were cherished visits from her father as he joined her in her Parisian exile: "pleasant days of joyous *camaraderie* and *flanerie*" as they strolled the rue de Rivoli and the Tuileries, had dinner at various cafés, and then went to the theater. Her father's time in Paris gave him respite from the anxiety of Covent Garden and the jealous tirades of his wife (by now he was reputed to be a philanderer), and they released Fanny from the routine of her studies. They were "golden" days in her calendar, moments of elation as her father escorted her to *déjeuner à la fourchette* at smart cafés and on walks through the Paris streets.[51] During these summer days with Charles, she felt that father and daughter were no longer adrift on the open sea, as they had been in the picture at Blackheath. Safe on the imaginative and magical island that was Paris, Fanny told him about her reading and her success in the amateur theatricals not exactly encouraged by Mrs. Rowden (they were not in line with her strict Methodism) but tactfully ignored as the girls were rehearsed by Mademoiselle Descuilles, the principal teacher, in a production of Racine's *Andromaque*. Kemble played Hermione in what she believed was an electrifying performance. But Mrs. Rowden thought otherwise and told her at bedtime that her parents need never worry about her going on the stage since she "would make but a poor actress,"[52] a remark probably designed to squash such an ambition since she was familiar with the Kemble family's desire to keep their children off the stage.

When Fanny was a little past sixteen, as she described herself, "a very pretty-looking girl, with fine eyes, teeth, and hair, a clear, vivid complexion, and rather good features,"[53] she returned to the family's summer cottage at Weybridge, and to her mother. Wearing a chic straw hat bought for her by her father and sporting a social self-possession that she never lost, she fell into Thérèse's arms as she descended from the coach, her fear that she would be unwelcome quickly assuaged by the warm embraces of the family. But she relapsed quickly into the earlier pattern of boredom and rebellion. On the weekends her father arrived from Soho Square, and that cheered her a little, but during the week there was, quite simply, nothing for her to do. Thérèse Kemble was happier than she had ever been, but she proved a dull companion for an intellectually curious sixteen-year-old girl who had just spent four years studying French and Italian literature and exploring vibrant post-Napoleonic Paris. Surrounded by fruit trees and flower gardens and fronted by the River Wey, the cottage faced beautiful woods, and Thérèse no longer talked of moving. The furniture remained in place. The future of her restless daughter remained the only difficulty.

After four years of disciplined study, Fanny now followed no systematic program of work but began "an epoch of indiscriminate, omnivorous reading" that lasted until she went on the stage in 1829.[54] She continued to read Walter Scott and Byron, tastes indulged while at Mrs. Rowden's, and in an arrangement common for intellectually ambitious young women in the early nineteenth century she was guided to Goethe and demanding translations of Italian by her brother's tutor, Dr. Malkin. She also began what she describes in self-deprecating fashion as the "objectionable practice of scribbling verse without stint or stay."[55] Reading German literature, writing poetry, fishing in the Wey, and taking lessons in piano and voice from her mother, Kemble in these few years led a life that was deceptively calm, her only acknowledged misery the nervous terror to which she was reduced by her mother's impatience with her contralto voice. But her days were aimless: her parents, having determined that their intellectually gifted elder daughter should be well educated and not tempted by the stage, had no idea what to do with her. Adelaide remained a bore, her nine-year-old brother Henry was uninteresting, and she missed the intellectual companionship of her brother John Mitchell, away at Cambridge, a member of the famous Apostles, a close friend of Alfred Tennyson, a devout worshiper of John Stuart Mill, and a firm advocate of the philosophy of Jeremy Bentham.

Unexpectedly, in the spring of 1827 when she was seventeen, Kemble's intellectual and emotional life changed forever during a visit to her aunt, the widow of John Philip Kemble, who had returned to England from Switzerland after his death in 1823 to live at Heath Farm in Hertfordshire, a comfortable and elegant house on the estate of Lord Essex, one of John Kemble's patrons. It was at Heath Farm that Kemble met the eccentric, intellectual thirty-year-old woman who became a deeply loved friend, confidante, and advisor. On rambling walks through the Hertfordshire countryside began what Kemble termed "the love bestowed upon my whole life by Harriet St. Leger."[56]

The Gaze of Every Eye

I resolved to go the play. It was Covent Garden Theatre ...
when I came out into the rainy street, at twelve o'clock at
night, I felt as if I had come from the clouds, where I had been
leading a romantic life for ages, to a bawling, splashing, link-
lighted, umbrella-struggling, hackney-coach-jostling, patten-
clinking, muddy, miserable world.

— Charles Dickens, *David Copperfield*

Giving Up Byron

Harriet St. Leger was unlike any other woman Fanny Kemble had ever met. A member of a reclusive Anglo-Irish country family, she lived at Ardgillan Castle, a fine eighteenth-century manor house set close to the cliffs about fifteen miles north of Dublin. The daughter of the Hon. Richard St. Leger and a granddaughter of Viscount Doneraile of County Cork, she had lived at the castle for some fifteen years with her sister Marianne and Marianne's husband, a Church of Ireland cleric, at the time of meeting Kemble. Harriet was tall, angular, and athletic, with cropped chestnut hair and fine gray eyes, and eccentric in many things, none more so than in her clothes. Dressed in men's hats and boots especially made for her in London, beautifully cut black and gray cashmere dresses, trim-fitting short waistcoats, and immaculate collars and cuffs, she looked like an androgynous and beautiful young man. To Kemble, she was a modern Atalanta or Diana, the Greek mythology wood goddesses known for hunting and aversion to marriage. To Frances Power Cobbe, the prominent Victorian antivivisectionist and intellectual, who grew up not far from Ardgillan Castle, she was "a deep and singularly critical thinker and reader [who] had one of the warmest hearts which ever beat under a cold and shy exterior." Cobbe adds that Harriet's fondness for male clothing (especially black beaver hats) made her as peculiar in the eyes of her neighbors as the notorious Ladies of Llangollen were in theirs—Lady Eleanor Butler and Miss Sarah Ponsonby, learned and literary Regency women who were renowned for living openly as a lesbian couple.[1] According to Cobbe, "All the empty-headed men and women in the county prated incessantly" about Harriet's "offensive garments."[2]

Eager for affection and intelligent companionship, Kemble discovered in Harriet much that had been missing from her life: as Cobbe puts it, "the iridescent genius of Fanny Kemble in the prime of her splendid womanhood" was drawn to seek Harriet's sympathy.[3] Whether their friendship was explicitly homosexual remains uncertain without plausible evidence—and there is none—but their feelings as expressed in the letters they exchanged for the next fifty years are charged with homoerotic intensity. Robert Bernard Martin characterizes their friendship as one of "great intimacy, best described as love, made up of many components,"[4] and given Kemble's vibrant personality, it is easy to imagine that just as she was drawn to Harriet's spare elegance of mind and body, so Harriet was attracted by Kemble's magnetic physicality. Missing Harriet in February 1830, and at the height of her newly minted theatrical celebrity, Kemble wrote to her, "How I wish you and I had wings, and that Heath Farm belonged to us!"[5] There, if not to live exactly as the Ladies of Llangollen, she knew she would find in Harriet the tenderness and intellectual challenge that had been absent from the Weybridge cottage, the niceties of French schooling, and the training in drawing room graces offered by Thérèse Kemble. Harriet found in her "gorgeous friend" (which is how Frances Power Cobbe described Kemble)[6] an unaffected desire to be instructed and to be loved. At Heath Farm in 1827, they walked together everyday and often talked well into the night, Fanny responding avidly to Harriet's speculative habits of thought, her interest in metaphysical subjects, and her relish in debating abstract moral questions. Harriet forced her into more rigorous thinking than anyone she had encountered in Paris, and Kemble, in return, offered a joyous love of life that she hoped would cheer her "moping owl," her nickname for her friend. If Bellina Grimani had been a radiant maternal image when she was six, and if Dall was her comforting surrogate mother until her death when Kemble was twenty-four, then Harriet, at this moment, was the perfect, androgynous parent. She combined the unguarded, intuitive love that Thérèse Kemble provided when she was calm and the cultured intellect to which Charles Kemble always aspired. If with her parents and her teachers Fanny had been a performing daughter and student, then with Harriet she was an adoring acolyte.

In contrast to Thérèse, Harriet was equable rather than volatile; intellectual and austere rather than emotional and excessive; encouraging rather than unappeasable. She became an incisive critic of Kemble's mind and writings, a meticulous reader of the verse and a play about Francis the First that she was writing at the time, and she was a delighted audience for her impromptu entertainments. On one of their epic walks around the countryside, Harriet listened, enraptured, while Kemble sang her version of Carl Maria Von Weber's *Oberon* that she had just heard performed at Covent Garden, sitting in the manager's box, which she did with her mother two or three times a week. As payment for this bravura feat of musical memory, Harriet took them to lunch at a local alehouse where they tucked into bread and cheese, drank beer, and hid themselves from friends' carriages as they rumbled past the window. Encouraged by the emotional acceptance and intelligent comradeship she had missed at home, Kemble flourished and now began to confide in Harriet the history of her troubled childhood, the uncertainty of her present life, and her ambitions for the future. Precisely because she was *not* her mother, Harriet could offer the serious guidance that Kemble needed if she were ever to harness her multiple talents.

After she had known Harriet for almost a year, Kemble confided that she felt herself unfit "to marry, to make an obedient wife, or affectionate mother" since her mercurial imagination would disqualify her for the everyday business of running a household; indeed, right up until the time she became the wife of Pierce Butler in Christ Church, Philadelphia, on June 4, 1834, she continued to express to Harriet her doubts about her suitability for marriage.[7] Determined to remain unencumbered (perhaps in emulation of Harriet St. Leger's idiosyncratic independence), in the summer and autumn of 1827 Kemble read constantly, plunged one day into the lush language of Byron's *Manfred* and the next lifted into the simple splendor and inspiration of Jeremy Taylor's *Holy Living*. Tramping the countryside with Harriet when they were at Heath Farm or fishing with her mother in the River Wye, she worried little about her future. But she was full of passionate feeling, and the two people to whom she was now most attached, Harriet and her father, were not always present when she needed them; her friend was often back at Ardgillan Castle and her father was seriously distracted by the financial mess at Covent Garden. Kemble continued to write reams of verse, but despite her relative serenity and Harriet's encouragement, she did not shape it into publishable work. She knew how miserably she was wasting her talents, but, separated from Harriet, she became depressed and lazy.

The companionship of her older brother, John, was no longer a consolation since he was at Cambridge, although he occasionally came down to London accompanied by his fellow students Alfred Tennyson and Arthur Hallam; her younger brother, Henry, was at school with Dr. Malkin in Bury St. Edmund's; and her sister, Adelaide, was of little interest since she was only thirteen. Kemble spent almost a year doing little but lazing around the Weybridge cottage, writing poetry and finishing her five-act play, *Francis the First*. Initially conceived as a historical novel, it dramatizes the story of the early sixteenth-century French king of France and his mother, Louisa of Savoy. Kemble followed the pattern of Elizabethan drama and mixed historical events, family discord, lovers' quarrels, and tragic resolution, but she knew it was not successful. Always an astute critic of her own work, she later judged it full of "stilted declamation," lacking any valuable dramatic construction, and devoid of poetic merit. The play was eventually performed at Covent Garden in March 1832, and its brief success and the considerable amount of money John Murray paid to publish it Kemble accurately and ruefully attributed to the curiosity of London audiences about her celebrity.[8] But in terms of Kemble's volatile relationship with her mother, there are several intriguing things about *Francis the First*: in the first place, the most powerful character in the play is Francis's mother, and in the short-lived London production Kemble chose to play this part, an ambitious, vengeful, and jealous woman so possessive of her son that she tries to poison his beloved, who warns her, at the end of the play, "Hark you, madam! / 'Tis time you lay aside the glittering bauble, / Which, hourly, in your hands grows mores respectless;— / I speak of power." In the second place, Kemble dedicated the play to her mother. In writing a play about a dominant mother, in deciding to perform this role herself, and then dedicating the play to her own mother, Fanny expresses some deeply ambivalent feelings about the powerful, volatile, and destructive personality of Thérèse Kemble.

Unexpectedly, in the spring of 1828, Kemble's rudderless existence was steered to one of the happiest times of her life: a year spent in Edinburgh with her cousin, Harriet Siddons, who was an attractive and intelligent former actress and the widow of Sarah Siddons's youngest son, Harry, who had been an actor and manager of theaters in Dublin, Glasgow, and Edinburgh. After the death of her husband, Harriet Siddons continued management of the Theatre Royal, Edinburgh, and the practice of promoting Scottish drama that conveyed strong nationalistic messages, an enterprise in which she and her husband had been supported by Walter Scott. After Harriet Siddons visited the Kemble house in Buckingham Gate and became concerned about Fanny Kemble's restlessness and bad temper, Harriet suggested that Kemble spend some time with her in Scotland, sensing, astutely, that a separation from Thérèse Kemble would provide good medicine, if not a cure. Looking back on this time in her memoirs, Kemble notes that just before she went to Edinburgh her life at home had become "difficult and troublesome, and unsatisfactory to others; my mind and character were in a chaotic state of fermentation that required the wisest, firmest, and gentlest guidance. I was vehement and excitable, violently impulsive, and with a wild, ill-regulated imagination."[9]

Later in Kemble's life, many others besides Harriet Siddons were distressed by her unpredictable personality, her impulsive vehemence, and her morbid self-absorption. Harriet Martineau, for example, when she met Kemble in Philadelphia in the early days of her marriage, was disturbed by what she perceived to be a perverse "sporting" with her privileges: she declared that Kemble was "finely gifted" but undisciplined, unprincipled, and self-centered.[10] To be fair, this judgment must be placed in the context of Martineau's severe standards when assessing other nineteenth-century women; if figures such as Mary Wollstonecraft (about whose amorous adventures Martineau was particularly scathing) failed to subordinate erotic passion to intellectual work, they fell short. But the judgment of others, much closer to Kemble, suggest that Martineau was, in part, correct. For example, when Pierce Butler and Fanny Kemble were engaged in the last of many wrenching quarrels that had led previously to reconciliation but in this case precipitated divorce, Elizabeth Sedgwick, sister-in-law of Catharine Sedgwick and always a loyal friend, warned Kemble in June 1839 that she must try to discipline the irrational behavior that was so clearly the inheritance of her mother's psychological illnesses or she would be destroyed by it.[11]

As Kemble recalls it, "to the anxious, nervous, exciting, irritating tenor of my London life succeeded the calm, equable, and all but imperceptible control of my dear friend."[12] The power of Harriet Siddons over Kemble was clearly different from that of Bellina Grimani, always present in Kemble's memory, and emotionally distinct from that of Harriet St. Leger, now her beloved friend. If Bellina Grimani was her aesthetic muse and Harriet St. Leger her Diana, then Harriet Siddons became her goddess of the hearth and home. Kemble could see the benevolent influence that she had over her own children, which she knew to be the result of her wisdom in dealing with them. A flirtation with Harriet Siddons's twenty-year-old son, Henry, for example, was dealt with very differently by Harriet Siddons than it would have been by her own mother: Kemble knew that her mother's hysterical apprehensions would probably have precipitated a childish engagement, whereas Harriet Siddons seemed oblivious to any danger. The result was that Henry Siddons went off to India with Kemble's name engraved upon his sword, and that was that, leaving Kemble still "idolatrous" about his mother and turning her attention to the talk about government that she was allowed to hear in the Siddons drawing room. The theater gossip of London was replaced by debate about Scottish politics.

In 1828 Edinburgh was the splendid capital of Scotland. Figures such as Walter Scott, Sydney Smith, Henry Brougham, and Francis Jeffrey were at the center of Scottish literary and intellectual culture, which was dominated by the *Edinburgh Review*, a journal founded in 1802 by a group of young lawyers led by Brougham and Jeffrey. Moreover, the intellectual life of Edinburgh had benefited in part from the Napoleonic Wars since students unable to study in France were drawn to the University of Edinburgh, whose reputation had been established in the mid- to late eighteenth-century Scottish Enlightenment. Harriet Siddons, gracefully learned, socially prominent by virtue of having descended from the social secretary to the Young Pretender, and with none of the green-room taint that often stuck to actresses, opened her drawing room to the Edinburgh intelligentsia. In the elegant gray stone terrace house on Windsor Street, set high over the city with a view of the Water of Leith, Kemble was exposed to conversation engagingly different from that to which she was accustomed. Undeniably, Charles Kemble's informed interest in sculpture, philology, and literature redeemed him from showy vulgarity, but the talk at home was almost always about the theater. In Edinburgh, all matters of public interest were discussed from the most liberal and enlightened point of view (Kemble thought), and in her memoirs she acknowledges the great advantage for an intelligent girl of her age to hear "such vigorous, manly, clear expositions of the broadest aspects of all the great political and governmental questions of the day."[13] Among Harriet Siddons's closest friends were two brothers, George and Andrew Combe, who shared a house on Northumberland Street, near her Windsor Street home. George Combe was a lawyer and phrenologist who was later consulted by Prince Albert with regard to the royal children and asked to examine their heads; Andrew was a physician whose writings on physiology, hygiene, and physical education were influential during the Victorian period. In 1833, George Combe married Sarah and William Siddons's daughter Cecilia, and after Kemble left Edinburgh she maintained a close correspondence with the Combe family.

When not sitting at the feet of the Combe brothers, Kemble tramped up and down the hills around Edinburgh, singing to herself the Scottish ballads that she was just beginning to learn and visiting the fishing villages that spread out from the city. She loved the wild beauty of the ballads, the terror and pity of their stories, the Jacobite songs of noble heroism, the pathetic and humorous songs of Burns. The ballads were to her "the deepest and freshest sources of poetical thought and feeling," and throughout her life her friends were often treated to an impromptu concert delivered in her rich contralto voice.[14] Singing, or reading while walking, always remained a pleasure for Kemble. When she was living at 79 Great Russell Street in London in 1831 (the house had belonged to John Philip Kemble and had been bought by her father with profits made from her Covent Garden success), she would walk around sooty Russell Square reciting her lines for the part of Lady Teazle in Sheridan's *School for Scandal*; when she took up Alpine walking in her fifties, she would tramp along singing so loudly that she became known to the Alpine guides as the peculiar Englishwoman who sang in the mountains. In Edinburgh, then, listening to the "manly" talk of Edinburgh's professional classes and singing sad Jacobite ballads on her lonely walks, Fanny Kemble developed the "graver turn of thought" that had been initiated by Harriet St. Leger.

She vowed, first, to give up reading Byron, influenced in part by the contempt of Francis Jeffrey for the Romantic poets, Byron in particular. Jeffrey and other members of the "manly Edinburgh circle" became an important influence on her literary tastes; Jeffrey had particular power as the literary editor of the *Edinburgh Review* and as a close friend of Harriet Siddons. Giving up Byron was a tremendous sacrifice and required great effort since she loved the way poems such as *Cain* and *Manfred* excited her emotionally. But she also knew that the exhausting frenzy they produced in her was alarmingly similar to the feelings she and her mother experienced when they were fighting with each other. Moreover, Thérèse Kemble possessed, in the words of her daughter, an "extreme admiration" for Byron. When Kemble went to Edinburgh, she not only matured emotionally, she also re-formed her literary tastes. From her thrilling immersion in the lives and works of the Romantic poets—when Kemble was in Paris from 1821 to 1825, Byron was in Italy with Mary and Percy Shelley and Leigh Hunt, and Kemble would have fantasies of an imaginative link with these glamorous figures—she transformed her infatuation with Byron into admiration for Wordsworth, just as the century in which she lived shifted its cultural and moral attitudes from Romantic to Victorian.

In essence, she left behind her tumultuous Regency childhood and grew up to become a Victorian young woman. She termed herself "un enfant du siècle," a wild girl produced by the wild spirit of the age, and for her Byron was the poetic voice of that spirit. He shaped into verse the revolutionary passions that were sweeping Europe but, Kemble came to believe, at the historical moment when he "was growling and howling, and Shelley was denying and defying, Scott was telling and Wordsworth singing things beautiful and good, and new and true."[15] At the end of her Edinburgh year, she was far less a howling, defiant girl and much more a contemplative, settled young woman. After two years of not reading Byron she was no longer enthralled by him, and she claimed that the new, early Victorian generation was not either, since it was now reading Thackeray, Dickens, and Tennyson. Her letters to Harriet St. Leger warn of the dangers posed by Byron's verse and ideas to "young brains." Rather primly, she announces that his "despondent, defiant, questioning, murmuring, bitter, proud spirit" acts powerfully and dangerously upon young people, and her characterization of Byron's spirit can be substituted easily for a description of own state of mind before she went to Edinburgh. In the grip of what she calls her "blue devils"—defying authority, fighting with her mother, and rebelling against all rule—she seemed, before, a true *enfant du siècle*. After the Edinburgh year, she anticipated and obeyed the narrator's call in Thomas Carlyle's *Sartor Resartus* (published in 1833–34) to "Close thy Byron; open thy Goethe!"

In the spring of 1829 Kemble returned to London, her mind having developed "a rather serious bias" and her reading having turned almost entirely to sermons and religious essays.[16] She found her parents overwhelmed with anxiety about the financial state of Covent Garden and her father the principal litigant in the suit brought by shareholders against the proprietors of the Theatre for unpaid debts. These legal quarrels, which quickly entered the Court of Chancery, a nineteenth-century civil process designed to provide remedies where the common law failed to do so, affirm Tracy Davis's observation that nineteenth-century "theatre practitioners operated in their own self-interest, and not for the greater glory of dramatic literature, theatre aesthetics, or proletarian culture."[17] Chancery was generally concerned with contracts, trusts, and disputes in which it was difficult to apply a specific body of law, and the term "Chancery" became synonymous with lengthy, expensive, and surrealistically bizarre legal processes.[18] It seemed to Kemble when she returned to London from Edinburgh that her parents were on the road to Chancery ruin, steeped in depression about their "miserably uncertain circumstances."[19]

Desperate for ways to resolve the financial crisis, Charles Kemble spoke of sending his wife and children to live cheaply in the south of France while he continued to work in London and to seek acting engagements on the Continent. Then, in the autumn of 1829, when he was absent on a professional tour in Ireland and Thérèse and Fanny were sitting at home in Buckingham Gate, Thérèse suddenly burst into tears and announced that the dreadful day had come at last. Faced with unpayable bills for rates and taxes, the shareholders had decided that Covent Garden Theatre must be sold. It was plastered with placards and bills of sale, and hundreds of people who worked at the Theatre would be unemployed. In her memoirs, Kemble describes herself at this moment as "seized with a sort of terror," feeling cursed like Tennyson's Lady of Shalott.[20] She wrote immediately to her father that she would seek work as a governess, a reasonable enough suggestion given her education and social class. Her mother, however, after she had pulled herself together, proposed a less dismal future for Fanny: the family should abandon temporarily its desire for none of the Kemble children to become actors. The most talented of the four would be transformed into a Kemble ingenue. As Kemble put it plainly to her friend on September 24, 1829, "My dear Harriet, I am going on the stage."[21]

The Skeleton in the Kemble Closet

In 1831, Fanny Kemble wrote in her unfinished autobiographical manuscript, "Before my Aunt Siddons's time, women on the stage I believe generally led immoral lives. Their position naturally affords greater temptations and greater facilities for irregular conduct than any other career."[22] Although Kemble wished to believe that by the time her aunt had become the revered tragedienne Sarah Siddons actresses no longer led "immoral lives" or were *thought* to lead such lives, the devotion of the Kemble family to maintaining their impeccable respectability suggests the contrary. Sarah Siddons may have been a paragon of virtue, but the association of actresses with sexual immorality preceded her late eighteenth-century celebrity and flourished well into the nineteenth century. She was the exception to the "irregular conduct" found in the racy world within and without the London theater and the title of a book published in 1792, *The Secret History of the Green Room: Containing Authentic and Entertaining Memoirs of the Actors and Actresses in the Three Theatres Royal*, defends its promised revelations: "Were we to dissemble the vices which stain the private life of too many Performers, the full merit would not appear of the virtuous few who escape untainted by contagion."[23] Without question, the Kemble family belonged to "the virtuous few." With the sensational exception of one member of the family whose private life was "stained," if not by "vice" then certainly by some dubious behavior, all the Kembles were lauded for their decorous, well-regulated, and industrious lives. Although the profession of actress retained the licentious aura with which it was regarded in the late eighteenth century, when she became an actress, Fanny Kemble was placed on a moral pedestal from which she was never dislodged in her lifetime. She exemplified the unspotted character of the Kemble dynasty.

However, Sarah Kemble Siddons had a sister, and Fanny Kemble another aunt, whose sensational life symbolized everything that the Kemble dynasty sought to suppress and whose existence is unacknowledged in Fanny Kemble's autobiographical writings. Known at different times in her life as Ann Kemble, Ann Curtis, Ann Julia Hatton, and "Ann of Swansea," she was born on April 29, 1764, in Worcester, the seventh child and fourth daughter in the family. Said to have been born with physical drawbacks that do not seem to have hampered her sexual appeal—lameness, a squint, and the large Kemble frame that in Sarah Siddons's case became a majestic stage presence but in Ann's led to a sort of lumpy largeness—Ann Kemble played minor roles in companies touring the provincial circuits until the age of nineteen. She left the stage in 1783 when she married an actor named Curtis, who turned out to be a bigamist, and in the same year she began what was termed "lecturing" on "chastity and other delicate subjects" at one of the most extraordinary edifices ever to grace Pall Mall: a charlatan sex palace called the Temple of Health and Hymen. *The Secret History of the Green Room* declares that this "vicious woman, who would not conform to modesty . . . read lectures in Dr. Graham's Temple of Health, at which decency would have blushed; and notwithstanding she disgraced her relations in many respects, she expected their countenance and support."[24]

The Temple was presided over by James Graham, a handsome Scottish charlatan who has been described, variously, as a therapist, a showman, and a quack. Contemporary accounts of his Temple and what it offered indicate that he resourcefully combined all three roles.[25] With its Greek temple architecture, its five Egyptian sphinxes, its "Great Apollo Apartment," a darkened chamber through which the vital essences of Apollo himself were said to circulate, its exhibition of instruments purported to restore animation to persons recently dead, and its scantily costumed "gods" and "goddesses" (played, mostly, by unemployed actors and actresses), the Temple provided dramatic spectacle, rickety science, dreamy music, and a titillating sex show. Dominating the Temple were two displays: a "magnificent and most powerful Medico-electrical Apparatus" that offered a gentle form of electric-shock therapy and a "celestial bed" that promised to produce maximum sexual pleasure and immediate conception.[26] As they wandered around the Temple, visitors were encouraged to buy Graham's "Three Great Medicines": Electrical Ether, Nervous Aetherial Balsam, and the Imperial Pills. Should the medicines have failed to appeal, Graham offered to bury his clients up to the chin in fresh mold.

The gigantic "Apparatus" consisted of an enormous metallic conductor, some eleven feet long and four feet in circumference, connected by the body of a brilliantly painted fiery dragon to an equally large cylinder, in front of which was an elaborate, insulated throne on which the patients sat, their rheumatism and dyspepsia dispatched by the electrical currents that Graham sent their way. If their ailments were of a more sexual nature, then the celestial bed was the next stop. Twelve feet by nine, covered by a mattress "filled with the strongest, most springy hair, produced at vast expense from the tails of English stallions which are elastic to the highest degree,"[27] it was supported by forty pillars of brilliant glass in variegated colors. Above the bed was a super-celestial dome that was touted as being a "grand reservoir of those reviving invigorating influences which are exhaled by . . . the exhilarating forces of electrical fire." This fire, combined with music and the balmy odors of aromatic ethereal essences (a form of eighteenth-century aromatherapy), caused "immediate conception" and a powerful agitation of "the delights of love" for any couple willing to fork over fifty pounds to Graham, whose showmanship catered brilliantly to a late eighteenth-century public eager for quick fixes for aches and pains and sexual malfunction.

Since the Temple employed actors and actresses to play such roles as apothecaries and goddesses of health (among them Emma Lyon, who went on to become the mistress of Charles Greville, the wife of Sir William Hamilton, and then the mistress of Horatio Nelson) and the goddesses of health were available for assistance in the celestial bed, it is probable that Ann Kemble did more than offer lectures at the Temple of Health. Whatever the form of her assistance to James Graham, however, it proved less than successful; in 1783 an advertisement appeared in the London newspapers soliciting "Donations in Favour of Mrs. Curtis, Youngest Sister of Mrs. Siddons." Her "talents for the stage" having been rendered useless by "misfortune" and desiring to become "a useful member to Society," she entreated some deliverance from financial distress. The appeal concluded with the statement that Mrs. Curtis was the youngest sister of Messrs. Kemble and Mrs. Siddons, whom she had repeatedly solicited for some "relief" and who had flatly refused her. She hoped that the public, having liberally supported her brothers and her sister, would now come to *her* aid.[28] Apparently it did not, for the next we hear of Ann Kemble is her injury in a bagnio (a common term for brothel) in the Covent Garden Piazza; according to a contemporary newspaper item, a pistol was "presented" to her by her male companion, whereupon he "pulled the trigger, and lodged the contents in her face! Her right eye was driven from the socket, and her face exhibited an indescribably shocking spectacle!"[29] The newspaper concluded by defending what it termed her "avocation": if it has been "*immoral*, it has been excited by poignant distress, for she was obliged, even by the sacrifice of her person, to provide 'for the calls of the morrow!'" As things turned out, Ann Kemble was injured far less seriously than the account suggests, and the next day she put a notice in the newspaper to that effect. An unsuccessful actress, driven by "poignant distress" to her "avocation," she exemplifies the popular association of actresses and prostitutes that Tracy Davis, in her study of the position of the actress in Victorian culture, complicates through exploration of the importance of issues of class and gender.[30]

In the early 1790s Ann Kemble married William Hatton, a maker of musical instruments, who took her to New York where she had some success as a songwriter and librettist for two productions staged in the John Street Theater.[31] By 1800 she was back in Great Britain operating a hotel in Swansea, whereupon she transformed herself into "Ann of Swansea" and published thirteen works of virtually unreadable gothic fiction between 1810 and 1831, despite the fact that some of her language was so "indelicate" reviewers were reluctant to believe it proceeded "from a female pen."[32] The title *Secrets in Every Mansion: or, The Surgeon's Memorandum-Book; a Scottish Record* (1818) gives some idea of her novels. In her last years, her small income was supplemented by an annual stipend of twenty pounds granted by Sarah Siddons on the condition that she live at least one hundred fifty miles from London, a bequest of twenty pounds annually from her father, and a legacy of sixty pounds annually left by John Philip Kemble in his will. She died in 1838, the year that her niece Fanny Kemble Butler traveled to Georgia to visit her husband's cotton and rice plantations.

When Fanny Kemble announced to Harriet St. Leger on September 24, 1829, that she was going on the stage, even if she had no knowledge of the scandalous details of the career of her aunt Ann, she knew that she was entering a profession in which she would be subject to moral censure, to patronizing exclusion, and even to charges of sexual promiscuity. The transgressive life of Ann Kemble, censored from the Kemble family narrative, lived on to shadow the career of her niece.

Fanny Is Brought Out

As preparation for going on the stage, Fanny Kemble was immediately immersed in a three-week course in stage acting that her mother had devised for her. Drawing on forty years of experience in the theater that had begun when she was a chirpy six-year-old at Drury Lane, Thérèse Kemble had a great deal to teach, and Fanny had a great deal to learn.[33] Thérèse knew from experience that Fanny was an accomplished singer (thanks to her instruction) and also an enthusiastic participant in family charades, but she was not sure how well this physically unimposing girl might project herself into the vast spaces of Covent Garden, nor if she had the discipline and fortitude to turn her talent for self-dramatization into a professional career. She asked her to read something from Shakespeare.

For this family audition, Kemble chose one of Portia's speeches from *The Merchant of Venice*. The more somber turn of mind she had adopted since returning from Edinburgh had occasioned some lessening of her identification with the bereft Miranda; now, she developed a grave admiration for Portia's measured temperament and considered her an embodiment of ideal womanhood—generous, affectionate, and wise, in many ways not unlike Harriet Siddons.[34] Her favorite speech was the one addressed to Bassanio, after his successful choice of casket, in which Portia submits "with all her heart . . . the woman of women."[35] In light of Kemble's later battles with her husband about the proper nature of wifely obedience, it is ironic that she loved a speech that concludes with Portia's humble acquiescence to the direction of "her lord, her governor, her king" (3.2.165-66). At this moment, however, she composed herself as best she could before her demanding mother, and modestly delivered her lines. Thérèse was neither impressed nor encouraging; she admired the dignified delivery but she was surprised by the timid approach. If Kemble were to work some box-office magic, they needed a little more dramatic fire.

Since *Romeo and Juliet* was a perennial Covent Garden favorite and Juliet more suited to Fanny's girlish appearance, Thérèse suggested she read the speech at the beginning of Act III, Scene 2, in which Juliet pours out her longing for Romeo: "Come, gentle night; come, loving, black-brow'd night, / Give me my Romeo." This was very much better than her Portia speech, probably because Kemble was so terrified her mother's disappointment would destroy her chance to help Covent Garden (and her father), she put all her passionate anxiety into the reading. When Charles Kemble returned to London the next morning, he was instructed to take his daughter to a darkened Covent Garden to test her voice. Set down, as she remembers it, in the midst of the twilight space of the empty stage with her father's image shrouded in the gloom of the empty pit, Kemble entered into the spirit of the thing. Her contralto voice resounded through the great vault of the enormous theater and she found herself carried away by the inspiration of Shakespeare's verse. She felt herself acting Juliet as she never would again, "for I had no visible Romeo, and no audience to thwart my imagination."[36] As she reconstructs in her memoirs this tumultuous moment in her dramatic life, she invests it with a powerful theatricality. She performs only for her father, both of them half lit, she on the empty stage, he in the shadowy pit. But secreted in a private box and invisible to Kemble was an old friend of her father's, identified in her memoirs as "Major Dawkins, a man of the world." When she sank to one knee, drove the dagger into her heart, smiled with a look of triumphant defiance, and fell flat on her back, he quickly sent a note to Charles Kemble: "Bring her out at once; it will be a great success." Her first performance for her father, dedicated to him with unquestionable love (unlike the problematical dedication of *Francis the First* to her mother), was a tremendous hit.

When she acted Juliet at this moment before her father and felt the role in every nerve of her being, she lived entirely in the verse. With no bumbling and improbably middle-aged Romeo of the sort she later encountered in her provincial touring, and with no restless London audience given to talking, swilling ale, and wandering around the theater it usually inhabited from six in the evening until midnight, she was alone with the poetry and her imagination. This is what mattered most, and always, to Kemble. Quite simply, she adored Shakespeare. Woven into the fabric of her emotional and intellectual being, his plays provided her with powerful references for evoking the drama of her life, and she never lost her intense delight, as she put it, in the "act of rendering Shakespeare's creations."[37] Quoting with perfect accuracy from the plays in her letters and in her conversation, deploying with elegant precision his images in her memoirs to set a scene, characterize an individual, or evoke a moment, Kemble brought to the audition for her father this passionate love of Shakespeare. When she began her dramatic readings fifteen years later, she garnered all this love and all her training to produce some shattering effects, which were commemorated by one of her dearest American friends, Henry Longfellow, in a sonnet that concludes with the lines, "Oh Happy Poet! By no critic vext! / How must thy listening spirit now rejoice / To be interpreted by such a voice!"[38]

The preparation for the "bringing out" began on the very afternoon of her Covent Garden audition, with Charles Kemble as an assistant instructor to Thérèse. Their raw material was what Fanny describes as "the dramatic element inherent" in her "organization," but she knew little of the fundamental business of stagecraft: how to move around the stage, how to project her voice, how to work with the company. The "attitudes," the late eighteenth- and early nineteenth-century fashion for the actor to hold a physical position expressive of a particular emotion—supplication, astonishment, anger, disgust, and so on—presented a particular challenge. These were derived from classical models of rhetorical gesture, and Kemble's talent was for spontaneous outbursts of feeling, not for carefully calibrated turns of the neck. But she soon developed her own characteristic attitudes and audiences loved her for them, such as the moment when Juliet waits for the nurse and a message from Romeo; she would lean on the back of her chair, gaze out of an open window, her ardent yearning expressed in a minute or so of sculpted, frozen movement.[39] As Rebecca Jenkins points out, in a theater the size of Covent Garden (there were approximately 2,800 seats), only those in the pit and in the boxes closest to the stage could expect to hear and see the nuances of speech and facial expression; the attitudes were essential for "telegraphing emotion through physicality—body-line, vigorous movement and mime."[40]

Fanny Kemble's supple display of this technique when she made her debut as Juliet in October 1829 suggests a developed formal expression of her tendency from childhood to release her feelings through the body. Whether garnering attention from passersby as she danced for their amusement in the Bayswater garden, cavorting on the roof of her French school, skipping for miles across the Scottish hills, or furiously riding her horse along the banks of the Schuylkill River in Philadelphia, Kemble conveyed through contrived physical attitudes the passions that she often censored from her writings, or expressed less coherently through language. Undeniably, she was an extraordinary conversationalist, feared by some for her brusque impatience with slower minds than her own, and she was also a brilliant correspondent (to which the letters of Harriet St. Leger attest in their grateful acknowledgment of so much news, so much information, so much sheer life). Moreover, she was a skillful and fluent writer of prose, as one can see from

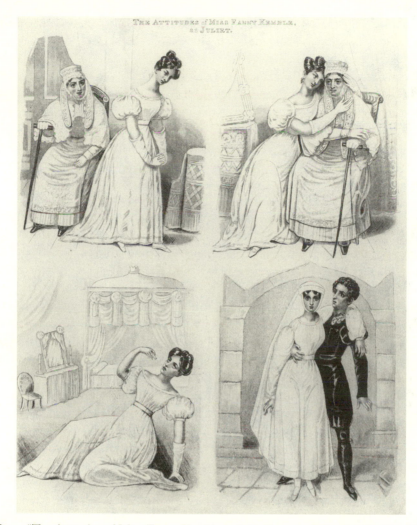

Fig. 7. "The Attitudes of Miss Fanny Kemble as Juliet," engraved shortly after Kemble's debut in 1829. © National Portrait Gallery, London.

her memoirs and essays. Yet she was often wary of confidences, and at her most unhappy (even in the early months of her marriage) she tended to put on a show of emotional contentment for her friends. She edited the letters that constitute her autobiographical writings, and her memoirs do not always state directly what seems to be expressed in her less guarded description of physical movement. The capering as a child signals a desire for attention in the Kemble family world of narcissistic devotion to one's reputation; the escapade on the roof, a wish to be recognized as a brightly intelligent young girl; the tramping through the Scottish hills, a joy in being free of her mother's neurotic compulsions; the reckless riding, a furious resentment of her husband. To be sure, these feelings are conveyed powerfully in her writings, but they gain intensity through Kemble's description of physical action. Emotion is telegraphed through Kemble's movements, just as, onstage, the feelings of her characters were expressed through her elegant "attitudes." In a complex affiliation of theatrical technique with individual feeling, Fanny Kemble may be said to have "performed" her passions in her writings through a vivid evocation of physical movement. In a similar and complex manner, she defends herself against charges that her attitudes were too studied by declaring she first saw things and feelings in her mind as "pictures" before executing them on the stage.[41]

After her career was long over, Kemble attributed the accolades that were heaped upon her not to any mastery of the attitudes but to an intuitive talent for expressing histrionic passion and to the strict training from her parents. She knew, and was never reluctant to admit, that her early performances had been uneven and erratic, that they had depended more on her emotional state at the moment she stepped onstage and less on disciplined technique. However, contrary to her self-assessment that the performances were sometimes uncontrolled, some critics felt that her acting was calculatingly cold. The innovative attitudes were seen by the critic for the *Spectator* in 1829, for example, as unnatural: "they border a little too closely on distortion. In expressing dignity or high resolve, we think her particularly unhappy. She uniformly points her toe, in what dancing masters call the fourth position, and throws back her head, till her attitude presents a perilous deviation from the perpendicular."[42] The *Spectator* also criticized what it saw as an unnatural manner of reading: much as the critic admired the "the musical sweetness of Miss KEMBLE's voice," the endowment was "not without its perils."[43]

Applauded or not for her technique, Fanny Kemble was acting in accordance with some of the conventions of the school of performance in which she had been reared by virtue of growing up in a household thick with discussions of acting, philosophical approaches to character, and dissection of current critical standards. This is the "school" of John Philip Kemble and Sarah Siddons, which, according to Joseph Donohue, reflected dominant aesthetic tendencies of its age. Fanny Kemble's uncle and aunt, although often seen primarily as classical actors shaped by late eighteenth-century standards of performance, should, Donohue argues, be seen as members of the "Romantic school" by virtue of an interpretation of character based on subjective response: "The aesthetic impression derived from such an emphasis is that a character is by nature individual and so his response in a given situation is necessarily unique. Consequently the audience identifies sympathetically with the character, sees the world through his eyes, and ultimately finds the meaning of the play inseparable from, and in fact the same as, the meaning of the character's responses."[44] If nothing else, Fanny Kemble brought to her performances the "subjective response" that Donohue identifies, an interpretation of character attested to by her reviews.

October 5, 1829, the night of her "bringing out," was a triumph. Knowing she would get through the day with a minimum amount of nervous anxiety if she followed her usual routine (her regular remedy for calming her nerves), she practiced the piano, walked in St. James's Park, did a little reading, and set off early to drive to the theater with her mother and Dall. After a few minutes of terrified inertia in the wings and a push from Dall, she got onstage, and after mumbling through the first scene, all was well. By the time that she stepped onto the balcony, she felt herself "transported into the imaginary existence of the play," and in a significant instance of Kemble's awareness of how her feelings were expressed through the body, she adds that "the passion I was uttering [sent] hot waves of blushes all over my neck and shoulders."[45] The reviewer for *The Times* declared he had never seen a more triumphant debut; perhaps Kemble appeared a little too "instructed" but no one could claim her talent had been created by the Kemble training. He predicted that she would "prove a great acquisition to the dramatic strength of the theatre."[46] Thomas Noon Talfourd, a barrister and avid theatergoer, wrote that Kemble "repudiated with genius" all previous interpretations of the role through using none of the "girlish prettinesses" on which other actresses relied, and by showing her audience that Juliet was a heroic young woman; he especially liked her gift for integrating the Kemble training with a more naturalistic style. When she "erected her head, and extended her arm with an expressive air which we never saw surpassed in acting,"[47] this was the Kemble manner at work, but Fanny had somehow managed to forge a new way of doing it, to fuse successfully, at least at this moment, her father's stately technique with her mother's passionate feeling. This fusion is attested to by a letter written by a prolific nineteenth-century playwright, John Poole, who saw Kemble in *Romeo and Juliet* three times: "It would be a waste of words to enter into minute criticism upon her performance—you will understand me when I say that it *is worthy of the name she bears.* . . . That she has been instructed is obvious; but her own natural genius is perpetually flashing out, and the instruction she has received does no more than regulate its fury . . . we may say we once more possess a female tragedian of super-eminent genius."[48]

Charles Greville, intimate of statesmen and wry memoirist of late Georgian and early Victorian society, was less enthusiastic. He declared both Kemble's acting and physical appearance a disappointment: her voice was good, but colored too much with the Kemble drawl; the pathetic gestures that so moved Thomas Talfourd excited no emotion in him, although he conceded that since she was young and clever she might become a "very good, perhaps a fine actress." Most damagingly for Greville, she lacked the "pathos and tenderness" of the most acclaimed Juliet of the early nineteenth century, Eliza O'Neill (1791-1872), an Irish actress who, after claiming the part as her own for five years after her debut in 1814, married in 1819 and retired from the stage. More positively, Greville pronounced Kemble's performance as Julia in *The Hunchback* "very good and a great success. Miss Fanny Kemble acted well—for the first time, in my opinion, great acting." The author of *The Hunchback*, James Sheridan Knowles, also liked the Julia performance: "I owe her such a personation of my heroine, as—proud though I was of my offspring—I did not think that heroine afforded scope for. Her 'Julia' has outstripped my most sanguine hopes."[49] But Kemble's physical appearance troubled Greville: at least twice in his memoirs he laments her unfortunate dissimilarity from Sarah Siddons: where her aunt was statuesque and graceful, Kemble was "short, ill-made, with large hands and feet," and her skin, browned by the sun and pitted by the traces of smallpox, was "dark and coarse."[50]

Two other nineteenth-century theater critics liked nothing about Kemble's acting. Mrs. C. Baron Wilson confirms what Kemble herself always conceded about her style: it was "of a kind peculiarly entitled to be designated as spontaneous or gifted." Mrs. Wilson believes her to have been a "born artist, yet something too wilful withal," a comment that points to the inheritance of a dramatic temperament from Thérèse Kemble. Mrs. Wilson concedes that she had been well trained, as indeed did all the critics, but she chides her for a contrary refusal to observe that training, for doing what she fancied when the moment came for displaying its results in practice: "When there was little to say or do, she took no pains, but did it awkwardly, or anyhow; when there was much to be said or done, she came out in the finest manner."[51] H. Barton Baker, historian of the English theater, summing up in 1883 the century's parade of actors, declares that despite the "overflowing houses" that helped Charles Kemble pay off £13,000 of his debts (now about £83,000), Kemble was not a genius: "she had no true sympathy for her art, and has been chiefly conspicuous, after her short-lived triumph, for casting scorn and contempt upon everything and everybody connected with it,"[52] an assessment that, although exaggerated, points to Kemble's undisguised dislike of the theater.

The overflowing houses meant a good income for the Kembles and a restoration of financial stability for the Theatre.[53] In her first season Kemble was paid £30 a week (now, close to £2,000): this was almost triple what Sarah Siddons had received at the zenith of her career, and her father gave her an allowance of £20 a week out of her weekly earnings. In her own words, she quickly went from obscurity as an insignificant schoolgirl to fame as an "object of general public interest."

The rapid presentation of the seven roles she played in her first season meant many daily newspaper notices; these were roles well-known to Covent Garden audiences since they had been done to a turn by Siddons, and part of Kemble's draw was the audience's interest in comparing aunt and niece.[54] But Fanny, so different physically and temperamentally from her majestic aunt, had no desire to mimic her style. She was determined to forge her own, one that combined the dramatic fire and theatrical technique of her parents, an ambition that signals the beginning of her lifelong revision of assigned roles, allotted parts. Her Kemble lineage and identity were inescapable, but she appropriated this inheritance to construct a reputation both professionally and personally far different from that of her aunt Siddons. Moreover, much as she relished the attention she received in London society after her debut as successor to her aunt Siddons, she regarded Siddons as a chilling example of what could happen to actors when they left the stage. Perceiving in her aunt an emotional deadness and social indifference, Kemble strongly denounced the almost narcotic dependence of many actors on the adulation of the audience.

She was not the first to perceive her aunt's emotional inertia after she retired. Thomas Moore, the Irish poet and Kemble's friend after she became a celebrity, noted in June 1828 after a visit to Siddons that she had confessed to only one profound regret in leaving the stage—that she was no longer able to enjoy a "vent for her private sorrows which enabled her to bear them better." Admitting to Moore that she had received critical acclaim for the strength of her acting that should have been understood more correctly as emotional release, she also complained of the great boredom that came upon her in the evening: at the hour when she would have been preparing herself to meet a crowded house she now found herself sitting drearily alone.[55] Kemble intuitively grasped the example in her aunt of the dangers to herself if she allowed the emotional excitement of acting to become addictive; she had the model of her mother's turbulent behavior in front of her. But where Thérèse was unable to cope with her neurosis, Fanny's instinct for psychological self-preservation led her to create unbendable rules and almost punitive schedules for herself. At the theater, she vanquished nervousness by preceding her performances with an established round of duties and pursuits: she would read an instructive sermon, walk vigorously around the nearest London square (depending on where the Kembles were living at the time), and rest for a prescribed period every afternoon. Not always successful in calming her nerves before the theater and not always the mistress of her neuroses, she nevertheless made valiant efforts through the adoption of what she called her "monotonous habits" to forge a managed life.

The first few months after her debut were filled with bouquets, adoring letters, and socially impressive invitations. Thomas Lawrence's sketch of her appeared in shop windows, as did plates and saucers painted with images of her as Juliet; male admirers took to sporting buff-colored neck handkerchiefs with lilac-colored images of Lawrence's sketch printed on them. Most men adored her, although Tom Moore, at their first meeting, thought her rather affected, her voice a little too "Siddonian" with the sentences "rounded off most formidably."[56] But Arthur Hallam, her brother's fellow Apostle at Cambridge who died young and became the subject of Tennyson's *In Memoriam,* was one of her most fervent admirers: he called her his "divine Fanny" and announced dramatically that he meant "to live in her idea." At Covent Garden, he refused to share his opera glasses with his friends since he had them trained permanently on Fanny, and he left the theater "raving" with inspiration for adoring sonnets.[57] (According to Jack Kolb, Fanny Kemble is the subject of one of Hallam's undated sonnets, "To an Admired Lady.")[58] Monckton Milnes, another Cambridge Apostle who became Kemble's lifelong friend, fervently declaimed she was "far too good for her Romeo." He wrote to his mother that when Fanny fell flat on her back (one of her best attitudes), "the impression was quite awful."[59]

Kemble's name also began to appear regularly in gossip columns that recorded her social triumphs as she danced and chatted her way through London society. With a carriage of her own, no longer did she trudge through the muddy London streets, when she was in need of exercise. With her own horse, she was able to take daily lessons at Captain Fozzard's riding school, one day scrutinized carefully by a stately middle-aged woman and a dainty young girl even shorter than herself: the Duchess of Kent and Princess Victoria. When not showing off for royalty at Fozzard's—her favorite trick was to gallop around the ring, very fast, with her hands on her hips—she would ride in Rotten Row, her diminutive figure and commanding control the object of admiring gazes of young men lolling on the rails who had seen her at Covent Garden the night before.

With her newfound wealth she bought a splendid horse for her father and an army commission for her thirteen-year-old brother Henry. Her talented sister, Adelaide, was given the chance to display her voice for the theater and literary luminaries who had come to pay court to Kemble, and even Thérèse began to enjoy herself. Elegantly dressed and full of spirit, she became a chaperone for her famous daughter as she cut her witty swath through London salons and dining rooms, but Fanny preferred to be accompanied by Charles Kemble: she complained that her mother got sleepy and tired too early, whereas her father flirted and talked with all the pretty women he could corner, and did not care at what hour they went home. Especially nice for Fanny was the chance to throw out her faded, threadbare, turned and dyed frocks, and buy herself beautiful clothes. And the money she was earning for the Theatre enabled the design and making of some gorgeous

Fig. 8. Miss Fanny Kemble as Portia. Fanny was particularly proud of her costume for this role. V&A Images/Theatre Museum.

stage costumes, something in which she always took a great interest and delight. Two dresses especially made for her Portia in March 1830 were "really beautiful," she reported to Harriet St. Leger.[60] All her life, Kemble was never reluctant to dress for the part. During her five years as an actress, she often paid as much attention to the details of her costumes as to the nuances of her performance, and in her married life in Philadelphia, she amazed her neighbors with riding outfits that featured Turkish trousers. When she began her Shakespeare readings in 1847, the sumptuous luster of her black velvet and white satin dresses contributed to the brilliantly dramatic effects she produced through her declamatory style.

From October 1829 to August 1832 Kemble was, in her own words, "sought and petted and caressed by persons of conventional and real distinction, and every night that I did not act I might, if my parents had thought it prudent to let me do so, have passed in all the gayety of the fashionable world and the great London season."[61] The crowning accolade came on November 1, 1830, when she acted Lady Townley in Farquhar's *The Provoked Husband* before King William and Queen Adelaide; the next day she received a present of the queen's portrait chased with diamonds. Looking back she wondered how useful a preparation all the tinsel, spectacular success, and giddy popularity was for the "duties and trials" of her later life," but at the time she relished it all. She was twenty years old, physically robust, bursting with energy, and very witty, and even if her "ill-made" figure and "coarse" skin ruled her out as a beauty, she was clearly very attractive. Even her relationship with her mother improved to the extent that after the debut Thérèse Kemble entertained guests at a dinner party with details of the transformation in her daughter from unmanageable child to someone quite altered and reformed.[62] On October 29, 1829, three weeks after she came out as Juliet and only six weeks after her mother had the brilliant idea of putting her on the stage, the Covent Garden company presented her with a gold bracelet, "in admiration of her distinguished talents and with thanks for her exertions on behalf of the company." She had saved them all and changed the course of her life from wishing to become a famous poet to reconciling herself to the fact that she was a famous actress.

Fame

In her memoirs, Kemble tells her readers that she went on the stage out of gratitude to her parents and in conformity to their will, that she was compelled to help them by every means in her power. But to Harriet St. Leger she disclosed more private and less dutiful reasons. A few weeks before Harriet Siddons rescued her from the lassitude of her London life and the compulsive attentions of her mother, Kemble wrote to Harriet St. Leger in February 1828 that she was unwilling to undergo the "drudgery" of writing for her bread, even if her wits, intelligence, and literary talent might lead to publication. She confessed she was "engrossed with the idea of exercising and developing the literary talent which I think I possess. This is meat, drink, and sleep to me; my world, in which I live, and have my happiness."[63] But the prospect of writing to earn a living was daunting, virtually impossible: earning "hard money after a very hard fashion."[64] As an instance of the unhappy life of the impoverished female poet, she offered the grim example of Felicia Hemans.

Despite the fashion for "poetesses" in the literary marketplace in the 1820s, some struggled mightily (and at the expense of their writing) to support themselves and their families; if they were lucky, they were shielded from a garret existence through financial dependence on their fathers or husbands, or through enjoyment of a social privilege that exempted them from serious want. Kemble had neither the desire for deprivation nor the prospect of long-term support from her father. Felicia Hemans (1793–1835), the image for Kemble of what she could not endure and proclaimed by the *Literary Chronicle* in 1826 as the "finest woman poet of the day,"[65] furiously wrote verse in the spare moments when she was not taking care of five children by herself (she had been abandoned by her husband). Hemans bitterly notes that her "life after eighteen became so painfully, laboriously domestic, that it was an absolute duty to crush intellectual tastes. . . . I could neither read nor write legitimately till the day was over."[66] After reading Hemans, Kemble harshly announced that she was unsympathetic to excuses for inferior work on the grounds of material deprivation. Although she found some of the verse sentimentally beautiful, she considered most of it feeble, mundane, and erratic: produced under "hasty conditions," it lacked intellectual substance and logical exposition.[67]

Kemble's unfriendly dismissal of Hemans is colored by her growing recognition that she had neither her talent nor her resilience, and she also knew that her poems did not compare well with those of Elizabeth Barrett, whose first volume of verse had been published in 1826. Kemble was no fool and she understood perfectly that women poets *were* capable of writing intellectually substantial poems; she was just not confident she was one of them. Moreover, she could not help comparing her financial situation as it was in the spring of 1828 (dependent on a father whose comfortable income was being drained by Covent Garden Theatre) with that of Elizabeth Barrett. The precocious daughter of a wealthy father who supported her writing life (at least until she ran away with Robert Browning in 1845), indulged her neurasthenic illnesses, and shielded her from the marketplace, she endured no material struggles. Lastly, in assembling the case for why she could not *afford* to become a poet, Kemble also had in mind the career of her friend Caroline Norton. The granddaughter of Richard Brinsley Sheridan and the wife of a Whig politician, she published her first collection, *The Sorrows of Rosalie,* in 1829 when she was a prominent society beauty, famed for her eminent social connections, spry wit, and intellectual distinction. Kemble, then, reviewing her chances for success in a literary marketplace where she would have neither a wealthy father nor aristocratic connections, concluded she would be better off working as an actress. After all, she argued to Harriet St. Leger, "The stage is a profession that people who have a talent for it make lucrative, and which honorable conduct may make respectable."[68] As an actress, she would place herself "beyond the fear of want," and an acting career was closely allied in its performing nature to the work of an author. In sum, even if the stage was not her first career choice, it was one made with agency, forethought, and not solely under pressure from her parents.

The myth of a vulnerable, bookish girl reluctantly transformed into a glamorous star possessed considerable drawing power for the box office, and an anonymous American account of her English fame that prefaces the 1833 New York edition of Kemble's play *Francis the First* describes her as "*sacrificed* unto fame." As the author of "many pieces of fugitive poetry lofty in their elegance," and as the stellar and magnetic center of London society through the "elegance of her conversation, and the fascination of her manner," Kemble, in this rapturous tribute, becomes an offering on the altar of the wreck of Covent Garden Theatre. The memoir announces that she forsook "the domestic seclusion of which she was the most accomplished ornament," propped up by her talents the falling fortunes of her house, and restored "to the declining years of her parents, the comfort in which they had always lived."[69] In this heady tale of sacrifice to her parents' security, Kemble seems to step out of sentimental nineteenth-century melodrama, a role she soon began to rewrite as a means of self-accommodation to a different career from that she had imagined and desired for herself.

Anecdotes of racy life both backstage and in the galleries and the scandalous career of Ann Julia Kemble attest to the considerable risks to reputation involved in being an actress. Kemble always emphasized the impeccable sobriety of her own family, and they, in turn, always shielded her from the green-room bawdiness so readily associated with the life of an actress in the popular imagination. In 1878, when reviewing the first volume of Kemble's memoirs, Henry James majestically verifies the success of her family in transcending nineteenth-century popular ideas about the theater and actors, and, by implication, in repelling any salacious affiliation with Fanny Kemble's unmentioned aunt. James confesses himself so impressed by the "serious side" of Kemble's mind, by the "original, positive, interrogative, reflective, generous, cultivated" nature of her intellect, by "the complete absence of any touch of Bohemianism in her personal situation," that he finds it almost impossible to believe she had been "a young lady of the footlights."[70] By the time he wrote this review, of course, he had been Kemble's devoted admirer for five years and had enjoyed many opportunities to be provoked and delighted by her reflective and cultivated intellect.

In her second year of acting at Covent Garden, Kemble notes in her journal, she had talked with Dall about her undiminished dislike of the stage. She had explained to her aunt that it was not acting itself that was so disagreeable to her but "the public personal exhibition, the violence done (as it seems to me) to womanly dignity and decorum in thus becoming the gaze of every eye and theme of every tongue."[71] Unspoken, but acknowledged here, is the association in early nineteenth-century society of actresses with prostitutes. If, in the late 1820s, a young woman became an actress, or as James puts it rather fussily, "a young lady of the footlights," she entered a profession whose practices dangerously resembled those of prostitution. Actresses performed in public spaces for the entertainment of others, their appearances were integral to their marketability, they were paid to be looked at, and they were perceived as having rejected the domestic life of hearth and home for the public life of applause and the theater. This is not to say that actresses were seen as literal prostitutes; rather, as Tracy Davis argues, the two professions were perceived as parallel, not equated or interchangeable. Moreover, open prostitution for any female performer would have meant instant dismissal by the theater manager.[72]

It is also important to remember that issues of social class were tremendously important in how actresses were regarded by the public: an educated, upper-middle-class, cultivated, and well-paid member of England's most distinguished theatrical family was a different kind of actress from the lowest-paid chorus singer or ballet dancer. Among actresses, significant differences between social background, types of roles, kind of training, and range of income created entirely different social and cultural responses to the term "actress." Sarah Siddons, the great tragedienne, rose so regally above her audience—she was both tall and faultlessly respectable—that it is impossible to imagine her as touched by the raffish element that hung around Covent Garden after one of her wrenching performances. Similarly, her niece inhabited a spotless moral sphere in the popular imagination: whatever else people might have said about her—she was too short, her complexion was bad, her manners high-handed—no one could say she was louche. The difficulty for the morally impeccable actress was that she found herself in physical proximity to the women who patrolled public houses, public gardens, and neighborhoods such as Covent Garden, notoriously the home of London's liveliest brothels. Lastly, in the late Georgian period, no London theater, however distinguished its history or elevated its offerings, was free of prostitutes in the auditorium. In 1832, a Parliamentary Select Committee on Dramatic Literature observed, "If there are any places in the world where indecency is openly and shamelessly exhibited, it is within the walls of the great monopolist houses. . . . It is there not only exhibited, but encouraged; not only encouraged, but defended as a means of attraction far more potent than the charms of that fair incognita the 'legitimate drama.'"[73] When Kemble married and settled in Philadelphia, society was slow to accept her, not because *she* was perceived as morally suspect but because actresses, as a social group, carried with them the aura of something not entirely decent.

In October 1829, Kemble stepped onstage at a transitional moment in London's theater history. The monopoly of the two patent theaters was beginning to face strong interrogation and the classical style of Kemble and Siddons was being challenged by the dynamic acting of Edmund Kean and William Macready. The significant alteration in the concept of dramatic character that Joseph Donohue sees emerging in the late eighteenth and early nineteenth centuries—"an increasing emphasis on the character's subjective mental state"—continued even during years of innovation that involved "the greater development of illusion and spectacle as qualities of production."[74] Fanny Kemble practiced a style that projected her characters' "subjective" mental states, but she did so in a theatrical culture of illusion and spectacle. A Covent Garden playbill from November 9, 1829, indicates the kind of theatrical evening that was replaced in the Victorian period by less elaborately varied offerings and by sets that aimed at domestic verisimilitude with richly detailed interiors. The playbill offers, first, the overture to Mozart's *The Magic Flute*; this was followed by *Romeo and Juliet*, highlighted as featuring the sixteenth appearance on any stage of Miss Fanny Kemble and as presenting in Act V the funeral procession of Juliet and a solemn dirge; and Shakespeare was followed by "the Melo-Drama of *The Woodman's Hut*." Early in the next year, on February 10, Fanny's Belvidera in Otway's *Venice Preserv'd* (one of Sarah Siddons's most famous roles) was followed by something a little racier, a farce titled *A Husband's Mistake, or The Corporal's Wedding*, and Edward Moore's *The Gamester*, in which she played Mrs. Beverley, was followed by a new musical romance, *Robert the Devil, Duke of Normandy*. In the years following Kemble's debut, pantomimes of the sort that featured panoramas of "The Suspension Bridge at Hammersmith" and "The Zoological Gardens in the Regent's Park, in which will be introduced some very extraordinary birds and beasts, the largest ever seen in this Kingdom," were replaced by less extravagant and expensive offerings.[75] Melodrama became more genteel, pantomimes less vulgar, and Shakespeare performed more in the internalized, psychological style of William Macready, who managed Covent Garden from 1837 to 1839, and Drury Lane for two years in the early 1840s. Although he admired some of Fanny's polished technique, Macready essentially ridiculed "the teapot school," which Kemble herself had aimed to revise, since, as she writes in her 1863 essay "On the Stage," she had never been happy with the fashion for actors to perform "every emphatic word underlined and accentuated, lest they should omit the right inflection in delivering the lines."[76]

Fanny Kemble believed that acting had two elements: a power of imagination and a vigilant presence of mind; in the first, the actor might feel real grief (as she herself did when acting Juliet), and in the second, the actor deploys a self-aware watchfulness over what she or he is doing. This double process always interested her, and she related it to the performance of comedy and tragedy. In her memoirs, she argues that tragedy is always an emotional experience for the actor and comedy "decidedly a more mature and complete result of dramatic training."[77] Consciously or not, and consistent with the model of profound difference between her parents that was always in her mind, she aligned the emotional abandon of tragic acting, as she understood it, with her mother, and the mature, trained approach needed for comedy with her father. She makes these rueful confessions in her memoirs, conceding that she was a respectable enough tragic actress but a very poor comedic one. Forty-five years after the spectacular transatlantic success that took her from that fateful morning in the darkened Covent Garden Theatre in September 1829 to her farewell performance at the Park Theater in New York in June 1834 just before her marriage, it seems as if she was still auditioning for her parents.

3

Reform and Romance

Come all you cotton-weavers, your looms you may pull down;
You must get employ'd in factories, in country or in town,
For our cotton-masters have found out a wonderful
    new scheme,
These calico goods now wove by hand they's going
    to weave by steam.
    —John Grimshaw, *Hand Loom v. Power-Loom*

On Stephenson's "Rocket"

In the summer of 1830, following the custom for Covent Garden actors to tour the provinces after a successful metropolitan season, Fanny Kemble and her father set off for Bath, Glasgow, Edinburgh, Dublin, Liverpool, Manchester, and Birmingham. Dall accompanied them as Fanny's chaperone and Thérèse occasionally joined the group when they were invited to a country house for the weekend. Back in London, the Tory party was nearing the end of a quarter century's control of government, and by the autumn of 1830 their leader, the Duke of Wellington, had lost a vote of confidence in the House of Commons and been forced to resign. His efforts to persuade his party to adopt parliamentary reform, however diluted from the clamorous demands being voiced by a politically ambitious middle class, proved fruitless, and the Whigs, led by Lord Grey, came into power. In an uneasy and fearful atmosphere created by a wave of revolutionary feeling that seemed to be sweeping across Europe (in the summer of 1830 the French dethroned Charles

X and set up Louis Philippe in his stead, the Belgians proclaimed their national independence from Holland, and Poland and various German principalities were making nationalistic noises), the Whigs knew that if they were to retain control of government, they needed to broaden the electoral franchise and redistribute parliamentary representation in the form of electoral constituencies throughout Britain, particularly in the heavily industrialized cities of Liverpool, Manchester, and Birmingham.[1] Traveling to all these cities on her 1830 summer tour, Fanny was exposed to a stark contrast between the misery of working-class people made desperate by unemployment and the privilege of the northern upper-class families who opened their country house doors to the youngest, most charismatic Kemble. As she listened to morning room debates about enlargement of the electorate on the basis of property taxes, the elimination of "rotten" boroughs, and the enfranchisement of presently unrepresented constituencies such as Manchester, she began to develop political opinions that were notably surprising in a twenty-year-old actress. Appropriating for her own purposes the role of celebrity Kemble actress, she ventured into the predominantly male sphere of political opinion, albeit in unassuming fashion.

The summer began at Bath, which was tolerable since her "Romeo" was a Kemble cousin with the family voice and enough experience not to mutilate Shakespeare; in its grim and grimy way, she found Glasgow interesting and was especially taken by the dark and handsome square where she lodged; Edinburgh was a delight since there she was reunited with Harriet Siddons and breakfasted with one of her literary heroes, Walter Scott, who was "kind, cordial, affectionate." Scott recorded in his diary for that day (June 17), "Miss Fanny Kemble has very expressive though not regular features, and what is worth it all, great energy mingled with and chastened by correct taste."[2] Dublin was her much-anticipated joy because at Ardgillan Castle, situated high on the cliffs beyond the city, she was reunited with Harriet St. Leger, whom she had not seen for four years. Up above the rocky shore, sheltered by bracken from the wind, was a kind of sylvan recess "whose hollow depth, carpeted with grass and curtained with various growth of trees, was the especial domain of my dear Harriet." In this hiding place, they lay on the grass, smelling the sea air and arguing about "things in heaven, and things in earth, and things beyond heaven . . . till we were well-nigh beside ourselves."[3] Even if Kemble was now a celebrity in need of protection from the crowd of male admirers who blocked her way to the carriage when she left her Dublin hotel on the way to Ardgillan, to Harriet she revealed herself as an ardent young woman who needed Harriet's measured guidance and loyal affection. She was miserable when after only a few days of respite from acting and time with Harriet, the tour called for her to exchange her "beloved Plato in petticoats" for her playhouse work in Liverpool.

It was in this bustling port that she began to notice signs of working-class discontent—men with surly faces huddling in doorways and women with shawls wrapped tightly around their shoulders glaring contemptuously at her carriage. This is not to say that the London streets she knew so well displayed no evidence of lower-class social misery. Even if she moved only within the confines of the West End, almost every day she witnessed urban misery—famished street sweepers and half-naked children huddling under the porticos of Covent Garden, scrawny young women peddling their bodies around Soho Square, beggars sleeping in Hyde Park—but Kemble had tended to think this was a misery endured, rather than a poverty protested. Her views of England's social ills had, for the most part, been shaped by those of the politicians and writers with whom she had mingled at places such as Holland House, the great Whig salon presided over by the formidable Lady Holland where, according to Thomas Macaulay, "the last debate was discussed in one corner and the last comedy by Scribe in another."[4] She had overheard heated conversations about the best way to manage the social discontent that seemed to be outstripping the expansion of England's mercantile glory. The Edinburgh year, too, had given her the chance to listen to the "manly" exchanges of the Combe brothers about Scottish and English politics. But until her travel to the industrial north, Fanny Kemble's political positions, inasmuch as she possessed them, had taken shape from listening attentively to political talk, which was an appropriate role for a young woman of twenty, however famous or thoughtful. Now, however, by virtue of her fame, her family connections, and her first theatrical appearances in the north of England, she developed a political awareness through exposure to scenes of industrial protest that in London had been only the subject of newspaper stories, parliamentary reports, and periodical articles. What she had heard discussed at Holland House and what she had read about in *The Times* was now enacted before her eyes in a pageant of political protest that began with weekend visits to Heaton Hall, the country house nestled in the foothills of the Pennines, near Manchester, that was the property of the Earl of Wilton.

The mother of Lady Wilton, the Countess of Derby, had been an actress, and as Elizabeth Farren had become a close friend of John Philip and Charles Kemble. At Heaton, Kemble found the house and her hosts charmingly seductive and the family quickly began to spoil her, especially Lady Wilton, who dressed her in her own expensive riding clothes, urged her to ride her favorite horse, and took her everywhere she went. Always responsive to the affectionate interest of older women, Kemble loved the attention, the clothes, and the riding. In return she participated vivaciously in all the lavish entertainments that were planned for the Heaton houseguests. One of these diversions was a ride on a fifteen-mile experi-

Fig. 9. George Stephenson, by Samuel Bellin, after John Lucas, ca. 1830s. Fanny rode with him on his "Rocket" in 1830. National Railway Museum/Science and Society Picture Library, London.

mental line of railway that was being constructed between Liverpool and Manchester under the direction of George Stephenson and driven by his prototype steam locomotive, the "Rocket." The entire railway line was to be inaugurated later in the summer, and this preview was arranged especially for the guests of Lord and Lady Wilton. Stephenson's project was underwritten by a group of Liverpool mer-

Fig. 10. Stephenson's "Rocket," 1829. National Railway Museum/Science and Society Picture Library, London.

chants, and its rapid financial and popular success made it a model for hundreds of lines constructed after 1830. In a letter to Harriet St. Leger written from Liverpool on August 26, 1830, where she had just arrived after a long stay at Heaton, Kemble entertained her with a detailed narrative of her first ride on a railway.

The party of sixteen entered a long-bodied vehicle, a sort of uncovered single-decker bus that was pulled by a small engine consisting of a boiler and a stove that was fed water from a barrel filled just enough to take them fifteen miles. The whole machine, Kemble was amazed to report, was no bigger than a common fire engine. She was enthralled by the way the pistons propelled by steam moved the wheels, and she was flattered by the attention Stephenson paid her when he seated her beside him on the bench of the engine. In the twenty-first-century world of jet travel, it is difficult to imagine how extraordinary this must have seemed to people accustomed to the noise and bumpiness of carriages, the snorting of horses, the dirt of muddy roads—indeed, to the sheer fatigue of any journey involving more than twenty-five miles. For Kemble, the engine was "a magical machine, with its flying white breath and rhythmical, unvarying pace." It raced between the mossy rocks, skimmed on a kind of floating rail across a swamp at the rate of twenty-five miles an hour, and streamed across a magnificent viaduct of nine arches. Stephenson was much taken by Kemble's fearless interest in the entire project and he explained to her the whole construction of the steam engine: in a gently ironic way, she boasted to Harriet that he "said he could soon make a famous engineer of me" and she added that she was "most horribly in love" with him. She described him as a man of about fifty, his face "fine, though careworn . . . his mode of explaining his ideas is peculiar and very original, striking, and forcible. . . . He has certainly turned my head."[5] As, indeed, she had turned his.

At this historical moment when Kemble thrilled to the power of steam and flirted with George Stephenson on the railway ride that would soon link Liverpool and Manchester, the hand-loom weavers of northern England were in a desperate state. As G. D. H. Cole and Raymond Postgate observe, by 1815 they were "already at starvation point; for the introduction of the power-loom had pushed them into a position in which they could get work only by reducing their wage-claims to a desperately low level."[6] Throughout the 1820s, they had managed to survive due to marginal employment and a high level of prices for British cotton. But by 1830, more and more employers had installed power looms to cut costs and the hand-loom weavers were given only the residual work that could not be handled by the weavers in the factories. When Kemble rode out on splendid Saturday mornings from the Wilton house into the countryside, she could see in the distance wisps of black smoke rising from the chimneys of the newly built mill towns of Old-ham, Rochdale, and Bury that were only about five miles from Heaton Hall, and her exhilaration in the morning's ride was tempered, for a moment, by a growing awareness of what was beyond the extensive acres of the Wilton family. When she actually entered Manchester itself, the sobering difference between her own enthusiasm about steam power and the despair of the hand-loom weavers about the influence of industrial technology on their working lives was presented to her in a shocking tableau of social protest. In mid-September 1830, she saw the source of the wealth that enabled, in part, the middle-class audiences to flock to her performances in the industrial north.

Again, she was at Heaton, this time for a grand house party that included the Duke of Wellington, Mr. and Lady Harriet Baring (of banking fame), Henry Greville, the intellectual exquisite and influential courtier, and two celebrated society beauties, Anne and Isabella Forrester, whose figures and wardrobes Kemble found most interesting: she reported to Harriet that they had quite beautiful bodies and dressed so as to display them to full advantage. They wore skirts shorter than the current fashion to show their aristocratic feet and ankles, and their bodices were cut so low on the shoulders and bosom that virtually nothing was concealed: Kemble confessed that she wished Isabella's gown might slip entirely off so that she could see her "exquisite bust." Her own appearances at this house party were also quite spectacular, staged out of necessity but performed with dazzling theatricality. When she was acting in Manchester, she needed to leave Heaton after an early dinner prepared by the Wilton family's famous chef, a Monsieur Rotival, and would appear in the dining room dressed in full theatrical costume. She recalls in her memoirs that when she was performing Belvidera in Otway's *Venice Preserv'd* her entrance in a medieval-style gown made of black satin and velvet with a sweeping train, her dark-brown eyes and hair set off by an elaborate hat covered in black ostrich feathers, was especially stunning for her fellow guests. Kemble presented her covered-up glamor as a contrast to the deceptively simple arts of the Forrester sisters.

This whole "gay party" set off on the morning of September 15 for Liverpool. Lord and Lady Wilton had arranged for their Heaton houseguests to attend the official opening of the railway line to Manchester, on whose partial track Kemble a few weeks earlier had sailed through the air, thrilled by the extraordinary exhilaration of this new experience and the attentions of George Stephenson.

Enormous crowds lined the track, eager to see Stephenson's "Rocket" rush by and to catch a glimpse of the Duke of Wellington and other dignitaries onboard. Kemble was taken to "the height of her ecstacy" by the speed, although the terrified screams of her mother (who had joined them for this historic weekend) dampened her delight. Not far out of Liverpool, the train halted to take on a supply of water and several men jumped out to take a look, Lord Wilton among them, as well as William Huskisson, Member of Parliament for Liverpool since 1822. An engine on the adjacent line suddenly gathered speed, sending all but Huskisson out of its way with the result, as Kemble described it, that he was "instantaneously prostrated by the fatal machine, which dashed down like a thunderbolt upon him." The Duke of Wellington declared immediately that it would be unseemly for the train to continue to Manchester and that he wished to return to Liverpool. Shocked by what she had witnessed, Kemble felt uncertain about what was best, but she was convinced they should continue when she heard Lord Wilton remind the group that "the whole population of Manchester had turned out to witness the procession, and that a disappointment might give rise to riots and disturbances."[7] The fear of protests was well founded, although Lord Wilton's speculation about the cause of protest was entirely wrong. The workers gathered at the Manchester railway station were there to demonstrate against the industrial technology that had produced the train, not to register their disappointment about the failure of the Duke of Wellington to make an appearance.

In her memoirs, Kemble vividly evokes the scene in Manchester as the train pulled into the station. The terrible injuries suffered by William Huskisson (he died almost immediately after being struck down) transformed the spirit of the excursion from celebration to mourning.

> After this disastrous event the day became overcast, and as we neared
> Manchester the sky grew cloudy and dark, and it began to rain. The vast
> concourse of people who had assembled to witness the triumphant ar-
> rival of the successful travellers was of the lowest order of mechanics and
> artisans, among whom great distress and a dangerous spirit of discontent
> with the Government at that time prevailed. Groans and hisses greeted
> the carriage full of influential personages, in which the Duke of Wel-

lington sat. High above the grim and grimy crowd of scowling faces a
loom had been erected, at which sat a tattered, starved-looking weaver,
evidently set there as a *representative man*, to protest against this triumph
of machinery, and the gain and glory which the wealthy Liverpool and
Manchester men were likely to derive from it.[8]

First setting the dramatic scene with a description of gloomy and drizzly
weather that matches the sullen mood of the assembled workers, Kemble next
evokes the anger of a crowd seething with discontent and voicing its resentment in
groans and hisses directed at the assembled personages as they disembarked from
the train. At center stage is the figure of the "tattered, starved-looking weaver"
seated at a loom high above the lowest order of mechanics and artisans, a "representative man" as Kemble emphasizes. In a form of political theater, an emaciated
weaver is presented by his fellow workmen as a shaming emblem of the plight of
all Lancashire hand-loom weavers who had been reduced to virtual starvation
through the arrival of steam-powered machinery. Kemble's complex responses to
the scene are registered, on the one hand, in a quick dismissal of the men as "the
lowest order of mechanics and artisans" and, on the other, in her ironic description
of the purpose of the protest: to speak of the "gain and glory" of wealthy businessmen is to question, however mildly, their motives and their morals. After witnessing a scene of grim political protest, whose theatricality gains intensity through
Kemble's discursive arrangement of the scene, she responded to it in a manner
that would have been unusual in a less intelligent and politically curious young
actress, but in her case does not surprise. She was becoming seriously interested in
the English national debate about parliamentary reform, and six weeks after the
unforgettable scene at the Manchester railway station, she wrote to Harriet that
"our own country is in a perilous state of excitement, and these troubled times
make politicians of us all."[9]

When Lord John Russell, who had replaced Lord Grey as prime minister, rose
in the House of Commons on March 1, 1831, to bring forward a bill to amend the
representation of the people of England and Wales, his speech initiated one of the
greatest constitutional debates in British history and led, eventually, to the passing
of the first Reform Act in 1832. Under the provisions of this act, which enlarged
the franchise on the basis of property taxes, the electorate was increased by nearly
80 percent, fifty-six "rotten" boroughs (those controlled, primarily, by absentee
landowners) were eliminated, and forty-three previously unrepresented boroughs,
including Manchester, were given representation. After considerable political negotiation and maneuvering by Russell and his Whig colleagues, the bill managed

to pass its first reading on April 14. Kemble reported to Harriet that following the positive vote on the first reading, London's lord mayor ordered illuminations for the entertainment of an immense crowd "of the lowest order," some of whom became dissatisfied with the quality of the illuminations and took to breaking windows in the West End. She noted in her private journal on April 27, 1831, that London was "one blaze of rejoicing for the Reform Bill triumph; the streets are thronged with people and choked up with carriages, and the air is flashing and crashing with rockets and squibs and crackers."[10] In an even more private document than her journal, fragments from an autobiographical manuscript written in 1831 and now housed in the British Library, Kemble reveals her strong interest in these momentous political events.

She writes that she finds herself troubled by a contradictory "vein of hopefulness": she fervently hopes that "the spread of enlightenment and general progress" in the country will achieve reform without revolution; this hopefulness was consistently being undermined, however, by the alarmed talk of her aristocratic friends, all of them anti-reformers, and all of them predicting violence and anarchy if the bill were to be passed. She went so far as to write what she called "a flaming speech for an imaginary peer" that expressed her ambivalent views about reform: approval of the principles but reservations about the implementation. It seems that she kept most of this political thinking to herself; in late May 1831 Harriet voiced her disappointment that such an intelligent and astute young woman seemed to have no opinion of the political state of the her country. Kemble responded by saying she had other things to care about (mainly the perennial worry about Covent Garden's survival), but she did concede that the Reform Bill, modified as it now was, had her "best prayers and wishes" since it might restore the social order being upset by protests in Kent and Sussex. She accurately predicted that once the lower classes discovered reform had not brought immediate relief from economic hardship, they would again become restless, and she added that she was increasingly despondent about the "battle-field" that society seemed to have become, with everyone at political odds with one another. She found it strange and deplorable there was no "moderating" party, and she wished that popular literature might engage itself with social issues (she had to wait until the 1840s for the emergence of fiction that addresses the problems of working-class life). She was particularly dispirited by a play by her friend Caroline Norton that she saw in May 1831 since she was in sympathetic accord with its intention to provoke sympathy in the audience for lower-class suffering.

Kemble found it abominable. Despite being moved to tears by the sight of people eating nettles and cabbage stalks, she thought it resembled far too closely a scene in Newgate prison, which she had recently visited in the company of Elizabeth Fry, the philanthropist and advocate of prison reform. She had felt sorry for the prisoners and "ashamed" for the visitors, and when she came home from Norton's play, she wrote, "Destitution, absolute hunger, cold and nakedness are no more subjects for artistic representation than sickness, disease, and the *real* details of idiotcy, [*sic*] madness, and death"; "beggary and vice," she announces, are not the proper work of the dramatist.[11] But however imperfect as art from Kemble's perspective, Norton's play was part of an important literary engagement with social problems that began in the early 1830s and flourished in the 1840s with the novels of writers such as Elizabeth Gaskell, whose *Mary Barton* (1848), for example, with great sympathy and in harrowing detail, represents the plight of Manchester factory workers. Kemble's own political thinking, as found in her letters to Harriet St. Leger at the time and in the autobiographical fragment, was impelled, in part, by that same engagement, by a sincere sympathy for lower-class suffering and a guarded advocacy of reform.

As Stephenson's train pulled into Manchester and Caroline Norton's characters ate cabbage stalks, a decade was beginning in which working-class protest against inhumane factory conditions and the absence of a vote accelerated. The 1832 Reform Bill, about which Kemble was so ambivalent and for which working men had agitated, denied them enfranchisement, and despite the Factory Act of 1833, which reduced the working hours for children employed in the textile mills whose smoke Kemble could see from Lord Wilton's acres, trade union organization and strikes proliferated. Economic depression in the late 1830s and 1840s led to mass unemployment and to the terrible hardship described by writers known as "social problem" novelists: in addition to Elizabeth Gaskell, authors such as Charles Dickens and Benjamin Disraeli disclosed to their middle-class readership scenes of poverty, disease, and a divided nation that, in some instances, shocked readers into social action. Early in 1837, working-class dissatisfaction with the inequities of the 1832 Reform Bill coalesced in the People's Charter, a document that gave name to one of the most famous political movements of the early Victorian period: Chartism. Among other things, the charter demanded votes for all men, abolition of the requirement that Members of Parliament be property owners, and a secret ballot. On July 12, 1839, a petition bearing 1,280,000 signatures supporting the charter was presented to the House of Commons, where it was rejected by a vote of 235 to 46. The political theater that Kemble had seen performed in the Manchester railway station in 1830 was defeated in its much greater and longer-running expression by the end of the 1840s: Chartism eventually petered out, vanquished by a number of factors, among them an eventual loss of heart brought about by so much rejection and a violent suppression of demonstrations by the authorities (in one riot, twelve Chartists were killed).[12]

At the beginning of the socially volatile 1830s, there was also unsettling talk of reform in the world of the theater when, in early 1831, the monopoly patents of Drury Lane and Covent Garden came under attack in the House of Commons. Consistent with the reforming principles that demanded enlargement of the franchise, Whig politicians began to advocate that the right to act legitimate drama be granted to anyone wishing to open a playhouse. Charles Kemble testified before a parliamentary committee and delineated the evils, as he saw them, that would result from granting the right to all and sundry to present the great works of English drama. He argued that the companies of superb actors would be broken up, the best plays would no longer find adequate support, a school of fine acting would be lost, and no play of Shakespeare would be properly performed. In the long run, his cause was defeated, and in 1843 the monopoly held by Drury Lane and Covent Garden was broken. While the future of the English theater was being debated in Parliament, Fanny Kemble was contemplating an engagement to the first of the few men figured in her memoirs whom she acknowledges she found attractive.

Dangerous Fascinations

After the summer tour of 1830, Fanny and her father returned in October to Covent Garden, there to repeat the triumphs of her first year. In their absence, Thérèse had moved the family to the house at 79 Great Russell Street that had been owned by John Philip Kemble, right next to the British Museum, and Fanny, reproved by the weight of learning housed next door, vowed to forswear paying and receiving morning visits, to walk regularly around Russell Square, and to apply herself to the goal of becoming proficient in German. With the sad example of her aunt Siddons before her, she was determined to avoid the engrossing and addictive excitement of her profession, and she was delighted with the room Thérèse had decorated for her on the fourth floor of the house. There, sequestered with a view over the chimney pots of Bloomsbury, Kemble settled down to serious study.

In November, however, she was distracted from her program of self-improvement by the departure of her brother John Mitchell for Spain, where he aimed to join a rebel group seeking to overthrow the royal government. He had gone to Cambridge with the intention of becoming a lawyer, but, fired by radical political debate, he neglected his studies, took to haranguing his family with lectures about the evils of inherited privilege, the established church, and the military, and left Cambridge without taking his degree after the examining committee refused to accept his arguments against Locke as evidence of his actually having *read* Locke. His most worrisome act of rebellion was his going to Spain to fight on the side of a rebel, General Torrijos; his close friend Alfred Tennyson memorialized the expedition in a sonnet in which he hails him as a "later Luther," spurred with "fieriest energy." For a while, during the winter of 1830–31, this later Luther faded from sight into the morass of European revolutionary politics, and the Kemble household was preoccupied with an effort to trace his whereabouts. Thérèse was hysterical, Charles monumentally calm, and Fanny distracted by her German lessons and English political reform. But the affair fizzled, the would-be revolutionaries perilously got themselves back to England in May 1831, and John Kemble went on to lead a surprisingly sedate life as a distinguished Anglo-Saxon scholar, editor of the *British and Foreign Review*, and successor to his father as examiner of stage plays (a pleasant, if not very lucrative, sinecure).

Despite John Kemble's worrisome absence from England, things brightened up in December when Harriet St. Leger made a rare three-week visit to London, braving the noise and fog she so detested. Christmas Eve 1830 saw a jolly family reunion at Sarah Siddons's house where some three dozen Siddons relatives gathered around her when she came downstairs and Kemble was reunited with her dearest friend from the Edinburgh year, Harriet Siddons. During this winter, Thérèse Kemble continued to be bitingly critical of her daughter's work, despite the general acclaim and adulation she received from audiences and the press. In January 1831 Kemble confessed to Harriet St. Leger that her chief happiness in acting one of her new roles (Bianca in Milman's *Fazio*, an Italianate tragedy with some intensely dramatic moments) was the approbation of her mother: "She is a very severe critic, and, as she censures sharply, I am only too thankful when I escape her condemnation."[13] Consistent with her aim to lead a more disciplined life, she resolved to study her profession more seriously than she had before, and she challenged herself by taking on some of her aunt's demanding roles, particularly Constance in *King John* and Lady Macbeth. Reviews, for the most part, confirmed Kemble's discomfort in these parts: she lacked the emotional and physical maturity to carry them off. Her social life in London also took a slightly weightier turn; rather than dancing through the night or going to a glittering dinner party, she spent more time in her study, often talking seriously about Shakespeare's heroines with Anna Jameson, the social critic and art historian who dedicated her book on that topic to Kemble when it was published in 1832, or discussing with her the merits of Shelley's *The Cenci*—Kemble found the subject of the drama "hideous" but Shelley's verse superbly moving. For many years afterward, Kemble and Jameson stayed in close contact: in her letters to Jameson, Kemble frequently confessed her despair that she was wasting her intellectual talent, and, when they met, she always responded enthusiastically to Jameson's interesting and informative conversation.

In the spring of 1831, Kemble agreed to participate in some private theatricals to be presented at Bridgewater House, the London home of Francis Leveson-Gower (later Lord Ellesmere), a neighbor from the Kemble family's Weybridge days in the late 1820s. One of her fellow actors was a young man named Augustus Craven, and the entanglement that ensued suggests the possibilities for romance that were endemic in the performance of private theatricals. As Catherine Burroughs observes, private theatricals, "often rehearsed in the context of a house party that could go on for several weeks," allowed "a great deal of playfulness and delight in the act of improvisation."[14]

Playfulness and delight are certainly the promise held out by the theatricals performed in Jane Austen's *Mansfield Park* (published in 1814). In this narrative of an English gentry family (the Bertrams) and the eventual expulsion of sophisticated outsiders to whom its members are dangerously susceptible, the younger members of the family get perilously involved in private theatricals. In the absence of their father, who has gone off to Antigua to attend to the family sugar plantations, they respond enthusiastically to a plan for amateur acting proposed by a visitor, about whom Austen drily notes, "Happily for him a love of the theatre is so general, an itch for acting so strong among young people, that he could hardly out-talk the interest of his hearers."[15] The only impediment to the plan is the opposition of Edmund Bertram, who declares he does not wish to observe "the raw efforts of those who have not bred to the trade,—a set of gentlemen and ladies, who have all the disadvantages of education and decorum to struggle through."[16]

A number of key words in Edmund's moral disapprobation of actors and acting convey an attitude toward the profession that prevailed at the time within the conservative gentry. The theater business was just that—a business, a "trade"; actors are not "gentlemen and ladies"; and actors lack "education" and "decorum." By contrast, in the country houses of the aristocracy where all the Kembles were well received, theatricals were never thought immoral: for instance, John Philip Kemble's wife, Priscilla, wrote to him in 1803 about a splendid house party she had just attended at the estate of the Marquis and Marchioness of Abercorn. The guests included the Prince of Wales, the Duke and Duchess of Devonshire, and Lady Melbourne and her family (just a few of the over forty persons present), and Priscilla Kemble had been given the entire "direction" of the theatricals.[17] Edmund Bertram's objection in Austen's novel to some racy fun designed to liven up a dull country house reveals the importance to a particular social group of maintaining recently forged class privilege. Austen's description of the Bertram family suggests the moral resistance of their conservative class to the theatrical high jinks not only tolerated but welcomed by the Marquis and Marchioness of Abercorn. At Mansfield Park, Austen implies, one needs to remain unobtrusive since the social, cultural, and political power of the English gentry was not, by far, as entrenched in English life as that of the aristocracy. Priscilla Kemble's aristocratic hosts (at ease with the Prince of Wales) did not object to the fame culture identified by Leo Braudy that emerged in the Romantic period, in which political figures such as Napoleon arranged themselves on European battlefields and literary figures such as Byron performed their poetic lives on London's social stages.[18] Kemble was welcomed into this fame culture—as a celebrated actress, sparkling wit, and freshly minted ornament of the Kemble dynasty—and she was a dazzling trophy for the private theatricals being staged in the summer of 1831.

The play was *Hernani* by Victor Hugo. Inspired by Spanish tragedies and featuring a passionate love affair between the principals, Hernani and Dona Sol, it had been premiered in Paris on February 25, 1830, and translated into English by Leveson-Gower's son, Francis Egerton. Rehearsals took place at the family's rented country estate near Weybridge, Oatlands, which was owned by a certain Edward Hughes Ball Hughes, a man notorious for his fabulous wealth, extravagant wardrobe, and profligate spending. The latter tendency forced him to rent Oatlands to Leveson-Gower. The first thing Kemble did when she arrived at Oatlands in mid-May for the grand house party devoted to rehearsals was to fly down familiar paths to the cottage where she had spent many months with her mother after she returned from school in Paris. The desolation of the cottage upset her—the grass was knee deep, the shrubs so carefully pruned by Thérèse trailing their branches, and her honeysuckle vines all torn down—and she retreated to the familiar circle of her fellow houseguests, among whom were social and political luminaries with whom she was now on intimate terms, Henry Greville and Lord John Russell among them. Poor John Russell, Kemble notes, had to bear all the attacks of the "anti-Reformers"—he did it with "great good humour however and with the well satisfied smile of a man who thinks himself on the right side."[19] Oatlands was idyllic: glorious sunsets, walking in the beautifully tended gardens, riding with her host and discussing the Romantic poets ("a very pretty and proper discourse for such a ride," she noted), and feeling, as she put it in her memoirs, her first painful pangs of an "ephemeral love."

It is reasonably certain that during this time she fell in love with Augustus Craven, the grandson of Elizabeth Berkeley Craven who at the end of the eighteenth and early nineteenth centuries had been a prominent figure in the group of women who organized, wrote, and acted in private theatricals.[20] An eager amateur actor, Augustus Craven had an enthusiasm to match that of the group in *Mansfield Park*. When he read his role of Hernani (Kemble played Dona Sol) at the first rehearsal, Kemble was impressed by his performance even if she found it wanting technical experience. In her memoirs, Kemble remains discreet about any more

intimate feeling for him, other than to make an unhappy note in her journal written six months after this idyllic May and June that she was reluctant to accept an
invitation to Oatlands, since "Everything is winter now, within and without me;
and when I was last there it was summer, in my heart and all over the earth."[21]
In this particular part of her journal, however, she had just recorded her father's
battle with "inflammation of the lungs": her mother was utterly distraught, Fanny
and her brother Henry had lain down on the sofa in her room and cried together
throughout the whole afternoon, and the feelings of wintry cold and desolation
might be attributable to worry about her father's illness.

However, copies of Kemble's letters to Harriet St. Leger written in June 1831
that are included with the fragments of Kemble's autobiographical manuscript in
the British Library do seem to confirm that she was in love with Craven, perhaps
secretly engaged to him.[22] On June 30 she wrote the following: "I write to tell you
and how I wish I could tell it instead of writing that I have made an engagement
not for London or the provinces—not for a season or a year but for all time and all
places and have promised to leave my home."[23] It is easy to imagine that this refers
to an engagement to marry Craven. The letter continues, "I think any woman of
sense or good feeling would be the first to say 'no' to any plan involving the trial
of the affections of the man she loved by anxiety care toil or regret or by rashly
embarking with him in a venture where all his love might hardly enable him to
bear the daily burden of living on narrow means." If, indeed, she was trying to tell
Harriet that she had contracted herself, privately, to Craven, then she was also
admitting that there might be impediments to the marriage and that if he had
insufficient income to support her, she would let him go. It is also possible that his
father, Keppel Craven, objected to marriage to an actress, however morally impeccable and untouched by the green-room, and threatened disinheritance. Whatever
happened, Kemble remained discreet about it, and all we have is her candid confidences to Harriet about an engagement "for all time" and about her belief that a
woman "of sense or good feeling" would reject a plan that tested the affections of
a man she loved.[24]

Kemble was far less discreet when admitting her dangerous infatuation with
Sir Thomas Lawrence, a man older than her father, a famous painter, and a Prospero figure in search of a young woman on whom he might practice his romantic
magic. Lawrence reentered the Kemble family orbit at the time of Kemble's Covent Garden debut after many years of estrangement, bringing with him a scandalous history of romantic involvement with the two daughters of Sarah Siddons,
Sarah and Maria. On intimate terms with the famous mother through having
painted her portrait, he proposed to her eldest daughter, Sarah, was accepted, and
then, according to Kemble, became "deeply dejected, moody, restless, and evident-

ly extremely and unaccountably wretched." In a violent scene with Sarah's mother he confessed that Maria, rather than Sarah, was the real object of his affection, and he begged to become engaged to her. "How this extraordinary change was accomplished" Kemble confessed herself unable to fathom, but it happened, and Maria Siddons became engaged to her sister's fickle lover. Then in a cruel development that left Sarah Siddons bereft of her two daughters and Thomas Lawrence deprived of a betrothed, both sisters quickly became ill with consumption. Maria extracted a deathbed wish from her sister that she would not marry Lawrence, and shortly thereafter Sarah herself died. This sensational narrative ended in the permanent banishment of Lawrence from the Siddons household.

Aged sixty when Kemble was just about to appear at Covent Garden, Lawrence met Charles Kemble by chance on the street and quickly ingratiated himself with the family by offering his services as they prepared her for the stage. He soon became a devoted member of Kemble's theatrical entourage. He designed

Fig. 11. *Sir Thomas Lawrence*, by George Thomas Doo, after Sir Thomas Lawrence, 1786. © National Portrait Gallery, London.

Fig. 12. *Cecilia Combe, Sarah Siddons, Charles Kemble, Maria Siddons,* by Richard James Lane, after Sir Thomas Lawrence, 1830. The lithograph features Sarah Siddons surrounded by her daughters Cecilia and Maria, and their uncle Charles Kemble. © National Portrait Gallery, London.

her costumes, adjusted her wigs, made pencil drawings of her, and sent sensitive and detailed evaluations of her performances. These critiques Kemble took very seriously, and in return she wrote him many flowery letters of thanks, apologizing for trespassing on his time, offering explanations for her "defects," and begging for his patience. There is a touching fear of her mother expressed in these letters, as well as gratitude for his much less harsh review of her work: in a letter from late 1829, for instance, she writes that sometimes when she thought she was "acting well and carefully that severe judge my mother has destroyed all my flattering self-approbation with a word."[25] Lawrence's swain-like attentions were noted by Tom Moore, the Irish poet and acquaintance of the Kembles, who wrote in his journal that when he saw Kemble as Belvidera in Otway's *Venice Preserv'd* on December 23, 1829, Lawrence was in a box, "full of anxiety and delight." Whenever Lawrence looked his way, Moore made it a point to clap enthusiastically, although he thought Kemble's acting unmoving, even if clever. Lawrence had also been among the adoring company a month earlier when Moore dined at the Kemble house: Fanny and Adelaide made a point of singing some of Moore's duets, for which he was properly grateful, and he much admired the contralto voice of "the young Juliet."[26]

A few months after this musical evening, Lawrence died suddenly, in circumstances sufficiently mysterious, Kemble recalled, "to give rise to a report that he had committed suicide."[27] Four days before his death, on January 4, 1830, he wrote to a friend thanking her for praise of Kemble's performance as Belvidera; he added that he saw no signs of vanity in Kemble, that she was much more beautiful in private than she was onstage, and that he had "almost a father's interest for her, and a father's resentment towards those who will not see the promise."[28] Kemble felt the shock of his death tremendously, but she also believed, in retrospect, that his death was "fortunate" for her rather than otherwise. Attracted to and flattered by his intense and adoring interest in all she did, she was entranced by a famous, charming older man with melancholy good looks, gentle manners, and extraordinary romantic history. A "very dangerous fascination" took hold, and she confessed in her memoirs that as a very romantic girl, if she had sat for the portrait of Juliet he was planning to make of her, she would have "become in love with him" and acquired the unhappy distinction of being the fourth member of her family "whose life he would have disturbed and embittered."[29] Fifteen years later, she looked back in amusement at her "fascination" and wrote to Harriet St. Leger that Lawrence was probably in heaven "staring with his one eye at womankind in general, just as when he was on earth 'man-fashion' as he went about among the girls, making love to such of them as he fancied."[30]

Kemble always believed that no painter captured her essence as Lawrence had done since he could see her spirit in her face, a judgment that makes one wonder if she had seen Lawrence's portrait of the Countess of Blessington, painted in 1821, that now hangs in the Wallace Collection. Lawrence's much-reproduced portrait of Kemble is uncannily similar to this earlier painting: the hands are differently arranged but the dress, the hair, and the general pose are notably alike. However, Kemble had a rather dim view of the other Lawrence portraits with which she was familiar: she sighed, as she put it, for the simple grace and unaffected dignity of Reynolds and Gainsborough.[31] Believing that before his death his portraits had been overestimated and that after it they had been undervalued, she traced the shortcomings of his work, as she saw it, to his adherence to "the false and bad style which, from the deeper sources of degraded morality, spread a taint over all matters of art and taste." In these aesthetic judgments, she expresses her loathing of the Prince Regent's taste and dismisses as vulgar and unrefined his hideous pagoda pavilions, grotesque and monstrous decorations, and royal palaces lacking proper royal magnificence. And she ridiculed Lawrence's portrait of the Prince Regent: a corpulent body girthed in stays, a dancing master's leg, a

Fig. 13. *Frances Anne Kemble*, by Richard James Lane, after Sir Thomas Lawrence, 1829. Fanny believed no painter ever captured her "essence" as did Lawrence; she was probably unaware of the similarity of this portrait to that of Margaret, Countess of Blessington. © National Portrait Gallery, London.

frizzled barber's block head—all this she believed was "enough to have vulgarized any pencil."[32] Kemble wrote her memoirs as a mature Victorian woman, and in these judgments we hear the familiar tone of Victorian distaste for Regency excess, although, of course, the Prince Regent was disliked, caricatured, and satirized by plenty of people in his own time.

Fig. 14. *Margaret, Countess of Blessington*, by Sir Thomas Lawrence, ca. 1822. © By kind permission of the Trustees of the Wallace Collection, London.

In July 1831, Kemble set off on her second provincial tour, this time to southwest England, performing first in Bristol with the usual motley crew of unpredictable actors assembled for the arrival of the famous father and daughter. In Bristol the nurse in *Romeo and Juliet* so mangled her lines that she made Kemble nearly scream with laughter as she went into her trance—it was altogether a "shocking hash." A fellow actor in *Venice Preserv'd*, knowing hardly any of his lines, extemporized so wildly that she could barely utter her own; failing to deliver any of the play's words, he stamped, bellowed, rolled his eyes, and wrenched her around so badly that she found herself exhausted at the end of the play by his quavering and

violence. This summer trip also gave Kemble the chance to explore the countryside, do some hill climbing around Portsmouth with her father, and breathe the
fresh sea air that was so good after the London fog. This summer there were no
steam-powered adventures and no scenes of industrial protest. More and more,
Kemble began to echo her mother's dislike of the city and complained to friends
of feeling enclosed by paved streets and brick walls, of longing for the earth, sea,
and sky spread around her, as things had been in Edinburgh four years before
when she had climbed the heather-banked hillsides and looked down upon the
city she loved so much, her spirits soaring with the wind from the River Firth.

The more she acted and the more she saw of the lives of other actors (the
vanity of the metropolitan stars, the ineptitude of the provincial casts), the more
she articulated her loathing of the profession. But she knew also that if she were
to leave it, she would relinquish her financial independence and her glamorous
social connections—the world of beautiful dresses, elegant country houses, chats
with Thomas Macaulay—to say nothing of the serious dent in the Kemble family
fortunes that would be felt by her departure from the stage. Finally, she knew that
if she were to leave the theater because of marriage, she would become entirely
dependent on her husband since whatever she had earned prior to her marriage
would come under his control. Three years later, she married a very wealthy man
and as Mrs. Butler immediately became his financial dependent, having signed
over to her father the money she had made as an actress, which, at the time, seemed
to suit her very well since she was desperate to leave a profession she found utterly
degrading to women. Seeing how another actress was treated by a mainly male
audience brought this home to her.

When she returned to London for the winter season of 1831 she went with her
family to see a Miss Phillips make her debut at Drury Lane. Miss Phillips, through
terrible stage fright, performed very badly and Kemble felt sorry for her, but she
was made even sorrier by the sight of a young woman like herself turned into the
pitiful object of male inspection. She says that when she saw "the thousands of
eyes of that crowded pitful of men, and heard their stormy acclamations, and then
looked at the fragile, helpless, pretty young creature standing before them trembling with terror, and all woman's fear and shame in such an unnatural position,"
she marveled "how I, or any woman, could ever have ventured on so terrible a trial,
or survived the venture. It seemed to me as if the mere gaze of all that multitude
must melt the slight figure away like a wreath of vapor in the sun, or shrivel it up
like a scrap of silver paper before a blazing fire."[33] That Kemble had been able to
venture "on so terrible a trial" and had endured it to become famous and wealthy
suggests that however emotionally vulnerable her state of being and however tem-

peramentally erratic her behavior, she possessed an imperishable sense of self that sustained her through her life.

Early in the new year of 1832, Kemble finished *The Star of Seville*, a play she had been writing since she was sixteen and a work for which she had the utmost contempt, calling it utter trash, as dead as can be, and inferior to her first play, *Francis the First*, about which she was also unenthusiastic. On January 14 she read it to her family with mixed results: her mother cried a lot and her father, Dall, and brother John thought it beautiful, but it seemed to her that they slept through the latter half of the reading. The only people who appeared to like *The Star of Seville* were Elizabeth Barrett and Anna Jameson: Barrett wrote to Jameson on May 2, 1837, "Yes! The extracts from Mrs. Butler's play, in the Athenaeum, *are* very beautiful—and so are some others which I have seen in another paper."[34] Barrett also liked *Francis the First*, although she had some reservations about the verse: she wrote to Hugh Stuart Boyd on July 10, 1832, that she would like him to read it, since "It seems to me to be a very clever and indeed surprising production as from the pen of a young person . . . the poetry is seldom good as poetry. . . . There are however some beautiful passages."[35]

Kemble's life of acting at Covent Garden, of dinner parties, and of dances continued, although a little less frantically than before, marked by such events as riding with her brother Henry in Hyde Park and being joined by Lord John Russell "peering out of voluminous wrappers." The interest in politics that had been aroused when she had traveled in the north of England in 1830 became more intense as the Reform Bill came up for its final vote in the House of Commons, and Kemble began to speak disparagingly about the unpolished arrivistes who, she believed, would soon be crowding into Parliament. She developed these views when she was in America in early 1833, writing in her journal that she would not be in the Reform Parliament for "ten thousand pounds! . . . Oh, shame, England, shame!—Poor England!" She embellished this strong sentiment with some lines titled "A Rhapsody," in which the poem's speaker is personified as England, who declares she will reign as long as the "crawling ivy" (an image of parasitical Reform-licensed politicians) does not destroy the "oak" (an image of old, feudal England). Her "downfalling" will come when mud is thrown on the ermine of the king and "boxers and bankrupts" sit in Parliament.[36]

There seemed no end to the financial worries about the Theatre, compounded now by Kemble's nagging conviction that if she stopped acting she would remain neither financially independent nor unmarried. Now more resourceful than she had been when she first went onstage, she began to harbor a plan for going to America to make as much money as possible, return to England, and invest her

funds as a secure income for life. But on the last day of February 1832, her father signaled that her plans for America would be realized sooner than she had
anticipated. In a scene that seemed to repeat her mother's anguished announce-
ment of two and a half years earlier that they were ruined, he announced that her
brother Henry's horse must be sold, and that the "crumbling fabric" of the Theatre,
in whose patching Charles and Fanny Kemble had exhausted themselves, was
about to entangle them all in a kind of financial death throes. Charles Kemble
declared that to keep the family finances afloat, he and his daughter must work
incessantly in London and in the provinces, with reduced salaries and reduced expenses. Fanny felt it pitiful that her father clung so tenaciously to the theater that
was destroying them, and she wondered to herself if it was because his own name
and the names of his famous brother and sister were graven on its very stones. She
concluded her unhappy diary note for that fateful day with a prayer that they all
remain healthy, that they not be separated, and that they not have to "go off to that
dreadful America"—at least not quite yet.

Despite the fact that the complex quarrel between the Covent Garden partners came out of the Chancery court with some benefit to Charles Kemble, he remained deeply in debt. Fanny felt the Theatre was some kind of malignant disease,
eating their lives away, and her only consolation was to read and reread *King Lear*,
which seems particularly poignant given the broken state of her father who was
tragically bereft almost to the point of resembling Lear at his most distraught. The
few performances of *Francis the First* in April boosted the family coffers temporarily, but by the middle of June the situation was so grim that the only salvation
seemed to lie in an American tour. The family agreed that Charles, Fanny, and
Dall would leave for New York in early August.

Fanny Kemble's last Covent Garden performance took place on June 22, 1832
(she played her favorite role, Julia in Knowles's *The Hunchback*). They were to sail
from Liverpool, and Charles Kemble decided that they should first go to Edinburgh. This idea delighted Fanny, since she would see the woman who had rescued
her from her mother's distressing influence in 1828: Harriet Siddons. On Kemble's
last day in Edinburgh, July 14, she climbed up into the heather-banked hills outside the city, together with three old friends and admirers, Mr. Murray, Mr. Allen,
and Mr. Byrne, who vowed they would establish annual ceremonies on July 14 and
on her birthday, November 27, until her return from America. After the stop in
Edinburgh, Charles and Fanny acted in Liverpool, eager to make as much money
as possible before they left, and Harriet St. Leger joined them for a few last days.
On August 1 they set sail for New York. As Kemble remembers the day in her
memoirs, "I was leaving my mother, my brothers and sister, my friends and my
country, for two years. . . . I was going to work very hard, in a distasteful vocation,

among strangers, from whom I had no right to expect the invariable kindness and indulgence my own people had favoured me with."[37] She was almost twenty-three and famous, but she was deeply depressed by her father's troubled spirits and felt she was just receiving her "first sharp, smarting strokes in the battle of life," those "gashes" that even when healed leave nasty scars.[38] Exiled from England and her family by virtue of her father's never-ending financial difficulties, she became his sustaining Miranda as they set sail for America, the child from the portrait she had seen when she was six years old. She spent the transatlantic voyage making friends and entertaining her fellow passengers, and she arrived in New York on September 5 after thirty-two days at sea, ready once more to play her part in the Kemble family romance. By virtue, however, of the considerable social and professional experience occasioned by her celebrity, she now began to play that part with an ironic resistance. Her performances as a Kemble daughter found expression not merely on the stage: when she arrived in America, she began keeping a journal and its self-reflexive stance discloses her increasing authority over her own life.

Before leaving England, she had confided to Harriet St. Leger that the sea voyage would be her first real holiday since she had first gone on the stage. The previous three years had been tumultuous ones in the political life of the nation as it negotiated its perilous way through working-class discontent and agitation for parliamentary reform. These same years had seen Kemble navigate her journey through theatrical celebrity, "ephemeral" love, romantic infatuation, and, as always, the perilous mess of the family finances. This navigation, however, had enabled the development of a political voice and when she arrived in America, she deployed it to articulate feminist positions that hitherto had been expressed primarily in the realm of her private life.

4

Seeing the World

You are living, you are seeing men and things, you are seeing the world. . . . I know of no one whose life has such promise in it as yours.

—Washington Irving to Fanny Kemble, April 1833

Writing About America

When Fanny Kemble boarded the sailing ship *Pacific* in Liverpool on August 1, 1832, bound for New York, she and her fellow passengers faced a voyage of almost five weeks. It was not until 1838, when the *Great Western* made the trip entirely under steam in a space of fifteen days, that transatlantic travel harnessed the power so thrilling to Kemble as she rode beside George Stephenson on his marvelous new "Rocket" in the summer of 1830. Five weeks at sea and two years in America called for careful planning, and the Kemble party arrived in Liverpool with twenty-one huge trunks. Kemble came equipped with her extravagantly beautiful theatrical wardrobe, many fashionable dresses, a pile of reading matter that ranged from the Bible to a life of Byron, and several nightcaps and Bible covers ready for embroidery onboard ship. Like many nineteenth-century young women who embarked on a journey that would keep them out of England for a long time—perhaps to India as the wife of an army officer or to the West Indies as a missionary—Kemble also took onboard everything she would need for keeping a detailed journal: much writing paper, pens in good order, plenty of ink, and a small portable writing desk. The writing that she did on the *Pacific* shaped the beginning of her first major publication after *Francis the First*, a narrative of one year in the life of an actress in America, *The Journal of Frances Anne Butler*, published in 1835 under her married name.[1]

In addition to the Kemble party and other first-class passengers, the *Pacific* carried a considerable number in steerage. For many of these, this was a one-way trip driven by a desperate need to escape unemployment and financial hardship. The English, Irish, and Scottish working-class passengers hoped for land, for work, and for release from labor unrest and political disappointments such as that delivered to the Chartists by Parliament when it rejected their petition for male suffrage and reform of corrupt elections. In fact, in 1832, more emigrants sailed for America from the British Isles than in the other six years between 1827 and 1833.[2] For many of the first-class passengers, this was also a journey undertaken for economic reasons. The *Pacific* carried British merchants to America who were in search of new markets for their commodities and American businessmen returning home after overseeing their European interests. Kemble and her father, of course, had embarked on their own moneymaking venture—one more effort to prop up the faltering fortunes of Covent Garden.

The *Pacific* was a comfortable ship, at least for those in first class. They ate well (every luxury imaginable, Kemble notes in her *Journal*), their meals provided, in part, by the cow, geese, and ducks that created in one section of the ship the noises and smells of an English farmyard. There were spacious separate staterooms for the gentlemen and ladies, and, although they were small, the berths were comfortable—clearly more roomy than those on the *Britannia,* the steam-packet that carried Charles Dickens to New York ten years later in 1842. Dickens describes his cabin as "utterly impracticable, thoroughly hopeless, and profoundly preposterous," bearing no resemblance whatsoever to the "gorgeous little bower" that had adorned the ship's plan in an agent's counting house in London.[3] Kemble took immediately to her own little cabin on the *Pacific* and, as soon as she got settled, drew up a scheme of exercise, self-improvement, and journal keeping for the next five weeks. When she was not laid up with seasickness (this did not happen very often since she was physically quite tough), every morning she did needlework, translated German fables, studied Dante in Italian, or read Tom Moore's life of Byron that both fascinated and repelled her (his gift for satire she found "keen and true," his egotism "heartless").[4] Determined not to abandon her recently devised scheme for a more serious life, she wrote regularly in her journal, although the shipboard conviviality sometimes interfered with her rigorous schedule for reading and writing. She produced nothing like the sustained work managed by the industrious political journalist Harriet Martineau, who went to America in 1834. Immediately upon embarkation, Martineau set up her portable desk on deck, sat there in almost all weather, and wrote a book about how to gather material for a travel narrative when one arrives at one's destination (*How to Observe Manners and Morals*, published in 1838). Martineau also wasted no time after she arrived. *Society in America* was published in 1837 and *Retrospect of Western Travel* in 1838, both incisive, forthright impressions of American life. A formidable figure in English intellectual and political circles, Martineau had an intimidating personality that was well-known to Kemble, who wrote to Anna Jameson from Philadelphia in October 1834 that she admired Martineau's genius "greatly" but predicted that if they met, she would be "an object of much superior contempt to that enlightened and clever female Radical and Utilitarian."[5]

Kemble's prediction of how Martineau might feel about her was correct. In her *Autobiography*, Martineau recalls that when they did meet in 1834, shortly after Kemble's marriage to Pierce Butler, she found her spoiled and self-destructive. Acknowledging that Charles Kemble and his daughters were "full of knowledge and accomplishment . . . experienced in all manner of social intercourse," she believed there was "an incurable vulgarity clinging to them, among all the charms of their genius, their cultivation, and their social privileges."[6] For her, they saw life too much in the light of stage lamps rather than in the light of day. When Martineau came to Philadelphia, Kemble showed her proofs of her American *Journal* and asked her to attend the christening of her first child, Sarah Butler, born on May 28, 1835; despite Kemble's overtures at friendship, Martineau declared however much she "really strove hard to like and approve [of] her," she found so radical an "unreality" about her that her interest "died out completely." Censoriously, Martineau announces in her *Autobiography* that she believed all of Kemble's notorious misfortunes were "self-inflicted." Either because she could not see the unhappiness and frustrated intelligence screened by the brittle demeanor that Kemble began to assume soon after her marriage or because she did not wish to see such things, Harriet Martineau dismissed Kemble from her own much less volatile life.[7]

On her way to America, Kemble's shipboard plan included vigorous walking after lunch: consistent with her robust approach to the female body, on the *Pacific* she marched up and down the decks (in London she had ridden almost every day in Hyde Park or tramped through the parkland of various grand houses in the countryside). The pasty complexions and poor posture of American women appalled her and affirmed her feminist belief that women must refuse pampering and maintain their health through exercise. She argued that well-regulated digestion and circulation contributed to a healthy "nervous system" and that it was impossible to "possess a healthy and vigorous mind in a diseased and debilitated body." Always hopeful that the nervous instability that plagued her mother and herself could be steadied through regular physical activity and a disciplined daily schedule, she advocated "exercise, regularity, and moderation in diet and sleep" for all women.[8]

Onboard ship, she was the life of the party not merely because of her charismatic celebrity but also because she danced, sang, and played the piano with an inexhaustible verve that outdid everybody else. A day of serious study, healthy meals with plenty of fruit and vegetables and no sticky pastries, an evening of singing and dancing, capped by a good night's sleep—this was her sensible ideal. And onboard ship she realized it, except for moments when she was tearfully frightened of what awaited her in America: for a two-year period she would be separated from her friends, her family, and her country, and a profitable outcome for the trip depended almost entirely on her success in a profession she despised. In a characteristic expression of her struggle to curb her emotional excitability and of her desire to have her father's "theatrical" discipline quench her mother's "dramatic" outbursts, at one point on the voyage she wrote some lines of verse that call for "stern control" in banishing from the mind all "forbidden thoughts." But despite the brave effort to manage her anxiety, she arrived in New York in a sobbing frenzy, barely able to lift her eyes to the American coastline.

As the steamboat conveyed her into the mist of New York harbor, she became hysterical when she lost sight of the *Pacific*, and when she arrived at the American Hotel not far from the Battery in lower Manhattan, she was choked with sobs. Her wrought-up state was exacerbated by her unhappiness with the hotel itself. She quickly pronounced the rooms a mixture of "French finery, and Irish disorder and dirt," the wine "exorbitantly dear," and the housing of servants nonexistent since they seemed to be sleeping all over the hotel.[9] Her depression lifted with some cake and iced lemonade, however, and she spent the rest of the day playing the piano, venting her dissatisfaction with the hotel, and reading a little Dante. She vowed "to do everything in the world that can be done," including work on her German, which she declared she would "*persecute*."[10] In the early 1830s the thriving city of New York, spread around the lower end of Manhattan island and bisected by a bustling Broadway full of shops and thronged with fashionably dressed women, was a splendid place for her to begin to see and do everything in the world that could be seen and done even if, to her critical eye, the shop assistants were cheeky and American women wore far too much French silk and embroidery. Soon after the Kemble party was all settled, Fanny explored the many opportunities for exercise the countryside around New York offered—delicious horseback outings through Brooklyn, for example, where she trotted like "a gentleman" and felt her spirits sparkle "like champagne."

Fanny Kemble's arrival in America had been preceded by a steady stream of English travelers who, following the end of the Revolutionary War, began their

Fig. 15. American Hotel, Broadway. James Smillie, after Charles Burton, 1831. Fanny and Charles Kemble stayed here when they arrived in New York in August 1832. Fanny was not pleased with the service. I. N. Phelps Stokes Collection, Miriam and Ira D. Wallach Division of Art, Prints, and Photographs, New York Public Library, Astor, Lenox and Tilden Foundations.

ambiguous assessment of the former colonies now transformed into a vigorous nation. Most of these travelers kept detailed journals and wrote long letters, some merely to record impressions for their friends and families, and others with the aim of publishing books on their return to the mother country—figures such as Frances Trollope, for example, whose controversial *Domestic Manners of the Americans* appeared in 1832. A little later, the work of well-known transatlantic travelers helped shape English ideas about America: for instance, Charles Dickens's *American Notes* in the 1840s, Isabella Bird's *The Englishwoman in America* in the 1850s, and Anthony Trollope's *North America* in the 1860s. Kemble, then, when she began writing her journal onboard the *Pacific* and adding to it as she traveled the Northeast from Boston to Washington, joined a group whose work often offended American readers and sometimes assured the English that their lost colonies were paying for their disobedience with shambling democracy and barbarous social and cultural mores. Hypocrisy about slavery, rude table manners, the use of spittoons, and the absence of a decent artistic culture became punctuating motifs in this writing.

Many things about America delighted Kemble—the glorious scenery along the Hudson River, the pure fresh air that immediately invigorated her father, the "unmingled good will, and cordial, real kindness" with which she was received— but in her American *Journal* she was not shy to express her unhappiness with the "peculiarities" of the country in which, as things turned out, she was to spend roughly a third of the rest of her life (at different periods and for varying lengths of time). Much of her criticism concurs with prevailing English attitudes, but she brought a fresh perspective to the American experience. As a glamorous young actress whose adulation was surpassed only by that heaped on Dickens in the 1840s, she packed her *Journal* with entertaining anecdotes of actors so terrified they became utterly mute when she stepped onstage, of politicians practiced in the art of flirtation, and of literary figures who listened graciously to her ideas and encouraged her in her writing. The *Journal* also chronicles the growth of a political awareness that began when she saw the emaciated hand-loom weaver in the Manchester railway station and that continued as she fashioned imaginary speeches against the Reform Bill. Kemble's arrival in New York precipitated her literary entry into a body of commentary about America.

Tom Moore, one of Kemble's close friends, had crossed the Atlantic in 1803, and the angry poems he published recording his impressions probably contributed to her tears when she arrived in New York. His verse would have led her to expect corruption and decay, obsessed as the poems are with the metaphorical presentation of America as a degenerate body so dissipated by disease that the country is in a state of terminal rot. Moore claimed that before his arrival he treasured a sanguine vision of "man's new world of liberty," but "not one gleaming trace" of that ideal could be found.[11] America had become infected with French individualism and English radicalism, polluted by what he terms "Gallic dross" and "mob-mania." These images, produced in part by the English fear of revolution that was so powerful during the Napoleonic Wars, emerge strongly in a poem titled "Columbia" that presents America as an infected female body: "Even now, in dawn of life, / her sickly breath / Burns with the taint of empires near their death . . . / She's old in youth, she's blasted in her prime."[12] Diagnosing America as fatally diseased, Moore traces this condition to the peopling of the country with "the motley dregs of every distant clime," the quasi-criminal outcasts of Europe who, rather than building on the idealistic foundations of the Declaration of Independence, have dragged America down to the point of anarchy. He also takes aim at that favored target for English travelers—democratic principles articulated in the Declaration contradicted by the existence of slavery—by satirizing the "weary statesman" who flees "From halls of council to his negro's shed. . . . And dreams of freedom in his slave's embrace."[13]

Moore's intemperate attacks were modified somewhat by English writers who followed him to America in the 1820s. Although uniformly disgusted by the table manners and perplexed by the existence of slavery in a nation founded on ideals of liberty, these travelers admired the vigor and natural wonders of their former colonies. Kemble's *Journal* shows that although she might have shared some of Moore's conservatism, she was much more appreciative than he of the social generosity of her American hosts and much more responsive to the natural beauty of the Northeast. Essentially, her earliest attitudes toward America were ambivalent: at best they were delightedly enthusiastic and at worst they were snootily dismissive. These mixed feelings were clearly divined by her parents, as we can see from a note in the diary of Charles Greville, who, shortly after the publication in England of the *Journal*, observed that Charles and Thérèse were obsessively occupied with the puzzling discrepancies in their daughter's book—her father thought it "full of sublime things and vulgarities" and her mother was "divided between admiration and disgust."[14]

Kemble's ambivalent responses to American society are, in quite surprising ways, similar to those of the radical journalist and reformer William Cobbett, who brought with him to America ideals he believed the industrial revolution had erased from English life (he first arrived in America in 1791). Cobbett delighted in a new world free of unearned privilege and he ignored what other English writers perceived as social rawness and cultural barbarism. He made three trips across the Atlantic, the first as a corporal in the Revolutionary War, then two years after the war as a civilian traveler, and, finally, as a fugitive from imprisonment as a supposedly dangerous rabble-rouser. It was his third visit that produced *A Year's Residence in the United States of America*, published in 1819, part political pamphlet and part guide for yeoman immigrants of the sort who, traveling steerage, accompanied Kemble on the *Pacific* from Liverpool to New York. Cobbett argues that the forefathers of the present generation of Americans brought with them to the colonies sterling English values of honesty, industry, and hospitality. By the beginning of the nineteenth century, however, these values were being eroded in England by what Cobbett characterizes (along with many others) as a grasping, materialistic society, devoted to profit making and tax gathering.[15] He offers his readers a useful chapter on growing turnips on Long Island, an enthusiastic description of the civil but never servile ways of the American laborer, and much political protest against the English system of taxation. Governed by political critique of his mother country, Cobbett envisions America as a pastoral fantasy of what he imagines England once was but is no more because of greedy businessmen and politicians, those "boxers and bankrupts" who figured in Kemble's poem about the 1832 Reform Bill.[16]

Writing some fifteen years after Cobbett, Kemble shared most of his views despite the transparent political difference between them. Although she became cross when she first arrived in New York when impertinent visitors walked in and out of the Kemble sitting room "without leave or licence," and although she felt that the language used in society was "unrefined, inelegant, and often ungrammatically vulgar," she responded genuinely to the affectionate generosity of her American friends. She also vehemently insisted that America was "in one respect blessed above all others" and that was in the absence of poverty: through a greater degree of social equality than that to be found in England, "none here need lift up the despairing voice of hopeless and helpless want"[17] (as she had seen them do in the Manchester railway station). And her observations about the way America was treating its indigenous population are notably similar to those of Cobbett. Cobbett thundered against the "very questionable soundness" of grand ideas about western expansion of the American empire and its accompanying "taming of the wilderness."[18] On a visit to Hoboken just two weeks after her arrival in New York, Kemble noted in her *Journal* that the European "work of extermination" of "the child of the soil" was a "very singular and painful subject of contemplation."[19] She was no radical, yet her contempt for money-grubbing businessmen who were shoving their way into a reformed House of Commons (as she saw it) and her admiration of American social freedoms suggest that she was forming her own political views.

Kemble's early writings about America also include much controversial commentary about women, which signals the emergence of a feminist voice characterized by the forthrightness and independent spirit that would carry her through many difficult years ahead. As I shall demonstrate later in this chapter, she protested the legal and cultural subordination of women to their fathers, husbands, and brothers, and she did so in a manner that alarmed many of her American readers. She saw this subordination as an insidious protectiveness that rendered American women supine and dull; in a sense, she wanted them to be more like herself, or at least more like what she aimed to be—resilient, autonomous, and unafraid, all "dramatic" emotion subordinated to "theatrical" discipline.

In her first winter in New York she loved to walk at night along Spring Street (now part of fashionable Soho), and she relished the fresh wind from the north, the glittering moon, and the way she could speed along without interference from a protective, bothersome male figure: "How I do like walking alone—being alone; for this alone I wish I were a man," she wrote to Harriet St. Leger.[20] Racing along the lower Manhattan streets, released from the physical and social constraints placed on women, led her, really for the first time, to express explicitly feminist

ideas. To Harriet she had certainly confided her reservations about marriage, saying that should she marry, she would, somehow, retain her financial independence,
but now she articulated testy annoyance with the cosseting of women that she
witnessed in America. The only person she liked to walk with in New York that
winter was her father, which is no surprise: at sunset, they would go to the Battery
and admire the brilliant orange of the sunset and the violet color of twilight. In
the icy wind whipping off the Atlantic, they huddled together, marveling at skies
unseen in England.

The strong Tory opinions of a gentleman-traveler who arrived in America almost at the same time as Kemble, Thomas Hamilton, frame a book he published
on his return to England in 1833. Just when Kemble notes in her *Journal* that she
would not wish to be in a country run by upstart shopkeepers taking their seats in
Parliament as a result of reform, Hamilton was punctuating his conventional story
of the English traveler with a nightmare vision of America dominated by huge
manufacturing cities. Fear of an enraged working class dominates his thinking. He
warns that the American population would congregate in masses (and thus become
like Manchester) and that all the "vices incident to such a condition of society
will attain speedy maturity."[21] Military force will be powerless against the mob, he
predicts, and the rich man will have no place to look for security of his business
or his private fortune. Hamilton, like Tom Moore some twenty years before him,
saw America descending into anarchy, driven there by the same forces dreaded
by Moore: French-inspired political protest and English bourgeois materialism.
America was being populated by the criminal dregs of Europe, governed by vulgar
arrivistes, and ruled by merchants who paraded their wealth with their wives and
daughters supporting their "pretensions."[22] Kemble shared this view of pretentious,
newly rich manufacturers, but she also expressed strong feelings about the miserable working conditions of their employees. At a New Year's Day party in Baltimore
in 1833, for example, she responded heatedly to an American steel manufacturer's
defense of poor wages by saying that all over England, "this cruel oppression of the
poor, this forcing them . . . to toil in bitterness for their scanty daily bread, while
those who thus inhumanly depreciate their labour, and wring their hard earnings
from their starving grasp, grow wealthy on their plunder" were "the things that
make a nation rotten at core, and ripe for decay."[23] This forwardness in political
talk often alienated her American listeners and prompted them to couple her with
Frances Trollope, who, at the historical moment Kemble was both enchanting and
alienating her audiences, was preparing her intemperate attack on America.

In the late 1820s, Frances Trollope crossed the Atlantic for a three-year stay,
driven abroad by the financial difficulties of her husband and, with motives similar
to those of Charles and Fanny Kemble, determined to repair the family finances.

Trollope's moneymaking was spectacularly unsuccessful but she sailed home with much explosive material for a book. Her *Domestic Manners of the Americans* did not endear her to American readers, something she was the first to acknowledge in its afterword: "I suspect that what I have written will make it evident I do not like America. . . . I do not like them. I do not like their principles, I do not like their manners, I do not like their opinions."[24] She attacked Americans for gobbling their food, for spitting on the hems of women's dresses, and for betraying the ideals of individual freedom through the institution of slavery and the displacement of "Red Indians" from their lands: "You will see them with one hand hoisting the cap of liberty, and with the other flogging their slaves. You will see them one hour lecturing the mob on the indefeasible rights of man, and the next driving from their homes the children of the soil, whom they have bound themselves to protect by the most solemn treaties."[25]

Frances Trollope's bombastic attacks on American culture and society also rely on a familiar metaphor in nineteenth-century English writing about America: mother country and child colonies. Americans in the late 1820s, she argues, have inherited the spirit of independence stoutly fought for by their fathers, but they have not inherited the ability to become scholars and gentlemen because the mother country, through greedy desire to profit from her metaphorical children, so alienated them that in escaping her voracious grasp through revolution, they also rejected the benign influence of English civilization.[26] With these ideas, Trollope was trying to negotiate a difficulty presented to English writers by a nation that was both similar to their own in terms of race, culture, and language, yet different in terms of politics, manners, and social class. Caught between praise and condemnation, they invented a kind of family romance based on an image of England as a sometimes good and sometimes bad mother to rambunctious, amazing America.

Given England's eighteenth- and nineteenth-century perpetuation of the imperial nation as benevolent mother, it is not surprising that English writers who wanted both to explain the loss of their American colonies and to take pride in the new nation invented a story of enduring stability in the political bond between the two countries. The use of the image itself goes back, at least, to Edmund Burke, who in a March 1775 speech titled "On Conciliation with America" describes England as a fertile but exhausted mother whose body was now being fed by American trade. Formerly the selfless protector of her dependent colonies, England (and her empire) were now being sustained by "the very food that has nourished every other part into its present magnitude," and Burke argues that American trade should be treasured as the commerce that has fattened the empire.[27] Almost sixty years later Thomas Hamilton traced the origins of what he saw as an anarchic democracy back to the eighteenth-century English dispatch of her criminal population across the Atlantic. Then, in her "motherly care," Hamilton sarcastically argues, the mother country bled the colonies and replenished her own coffers with restrictive trade.

Frances Trollope's son, Anthony Trollope, writing about America in the 1860s, replaced what he saw as intemperate female attack on the lost colony with his more appreciative male analysis. He argues that the faults of his mother's book must be traced entirely to the gender of the writer: "No observer was certainly ever less qualified to judge of the prospects or even of the happiness of a young people. . . . Whatever she saw she judged, as most women do, from her own standing-point."[28] Although Trollope admitted that his mother wrote vividly, he believed that her ideas could only be wrong since she lacked the intellectual power to analyze the political system that produced the social absurdities she found so abominable.

Trollope initiated the analysis he believed most women, including his mother, were incapable of undertaking with a description of maternal England at the outbreak of the Revolutionary War: England was "as the mother bird when the young bird will fly alone. She suffered those pangs which Nature calls upon mothers to endure."[29] Young birds and former colonies need their independence, and Trollope's most fully developed transatlantic fantasy emerges in a kind of fictional tableau where America becomes the daughter who goes out into the world armed with the lessons of her responsible mother: "She is to go forth, and do as she best may in the world under that teaching which her old home has given her."[30] Trollope found America benevolent, civilizing, and morally impeccable, which could not be otherwise since she had been so wisely instructed by England. In sum, England reproduced her own splendid self in American culture and society. When Kemble began to write about America she quickly adopted the familiar mother country metaphor, lamenting the fact that England had not adopted "a more maternal course of conduct" toward America yet at the same time offering consolation to England by praising the new nation as "inheritor of her glory." America was a younger England, "destined to perpetuate the language, the memory, the virtues of the noble land from which she is descended."[31] Visiting Bunker Hill in April 1833, she reflected that it was all *English* blood that had been shed in the battle there, for try as Americans might to separate themselves from England, "they must still be the children of old England, for they speak the words her children speak by the fireside of her homes."[32]

Despite her political inexperience, Kemble produced some astute and lively commentary that contributed to the Victorian discourse about America, and she embellished the family romance created by English writers when she published her American *Journal*. As she envisioned the travel narrative that was taking shape, she realized she was more than a celebrity actress who happened to write verse and historical plays: each evening, as she reviewed her notes, she knew she was developing her skills as a social critic. If, when sailing from Liverpool, she had been the anxious daughter identified with her neurotic and dramatic mother and sent into exile with her theatrical father, when she traveled in America, she seemed to loosen these familial constraints. Fanny Kemble's world grew bigger, and although the influence of her mother's neurosis never left her, she became less dependent on Thérèse's approval of her work and less bothered by a duty to console the father she adored in his American exile. After a few days in New York, when she saw how well Charles was looking, she noted that half her regret "for this exile melted away."[33] As time went on, Kemble became more like America itself as it was mythologized by the English travelers who preceded and followed her: independent of the mother and unafraid to speak her piece.

Fanny Meets a Great Fortune

Philip Hone, a wealthy auctioneer and former mayor of New York, noted in his diary on September 4, 1832, that the "highly gifted daughter" of Charles Kemble had just arrived at the American Hotel, which was right next door to his handsome house. Within a few days, he had paid his respects and recorded his impressions: Fanny was "not very handsome," although she had a good figure, easy manners, and a sprightly intelligence. On September 15 he had the Kembles to dinner and neither Charles nor Fanny showed themselves to advantage, at least as far as Hone and his eager American guests were concerned: Charles was "stiff" and mainly interested in parading his polished deportment while Fanny behaved in a most "singular" and unfriendly fashion. Perfectly self-possessed, she talked extremely well but only when and to whom she chose; her air of indifference and nonchalance, Hone believed, would not make her a favorite with possible "beaux," and she monopolized the married men and ignored their wives. When she sang after dinner, Hone thought her voice remarkably similar to her personality: powerful but not sweet. The best he could say about her appearance was that although her features separately were not "good," combined, they made "a face of great and powerful expression."[34] When Kemble got home, she recorded *her* impressions of the evening: the dinner was "plenteous, and tolerably well dressed, but ill-served," the table lacked water and finger glasses, and the poky, old-fashioned piano stuck right up against the wall was tuned far too high for her contralto voice. She was glad to get back to the American Hotel.

Two nights later, on September 17, in the middle of a cholera scare that had recently hit New York City, the Kembles began their engagement at the Park Theater with Charles Kemble's *Hamlet*.[35] Philip Hone considered the performance fairly well studied, but, like Kemble himself, it lacked fire: Charles displayed a barrage of full-blown Kemble techniques—exaggerated delivery that seemed to introduce extra syllables into almost every word and marmoreal assumption of "attitudes" that held up the action. Along with most of the New York theatergoing public, Hone was impatient to see Fanny, and she appeared the next night as Bianca in Henry Hart Milman's 1815 tragedy, *Fazio*. Set in Florence, the play tells a story of robbery, supposed murder, and a wife's revenge for her husband's infidelity. Annoyingly for Kemble, the actor playing Fazio was so overcome with stage fright that he became speechless and unable to respond to her prompts, which rather ruined the first two acts; but by the third, when Bianca goes mad and dies of grief after discovering that her jealousy has caused her husband's death, she could, as she put it, get to work. She was a stupendous hit. Hone recorded that he never saw a New York audience so moved, astonished, and delighted; the last act exhibited "female powers" never before seen and even if she had uttered no lines, the expression of strong feelings on her face was a rich enough treat. He concluded that "we have never seen her equal on the American stage, and England has witnessed none since Miss O'Neil."[36] Most reviewers raved about the refined and calculated beauty of Kemble's attitudes, her melodious voice, and her eloquent features. The *American* was much taken with her "girlish figure dilating into queenlike dignity while sweeping to her revenge" and her "piteous distraction as she stood like the ideal forms of sculpture."[37] The *New York Mirror* declared that she had not disappointed the high expectations of an audience eager to see "the poet-actress, who so early in life has astonished and rivalled the finest and oldest poets of her day." Apart from her size—"petite" was the polite adjective in contrast to Charles Greville's opinion of Kemble as "ill-made"—she was enchanting: the large dark eyes half lifted to the audience and the low tones of a silvery voice at once seduced "every heart . . . we may safely assert that more brilliant effect has rarely if ever been produced on the American stage."[38] The only reservations about Kemble's performances appeared in the *New York Mirror* (perhaps written by a different critic from the person who attended Kemble's first night on September 18): on September 29, the *Mirror* asserted that Kemble lacked "fire and ardor. She flings herself into a stateliness of manner, when making only an ordinary remark, delivering her words with a lengthened and too deliberate attempt at stage effect; an error, we suspect, peculiar to the school of which she is such a rich ornament."[39] These failings, which suggest she was arranging herself in the "teapot" school of acting, were attributed to her

Fig. 16. Miss Fanny Kemble as Mrs. Beverley, Belvedera (Belvidera), Juliet, and Euphrasia, 1830s. Fanny performed these roles in her New York engagement. Billy Rose Theatre Division, New York Public Library for the Performing Arts, Astor, Lenox and Tilden Foundations.

mind being too "full of intellectual excellence." On this particular evening, at least, Kemble seems to have performed more in her father's mode of theatrical posturing than her mother's style of dramatic spontaneity.

Several nights later, Philip Hone saw Kemble as Lady Teazle but he found the performance quite unequal to her Bianca or Juliet (here he was in agreement with Kemble herself since she always felt she was never successful as a comic actress). However, her Julia in *The Hunchback*, which he saw a week later, showed an excellence "in the delineation of feeling highly wrought and impassioned."[40] The *New York Post* concurred, declaring that "a piece of more beautiful and perfect acting was never exhibited on our boards."[41] Walt Whitman was doubtless in that audience, for he recalled in later life that he had seen almost all her New York performances at the Park Theater. "Better than merely beautiful," superbly strong in her movements and her voice, Kemble was the stuff of legend: "Nothing finer did ever stage exhibit—the veterans of all nations said so, and my boyish heart and head felt it in every minute cell."[42]

The stunning success of the Kembles' New York engagement was registered at the box office: the average nightly take for the twelve days was $1,235 (now, just over $26,000) and the highest was on October 4 for Kemble in *The Hunchback*, which brought in $1,561.[43] Kemble's anxiety about leaving England was soon alleviated by the success of the New York venture, and although she felt depleted by New York's sultry fall weather (at the end of some performances she was half dead with heat and fatigue), she was invigorated by the exhilarating variety of her new life. Having come to like the Hone family more than she did at their welcoming dinner party, and to behave more pleasantly as a result, she rode out with them for picnics in Weehawken; Hone wrote in his diary after one of these outings, "The more I see of this wonderful girl the more I am pleased with her."[44] Boat trips up the beautiful Hudson to the house of a family friend living near West Point led to vigorous hikes around Peekskill; the walking reminded her of the tramps around Edinburgh. She shopped for ribbons on Broadway, ate ices at lively cafés, and whenever possible walked on the Battery in the early evening with her father. But as fresh, different, and exciting as her New York experience was proving to be, one thing remained unchanged: her distaste for the acting profession. After an especially tedious night at the theater, she wrote in her journal, "What a mass of wretched mumming mimicry acting is! . . . rouge, for the startled life-blood in the cheek of that young passionate woman; an actress, a mimicker, a sham creature, me, in fact."[45] Kemble's self-mocking tone, however, is far different from her anguished protest at being "cursed" like the Lady of Shalott. Three years of acting experience and social and professional acclaim had transformed her from a discontented, bookish young woman steered to the stage by her parents into a wry, composed presence with decided political opinions. As Washington Irving told her, she was seeing the world and she was using her sharp intelligence to shape her impressions into a publishable narrative. The identity as actress was being subsumed into the identity of social observer of America's systems of social class and its treatment of women.

On the dull, damp, and dreary morning of October 8, the New York engagement concluded, Kemble, her father, and Dall rose at a quarter to five to catch the six o'clock steamboat that would take them on the first leg of their ten-hour journey to Philadelphia and a booking at the Walnut Street Theater. At half-past ten they left the steamboat at a spot close to the New Jersey–Delaware border and boarded what was to Kemble's mind the most appalling coach she had ever entered. It was clumsy, wretched, and cramped, and she was almost smothered by her father's huge cloaks piled on the seat beside her. They jolted their way through a flat Delaware landscape she thought singularly unimpressive, dotted with desolate, untidy, and untended cottages. After fourteen miles in the horrendous carriage, everyone piled into coaches standing on a railway line—not drawn by steam like the Liverpool-to-Manchester railway, but by horses that took an hour and half to reach another steamboat on the Delaware River. At four o'clock in the afternoon they reached Philadelphia and settled into the Mansion House Hotel on Chestnut Street, desperate for rest before the opening the next night of their month-long engagement. Kemble immediately liked Philadelphia for its attractive eighteenth-century houses and its regularly intersecting streets. That it was less lively than New York did not displease her and she admired its substance, soberness, and dignity.

On October 13, feeling very much under the weather because of a cold, she came down to tea and found a personable young man sitting with her father, a Mr. Pierce Butler. She concluded her diary for that day with the following comment: "He was a pretty-spoken, *genteel* youth enough: he drank tea with us, and offered to ride with me. He is, it seems, a great fortune. . . . Now I'll go to bed: my cough's enough to kill a horse."[46] Butler's arrival at the Mansion House Hotel had been prompted by a letter from a New York friend, Henry Fitzharding Berkeley (dated September 23, 1832), that raved about Fanny's talents and charms: knowing her physical attractions would be of paramount interest for a young man notorious for his romantic conquests, Berkeley assessed Fanny as "pretty . . . large legs and feet, large hands, large arms. . . . Her eyes when flashing with spirit vividly beautiful . . . her mouth large with teeth of ivory, her nose straight."[47] On October 3, he wrote to Butler that Kemble's conversation, however, was a challenge: "she is very free but highly educated and accomplished, rather too much so for my way of thinking—because she puts you out of countenance by cursed apt quotations

. . . from horrible old Writers, and if you shew any French, kills you with Racine, if Italian knocks you down with Dante—Rather blue!! but not obtrusively so."[48] After Kemble and Butler were married, Fanny's wit and erudition often left Pierce fumbling for words, but despite the fact that she left no record of his physical attributes, said to be considerable, she was not reticent to confess how much she was sexually attracted to him.[49] Pierce was slim, short, and compact, a young man of "singular beauty and a certain refined charm of manner," according to the Philadelphia physician S. Weir Mitchell, who knew the Butler family and in later life became Kemble's close friend and ally. For Mitchell, Pierce possessed "the perfect amiability of a selfish man" and, in the words of one of Kemble's biographers, carried himself with the "the air of a well-bred fox."[50]

Until 1826, Pierce Butler had been known by the name of Pierce Butler Mease. One of six children of Sarah Butler Mease and Dr. James Mease, he was named Pierce in honor of his maternal grandfather, who had come to America from Ireland in 1766 as a major in the British army, married a South Carolina heiress, and fought with the Revolutionary army against the British in 1776. Major Butler participated in the Constitutional Convention, was elected twice to the United States Senate, and through his marriage acquired vast holdings in Georgia along the rich delta land of the Altamaha River: Butler Island, a rice plantation near Darien and Hampton, and Butler Point, a cotton plantation, on the northwest edge of St. Simons Island. He also devised a complicated set of legacies that disclosed his intense dislike of his son-in-law, Dr. Mease: any of his grandsons who changed his last name to Butler would become a joint heir to the fortune. When he met Fanny Kemble in 1832, Pierce and his brother, John, had already changed their names and had been known as Butlers for six years; at the age of twenty-one, Pierce had inherited one quarter of the income from his grandfather's estate. The remainder was divided between the unmarried twin sisters of his mother, upon whose death the bulk of the income would be shared between the Butler brothers. While waiting for this to happen, Pierce spent his time studying law in dilatory fashion at the University of Pennsylvania, riding and gambling, playing the flute, and paying calls on the Kembles at the Mansion House Hotel. Kemble's entries in her American *Journal* from October 27 to December 25, 1832, record a steady stream of visits from Pierce, who almost always arrived with a present: "Began practicing, when in walked that interesting youth, Mr. Butler, with a nosegay, as big as himself"; "That worthy youth,—insisted upon my accepting his beautiful large dog, Neptune"; "When I came into the drawing-room I found a beautiful work-box sent me by that very youthful admirer of mine, Mr. Butler."[51] The emphasis on Pierce's youth suggests that Kemble regarded him as emotionally immature even if she found him sexually attractive.

Fig. 17. Pierce Butler, ca. 1847. Courtesy of Hargrett Rare Book and Manuscript Library, University of Georgia Libraries.

On the day that Kemble met Pierce, however, she was indifferent to his attractions; the promise of riding enticed her but she was more interested in revising her journal, which she knew was more engaging than a lady's diary of polite commentary on the scenery, the fashions, and the social customs. Reviewing what she had written since she had arrived in New York six weeks earlier, she could see that three different subjects dominated her observations: first, the comparatively satisfied condition of the working classes in America; second, the raw nature of American culture; and third, the subjugated and unhappy state of American women. She knew that her commentary on these issues was sometimes casual and fragmentary but she could fathom the makings of a substantial publication. At this moment in her life when her acting had garnered every kind of financial and professional recognition that she could have hoped for, she decided to focus on the ambition she had put aside on the day her mother hysterically announced Covent Garden Theatre was covered in bills of sale: to become a published author. Ironically, this was also the moment when she met the man who treasured another ambition: to make Frances Anne Kemble an obedient Butler wife.

When she arrived in America, Kemble's ideas about social class had been shaped by the Kemble family's belief in its own elevated class position, her attention to political debate conducted by powerful politicians at places such as Holland House, and her quite recent exposure to class discontent produced by England's industrialization. Conservative in the way she cherished a belief in Kemble cultural superiority, she tended to the Whig side in acknowledging that reform needed to be accepted by the country if working-class unrest were to be contained, and she was outspoken in terms of her outrage at exploitation and suffering. Sometimes she favored the nostalgic fantasy that before industrialization the ruling classes never neglected their moral duty to the lower orders, and that those merchants and manufacturers shouldering their way into the House of Commons after 1832 thought only of profit and not of moral duty to their "hands." After a week in New York, she declared in her *Journal* that "universal suffrage is a political fallacy: and will be one of the stumbling-blocks in the path to this country's greatness."[52] But two weeks later, she enlarged her critique of oppression of the English factory population and she lightened her pessimism about universal suffrage. On a visit to rustic Hoboken, a pleasant relief from the rush and glitter of lower Broadway, Kemble observed what were to her significant differences between English and American working people. What impressed her most on this visit to New Jersey was the freedom of the American working man to enjoy nature, even on a workday. Crowds of "happy, cheerful, enjoying beings," well-dressed journeymen, laborers, handicraftsmen, and tradespeople, thronged the walks along the river and through the woods, flocked into the "pure air, the bright sunshine, and beautiful shade of this lovely place." Here she found the most splendid example of the sheer excellence of the American government: "the freedom and happiness of the lower classes." To emphasize her point, she contrasted these pastoral scenes with what would be happening to the English "miserable manufacturing population": rather than having time to wander in the Manchester fields, the factory hands would be confined to "unhealthy toil" from sunrise to sunset.[53]

Although she could not attribute the contentment of the American workers to their republican government, nor to an ideal of equality being expressed in political practice, she did concede that a republic was a noble, high, and pure form of government: the difficulty was in its realization, which is somewhat different from her earlier assertion that it is a "fallacy."[54] She attributed the happiness of the American working man and woman to the unsated need of American businessmen for workers to develop "the commercial and material resources" of the nation. Arguing that the working class was confident of its value as a labor force, was not subject to cruel exploitation by manufacturers, and was unafraid that its ever-swelling size due to the arrival of European immigrants would diminish its worth, she foresaw an ever-brightening future for cooperation between masters and workers. Although there is nothing original in Kemble's writings about American labor, it is notable that a highly intelligent and intellectually ambitious twenty-three-year-old actress was turning her mind to the world around her and shaping her observations into social commentary, even if that commentary was fairly commonplace. As Washington Irving predicted, she was seeing men and things—indeed the world—and she was taking steps to fulfill the promise identified by Harriet St. Leger and Harriet Siddons.

The speculation about working-class leisure prompted Kemble to think also about her own pleasures and, consequently, about the absence (as she saw it) of a fully realized American artistic culture: "Where are the picture-galleries—the sculptures—the works of art and science—the countless wonders of human ingenuity and skill . . . where are all the sources from which I am to draw my recreations?"[55] In common with many English travelers at the time, she argued that American culture lacked the foundation of a historical past. "Where are the poets of this land?" she asked herself when hiking along the Hudson. She wondered why the glorious scenery had not inspired verse like that of the Romantics, why the magnificent hills and majestic Hudson River did not call to poets to write hymns of praise to America's natural beauty. She found it strange "how marvellously unpoetical these people are! How swallowed up in life and its daily realities, wants and cares!" and concluded that republican forms of government are inimical to culture.[56] By the time Kemble's *Journal* was published in 1835, American readers were accustomed to this dismissive denigration of their literature and visual art, and they shook off her remarks as the snobbish thinking of a spoiled actress, but her unrestrained criticism of the sex generally treated with exaggerated deference was another matter.

Kemble's writings about American women exhibit a forthright feminist voice that from this moment in her life was never silenced, despite the best efforts of her husband. In the early sections of the *Journal*, remarks about American women mainly reflect her general dislike of American manners. For example, she was deeply bothered by a woman on the steamboat when she was crossing the Delaware to Philadelphia who snatched up a book she had placed beside her without asking permission. She found such behavior unceremonious and traced it to an unfortunate mixture of republican feelings of equality with resentful impudence and vulgarity. But she soon extended this critique of American female manners to lay the blame at the door of American men who treat women as fragile creatures in need of protection from their own rough ways. She was appalled by the way American women, when together, behaved so aggressively, talked so loudly, and with "such a twang," and she was distressed by the way they were treated, when with men, as exalted objects and thus as "comparative ciphers." Contrasting this state of things with relations between the sexes in England, where, she declared, married women exercised a dignified and graceful influence over society, she argued that in America, married women, because they were worshiped and kept apart, were denied authentic social, cultural, or political power. Exaggerated deference toward women was a form of patriarchal oppression. At virtually the same historical moment that Kemble was setting down her vigorous views of women's insidious subordination, Frances Trollope was observing that all the enjoyments of American men "are found in the absence of the women" and that because women are "guarded by a seven-fold shield of habitual insignificance," the only serious attention they seem to receive is from the clergy.[57]

In February 1833, riding around Weehawken, New Jersey, Kemble fell into leisurely debate with one of her party about the influence of religion on women's lives. First, she agreed with her nameless (male) companion that women, in general, do not have analytical minds and that their imaginations are more sensitive than those of men, and that because their "habits of thought, little enlarged by experience, observation, or proper culture," make women incapable of logical thought, they turn more readily to religion. In the body of the text in her published *Journal* she does not record what she said next. She leaves this for a long footnote where she inveighs against male refusal to consider the rational education "of the mothers of their children," attacks a system that relegates women to existences "burdensome to themselves and useless to others," and laments the abandonment of women's minds to the inanities of dinner party small talk. She winds things up by saying that if women's intellectual capacities are, indeed, inferior to those of men (perhaps in line with their physical inferiority), then at least women should be made as "wise in mind" as possible so that they may move beyond what they inherit from nature.[58]

Consciously or not, through the deployment of a long and impassioned footnote, she slyly subverts the Anglo-American patriarchal restriction of women to domestic matters by introducing her own political opinions with conventionally feminine disclaimers. By placing her sharp critique at the bottom of the page, away from the leisurely debate being conducted on horseback (and on the page proper), she performs a theatrical display of ignorant young womanhood withdrawing from the official public sphere of political discussion and making itself heard elsewhere (at the bottom of the page). Kemble's voice now becomes stronger, more opinionated, and more aware of how it might have been muted in the past. "Politics of all sorts, I confess, are far beyond my limited powers of comprehension," she announces disarmingly as she launches into some close analysis of the motives propelling American electoral politics in the fall of 1832: she felt that all was being driven by "the aristocratic desire of elevation and separation, and the democratic desire of demolishing and levelling. . . . Every man in America is a politician."[59]

In early 1833, on the last leg of their tour that would take her to Washington, Kemble left Philadelphia and the dogged attentions of Pierce Butler, which she now accepted and rather enjoyed. He seemed to have infinite time to devote to her wishes, and she relished riding with him along the Schuylkill and receiving the extravagant bouquets delivered daily to the Mansion House Hotel. The Kemble party arrived in Washington shortly after Andrew Jackson had been reelected, with an impressive majority of electoral votes, as president. When Philip Hone learned that she was to meet Jackson, he remarked that Fanny in the White House was rather like catching a canary in a mousetrap, an image that seems to suggest her indomitable personality would be quenched neither by the somber dignity of the building nor the office of the presidency. Kemble did not remain silent when she met Jackson. Politely, but insistently, she asked about his recently implemented policies: the "removal" scheme that drove most of America's indigenous Northeastern population beyond the Mississippi and filled their lands with European immigrants of the kind who had traveled with Fanny Kemble on the *Pacific* was in full swing. At the time of the Kemble visit, Jackson was embroiled in a fight with his Southern supporters (principally those in South Carolina) about a protective tariff that favored the Northeast, but he wanted to meet the alluring theatrical celebrity and her father. Describing him as "a good specimen of a fine old well-battered soldier" (a type she knew from her friendship with the Duke of Wellington), she noted his preoccupation with the South Carolina problem and his distaste for "scribbling ladies." According to Kemble, Jackson assured her that the whole of the "present southern disturbances" had their origin "in no larger a source than the nib of the pen of a lady." At the end of the day, Kemble noted wryly that if this "be true, the lady must have scribbled to some purpose."[60]

In the spring of 1833, she continued to explore the American social landscape and to enlarge her circle of American friends. After her experience with George

Stephenson in Manchester, she remained most interested in mechanical science and visited some ironworks at Cold Spring on the Hudson owned by a distant relative, Gouverneur Kemble. Shown the iron frames of large mill wheels, the machinery and process of boring the cannon, the model of an iron forcing pump, the casting houses, and all the "wonders" of manufacture, she felt that when able to see a scientific process at work, the hitherto technical terms were comprehensible. Her recounting of the Cold Spring experience affirms her speculation about why women's minds remain dull. Here she saw the workings of something conventionally thought to be uninteresting to women—an ironworks—and her mind was enlarged. It was an experience that almost exactly repeated her time on the "Rocket." But the significant difference between Manchester and Cold Spring is that after three years of artistic and financial success, Kemble had become more conscious of her identity as a working woman in a male-dominated world. As she lamented the oppressed condition of American women, she gained awareness of her own peculiarly privileged and shackled condition, an understanding that became acute on a holiday trip to New York State in the summer of 1833 following an acting engagement in Boston. She was the radiant center of a group that included her father, Dall, Pierce Butler, and the dangerously attractive Edward Trelawny, a glamorous figure whose stories of Shelley and Byron made him a charismatic companion. During this summer, Kemble became increasingly vulnerable to the seductive wooing of Butler, who aimed to separate her from acting, England, and her newly forged identity as an independent intellectual woman unafraid to say what she thought about social justice and sexual politics, even if she felt compelled to insert her subversive voice at the bottom of the page.

5

On the Brink

A woman should be her husband's friend, his best and dearest friend, as he should be hers: but friendship is a relation of equality, in which the same perfect respect for each other's liberty is exercised on both sides; and that sort of marriage, if it exists at all anywhere, is, I suspect, very uncommon everywhere.
> —Fanny Kemble to Harriet St. Leger, October 29, 1837

The marriage state is, and must be in itself, the closest bond of unions, and a state of the most entire and indissoluble friendship, that can subsist among mankind.
> —*The Married State, Its Obligations and Duties*, 1844

Seeing the Falls

When the Kemble party left Boston in the summer of 1833 on a holiday trip to Niagara, Fanny was delighted to leave the humid cities of the Northeast, relieved to be free of her duties in the theater (at least for a while), and eager to see the countryside in upstate New York. More and more, she felt the tension between various antagonistic forces her life: the hatred of acting and the need to work for the Kemble family; the feminist sentiments and the social codes that dictated female subordination to male governance; the desire to work on her writing and the demands of being a glamorous celebrity; and, finally, the tension between her passionate temperament (so much like that of her mother) and a desire for disciplined management of that temperament (which she associated with her father). Occasionally she found some lessening of the pressures that impinged upon her through the simple expedient of being alone, whether marching briskly through the New York streets, riding furiously through the New Jersey fields, or, when she could get away, hiking in the hills flanking the Hudson River.

Kemble was especially fond of the Hudson, and six months before departing for summer vacation in 1833, on a superb late autumn day in 1832 she embarked on a Hudson River steamer with Dall and her father for a visit to the village of Cold Spring. It was the kind of day Kemble found particularly invigorating, the brilliant sun turning her complexion a reddish brown and the wind whipping through her bonnet. Fifty miles north of New York, Cold Spring is on the banks of the Hudson, with magnificent views across the river to the hills around West Point, which lies nearly seven miles to the south on the other side of the river. Kemble felt fit, full of energy, and thrilled by the progress she was making on her American journal. The diary notes were fast taking shape as something she believed would rival Frances Trollope's just published *Domestic Manners of the Americans.* Trollope's tone was hard-edged and humorless, and hers, she knew, was droll and witty; where Trollope had only her aggressive dislike of America to offer her readers, Kemble believed she had a charming narrative of life as a young actress, through which she was threading her political critique of American ideas about social class and the role of women.

Back in Philadelphia she had left the smitten Pierce Butler. Fully aware that he was bent on winning her with his considerable attractions—wealth, good looks, languorous sexuality—she wished nothing more at this moment than to enjoy his attentions and his presents, and she had heard nothing of his rumored "profligacy." She did, however, know she was not welcome in Pierce's social circle and was glad to be away from the frosty dislike she encountered in Philadelphia drawing rooms. Pierce's friends were proving hostile and resentful, as the impressions of a young woman named Julia Kean suggest. Writing to her mother in December 1832, she describes an elegant ball at a Miss Willing's house where "the lions of the evening were Mr. and Miss Kemble, everyone crowded in the room where they were and everyone expressed their disappointment when instead of the graceful and elegant female they had seen onstage they beheld a dark complexioned, unhappy, diminutive little person, who looked as if she had been studying for some time the character of a witch."[1] The disparity between Kemble's stage and real-life appearances suggests the conflicts that pressed more and more upon her daily life: on the one hand, she received accolades for being the elegant actress who impersonated characters on the stage; on the other, she despised impersonation and wished to be recognized for what rested beneath the makeup, the costumes, and the attitudes—as she imagined herself, this was a confident young woman who desired only to be recognized for her intellectual accomplishments. One way that Kemble negotiated this conflict was to develop her own autonomous scheme of masking; in her social interactions and in her writing she presented to the world an assembly of attitudes that both concealed the conflict and expressed it, as one can see in her descriptions of hiking above the Hudson, of her various waterfall adventures, and of her visit to Niagara.

After arriving at Cold Spring, everyone set off for West Point, and when they had inspected the fort, Kemble announced she wished to climb into the hills overlooking the river. This was a rough hike, not a prospect that interested her father or Dall, but she was excited by the stony landscape that reminded her of the Edinburgh hills through which she had tramped, singing old Scottish ballads. She had been a fearless child, she was now a tough young woman, and she was determined to show America that women must be physically challenged, not sheltered like delicate plants. Philadelphia had already seen her riding out to the fields along the Schuylkill, her small, sturdy figure in absolute control of her horse, with Pierce Butler cantering beside her. Now she wanted the promised isolation of the windy hills above the river and was relieved that her father and Dall did not wish to go with her. Climbing alone would be like rushing along the streets of lower Manhattan on a crisp winter night, free of solicitous male protection.

In her memoirs, she describes scrambling for about an hour and waving off concerned shouts from below, and then arriving at the ruined ramparts of an old fort that looked out upon the fast-moving Hudson and the rolling hills of Putnam and Dutchess counties. When she recorded these moments in her diary later in the day, she says she felt her breath almost stop, her heart almost cease, and her awareness of self almost disappear in the awesome "beauty and wild sublimity" of what was before her: "I could have stretched out my arms, and shouted aloud—I could have fallen on my knees and worshipped—I could have committed any extravagance that ecstasy could suggest."[2] She adds that the scene "almost crushed my faculties." What is noticeable here are the words "almost" and "could have." Rather than flinging out her arms, projecting her vibrant contralto into the air, and falling on her knees into a worshipful position, she orders the faculties that remain uncrushed, and later in the day renders a theatrical account of what it feels like to be on the brink of such behavior. She performs both the management of ecstasy *and* its recounting in her text. Here, she may be said to assume in her writing the "attitude" of ecstatic submission to the sublime that would, perhaps, have overwhelmed her, had she succumbed to it in a "dramatic" actuality. Kemble in the hills over West Point creates a theater of the sublime: she is the performing actress at center stage, the director of the scene, and the ecstatic recorder of what *might* have happened had she let herself tumble down the tufted hillside to the banks of the Hudson.

During the eighteen months that began at this moment over the Hudson in November 1832 and that ended in Philadelphia in June 1834 when she married Pierce Butler, Fanny Kemble embraced her American experience. She trembled before Niagara Falls, shuddered at the sight of exhibited Native Americans in New York, mingled with the Boston intellectual gentry, and made many social conquests. Although she had never felt more physically strong and dazzlingly attractive during this time, she was increasingly troubled by the conflict between her distaste for the theater and no seeming alternative to this life other than marriage. One great sorrow also blighted her happiness during these eighteen months: the death of Dall in April 1834. But for the month before the coach accident that led to Dall's death, as the Kemble party traveled west from Boston through New York State to the Canadian border in the summer of 1833, a journey of almost five hundred miles by coach and boat through Schenectady, Utica, and the Mohawk Valley, the countryside depicted by James Fenimore Cooper in *The Last of the Mohicans* (1826), they all had a splendid time.

The group was composed of Fanny, Charles, Dall, and a fresh addition to Fanny's entourage, Edward Trelawny, an old friend of her father's. By this time, Pierce Butler had enrolled himself as a flute-playing member of the orchestra wherever Kemble happened to be performing and whenever he could leave Philadelphia, which seemed to be almost all the time. On this trip, he joined the Kemble party in Utica on its way west to Niagara. Trelawny had arrived in America in early 1833, bringing with him an extraordinary history of political and romantic adventures that he had recounted in his recently published sensational autobiography, *Adventures of a Younger Son* (1832). He joined Charles, Dall, and Fanny on June 30, 1833, on a visit to Gouverneur Kemble in Cold Spring, where they were to spend a few days before proceeding further up the Hudson to Albany. Trelawny quickly became a serious rival to Butler in securing Kemble's attention. She was immediately fascinated by his wild history and by his romantic good looks, which in many ways were not unlike her own: they were both swarthy and physically very strong, and they were both incorrigible performers.[3] Forty-one when he joined the Kemble party, Trelawny had met Shelley and Byron in Pisa, and claimed to have seen Shelley's boat disappear into a squall off Leghorn in July 1822 and to have snatched Shelley's unburned heart from his funeral pyre. In 1823, he sailed with Byron from Genoa to Greece, reputedly set up a harem of fifteen or so women in Athens, and, it was rumored, married the thirteen-year-old sister of a Greek warlord, Odysseus Androutses.

Fig. 18. *Edward John Trelawny*, by Bryan Edward Duppa, n.d. © National Portrait Gallery, London.

Few could enthrall Fanny Kemble to the point of silent and rapt attention for very long, but Trelawny succeeded immediately by telling her there was something in her spirit that reminded him of Shelley. Later, three weeks before she married Butler, he wrote to her, "From some real or imagined resemblance in person or mind, or both, you recalled his image so vividly to my mind that I was forced to admire you on the instant—and every day my admiration augmented."[4] According to Anna Jameson, if Trelawny ever loved anyone, it was Fanny Kemble, since she was "his ideal of womankind."[5] To Kemble, he was deliciously "savage":—"A man with the proportions of a giant for strength and agility; taller, straighter, and broader than most men. . . . His face as dark as a Moor's; with a wild, strange look about the eyes and forehead, and mark like a scar upon his cheek." His magnetic charm evoked a Byronic "idea of toil, hardship, peril, and wild adventure,"[6] but anything Byronic presented Kemble with a dangerous frisson: Trelawny had seen so much, traveled to so many places that to her were still unexplored, and had actually known the Romantic poet she still read, rather guiltily. Byron's moody fame and poetic fire imaginatively magnified her own dramatic nature, that part of her so much like Thérèse and so dangerous to her theatrical equilibrium. She found herself both infatuated with Trelawny and frightened by what he embodied.

Trelawny and Butler presented a stark physical contrast. Butler was fair and delicate, Trelawny dark, and brawny; Butler relied on his languid charm and wealth to win Kemble and Trelawny offered his romantic history, good looks, and thrilling talk, if not to gain her in marriage (whether he was actually divorced from the thirteen-year-old Greek girl with whom he subsequently had two children is uncertain) then certainly to monopolize her attention. But however much Kemble was attracted to Trelawny on this summer journey to Niagara, she eventually married a man who was not conventionally tall, dark, and handsome, not a wild figure from the Byronic romances that she put aside after her intellectually formative year in Edinburgh. Butler's delicate appearance, however, belied a willful, spoiled, and tyrannical personality. During these thrilling summer days he was a superb dissembler. Charles clearly favored Butler from the standpoint of financial security for the family but was almost as spellbound as Fanny by Trelawny's magnetism. Dall watched it all very carefully and by the close of this summer journey became seriously worried about Fanny's future.

The trip from Boston to Niagara had begun at Cold Spring, the place where Kemble had visited the ironworks and become as absorbed in the technological advances that were on display as she had been in Stephenson's "Rocket," and also where she had taken her "sublime" hike up into the hills. Now, on their last day at Cold Spring before proceeding up the Hudson to Albany, Kemble announced she wished to see the local waterfalls. Trelawny and a young man unidentified in Kemble's memoirs, but probably the brother of her host, rapidly organized an excursion. When they arrived she gazed ecstatically at a tree whose upper half was aslant over the tumbling water, and recalls that she had an "an uncontrollable desire" to clamber up the side of the fall so she might reach it. Trelawny sprang into action: he climbed up the rocks and stood on a ledge at the side of the falls, while the young man remained an anxious watcher below, holding her parasol and bonnet. Egging her on, Trelawny called down to Kemble and deftly steered her to the most perilous point of observation. Despite his guidance, however, she lost her

footing on a crumbling rock and grabbed hold of a sapling, which took her swing-
ing out over the waterfall. She was saved by Trelawny, who grabbed her hands and
hoisted her to safety. The scene is deeply theatrical in Kemble's recollection of it;
the reading audience senses the terror of losing one's footing on a slippery rock,
feels the thrill of being caught in Trelawny's brawny grip and swung out over the
roaring water, and shares the triumphant relief in waving at the young man with
parasol and bonnet who waits watchfully below. At the suspended center of the
dramatic action, Kemble is the performing daredevil, held tight by Trelawny, a
dashing cavalier who encourages her in daring physical adventure, offers vicarious
participation in his history of adventures with the Romantic poets, and embodies
a romantic alternative to the deceptively placid security offered by Pierce Butler.

In the section of her American *Journal* that describes this perilous adventure,
Kemble inserted a poem titled, innocuously, "Lines." She rarely interpolates her
verse into her prose writings, and when she does, it is usually for emphatic elabo-
ration. The diaries and correspondence with Harriet St. Leger that are the primary
material for her journals and memoirs are, by definition, informal writing, but
Kemble carefully controls their presentation: deceptively unguarded, the letters
are actually censored, and the interpolated commentary in the memoirs functions
as a kind of governing rein on what might be read as incendiary material. In her
writing for publication, as in all things, Kemble attempted to shape dramatic material into theatrical form, and this is something that Henry James understood
and noted in Kemble's obituary. He describes her verse as "all passionate and melancholy" and much less prized than it deserves to be, driven not only by a lyric
impulse but by what he terms "the genuine lyric need." It was in verse, as he puts
it, that she could express "the inexpungable, the fundamental, the boundless and
generous sadness which lay beneath her vitality, beneath her humor, her imagination, her talents, her violence of will and integrity of health."[7] Saying in lyric verse
what she cannot say, or will not say, in her prose, she releases what James perceives
as the "inexpungable."

Kemble's poems, however, are not merely careless outbursts of feeling: quite
the contrary, since everything that she allowed to get into print was almost always
performed for theatrical effect. The significant literary difference between her
verse composition and her letters and memoirs is what accounts for the expression
of passionate feeling that Henry James identifies. Poetry (particularly lyric poetry),
by virtue of its conventional association with feeling, invites both a loosening of
the emotional corsets and a refinement of that emotion into concise language.
By contrast, journal writing (especially that aimed at publication, as was most of
Kemble's) and letter writing (which constituted the bulk of her published memoirs) obviously demand a more casual arrangement of the prosaic stuff of everyday

life into engaging narrative. The seemingly uncensored emotionalism of Kemble's poetry suggests it was there, consciously or not, that she allowed free expression of the tempestuous temperament so similar to her mother's. It is as if poetry licensed the expression of what she was compelled to excise from the letters, the essays, and the memoirs. The principal speakers in many of the poems are unafraid to moan, beseech, and lament, and their emotional fearlessness imaginatively mirrors the physical daring with which Kemble jumped fences, scaled waterfalls, and danced till dawn.

The speaker in the interpolated "Lines," which were written right after Trelawny hoisted her away from danger and, for the moment, away from the deceptively passive attractions of the absent Pierce Butler, describes gathering an oak branch that "grows at home" but withers for lack of light, like some unnamed flower that weeps "because she may not meet the sun." The poem eroticizes the moment that the morning sun restores the flower associated with the English oak branch:

> And when he comes down from the mountain tops,
> Parting the forest with his hands of fire,
> He drinks her weeping, kissing all the flowers
> With passionate love, which makes them look so blushing.[8]

In part, this poem is a symbolic transformation of Kemble saved from crushing extinction by Trelawny's sun-bronzed hands into a woman unafraid of sexual desire (the English oak branch, the "hands of fire," and so on). It is revealing because with the exception of letters written to Butler when they were on the brink of separation, Kemble never refers explicitly to her own sexual feelings: in this poem she creates an image of a woman joyous to feel the pleasure of her own body. Trelawny's fiery sexuality is symbolized in imagery of the sun and her desire is figured in the blushing and the weeping. Soon Kemble responded to another kind of erotic appeal: the languid, more calculating sort displayed by Butler, who was to join Charles and Fanny while they fulfilled an engagement in Boston and who would be part of the group as it departed for Niagara.

The Boston performances were a spectacular success. Anna Quincy, daughter of the president of Harvard at the time, recorded that she was "wild" to see Kemble, and she was not disappointed. Kemble's physical grace, facial expressions, and "shrieks" and "starts" were all "admirable" as Bianca in *Fazio*; though her voice "had rather too much stage *tone*," it moved her audience to tears and horror. Quincy was particularly impressed by Kemble's attitudes—at the end of the play she stands "a perfect statue . . . the deathlike stillness that reigned over the crowded audience, every person seeming to hold their breath, was very striking."[9] At a party after the performance, Quincy was pleased and surprised by Kemble's modest demeanor, an indication of the expectations of vulgar behavior that shadowed the nineteenth-century actress: she can barely believe that the unassuming, delicate, and subdued creature is the actress she saw onstage. But, she adds, Kemble was "not handsome off stage. She has very fine eyes, with very black eyelashes and eyebrows, and fine teeth. Her complexion is coarse and her other features not remarkable."[10] Quincy expresses a further reservation about Kemble in comments that imply both the conventional moral suspicion of female performers and a kind of gendered pride that Kemble should have become so famous. Quincy is disappointed that Kemble chose to become an actress: "There is nothing in the world more beautiful, more striking, than such a gifted, graceful woman, yet while we feel proud of her powers, we cannot but regret to see them only employed in *acting*. However, if she is satisfied we have no reason to wish it otherwise."[11]

Kemble, of course, was far from "satisfied," but when she was offstage, in this summer of 1833, she was happy to be honored at the dinner tables of the city's intellectual gentry and to be out riding with Pierce Butler, often to the new burial ground at Mt. Auburn, just beyond Cambridge. Landscaped in a Romantic style, its high hills, deep ravines, and "dark, still, melancholy-looking meres" appealed to Kemble's imagination, and she and Pierce spent many days there, fitfully chaperoned by Dall. On July 11, 1833, she made an entry in her journal that was probably inspired by the late Romantic manmade "nature" she loved at Mt. Auburn: her remarks register her oft-expressed disgust with what she saw as an American indifference to nature—to her, it was "nothing short of amazing. . . . Wretched people!" They remind her, by contrast, as she sees them in the "crowded streets of their cities, those dens of Mammon," of Wordsworth's simple, noble figures who toil uncomplainingly in a harsh landscape.[12]

When the acting was over and the group left Boston, Kemble insisted that they stop at Trenton Falls, where she relied again on Trelawny to be her partner in risky adventure. The waterfall at Trenton was much more terrifying than that at Cold Spring and they crept along the narrow dripping edges of the precipice that overlooked the swirling waters. She wrote in her diary that she had never felt as afraid as she was when she walked along "this narrow edge of eternity."[13] Clearly inspired by images of water and danger, Kemble used these falls as the dramatic setting for a poem that recounts, over a period of twenty-six years, three episodes in the story of a woman's passionate responses to nature and disillusion at the hands of a faithless lover. The first stanza describes the speaker standing on the rocky ledge of the falls and gazing at the cauldron of swirling waters: "Love held my hand, and bade me nothing fear, / For life, and youth, and joy, and hope were mine, / And death and horror could not come me near, / I was so compassed with their arms divine." Given the accounts in her American *Journal* of how it is always Edward Trelawny, not Pierce Butler, who literally holds her hand as she hangs from a branch at Cold Spring, skips along the wet rocks at Trenton, and rushes to the edge at Niagara, one might think Trelawny is the principal figure of "Love." Pierce, however, was "compassing" her with promises of love, financial security, and release from her profession.

The speaker of the poem declares that on that brilliant day she was "full of happiness," as she looked "into the eyes that were my day" and felt her soul borne away in "eddying tumults of delight." In the middle section of the poem, Kemble alters the tone as the speaker, now suicidal, describes a second visit to Trenton Falls: "A devil dragged me ruthless towards the wave. . . . And thrust me downwards to that hideous grave." In an image that echoes and revises the fearsome thrill of standing on the rocky ledge, secured by "love" from falling into the waves, the speaker describes actually lying down "On the grim margin of that weary well. . . . Longing in nothingness thenceforth to dwell." In these perilous moments, Kemble reveals a paradoxical attraction to the brink of the abyss: exulting on a hillcrest over the Hudson River, suspending herself from a branch over the rushing waters at Cold Spring, or peering into the "weary well" of swirling waters at Trenton, she feels the suicidal pull of oblivion, respite from the sorrows and difficulties of a life beset by conflicting desires and demands. At West Point, however, she translated her sublime experience into performance and at Cold Spring she trembled with desire as Trelawny's brawny grip held her fast. At Trenton Falls, she came very close to suicide and to a loss of self in the eddying water.

It is impossible to date precisely the composition of this unsettling poem, although it first appeared in a volume published in Boston in 1859, by which time Kemble was fifty years old. Divorced from Pierce Butler for ten years, and liberated from the terms of the divorce settlement that had restricted her visits with her daughters to two months a year until their majority, she was now allowed to see them whenever she wished. The last two stanzas of "Written at Trenton Falls" evoke a third moment when the speaker has "lived to come and stand again / On the wild torrent's brim," but this time with "soul serene." She stands alone and symbolically upon the "stedfast rock" of God's peace, and the poem concludes with a prayer of thankfulness for the delivery from suicidal thoughts and for the return to her of her child, a reference, it is reasonable to assume, to her second daughter, Frances Butler (known always as Fan), since she reached twenty-one in May 1859.

Early in the morning of July 16, 1833, as the Kemble party was heading in its coach to Rochester for breakfast, Kemble felt a stunning blow that jolted her out of a doze. When she was fully awake she realized the coach was completely on its side, that she was uncomfortably curled up under the tremendous weight of her father, and that across from her, sitting bolt upright in the road, was Dall, "as white as a ghost, with her forehead cut open, and an awful-looking stream of blood falling from it." When her father lifted his "mountainous pressure" from her own bruised body, Kemble realized that her clothes were torn and her shoulder cut, that her father had suffered a very nasty gash on his leg, and that Dall was badly hurt. But when the injuries were examined by a local doctor, Dall was judged to have suffered a serious but not life-threatening wound, and in the American *Journal*, which concludes with her exciting arrival at Niagara Falls, Kemble does not mention her again. She leaves her reader to assume that Dall recovered from her injuries—as indeed Kemble probably thought she would in July 1833. But during the winter of 1833–34, Dall continued to suffer from aftereffects of the accident and she died in Boston in April 1834, probably from an undiagnosed brain injury. She was buried in Mt. Auburn cemetery, the romantic scene of Fanny and Pierce's courtship the year before.

Many English visitors to North America in the first part of the nineteenth century journeyed to Niagara, and their impressions create an enhancing backdrop for Kemble's entrance on the scene. Some of these English travelers fall into ecstatic swoons at the sight of the falls, and they lace their memories with language culled from early Romantic writings about the sublime. Kemble's old friend Tom Moore almost passed out, he claims, when he saw Niagara. After being appalled by what he saw as the social rot and cultural decay of England's lost colony, Moore found himself in ecstatic tears as he approached "the very residence of the Deity" when he arrived there in 1804. Overwhelmed by "devout admiration," scornful of those who turn the "ineffable wonders" of the falls into a scientific measuring of gallons of water, chastened by a feeling that all description is useless, Moore was, eventually, speechless. Another English traveler, Isaac Weld (neither a literary celebrity nor friend of Fanny Kemble's but a perceptive social observer nevertheless), who came to America to assess the new colony and publish a book about his impressions, declared in 1807, "No words can convey an adequate idea of the awful grandeur" of Niagara Falls. He collapses under a staggering sense of human insignificance, feels reduced to a minuscule speck in the immense creation.[14]

In the larger context of English nineteenth-century political writing about America, Niagara often gets evoked as a symbol of the awesome and frightening vigor of the new nation itself. Two prominent English women political writers, Anna Barbauld and Harriet Martineau, approach Niagara in this way, one metaphorically and the other literally. Their writings are models of the kind of work Kemble admired after she abandoned Byron but to which she suspected she was temperamentally unsuited: Barbauld is balanced, somewhat lofty, Martineau in-

Fig. 19. *Niagara Falls*, by Robert Havell, 1845. I. N. Phelps Stokes Collection, Miriam and Ira D. Wallach Division of Art, Prints, and Photographs, New York Public Library, Astor, Lenox and Tilden Foundations.

cisive, always practical. Barbauld's long poem, *Eighteen Hundred and Eleven* (published in 1812), ironically asks how Britain can "sit at ease" wrapped in domestic self-satisfaction while war rages in Europe and the "Midas dreams" of princely merchants crumble in economic depression. She finds but one utopian hope for the future: in America, English immigrants will plant a "finer sense of morals and of art," and "Milton's tones" will be mixed with "the roar of Niagara's fall" to produce a better world.[15] Symbolically, Niagara's ferocious power stands for the vigorous new nation. For Harriet Martineau, Niagara is a place that prompts musings on her own position as analytical observer. In 1837, she stood in a "thunder cavern" at Niagara. Untroubled by the wet whirlwind, the foaming flood, or the thunderous sound of water falling on the rocks, Martineau notes in the book she published after her return to England, *Society in America*, that she was watching "world-making." Rarely frightened by anything (she stoically endured years of chronic deafness, stomped through the Egyptian sands, and wrote fearlessly about almost any aspect of English culture and society that took her fancy), Martineau confidently found Niagara understandable in all its aspects, "like the systems of the sky . . . one of the hands of Nature's clock."[16] The sublime was not in her sensible dictionary, and neither was the fashioning of identity through theatrical self-presentation.

When Kemble arrived at Niagara she was in a "perfect frenzy of impatience." She did not wait for her father, Dall, or Pierce but rushed through the garden of the hotel and down to a steep footpath cut in the rocks, Trelawny close behind her. She sprang down the narrow footpath, urged on by Trelawny, separated "only by a thicket from the tumultuous rapids." Finally, she stood hesitantly just before Table Rock, seeing through the tree boughs the white glimmer of a sea of foam and knowing in her body the vertiginous attractions of standing on the brink, of the thrilling, terrifying possibility of going over into the rapids. This is how she describes the moment: "'Go on, go, don't stop,' shouted Trelawny; and in another minute the thicket was passed. I stood upon Table Rock. Trelawny seized me by the arm, and, without speaking a word, dragged me to the edge of the rapids, to the brink of the abyss. I saw Niagara."[17] She saw Niagara with Trelawny's strong arms around her, securing her from a fall into one of the most terrifying natural wonders in America. Dall, Charles, and Pierce are nowhere on the scene: her aunt, still rocky from the coach accident and injured much more seriously than anyone realized, understandably waited quietly until she could get to her room; Charles had no desire to get himself wet and his vanity ruled out much interest in the sublime; and Pierce held back, biding his time and confident his wealth and promise of marriage would, eventually, dispatch Trelawny's charismatic verve and fascinating talk. Trelawny was not wealthy; Kemble's earnings were not her own; and Pierce was rich and ready to marry. In the hotel that night, Kemble heard the noise of the falling cataract roaring through every chamber of the house and she felt the whole building vibrate incessantly with "the shock of the mighty fall." Her visceral thrill at standing on the brink seemed to be echoing in the sounds and movements of nature.

When the Kemble party left Niagara, Trelawny remained behind, determined, in some kind of Byronic ambition, to swim the river below the falls. As he described the experience to Claire Clairmont, Mary Shelley's half stepsister and the mother of Byron's daughter Allegra, "Nothing elates me so much—or exercises such power over my mind—as witnessing any of the elements at war—instead of shrinking at my own insignificance I dilate with high thoughts engendered by sublime scenes." After plunging into the river, Trelawny found himself being carried to the rapids, "which form a terrific whirlpool in which nothing that lives could float an instant," unable, finally, to tell how he regained the shore, after which time he spent two more years in America before returning to England in 1835.[18] A month after the thrills of Niagara, by August 1833, Fanny Kemble and Pierce Butler apparently had become engaged, although Kemble makes no reference in her memoirs to an engagement, which was rumored back in Philadelphia circles, according to Julia Kean, the young woman bitterly disappointed by Kemble's witchlike appearance when she first saw her: "The whole world is talking of the engagement of Miss Fanny Kemble to Pierce Butler of Philadelphia. I believe there is little doubt of its existence and we shall probably see this celebrated actress placed in one of the most elegant establishments in our country and leading that circle which now scarce deigns to notice her."[19]

Bewitching Fanny

Throughout the nineteenth century, Niagara Falls remained an essential stop for English travelers to America. Gazing at the falls was a peculiarly Victorian experience, as Rupert Brooke wryly noted in 1913 when he arrived there: he begged the friend to whom he recounted his feelings not to breathe a word of the fact that he had stared at "the thing" and had "the purest Nineteenth-Century grandiose thoughts, about the Destiny of Man, the Irresistibility of Fate, the Doom of Nations, and the fact that Death awaits us All."[20] As English nineteenth-century travelers made their way to Niagara, often through the same countryside that the Kemble party traversed in the summer of 1833, they also tried to get a look at how the former colonies were treating its "barbaric" indigenous population. The travelers had read about "savage" Indians in captivity narratives, stories that delivered sensational accounts of the brutal treatment of European settlers. Children get kidnaped by the Shawnee, women are scalped before their husbands' eyes by the Comanche, and all the tribes engage in cannibalism: as one captured European woman feverishly related after her release, "They appear to be very fond of human flesh. The hand or foot, they say, is the most delicious."[21] Many of the captivity narratives deal with the tribes that in the 1830s under Andrew Jackson's "removal" policy were transplanted permanently beyond the Mississippi. These vacated lands—like those in the lovely Mohawk valley that Kemble so admired—were usually taken over by European speculators, a move legitimated in Anglo-American eyes by the horror stories of Indian barbarism. English writers were uniformly pessimistic about the future of the Indian peoples, and Kemble shared this pessimism; when she caught her first sight of America's indigenous population, she felt a terrible horror at their history, their conditions, and their future, a horror felt by travelers before her.

When in Canada and the American Northeast in 1816 and 1817, Francis Hall, an English gentleman-traveler, ironically observed how rarely the "rights of the real proprietors of the soil" counted in Americans' convenient distribution of land.

He predicted, as did almost everyone else, that eventually their extinction was no less certain than that of the troublesome wild animals that roamed newly settled, white-controlled farms.[22] Never reluctant to attack American practices that enraged her, Frances Trollope lambastes Andrew Jackson (and Congress) for the legislation that removed (or "chased," in Trollope's terms) the "Indians from their forest homes." She declares that if the American character is to be judged by this shameful legislation, then "they are most lamentably deficient in every feeling of honour and integrity." Reinforcing the attack on hypocrisy that peppers most English nineteenth-century accounts of American life, she sarcastically adds that one may see Americans "one hour lecturing the mob on the indefeasible rights of man" and the next "driving from their homes the children of the soil, whom they have bound themselves to protect by the most solemn treaties."[23] When Charles Dickens arrived in 1842, he wondered how the intelligent Indian leaders he met could have been so foolish as to have signed away their lands, and he was particularly taken with a Choctaw chief he met on a steamboat from Cincinnati to Louisville. Surprised by this Indian leader's familiarity with the poetry of Walter Scott and by his handsome appearance (broad cheekbones, and "a very bright, keen, dark, and piercing eye"), Dickens contrasts him with the horrifically branded slaves he describes in his essay on American slavery that was published on his return to England. In a wave of hopeful nostalgia that erases America's history of slavery and pursuit of the Indian, Dickens calls for the restoration of "the forest and the Indian village" and the replacement of "streets and squares by wigwams."[24]

Fanny Kemble's first thoughts about the plight of the "Red Indian" were prompted by a visit to Hoboken on September 13, 1832, only ten days after her arrival in New York. Picnicking with the Hone family, she wondered aloud about the loveliness of the countryside and the "Red Children of the soil" who had freely steered their canoes through the New Jersey marshes until the "invaders" began their work of extermination. Her language, in recounting this moment, seems a little stale, as if taken from popular sentimentalizing journalism, and she paints a romantic picture of well-muscled young braves canoeing their way into the sunset and extinction. But within a year, her views changed from a kind of lofty nostalgia to a serious concern. After she viewed some paintings of Indians, and then actually saw them in the flesh for the first time, Kemble's writing became graphic and concrete. In January 1833, while in Washington, she viewed an exhibition of captured Indian artifacts—arrows, canoes, pipes, and paintings of Indian chiefs. The latter showed men who, in her eyes, were not handsome; their scornful mouths and cunning eyes make them far different from the noble, poetic creatures described by Dickens ten years later.[25] Kemble does not romanticize them. The most dramatic change in her views (and in her writing) came when she visited another exhibition—this time in New York and this time not of portraits of Indians but of the real, breathing thing. The celebrated young English actress, always the gaze of every eye, was part of a group that viewed a performance of Indian dignity against the backdrop of degraded captivity.

The exhibition of colonized or captured "natives," imperial curiosities, was a common popular phenomenon in the first half of the nineteenth century in England. "Hottentot" women, fierce "Bushmen," and sullen Aborigines, transported to England from their indigenous homes and placed on display, were regarded with mingled feelings of fear, amusement, and cultural superiority by English viewers. Americans soon began to display their own captured curiosities. Just before leaving for the trip to Niagara, Kemble went to view an Indian chief, "Black Hawk," and a few of his male relatives who were being exhibited in a building on the Battery near the American Hotel. She describes Black Hawk as sitting on a sofa, a shriveled old man, coldly calm and dignified, flanked by his younger brother and his son: in her eyes, "two young savages, with their fine muscular proportions." Black Hawk's dismal and humiliating condition, cooped up in a "hot-prison house" with narrow walls and forced to sit unmoving on a sofa as curious Americans passed before him, filled her with feelings of commiseration and disgust, and she was reminded of the abject condition of the women prisoners she had visited at Newgate with the philanthropist and prisoner reformer Elizabeth Fry. She describes Black Hawk in simple, unaffected language that is significantly different from her sentimental musings about the "Red Children of the soil" that were prompted by the picnic in rural Hoboken.[26]

The emerging political opinions about the subjugation of women and the restless state of the industrial working class that Kemble brought with her to America were honed by her actual experience—by her direct observation of the pampered isolation of American women and of the confident individualism of American workers. She expressed these clarified political opinions, a mark of her newly forged independence, in the direct and witty style that is a rhetorical hallmark of most of her American *Journal*. During her first two years in America, in addition to refining her political views on women and the working class, she also began to shape her uncompromising opposition to American slavery. Ironically, however, during the time that she was clarifying and voicing her positions on women, workers, Indians, and slaves, her constant companion was a man who, when he secured her in marriage, did all he could to silence her voice. Pierce Butler kept quiet during her rock-climbing adventures and merely murmured vague assent when she indignantly vented her opinions about "Red Indians," oppressed workers, and subjugated women. How quiet he remained when she began to talk noisily about the violence of slavery is open to question, but immediately after their marriage he demanded that she silence her abolitionist voice, that she hand over her unpublished American journal for his inspection and censorship, and that she remain sequestered at Butler Place, the family home nine miles north of Philadelphia, well out of the way of interfering abolitionist women. For a while, he prevailed.

Had Pierce Butler been with Fanny Kemble in New York on January 7, 1833, he might have possessed a clearer sense of the opposition he was to encounter. In her American *Journal*, she describes in moving detail a meeting on that day with a clergyman she does not identify; he came for dinner at the American Hotel and told stories of the flogging of slaves that "forced the colour into my face, the tears into my eyes, and strained every muscle in my body with positive rage and indignation."[27] In England, as a well-educated and intellectually curious young woman, Kemble had certainly read about American slavery and she was well acquainted with domestic debate about slavery in the West Indies, but to hear firsthand, from an eyewitness, about the penalties incurred in teaching a slave to read and write, about the dread of insurrection on the part of whites that kept the slaves in brutish ignorance, and about the brutal barbarity of the working and living conditions of slaves led her to record her belief that some day there would be a terrible "breaking asunder of old manacles." She predicted a fierce and horrible retaliation and revenge for "wrong so long endured—so wickedly inflected."[28]

It is not surprising, then, that when she met the New England novelist Catharine Maria Sedgwick she was drawn into immediate sympathy with Sedgwick's abolitionist opinions. Kemble's attraction to her (and perhaps hers to Kemble) is notably similar to the bond between Kemble and Harriet St. Leger. An older, intellectual, unmarried woman admires a younger, vivacious, intelligent one—and the younger woman, for at least the fourth time in her twenty-three years, seeks to win the approval and love of the older woman. Just as Kemble idealized the memory of Bellina Grimani, adored Harriet St. Leger, and worshiped Harriet Siddons, now she beguiled Catharine Maria Sedgwick into becoming a treasured, older female friend. Through her friendship with everyone in the Sedgwick family, Kemble enlarged her circle of cultured acquaintances, but to Pierce's mind, they were interfering do-gooders with ridiculous abolitionist ideas whose articulation in his household he aimed to prohibit when he married Fanny Kemble.

Kemble met Catharine Sedgwick and, subsequently, the rest of her prominent family, in early 1833. Catharine was the third daughter and sixth child of Theodore and Pamela Dwight Sedgwick. Theodore Sedgwick had a long and distinguished political career through his election, first, to both houses of the Massachusetts legislature, then to the House of Representatives, and, finally, to the United States Senate. He ended up as a Supreme Court justice. When Catharine became acquainted with Kemble she was forty years old, unmarried, and very close to her older brothers—Theodore, Harry, Robert, and Charles (it was to Charles's wife, Elizabeth, that Kemble wrote the unmailed letters that became the *Journal of a Residence on a Georgian Plantation*). Theodore Sedgwick, Catharine's brother, was convinced that Kemble "was the ablest woman I have ever seen—the most straightforward, masculine, controlling mind in a female head, and yet she is as feminine a creature in many things as I ever knew. In short, she is a vastly lovable person."[29] The Sedgwicks were Boston gentry: cultured, socially powerful, politically connected, and dedicated abolitionists. They were close friends of the Rev. William Ellery Channing, the prominent Unitarian minister and author of an important treatise against slavery, to whom they introduced Kemble when she arrived in Boston and whose writings on the conditions of slavery had a profound influence on her when she went to Georgia as the wife of a slave owner in 1838.

By the time Kemble met her, Catharine Sedgwick had already published several novels and didactic tales for young people. Studious and articulate about the power of gender in shaping the lives of American women, Sedgwick was easily moved to strong affection. When she met Kemble for the first time, she was drawn to the vivacious wit that animated her performances before an adoring social audience. They met in New York on February 14, 1833 (Sedgwick was on a visit to the city with one of her brothers), and her journal entry for that evening describes Kemble as a dazzling "gem," gleeful with the joy of "unbroken youth," singing with superb dramatic effect. But she wonders whether she is wrong in giving so much time and thought to her charismatic new friend: "My conscience is not *easy*—and yet I think that she who kindles the evening with the brightness that lit up the morning of life, who brings a melting influence to the frigid of forty, is an enchantress not to be resisted."[30] Very soon, rather than resisting her, Sedgwick was under the sway of Kemble's brilliance, noting in April 1833 that she can remember little of what is going on in her life except that Kemble has, "like a sun," cast everything else into shadow. Kemble's spellbinding warmth thawed Sedgwick's self-confessed emotional frigidity ("the frigid of forty"). Admitting that Kemble was "nature's cunning workmanship," designed to bewitch with her sparkle, she nevertheless allowed herself to be seduced, and although she never enjoyed the lifelong intimacy and tender love that Kemble felt for Harriet St. Leger, she resembled St. Leger in the way she adored, advised, and supported the younger woman.

All the Sedgwicks were proud of their friendship with Kemble and happy to introduce her to their Boston circle. On May 11, 1833, during her stay at the Tremont Hotel before the departure for Niagara, they went with her to dine at the house of Dr. George Parkman; the other two important guests were John Quincy

Adams, who until six years before had been the sixth president of the United States, and Daniel Webster, leading lawyer, powerful orator, and currently United States Senator from Massachusetts. Adams thought her surprisingly well educated and intelligent (for an actress), but disappointingly reluctant to talk about her own "poetical productions"; she seemed more interested in relating her feats of horsemanship and told him she had ridden that morning about thirty miles, and "leaped over many fences and stone walls."[31] Some of this time, she was riding and leaping over fences with Pierce Butler, although there is no record of his attendance at this particular dinner.

If Dall had lived it is possible that Kemble would not have married Butler, or anyone else for that matter. When she was touring the English southwest coast towns of Portsmouth and Southampton in the summer of 1831, she had received from Dall some sobering advice, based on her aunt's intimate knowledge of her niece's emotional makeup. Dall told her she should avoid marriage. Here are her reasons as Kemble recorded them in what she describes as an edifying talk about her future: "When you remain single . . . and choose to work, your fortune is an independent and ample one; as soon as you marry, there's no such thing. Your position in society . . . is both a pleasanter and more distinguished one that your birth or real station entitles you to; but that also is the result of your professional exertions."[32] Dall's realistic understanding of the Kemble family social position suggests how her commonsense nature must have provided a brake for her niece's impetuosity, how she must have exercised a steadying influence on her mercurial temperament, how her serenity gave Kemble respite from her mother's irritability and unpredictability. By including Dall's views of marriage in her memoirs, Kemble acknowledges that her own theatrical celebrity had elevated her into a higher social station than she might have enjoyed as an actress who was not a Kemble. Dall was also aware of the perilous condition of nineteenth-century women when it came to money; because of her own financially dependent position, as Thérèse Kemble's sister and Fanny's chaperone, she relied on the Kemble family for support. She knew that if a wealthy woman married, her fortune and income, if she continued to work, became the property of her husband. It was not until the middle of the Victorian period that English women were allowed to retain their own fortunes (and incomes) as a result of Parliament's passing the Married Women's Property Act. Despite the hardheaded advice she received from Dall in 1831, Kemble seemed to forget when she married Butler (or chose not to remember) that the money earned by hardworking, financially independent women like herself became the property of their husbands.

This serious talk with Dall did not stop Kemble from thinking about marriage—her own, if and when it should come, as well as the more general topic of what constituted an ideal relationship between husband and wife. She records in her memoirs that on January 27, 1832, she had enjoyed a long discussion with her family about the most desirable qualities in a husband, which had clarified her belief that the most successful marriage would be one like a piano duet for four hands. The wife would play all the brilliant and melodious parts (mainly treble) and the husband would be the governor of the harmony (mainly base). This image, in which the male harmony "really leads and sustains the whole composition and keeps it steady," because without such governance the treble "for the most part *runs to tune* merely, and wants depth, dignity, and real musical importance," discloses how she sought from others a guiding firmness for her erratic temperament. With Dall gone and nothing to replace her gentle discipline, two months after her aunt's death, Kemble rushed into what she must have thought would be a melodious marriage with Pierce Butler.[33] The dissonant tones of their life together were heard almost immediately in Kemble's letters to her friends.

Giving up the Maiden Corslet

How could the intelligent and vibrant young woman who had ventured to the edge of the abyss at Niagara Falls, wrapped in the arms of a man who had known Byron and Shelley, and who had sparred with John Quincy Adams and Daniel Webster marry a man regarded by many of his contemporaries as far less interesting than she? The memoirs and letters provide at least two reasons: first, marriage to a wealthy man meant she could leave the profession she despised; and second, she would be able to gratify her sexual desire for Pierce. It was for money and for sex, then, that she married, perhaps with some slim hope that Pierce would be the kind of husband she described in the letter to Harriet St. Leger that is quoted, in part, as the epigraph to this chapter. Kemble's feminist thinking would have led her to believe that she could be Pierce's "best and dearest friend," but when she discovered, soon after their marriage, that he refused to accept her as an equal and exercised no respect for her liberty, she was confirmed in her pessimistic view that a marriage where this were possible was, indeed, "uncommon everywhere."

Kemble married Butler, in part, because she was tired of having to make money in a profession she despised and because she believed he would provide the leisure for her to become a published writer. The dislike of acting that she had expressed well before she set foot on the stage strengthened when she arrived in America. On September 8, 1832, Kemble dined with a well-known actor and was disgusted by his vulgar posturing: "within and without an actor," he was a contemptible creature full of striving after effect, "a lamp and orange-peel in every action" (a reference to early nineteenth-century stage lighting). She might have tolerated his vulgarity but she found unbearable a genteel version of that vulgarity, the cosmetic disguise of something unappealing but nevertheless authentic.[34] Loathing the acting profession and the way that performances left their record solely in the memory of the audience, she was determined to leave her mark on the printed page. Actors were but "barren names" on a playbill; authors were creators of an art that could live permanently in the minds of their readers.

At the start of the trip to Niagara, it was obvious she was already assessing the benefits of marrying Pierce: she wrote to her English friend Anna Jameson, "I am already half moulded into my new circumstances and surroundings; and though England will always be home to my heart, it may be that this country will become my abiding place."[35] By October, it would seem that Pierce had proposed and that she had accepted, since she wrote again to Anna Jameson on the fifteenth of that month, "I shall not return to England, not even to visit it now—certainly never to make my home there again."[36] Financial security, however, was not the sole reason for Kemble's decision.

In the autumn of 1838, their marriage in tatters, Kemble wrote a notably cool-headed letter to Pierce in which she attempts to account for their incompatibility. This letter was one of several that were excerpted and included in the privately published statement that Butler, with the aid of his lawyer, produced after their divorce was granted in 1849.[37] She admits, first, that she had married him without using her judgment or observation "to ascertain whether or not we were likely to be companions and fellows to each other." Why, then, she asks, had they married? Her answer is given in the following: "The time is now evidently come when the sentiment which drew us together is waning and perishing away: this is natural;—it was of an order which can never long survive intimacy and possession; and they who have no other bond of union must, after a very brief space, cease to have any."[38] Strong sexual desire, what she calls a "sentiment," is, by virtue of its gratification, eventually diminished, and if a couple has nothing else in common (respect for one another's "liberty," for a start) the marriage will flounder.

When Fanny Kemble and Pierce Butler became engaged in the autumn of 1833, Charles Kemble, worried about money for his retirement, proposed a plan that would allow Fanny and Pierce to marry the following year (after completing her acting commitments in America), to have a brief honeymoon, and then to part, with Fanny returning to England to act for one more year with her father. Almost until the moment when they were to marry, and Fanny to sail for England, Pierce seemed to acquiesce to this proposal, but at the last minute he suggested another scheme: Fanny would remain in America and the money she had earned would be placed in a trust for Charles. Since the sum involved was $35,000 (approximately

Miss Fanny Kemble
Julia
in The Hunchback

Fig. 20. Miss Fanny Kemble as Julia in *The Hunchback*. Fanny Kemble performed this role in New York in early June 1834, a few days after her marriage to Pierce Butler. It was her last appearance on a stage until early 1847. © National Portrait Gallery, London.

a quarter of a million dollars by early twenty-first-century standards), Charles was not slow to agree.[39] In addition to Pierce Butler's securing a comfortable pension for his soon-to-be father-in-law (through Kemble's hard-earned money), Pierce's sisters reputedly granted an annuity to Thérèse Kemble. According to Rebecca Gratz, writing to her sister-in-law on July 20, 1834, this generosity "secures her [Kemble's mother] from any disappointment her daughter's retirement might occasion and thus the good and talented Miss K is rewarded for her filial piety. . . . The Butler family receive her very cordially so for the love of nature and romance we will suppose she is to be happy."[40]

On May 31, 1834, Kemble wrote to Sarah Perkins Cleveland that she was to be married the next Saturday and that, as Mrs. Pierce Butler, she would have "all the grave cares of matrimony" in her mind. She added that although her health was much better and her looks greatly improved since she left Boston, she was "not in very good spirits," something attributable, perhaps, to the financial negotiations that had preceded a final agreement between Charles and Pierce.[41] The wedding took place at Christ Church, Philadelphia, on June 7, 1834, with Charles Kemble in attendance; immediately afterward the Butlers embarked on a steamboat for New York where Kemble was to begin her last few days of acting in America. According to some witnesses, she wept all the way up to Bristol (about twenty miles north of Philadelphia),[42] and on the following Monday, her final performance in one of her most successful roles—Julia in *The Hunchback*—was witnessed by a would-be actress named Anna Mowatt. She noted in her diary that Kemble's name was on everyone's lips and her praises as "a most devoted daughter and truly excellent woman" echoed through New York's middle-class drawing rooms. She added that she had never seen any creature "so perfectly bewitching," so gifted with a magnificent voice, and so electrifying with her dark, flashing eyes.[43]

In early August the newly married Butlers went to Newport, Rhode Island, for a lengthy honeymoon, accompanied by Pierce's brother, John, and his wife, Ella.[44] Fanny Appleton, later the wife of Henry Longfellow, reported that Kemble wrote "her book of travels" during the day and waltzed "most gracefully" in the evening: "Her manners have become much more affable, and I must say she is capable of being truly fascinating. I have got very well acquainted with her and feel myself bound by the spell which attracts everyone to her." But Fanny Appleton did not like the way she dressed her hair (far too plainly) and reported that her face was "frightfully coarse to examine." Fanny Butler's taste in dress was judged "shocking" by everyone at the hotel: walking on the rocks in a muslin dress over yellow silk and wearing a transparent blond hat in a piercing wind was considered not only inappropriate but downright reckless. Fanny Appleton, on this particular afternoon, shielded herself from the wind in a "blankety shawl and boa."[45] Just two

Fig. 21. Old Butler Mansion on York Road, near Germantown, facing south, 1870. Kemble lived intermittently from 1874 to 1877 at York Farm, a small cottage across the road from the Butler mansion. Kennedy Watercolors, Historical Society of Pennsylvania, Philadelphia.

months after her marriage, Kemble was already behaving in the provocative manner that enraged her husband and shocked Philadelphia society: one of Andrew Jackson's "scribbling women," she wore what she fancied, arranged her hair as she wished, and declined the cosseting offered to American women by their male relatives. She had already appropriated and begun to revise the role of American wife as prescribed by sexual and gender politics.

By October, Fanny Kemble knew for certain that she was pregnant and in December, after spending several months with John and Ella Butler at their townhouse on Walnut Street, Fanny and Pierce moved to Butler Place, a small but handsome house on the Old York Road in Branchtown, about six miles north of Philadelphia. Built in 1790 by a Frenchman, it had been acquired by the Butler family in 1810. Set in three hundred acres of farmland, it was an imposing residence, although badly in need of the landscaping that Kemble undertook soon after her arrival.[46] She oversaw the planting of a long double row of maple trees that formed a grand promenade, the establishment of lawns and flower gardens, and, when she returned from Georgia in early 1839, the placement of red wooden tubs on each side of the driveway into which were planted oleander, lemon, and citron trees brought from the Butler plantations. Apart from planning the landscaping, however, she did little at Butler Place during her pregnancy but complain to her English friends that she was living in an intellectual wasteland and that no one to whom she "belonged" took the "slightest interest in literary pursuits." In response to a query from Harriet St. Leger after the birth of Sarah Butler in May 1835, she announced that she was doing no reading whatsoever, and that if she ever took up reading again, it would probably be "rambling, desultory, and unprofitable." She complained she had no stimulus of example, companionship, or sympathy and that she was incapable of study. But when Harriet Martineau visited Butler Place shortly after Sarah was born, Kemble showed her the proofs of the *Journal* that was about to be published, which indicates that despite her complaints, she had not abandoned her writing. She seems not to have concealed her restlessness from Martineau, conceding she had married hastily and unwisely, but Martineau believed Kemble's realization of her disastrous misjudgment was leading her to behave badly and that her domestic miseries, "terrible as they were," deserved no sympathy from her friends.[47]

For Anna Jameson, however, Kemble assumed the mask of settled wife, assuring her that she was well and happy, that her whole state of "life and being" had assumed a "placid, tranquil, serene, and even course, which, after the violent excitements of my last few years, is both agreeable and wholesome."[48] Behind that mask, however, Fanny's life was in turmoil, her struggle to curb her emotional

Fig. 22. Pierce Butler House, Old York Road, home of Owen Wister. This shows the Old Butler Mansion as it looked in 1936. Photo by Dr. John Faris. Society Photo Collection, Historical Society of Pennsylvania, Philadelphia.

volatility vanquished by the sheer misery and helplessness of her situation. Three months after the birth of Sarah, she told Pierce she wanted to return to England and that once he found a wet nurse, their daughter would not miss her mother since she was still an infant. Six months after the marriage she left Butler Place at six o'clock in the evening in search of a hotel room in Philadelphia. She returned at nine o'clock the same night, and remained officially united with Butler for the next eleven years, the humiliating failure of her marriage alternately draining her of strength and vitality or driving her to some brilliant writing and defiant behavior. What she did not say in her letters to her friends—or, rather, what she excised from those letters when she included them in her memoirs—she expressed in a poem that opens in the following way:

> One after one, the shield, the sword, the spear,
> The panoply that I was wont to wear,
> My suit of proof, my wings that kept me free,
> These, full of trust, delivered I to thee
> . . . I since have tried,
> In hours of sadness, when my former life
> Shone on me through thick gathering clouds of strife,
> To wield my weapons bright, and wear again
> My maiden corslet and free wings—in vain![49]

If those "wings" that kept her free, formed of her passionate response to suffering and racial injustice, had been clipped entirely by Pierce's domestic tyranny, then Kemble's story would be one of pitiable but not particularly memorable unhappiness. But it was his efforts to curb her spirit that drove her to "wield" the weapons she evokes in the poem, to wear again her "maiden corslet and free wings." He managed to edit some of the American *Journal* but was unable to prevent its publication; despite his best efforts to squash her writing career before it began, Kemble was launched as the author she had always wished to be—before she went on the stage, went to America, and met Pierce Butler. It remained her favorite role throughout her life, one that she never sought to revise or to rewrite.

The Outer Bound of Civilized Creation

One would imagine by the style that the authoress must be
very pert, and not well bred.
                                        —Princess Victoria, August 23, 1835

Fanny at Butler Place

Fanny Kemble Butler's American *Journal* created transatlantic outrage when it
was published in June 1835, just a week after the birth of her first child, Sarah
Butler, on May 28. English newspapers accused her of impertinent ingratitude,
and American readers thought her tone supercilious, her abolitionism naive. The
barrage of hostile criticism ranged from royal dismissal to wicked parody, but
none of this seemed to matter in terms of sales; the *Journal*'s immediate notoriety
probably spurred the sale of eight hundred copies in the first week by one New
York bookstore, Wiley and Long.[1] For many readers on both sides of the Atlantic,
the saucy style alone was worth the price. To her luster as a newly retired celebrity
actress Kemble could now add the notoriety of being the most recent English
traveler to enjoy generous hospitality from enraptured Americans and return the
favor with an amusing but lacerating critique of their customs, manners, and politics. For many American readers, the only difference between Frances Trollope
and Fanny Kemble was that the latter was younger, prettier, and had succeeded in
netting a rich American husband.

The possibility that Kemble might have married Pierce Butler to escape the
tawdry world of the theater gains credence when one reads the long review of her

American *Journal* that appeared in the *Quarterly Review* in July 1835. The anonymous writer makes Kemble the scathing subject of a vehement attack on actresses and attributes the vulgarities of style and subject to her life as a performer until her marriage. It is difficult to imagine that a nineteenth-century actress of Kemble's intelligence and education would not have wished to dissociate herself from the heated world of public display presented by the *Quarterly Review* in such a way as to encourage feelings of moral superiority in the reader.

> The life of an *actress*—the habits of individual thought, study, and exertion—the familiarity with bargains, business, and bustle—the various and ever-varying situations and society into which she is thrown—the crossings and jostlings of the dramatic *race* . . . the activity and firmness of personal character which are necessary to maintain her rights from the encroachments of rivals and the tyranny of managers—must all tend to blunt the feelings of youthful timidity, to weaken the sense of feminine dependence, and to *force*, as in a hot-bed, to premature exuberance, all the more vigorous qualities both of mind and body. An actress lives fast: her existence is a perpetual wrestling-match, and one *season* gives her more experience—and with experience, more of the nerve and hard features of the world—more than a whole life of domestic duties could do.[2]

Although this passage attempts to excuse Kemble's vulgar approach to American life as the inevitable consequence of having been an actress, it damns her by association on several significant grounds. First, an actress necessarily functions in the business world of bustling and bargains; next, she is a member of the "dramatic *race*," which implies she belongs to some kind of tribe (the Kemble family was sometimes tagged as "gypsy-ish" or "Jewish-looking" by its detractors); then, her feminine timidity and dependence are blunted by the "hot-bed" forcing of a vigorous mind and body, which implies unladylike awareness, even direct experience, of sexuality; and, finally, she lives "fast," toughened by the "hard features of the world." The social disdain for actors that the Kemble family had attempted to counter through education and cultured pursuits, that taint of the green-room from which Kemble's parents vigorously shielded her, and the association of actresses with louche sexual behavior still seem to track the reputation of "Fanny Kemble Butler," now retired from the stage, married to a wealthy American, and publishing her work on both sides of the Atlantic.

Having attempted to excuse Kemble's forwardness in choice of subject, the reviewer then offers an explanation for her vulgar literary style: "If she is at times colloquial to vulgarity, she is at others pompous even to bombast, and in both cases she is *acting* . . . the whole thing is arranged for *stage effect*. She is pompous, to prove that she can be dignified; and then she interposes trivialities, in order to appear natural. She wishes to show that she can play Lady Macbeth and Nell in the same volume."[3] In conclusion, the writer does allow that the *Journal* will afford considerable amusement; however, the sound principles of social and moral life that lie at the bottom of the whole work are "too often concealed or obscured by the exuberant vegetation of the rank soil and hot sky of the profession with which Mrs. Butler has become so entirely assimilated and so absolutely identified."[4]

Two things stand out here. First, the reviewer's perceptive analysis of Kemble's style, however unsympathetically conducted, affirms the theatrical quality of her writing. In the *Journal*, she is onstage, as the *Quarterly Review* suggests, playing for both tragic and pathetic effect, just as, as I have suggested previously, when she on the verge of abandoning herself to the sublime at West Point, she steps back, assumes an appropriate attitude, and *performs* the part of an early Romantic heroine awed by nature. Second, the *Quarterly Review* refuses Kemble the possibility of shedding her identity as an actress: indelibly marked (or stained in the pejorative scheme of things presented in the review), by being a member of the dramatic *race*, even if she has married a wealthy Philadelphian and withdrawn from the stage, she will always and forever be an actress, carrying with her the baggage of negotiation, jostling, forwardness, and vulgarity.

Until the publication of the American *Journal*, Kemble had, of course, been a performer, both on the stage and off. But from this moment onward, a time that coincides with the beginning of her married life, she begins even more consciously to assume attitudes of her own making, to wear masks, and to assume a variety of roles. Paradoxically, this is the moment when she had left the stage, but as the *Quarterly Review* must have made clear to her even more forcefully than before, she would always be Fanny Kemble, an actress with all the moral taint that encumbers such identity. One might assume also that since this is the moment when Kemble became Mrs. Pierce Butler, she would abandon or at least rely less on the assumption of roles. Quite the contrary seems to have happened: if, until her marriage, she had assumed various attitudes to impose the governance of the "theatrical" over the "dramatic" (that is to say, to curb the emotional volatility inherited from her mother with the cool discipline of her father), then, when confronted by the disastrous reality of her marriage, she appropriates the attribution of role-playing that is negatively attached to her name with the publication of the *Journal*. Defying the social approbation of Philadelphia society and the demands for obedience presented by her husband, she turns role-playing on the morally superior world and on the domestic tyranny of her husband. In a valiant feminist refusal to acquiesce in social hypocrisy and marital bullying, Kemble's assumption of masks becomes more marked. She becomes a skilled creator of roles designed not just to preserve her emotional sanity but also to challenge stifling codes of social and marital behavior. What had been in the American *Journal* pointed remarks about the subjugation of American women become in Fanny Kemble's life from the time of her marriage a feminist "acting out," as it were, of her feminist principles. In October 1833, the editor of the *Germantown Telegraph* announced that "he who weds [Miss Kemble] for an angel will discover, we opine, ere a fortnight that she is nothing more or less than a woman, and perhaps one of the most troublesome kind into the bargain."[5] When Fanny Kemble married Pierce Butler for an adoring and compliant husband she discovered, in perhaps less than a fortnight, that he was one of the most troublesome kinds of men: spoiled, arrogant, and contemptuous of his wife's desires for equality, respect, and friendship in their marriage.

Princess Victoria thought the *Journal* was "very pertly and oddly written" and, sounding somewhat like the reviewer of the *Quarterly Review*, added that if she had not known that Kemble was reasonably "well bred," she would have thought it the work of a vulgar little actress who had spent a few months touring America. But she did know Kemble was the author, maybe even remembered Kemble's exhibitionist feats at Captain Fozzard's Riding Academy, and it disappointed her that a "person endowed with so much talent as Mrs. Butler really is" should publish a book "so full of trash and nonsense."[6] However, only three weeks later, Victoria wrote in her diary, "I read in Mrs. Butler's journal which amuses me. There are some very fine feelings in it."[7] She gives no reason for her changed opinion, but when she first dipped into the *Journal* she might have read only the sections in which Kemble gleefully demolishes the social pretensions of her American hosts, and, when she returned to it, she might have admired the evocation of American landscape and the indictment of America's unjust treatment of its indigenous population and its slaves. Henry Greville, a longtime friend of the Kemble family, was certainly of this opinion; he noted in his diary on June 7, 1835, that he thought the landscape descriptions in the *Journal* well done and the writing amusing and eloquent.[8] Another Kemble family friend, Sydney Smith, wrote that "Mrs. Butler's Diary" was "much better than the reviews and papers will allow it to be. What is called vulgarity, is natural and useful contempt for the exclusive and superfine."[9]

The *Journal* was almost immediately satirized in an anonymous parody titled *My Conscience! Fanny Thimble Cutler's Journal of a Residence in America. Whilst Performing a Profitable Theatrical Engagement. Beating the Nonsensical Fanny Kemble Journal All Hollow.* About to honor Fierce Cutler with her hand in wedlock, poor Fanny Thimble has been driven to publication to get money to buy her wedding dress. The parody skewers Kemble for insulting her hosts and ridicules Pierce Butler for marrying an actress. After a breakfast of six muffins, seven eggs, and eight cups of coffee (Kemble was a voracious eater), the giddy narrator receives Mr. Cutler, according to her "dear, dear papa" a wealthy goose worth catching. Appalled by the American dislike of finger bowls and astonished by the preferred custom of having dinner guests wiped down by "a stout negro" equipped with a sponge dipped in whiskey and water, she attacks American manners and makes herself "a literary character" in a country where everyone believes the English "are born for poets, painters, actors, or chimney sweeps." Philadelphia outdoes the rituals and ceremo-

Fig. 23. "Dear Good Little Me." *Outlines Illustrative of the Journal of* ******A*******K****** (Boston: D. C. Johnston, 1835). Parodies of Kemble's American *Journal* ridiculed her self-satisfaction in overcoming adversity, here seasickness on the *Pacific*. American Literature Library, University of Virginia.

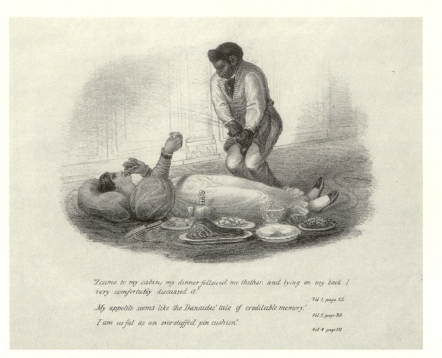

"I came to my cabin; my dinner followed me thither; and lying on my back I
very comfortably discussed it."
                                                              Vol 1, page 15.

My appetite seems like the Danaides' tale of creditable memory."
                                                              Vol 2, page 39.

I am as fat as an over stuffed pin cushion."
                                                              Vol 4 page 111.

Fig. 24. Fanny Thimble Cutler in her cabin on the *Pacific*. *Outlines Illustrative of the Journal of *******A******K****** (Boston: D. C. Johnston, 1835). Parodies also ridiculed Kemble's
prodigious appetite and robust good health. American Literature Library, University of
Virginia.

nies reserved for visiting presidents in welcoming Fanny Thimble. She receives a
five-hundred-gun salute, is cheered by five thousand marines, and rides through
the streets in a barouche drawn by an elephant, two lions, and sixty-six cream
horses. When she arrives at the Philadelphia fish market, the women working
there set up such a tumultuous racket that newly caught fish are brought back to
life and "spring once more into their native element." When she leaves the market,
"stout wenches" cram her carriage with tributes of minnows and sturgeon. Her
conquest of Fierce Cutler is complete.[10] What the author of the parody leaves
untouched, and probably could not have known, is that Pierce and Fanny had
fought furiously over what could be censored from the manuscript before it went
to the publishers; before even agreeing to publication, Pierce had insisted that he
be given editorial rights to eliminate what might offend Philadelphia society and
what might harm his wife's reputation.

Fanny Thimble Cutler's Journal offers an amusing parody of the animated and
biting style with which Kemble had not spared inept regional actors, noisy Ameri-

can women, or political hypocrisy. Performing jauntily throughout her text and with no thought of placating her audience, she castigates, amuses, and instructs. That her exuberant style and fearless opinions were immediately satirized testifies to her tabloid visibility in American popular culture and to the easy mark she offered as an actress. The parody shifts from reasonably good-natured spoofing (the part about the fish, in particular) to sour nastiness when it concludes with a fictitious letter to "Fanny Thimble" from the father of two young women in Baltimore who claim to have been slighted by the famous visitor. Ridiculing English actors, for him no more than gypsies, descendants of a "tribe" who sold old clothes, who think they can lord it over their American cousins, this irate father blasts both Pierce and Fanny by saying that if "a wealthy ignoramus chooses to lower the dignity of his family by marrying a third rate strolling actress," he should desist from forcibly introducing her into society."[11] The old rumor that the Kembles were Jewish gets rehearsed here (secondhand clothes traders, members of a "tribe"), as does the association of actresses with prostitution.

Despite the Kemble family's impeccable respectability, Fanny's spotless reputation, and Charles's stately manners, Fanny and her father were still tainted with the raffish air of a louche, itinerant existence: to term Fanny Thimble" a "strolling actress" is to put her on the street with her soliciting sisters. Parody exaggerates, but in the early days of her marriage Kemble received a frosty reception in Philadelphia: Pierce Butler had married beneath him; she was forward in company and shockingly unfeminine as she trotted down Walnut Street dressed in male riding clothes. Kemble eventually formed enduring friendships with some highly respected figures in Philadelphia such as the Rev. William Furness, who was pastor at the First Unitarian Church and an outspoken abolitionist, and her charm won over influential social figures such as Sidney George Fisher, but she never entirely warmed to Philadelphians, nor they to her: she felt they were hobbled by a "dread of opinion" and "desire for conformity" that made them distrustful, cautious, and flat conversationalists; they regarded her as abrasive, hysterical, and unfit to lead that "circle which had scarce" deigned to notice her before her marriage, Julia Kean's disdainful assessment of Kemble's suitability for Philadelphia society.[12]

When Fanny and Pierce returned from Newport, Rhode Island, in the late autumn of 1834, Pierce initiated his campaign to curb Kemble's independent spirit. His first move was to forbid publication of the American journal, a position he modified somewhat after Kemble's furious resistance. His price for publication was that he become its sole editor, and he excised anything that offended his propriety as the heir, with his brother, John, to enormous rice and cotton plantations in the South. Finding his censorship intolerable, Kemble assumed the role of defiant heroine. Only four months after they were married, following an anguished argument about her rights to her own intellectual work, she marched out of the Walnut Street house of his brother, where she and Pierce were staying while Butler Place was being renovated. In a note to Pierce she announced that she planned to sail for England, to seek refuge with her family, and to embark on a career as a poet and social critic. After several hours wandering the chilly streets, she returned, even more depressed and furious than when she had left: she was penniless, she had no one to whom she could turn in Philadelphia, and she was married to a man whose passivity had been a clever facade. Although the handsome earnings from her American tour were safe in the New Orleans bank and under Louisiana law could not be touched by Pierce without her consent, she had no access to the money since it was invested entirely in the annuity for her father. Undoubtedly, after some lengthy legal maneuvering she might have gained control of the money, but in a state of hysterical despair and with no legal counsel close at hand, she felt virtually stranded in America.

Having no American friends apart from the Sedgwick family to whom she could confide her anger and disappointment, she wrote in desperation to Anna Jameson, to whom Catharine Sedgwick had confided her fears about the marriage in May 1834. Conceding that Pierce Butler might be a "gentlemanly man, with good sense and amiable disposition," Sedgwick declares he was the infinite "inferior" of Kemble: "Poor girl, she makes a dangerous experiment; I have a thousand fears for the result."[13] In Kemble's letter to Jameson, written in October 1834, she articulated bluntly and clear-sightedly the difference between what she wished she were and what she was in actuality. She knew she was intelligent, that she was a talented, if undisciplined, poet, and that she was capable of writing powerfully about social conditions; she knew, in sum, that she could live as a Victorian woman intellectual, with or without a husband. But, as she confessed in this letter, rather than tackling some sustained work of social critique that would build on the clever insights of the American *Journal*, in the first year of her marriage she had read virtually nothing. Her only work had been to finish her play, *The Star of Seville*, which was published in 1835 without any interference from Pierce. There was nothing in its plot about the king of Spain, various nobles and merchants, and the romantic difficulties of its heroine that struck him as offensive.[14] In her letter to Jameson, Kemble expresses a revealing but impossible desire: "If I were a man in England, I should like to devote my life to the cause of national progress, carried on through party politics and public legislation."[15] This comparison between what she wished she were and, by implication, what she actually was touches on the frustration and sense of waste with which she viewed her married state. Rather than being a man in England devoting his life to national progress through political engagement, she was a married woman in America, devoting herself to an imperious husband and a new baby.

The first year at Butler Place was punctuated by a series of social failures occasioned, in part, by Kemble's mistaken choices of which roles to play in which setting. Imagining herself as a kind of English Lady Bountiful planted in the Philadelphia countryside, she arranged a colorful Fourth of July celebration in 1835. The Quaker tenant farmers and their families were horrified by the beer and wine and discomfited by a day devoted to pleasure rather than to work; viewing the hospitality as mere frivolity, a sign that Pierce's wife had nothing better to do than think about amusing diversions, they quickly left. The village lacked any poor she might visit, the children refused her offer to supplement their lessons at the local school, the dairymaid announced she had no intention of churning fresh butter every day specifically for the Butler family, and her neighbors drank water with their three o'clock dinner. That Pierce quickly assumed the habit of spending several nights a week in Philadelphia at his brother's house on Walnut Street did not help. After almost five years of being surrounded by admirers, of being welcomed into the best houses in London, and of being accustomed to scintillating conversation, Kemble was abandoned to the company of the baby nurse.

Although Butler Place was called a farm by the Butler family, it was a comfortable gentleman-farmer's mansion. Graced with Regency details such as fluted moldings around the ceilings, beautifully carved chair rails around the walls, and elegant marble fireplaces, it was a house Kemble wanted to turn into an English country retreat. But everything seemed too straight and utilitarian; footpaths led directly to front doors rather than meandering past flower beds, and rows of trees were set out merely to divide properties, not to beguile the eye in a pleasant avenue. She missed lovely Oatlands and the country lanes around Weybridge, the rides on crisp mornings at Heaton when she had set out with Lord Wilton, and the evenings when she had dazzled his guests with her wit and accomplishments. At Butler Place, defying the gender codes designed to protect American middle-class women from a harsh world, Kemble set off alone every morning for a four-mile walk through the rocky meadows and arid lanes around Branchtown. She spent the rest of the day caring for the baby, making copies of her *Journal*, and, for some unfathomable reason, learning double-entry bookkeeping and studying the mysteries of insurance. In her memoirs, she declares that she found the work tiresome but persisted since she liked to read about fire catastrophes and unlucky speculations; they were fodder for the plots for plays and novels that she would invent as she totted up columns of figures.

Discontented and rebellious, Kemble at twenty-six knew she had made a terrible mistake in marrying Butler. Little of this painful awareness enters into the published letters that she wrote to friends from Butler Place in the first year of her marriage, for the simple reason that when she edited these letters some forty years later as she assembled her memoirs, she methodically excised all mention of Pierce's name. Yet the tedium of her life governs her narrative, and as much as she attempts to downplay the unhappiness through the interpolation of retrospective commentary, she never omits the angry disappointment of these years. The commentary amplifies, revises, or corrects the earlier, epistolary record and it seems as if, through this temporal distance, Kemble aims to soften her rancor and despair. For instance, her 1835 letters from Butler Place disdainfully contrast the arid American countryside with the verdant English landscape, yet in her memoirs she tacks on to these letters enthusiastic descriptions of how the area around Philadelphia is now full of pleasant stone cottages, lovely flower gardens, and arable acres diversified with stretches of pretty wild woodland. To the desperate litany of complaints to her friends about her isolated, subjugated, and demeaned condition as the wife of Pierce Butler, she appends a long interpolation about the much-improved status of women in America over the previous half century. When she was twenty-two, she ruefully notes, the "woman's rights" question was barely aired; women's suffrage was neither demanded nor desired; married women's property was in the control of their husbands; and the "melancholy process of divorce" was saddled with virtually insurmountable obstacles. At the age of seventy-two, she celebrates the fact that American women are college professors, respected physicians, and practicing lawyers, and that they may more easily free themselves from tyrannical, abusive husbands. She thinks it wonderful that women can now lecture on formerly "unimaginable subjects" such as public prostitution and "free love."[16]

Looking back fifty years after the events she describes in her letters, Kemble constructs a wishful narrative for herself, a kind of rewriting of her life as a young woman. Had she stayed in England, she implies, she might have enjoyed the support of her intellectual women friends and taken advantage of the enhanced opportunities for women to become professionally independent. Compelled by loyalty to her father, however, she traveled to America where, desperate to get out of the theater, infatuated with Pierce, and deprived of Dall's wise counsel, she rushed into marriage. Covent Garden Theatre, scorn for a profession that in the popular imagination demeans women (as the *Quarterly Review* in 1835 made clear), hasty marriage grounded almost entirely in sexual attraction, and the absence of a supportive feminist culture—all these factors, combined, create an image of an existence *not* chosen. Compounding this construction of a life-that-might-have-been is her intelligent awareness of complicity in the dictates of patriarchal culture. In actuality, Kemble did have talent and promise as a writer (and she knew it), she did have women friends who encouraged her in her work (especially Harriet St. Leger and Anna Jameson), and she did have many male friends who paid tribute to her mind, wit, and style. Kemble's misery after her marriage originates, in part, in her knowledge that she failed to realize her potential, that she had been hobbled, perhaps, by fear that the emotional instability inherited from her mother would compound the challenge of a single life. Intensifying Kemble's self-awareness, at this moment, was a recurrence of the depression that she aimed always to govern through exercise and intellectual work. Her efforts now were not successful, and during the first year of her marriage her troubled mind was obvious to many who met her: Eliza Lee Cabot Follen, an author of juvenile literature and a friend of Harriet Martineau, wrote to Kemble's friend Sarah Perkins Cleveland in late September 1835 with reassurances that "Mrs. Butler's mind is one I doubt not that will work itself clear in time. Its excellences and graces seem to me intrinsic and lasting, while its faults are only accidental."[17]

In December 1835 Kemble wrote to Dorothy Wilson, Harriet St. Leger's companion, that she was "at first a little disappointed that my baby [Sarah] was not a man-child, for the lot of woman is seldom happy, owing principally, I think, to the many serious mistakes which have obtained universal sway in female education."[18] Determined that Sarah would be neither coddled nor patronized by virtue of her gender, Kemble fed her a diet rich in fruits and vegetables, had her tumbling around in the garden whenever possible, and reveled in her daughter's health and strength. She was tickled by the lack of resemblance to any of the Kembles and marveled that Sarah had "dark *blue* eyes." When Anna Jameson visited her at Butler Place in December 1837, she wrote to a friend in England that "Fanny's child is a sweet little being, full of health and spirits, but so fair and cherub like and so unlike herself that, as she says, she goes about like a Gypsey [*sic*] that had stolen a child."[19] Right after the birth of Sarah, Kemble wrote to Harriet St. Leger that she was busy with nursing, playing with a brace of puppies, and managing "a household of six servants."[20] Six servants, supplemented by three gardeners and a baby nurse, constituted a comfortable household for two adults and one baby, and the size of her domestic establishment suggests that Kemble had plenty of time to study and to write, had she been emotionally able to do so. Her spirits picked up a little when she resumed riding, shockingly soon after Sarah's birth according to her neighbors: she was determined not to sink into the acquiescent condition of new American motherhood in which women, as she saw it, became overprotected baby-feeding machines who were afraid of outdoor exercise and wanted only to laze on sofas in overheated rooms. After a good gallop across the fields, she wrote to Harriet that she was beginning to "to feel once more like my unmarried self," a sentiment that says a good deal about her views of her married state.

If her body began to regain its unmarried vigor, her mind, it would seem, was slipping into laziness: she admitted to Harriet, "I neither read, write, nor cast up accounts . . . my reading, if ever I take to such an occupation again is like, I fear, to be, as it always has been, rambling, desultory, and unprofitable."[21] Blaming Pierce by saying that those with whom she lived did not sympathize with her pursuits, she noted that she had on her table a volume of Marlowe's plays, a translation of Goethe's *Faust*, and an article on Victor Hugo's novels, all unread, together with various pieces of her own verse and "a long and vehement treatise against negro slavery, which I wanted to publish with my Journal, but was obliged to refrain from doing so, lest our fellow-citizens should tear our house down, and make a bonfire of our furniture." She included a copy of this "treatise" with her letter to Harriet.[22] What she does not reveal is that Pierce threatened to withhold his permission for publication of *any* part of the *Journal* if she insisted on including her writings on slavery. She had married a man who not only did not, as she put it ironically, sympathize with her own pursuits but also vindictively deployed his legally sanctioned power as an American husband to determine what she might say in public and where she might say it. He muffled the abolitionist opinions he had suffered in silence before their marriage, and he now enacted a punitive price for his deceptively compliant attitude.

One aspect of the sheer incompatibility of Fanny Kemble and Pierce Butler, except in terms of sexual attraction, is their deep division over the subject of slavery. When Kemble visited the cotton and rice plantations that were the source of the Butler family wealth, she claimed that when she married Pierce she knew nothing of his "dreadful possessions," a statement some have interpreted as meaning she did not know she was marrying a man who would soon become one of the three largest slave owners in America.[23] It seems more likely she meant she knew only of his "dreadful possessions" in theory, not in horrifying practice. The Butler estate in Georgia was renowned in Philadelphia society as notoriously large (it covered several thousand acres, was about eight square miles, and was diked and trenched and divided by ditches and a canal, into which the rice fields overflowed). Pierce's grandfather, Major Pierce Butler, had, like many late eighteenth-century planters, preferred not to live on his plantations. A prominent figure in Philadelphia society, he remained at his imposing mansion on Chestnut Street and left the supervision of his crops, and the seven hundred slaves who worked them, to experienced managers such as Roswell King and his son, who between them ran the Butler holdings for thirty-six years.

Although when he married Kemble, Pierce had not yet come into the Georgia inheritance, his potential fortune must have been known to her since she was ready to relinquish substantial American earnings for the support of her father and to authorize interest payments on this capital to be paid directly to her father, not to herself. She was, then, entirely dependent on her husband for support; should she leave him, she would be entirely dependent on her father. Ten years later in

1845, desperate to leave Pierce, she was appalled by the degraded financial position of married women: she realized that whatever she wrote was not her own legal property, and she ranted sarcastically to her friends about laws that licensed men whose wits would not keep them for a week without starving to claim as their own income earned by women so visibly their moral and intellectual superiors. Kemble was intelligent and not reluctant to ask questions, but in the case of the financial arrangements she agreed to before her marriage, she acted so impetuously that she left herself penniless.

During the summer of 1836, Kemble's behavior became increasingly erratic. Appearing to Pierce tiresomely resentful and to her neighbors eccentric and unpredictable, she assumed the role of social provocateur. Tired of tramping around the Butler acres, she took to walking the six miles into Philadelphia and back, an outrageous, even mad, figure to travelers on the Germantown road. Rather than shielding herself from the summer sun as did American women, she threw away her bonnets and became "coffee-colored," something she felt did not matter since she said her dark eyes and hair made her as dark as a gypsy. She wrote in her Georgian *Journal* that if she chose "to walk arm in arm with the dingiest mulatto through the streets of Philadelphia, nobody could possibly tell by my complexion that I was not his sister."[24] She spent hours in the garden trying to create English flower beds in defiance of the withering sun and ravenous insects, and she terrified the Butler gardeners as she raged against their neglect in not telling her that wild violets were growing along the wall by the kitchen.

At this time she announced to Harriet St. Leger that she would not sacrifice the health of the baby to the cause of "doing good" in the rice swamp (the Butler brothers inherited the Georgia plantations in April 1836), adding, however, that the "cause of the Southern negroes" was one occupation that would fully engage her "active energies and intellect."[25] She began to refer to Pierce not as her husband but as "the owner" of "Negroland," to voice a fearful insistence that she was not making use of her talents and that she was being denied the opportunity to set a noble example to others by freeing her husband's slaves, by educating them, and by paying them for their work: "Oh, how I wish I was a man! How I wish I owned these slaves! Instead of being supported (disgracefully, as it seems to me) by their unpaid labor."[26] Some relief from this impassioned frustration came when she spent the month of September 1836 with the Sedgwicks in Massachusetts, and in October "it was decided" by Pierce (as Kemble put it) that she, Sarah, and Margery O'Brien, the baby's nurse, should travel to England to visit her family. Kemble was eager to show off her healthy baby, to say nothing of her desire to get away from Pierce, Butler Place, and stifling Philadelphia. Pierce had been elected a delegate to the Pennsylvania Constitutional Convention after becoming actively involved in Philadelphia politics.[27] Tired of Kemble's tantrums and depression and rumored to be involved with other women, Pierce had no desire to take her to Harrisburg. Relieved to put her on the boat for Liverpool on November 1, 1836, he did not see her again for ten months.

London, Again

Four years and four months after Fanny Kemble left England to mend the family fortunes, she returned as Fanny Butler, married, wealthy, and glad to be away from her husband. The stormy passage to England was a twenty-eight-day nightmare, the most "formidable" of her eighteen transatlantic crossings, Kemble noted fifty years later. At the height of the storm, the convulsed plunging of the ship convinced her that they were all about to perish; as it reeled under what seemed to be an insurmountable shock, she was suddenly presented with what she describes as "the death-vision, so to speak, of my whole existence." Her life appeared not as a procession of events through the years but as a unified image of what she had been and what she had become. The vision was "indescribably awful," accompanied by a "simultaneous, acute and almost despairing sense of *loss*, of *waste*." Faced with what seemed to be impending death, she resorted to singing, very loudly, every English, Scottish, French, German, Italian, and Spanish song she could remember. Her repertoire "a very numerous one," she chanted throughout the night. Famous and wealthy, in flight from the despairing insight that she had wasted her life and lost her chance for literary success, Kemble sang against the storm and in defiance of an emotional turbulence that matched the pitching Atlantic. When she eventually got to London, she went to her parents' house at 10 Park Place, St. James's, close to Green Park, Pall Mall, and Piccadilly, and here she shared a room with Adelaide. Almost immediately she resumed a social life little different from the kind she had enjoyed before going to America.

Adelaide thought her "younger, and healthier, and happier than when I knew her before—and her spirits are untiring, *wonderful!* I sit in amazement at seeing anyone so happy for so long a time together."[28] It is no wonder Kemble was so extravagantly happy: apart from the evidence of baby Sarah, it was as if she had never left England. The Kembles doted on the baby, described by Adelaide as "very fair, with a determined expression and brows and eyes like my father," which amused Kemble since she had been unable to find any trace of her family in her child. The sisters were "out morning, noon, and night" and whole weeks flew by in a bustle that was deliciously exhausting.[29] Kemble's litany of complaints to Anna Jameson and Harriet St. Leger that she wandered in an intellectual desert, that she had become an indolent wife and mother, seems forgotten, the "death-vision" of her existence as lost and wasted replaced by vital engagement with London life.

For the next ten months, Kemble flung herself into a social whirl that suppressed the history of her marriage and returned her to a time before she had forfeited her independence for wealth and sexual attraction. She went regularly to the famous breakfasts given by the banker-poet Samuel Rogers at his lavish house in St. James's Square, danced with Edward Trelawny, her Byronic companion in adventures at Cold Spring and Niagara, enchanted new and old friends such as the Berry sisters and Sydney Smith, and charmed the great Whig salons of Lady Lansdowne and Lady Holland. When Kemble and Adelaide went out together in the evenings, they often sang together, Fanny's vibrant contralto blending beautifully with Adelaide's mezzo soprano. During this time, Charles Kemble gave his farewell performance at Covent Garden as Benedick in *Much Ado About Nothing*, a celebration derided by William Macready, the famous actor who loathed all the Kembles and their on- and offstage performances, as a sentimental honor for "an old coxcomb."[30] As she recalled the time in her memoirs, she was at the center of "a brilliant society, full of every element of wit, wisdom, experience, refined taste, high culture, good breeding, good sense, and distinction of every sort."[31] The difference between glittering Mayfair and dull Philadelphia seemed to erase four years of American fame and marital misery, the stormy vision of a wasted life was forgotten, and she became, once more, the darling of London society.

That she cut a theatrical swathe through London life is attested to by Jane Welsh Carlyle, who recalls the startling arrival of Kemble at the Carlyle House in Cheyne Walk in February 1837. Making his way with "the fair Intellectuals" (as Jane Carlyle ironically describes it in a letter to John Sterling), Thomas Carlyle is stunned to find "Mrs. Pierce Butler" bolting in "upon his studies, out of the atmosphere as it were, in riding-habit, cap and whip (but no shadow of a horse, only a carriage—the whip, I suppose being to whip the cushions with, for the purpose of keeping her hand in practice)—my inexperienced Scotch Domestic remaining entirely in a nonplus whether she had let in 'a leddy or a gentleman'!"[32] That Kemble dressed flamboyantly in male riding clothes and that she vigorously flourished her whip suggests the fondness for cross-dressing that became more pronounced after the marriage (a theatrical display of performed defiance against Butler's demands for feminine obedience); dressing as a man was one mode of snubbing Philadelphia society and turning its social prescription for correct feminine behavior upon itself. Hemmed in by the social demand to conform to prescribed codes, Kemble rewrote the roles and refashioned the masks to suit herself.

Later, in the spring of 1837, she behaved more sedately as she walked in Hyde Park with Wordsworth, now nearing seventy and paying a rare visit to the city.

Traveling once more to the country houses of her friends and realizing she would be happiest if she could live in the English countryside, she fought off thoughts of a foolish abandonment of Pierce and financial security, and swore to Anna Jameson that she would never desert America and her duties and that "henceforth England and I are 'Paradises Lost' to each other."[33] In the summer Thérèse Kemble moved to the Weybridge cottage, and Charles and Adelaide set off for Carlsbad in the hope that the waters would improve his health and that various social connections in the music world would launch Adelaide's career as an opera singer. During Fanny's absence in America, Adelaide's musical gifts, previously overshadowed by her sister's celebrity, had matured, and she was now recognized as a highly promising soprano. Kemble was left alone in London, but not lonely. She dined regularly with Sydney Smith, the witty essayist and one of the founders of the *Edinburgh Review*; she told him stories of her Edinburgh year and he amused her with barbed comments about all their friends. Invited in midsummer to Oatlands, the Leveson-Gower country house where in 1830 she had fallen in love with Augustus Craven, and knowing that Pierce was on his way to England, she expressed a powerful sense of impending loss in a poem titled "A Farewell: Written at Oatlands." The last two stanzas of the four-stanza poem read as follows:

> I shall fly no more on my fiery steed,
> O'er the springing sward,—through the twilight wood;
> Nor rein my courser, and check my speed,
> By the lonely grange, and the haunted flood.
>   …
> At fragrant noon, I shall lie no more
> 'Neath the oak's broad shade in the leafy dell:
> The sun is set,—the day is o'er,—
> The summer is past;—farewell!—farewell![34]

By the middle of August 1837 Kemble was in a seaside boardinghouse in Crosby just outside Liverpool, "to meet and to be met." Since the Pennsylvania Constitutional Convention would take only a brief adjournment, Pierce had informed her they would return almost immediately to America, dashing her hope that they might join her father and sister in Germany. After a brief visit to London, they were back in Liverpool in early September awaiting passage to America. Almost exactly nine months after Pierce landed in Liverpool, Fanny gave birth on May 28, 1838, to her second daughter, Fan, and the resumption of sexual relations with Pierce when he arrived in Liverpool compelled her to confront the rocky history and uncertain future of her marriage. Back in America, in late October, she wrote to Harriet St. Leger that she was exhausted after the voyage and that she was awaiting a summons from Pierce to join him in Harrisburg. After ten months apart from her husband, she knew he was devising more elaborate means than before to curb her public voice.

Living Alone

While in Harrisburg with Pierce, Kemble lapsed into a serious depression. Attending the convention debates pointedly reminded her of the eloquence to be found at a London dinner table, and the awkward rhetoric of the "uncultivated men, unlettered and ungrammared" who were Pierce's fellow delegates appalled her, although she did manage to concede that many of them were shrewd and sensible. She wrote dejectedly to Harriet St. Leger, rehearsing the complaints about her life that had been silenced by ten months in London: "I live alone—much alone bodily, more alone mentally; I have no intimates, no society, no intellectual intercourse whatever; and I give myself up, as I never did in my life before, to mere musing, reverie, and speculation."[35] Brought down from the exhilaration of London's sophisticated rush, tormented by the memory of how, in England, her mind had seemed to "flow back into its former channels," and unable to muster the energy on which she could usually rely to bring her out of depression, she sank into inertia.

Anna Jameson arrived in Philadelphia in November, a "short, sad visit" for Fanny, and her impressions of the Butler family give a very different story from the miserable picture Kemble had painted in her letters to Harriet: Butler Place was a most comfortable house, fitted up in true English style; Sarah was a sweet, spirited, and healthy child; and Kemble was "brimful of genius, poetry and power and eloquence, yet is an excellent wife, an excellent mother, and an excellent manager of a household."[36] Jameson marveled at the ferocity with which Kemble was reading, and discussing at length, a biography of Walter Scott, Thomas Carlyle's *French Revolution*, and a quite amazing amount of Milton: the *Treatise on Divorce, Areopagitica, Letters, Apologies for Smectymnus, Denunciations Against Episcopacy*.[37] The symptoms of Kemble's emotional instability are registered in her friends' very different impressions of her during this summer: when Kemble wrote to Harriet, she was at a very low point; when Jameson saw her she was in one of her exuberantly active periods. The emotional seesaw continued through the winter of 1837–38, with Kemble at one moment writing to Adelaide that her life flowed with uninterrupted monotony, and at another dispatching a vividly detailed letter to Harriet in which she presents an incisive critique of Harriet Martineau's *Soci-*

ety in America, which had just been published. The relationship between Kemble and Martineau had always been somewhat tense, and it continued to be so: Martineau could not tolerate Kemble's emotional skittishness, and Kemble thought Martineau's theories about female suffrage and community of property (Martineau was in favor of both) went too far. Kemble attributed Martineau's coolness to her inability to be as "thorough-going an abolitionist as the rest of her friends in America," and although they saw each other at odd times in the years to come, their friendship was always cool.

In July the Butler family, now composed of Fanny, Pierce, Sarah, and two-month-old Fan, left for Rockaway Beach on Long Island for a six-week respite from the oppressive heat of Philadelphia. Rockaway proved both a delight and a trial. Kemble loved the magnificent ten-mile beach and the sight of steamships about to begin or end their transatlantic crossings, but she loathed the enormous dining room of the large wood-frame hotel where they stayed, and she found nothing but constraint and discomfort in the perpetual presence of a crowd of strangers. The bathing arrangements were intolerable: she was carried down to the beach in an omnibus with other female bathers and had to undress in one of two small bathing huts set up by the water. Kemble loved an audience but not one composed of curious American women. Also at Rockaway was Philip Hone, the former mayor of New York whom she had met when she first arrived in America, and his impression of her at Rockaway attests, once more, to the vibrant intelligence that beguiled so many people. In his diary he notes that the American *Journal* never really offended him; he only thought it a pity that "a woman so brilliant and talented, who was capable of better things" should have blemished her literary reputation by allowing the publication of "inconsiderate, girlish remarks." Pegging her as a girlish Frances Trollope, he believed that her talents were worthy of better employment, which suggests he probably paid attention only to her tactless assessments of American manners and morals and ignored the persuasive power of her social critique. When they danced at a ball in Rockaway on August 10, Hone was bewitched by Kemble's flashing, expressive eyes and her brilliant talk, convinced again that it was the "circumstances of her early life" (the raffish world of the theater) that had encouraged in her "a self-destructive waywardness of thought."[38]

In late August, Pierce went back to Harrisburg and she traveled with the children to Lenox for a visit with the Sedgwick family, the only people, she announced dramatically to Harriet St. Leger, "among whom I have found mental companionship since I have been in this country."[39] She stayed at the Red Inn, which was used as the guest quarters for visitors to the Sedgwick family, and the following six weeks were packed with everything that delighted her: an absence of ceremony, vigorous horseback riding, much lively talk, and regular singing and dancing. The chance to be with the only Americans with whom she claimed to have any intellectual or emotional sympathy was enhanced by two other guests at the Red Inn: Mary and Fanny Appleton. The latter married Henry Wadsworth Longfellow and had fallen under Kemble's spell at Newport, Rhode Island, when the Butlers were on their honeymoon. Kemble's devoted admirer Catharine Sedgwick was "Aunt Kitty" to Fanny and to Mary Appleton, and Mary was as enthralled by Fanny Butler as her sister had been at Newport. She wrote from Lenox on September 5, 1838, that after breakfast Kemble would appear in the most marvelous riding costume, "white pants (*tout a fait a la mode des messieurs*) and habit, with a black velvet jacket and cap, very picturesque, and when mounted on her own fine steed a picture that puts Miss Sedgwick in raptures."[40] In the evening Kemble, dressed always in white muslin with bare arms and neck, would sing old ballads with such pathos and nervous excitement that she would visibly pale under her brown complexion. Enchanted by her talk, Fanny Appleton wrote that Kemble discoursed on "deep topics" so earnestly and intelligently that her face would be kindled "to wonderful shiftings beyond any countenance I ever saw. Her soul seems always boiling at fever-heat, and she reminds me in her various accomplishments and brilliant expressions of some gypsy Fenella. There is surely some southern, un-Saxon blood in her veins."[41]

Some of the animated evening talk concerned abolition, and with the looming possibility of a journey to the Georgian plantations now that Pierce and John had inherited the property, Kemble began to think more deeply about slavery—particularly in the light of her earlier reading of the writings of William Ellery Channing, to whom she had been introduced by Catharine Sedgwick in New York. Channing was pastor of the Federal Street Unitarian Church in Boston, an intellectual and spiritual leader of American Unitarianism in the nineteenth century, and admired in New England religious and artistic circles for his many published lectures, sermons, and essays. Kemble had read his influential book on slavery and thought it written with judgment and moderation, yet fired with abundant warmth and energy. The opening sentences of *Slavery* appealed directly to her strong sense of duty: "The first question to be proposed by a rational being is, not what is profitable, but what is Right. Duty must be primary, prominent, most conspicuous among the objects of human thought and pursuit."[42] Channing asserts that slavery is first and always a moral question. When Kemble set off for Georgia in the late autumn of 1838, shortly after the return from Lenox, her moral repugnance to slavery and her duty to oppose it were foremost in her mind. She wrote in her diary before leaving Philadelphia, "I am going to Georgia prejudiced against slavery, for I am an Englishwoman in whom the absence of such a prejudice would be disgraceful."[43]

When Pierce had read the "long and vehement treatise against negro slavery" that Fanny had wished to include in her American *Journal*, he reminded her that their present and future fortune depended on slavery, and he had sarcastically demanded to know just how she would conduct herself if she were living on a plantation. She had replied that she would welcome joyfully the chance to place their slaves "upon a more humane and Christian footing." When she recounted this exchange in her memoirs, she added that she had been unable to understand, at the time, "the amazement and dismay, the terror and disgust, with which such theories as those I have expressed . . . must have filled every member of the American family with which my marriage had connected me; I must have appeared to them nothing but a mischievous madwoman."[44] Yet her "theories" were hardly outlandish in the context of the English political circles in which she had moved before she came to America, grounded as they were in early nineteenth-century beliefs that dedication to Christian duty would bring about social and moral betterment, that under the direction and example of humane Christian governance, slaves should be emancipated, educated, and allowed to become self-governing members of the British Empire.

When Kemble married, she began living in a city renowned as a center of abolitionist activity. The Philadelphia Anti-Slavery Society, also known as the American Anti-Slavery Society, was founded in 1833, and on May 14, 1838, the second national meeting of the Anti-Slavery Convention of American Women opened at the newly built Pennsylvania Hall on Sixth Street, the home of John Greenleaf Whittier's antislavery newspaper, *Pennsylvania Freeman*. On the second day of the convention a resolution was passed calling for an end to slavery in the District of Columbia. On May 16, seventeen thousand pro-slavery protesters gathered outside the building and threatened violence against an integrated assembly. The mayor of Philadelphia shut down the convention and the women delegates marched from the hall in integrated pairs. Arsonists then set the place ablaze, which did not deter the women delegates, who assembled the next day in a nearby schoolhouse. Kemble did not attend this convention, in part because Pierce had expressly forbidden it and also because she was just two weeks away from giving birth to her second daughter. In an ironic aside to Anna Jameson in July 1838, she notes that "The friends of good order, in this excellent city of brotherly love, have been burning down a large new building erected for *purposes of free discussion*, because Abolition meetings were being held in it."[45] When Harriet Martineau heard of the Philadelphia outrages, she wrote to her friend that she never ceased to wonder "at the extent and intensity of the bigotry still existing in that city."[46]

On September 3, 1838, Thérèse Kemble died at her Weybridge cottage with her son John at her bedside. Charles and Adelaide Kemble were in Milan, making good headway in launching Adelaide's career as an opera singer, and Charles read of his wife's death in a newspaper that provided Europeans with English news. Kemble heard of her mother's death in a letter from a close family friend, and in her memoirs she makes little reference to it beyond a mere notation, which is consistent with the guarded discussion of Thérèse found in all her writings: while she paid tribute to her mother's energy and vitality, she also recorded the misery she inflicted on her children with her tantrums and impatience. At the time, too, Kemble was preoccupied with the pending journey south, to a part of the country where the whole manner of existence was repugnant to her. Her description of the eight-day journey to Georgia rivals in its evocation of the landscape the best of narratives written by English travelers in America. In the form of a very long letter to Harriet St. Leger, it begins with the departure by train from Philadelphia and concludes with the arrival at the low, reedy banks of Butler Island, where the wharf is crowded with Butler's slaves, jumping, dancing, shouting, laughing, clapping their hands, "and using the most extravagant and ludicrous gesticulations to express their ecstacy at our arrival."[47]

North to South

The train journey south through Delaware was a sustained offense to Kemble's sensible views about healthy eating and regular exercise. Since it was winter, the railroad cars were heated by anthracite-burning stoves, around which people crowded themselves; the aisles were covered by spit from the tobacco chewers; and the babies on the train were constantly being stuffed with heavy cakes by their sallow-cheeked and rickety-teethed mothers. Sarah's rosy, blooming complexion and her mother's insistence on feeding her only bread, milk, and meat puzzled these American women: how could a child look so healthy on such a meager, sugarless diet? After switching from the train to a steamboat to cross the Susquehanna, and then back to the train to take them to Baltimore, they embarked on another steamboat to take them down the coast, a journey that in Kemble's description began to assume the qualities of a trek through the wilderness. She consoled herself through most of it by reading *Oliver Twist*.

As they boarded a train at Portsmouth, Virginia, she encountered the first slaves she had ever seen and what had been a "theoretical" opposition to slavery, deeply grounded in her moral repugnance, became an actuality: dirty, poorly clothed, and walking with a kind of "lazy recklessness," they proffered, to Kemble's horror, a "little mahogany-colored imp" as a servant for three-and-a-half-year-old Sarah. The sight of the slaves made graphically real what she was heading for, and the desolation of the landscape, forlorn beyond anything she had ever seen, signaled to her the wasteland ahead. The vast swamp along which they passed was shadowed by melancholy cypress and juniper trees, their branches woven together with a hideous matting of giant creepers that "clung round their stems, and hung about the dreary forest like a drapery of withered snakes."[48] Nothing seemed to live or move in this "pestilential waste" except for rattlesnakes seeking cover in the reedy black ponds, and Kemble was relieved when they got to North Carolina and the flat pine barrens covered with wild myrtle.

When they reached their destination for that night, Kemble felt she had penetrated the innermost point of the southern wilderness: a forlorn and miserable inn offered them a dilapidated room with grime-smeared walls and dirt-covered windows, and they were served a chicken dinner swimming in black grease and accompanied by lumps of hot dough. At first light they reboarded the train and journeyed to the end of the railroad line, where they piled into three four-horse coaches. In midmorning, somewhere in the middle of North Carolina, they were fed begrimed eggs and stale bread covered in something that called itself butter, but which to Kemble resembled tallow. Little more than a year ago she had been dining at Holland House in London, and at Butler Place she had insisted on healthy and nutritious food for the whole family; this revolting stuff was even more offensive than the sweet and stodgy diet of the North she so disliked. At the end of this day, as the "dreary waste" around them suggested the "very shaggy edges of creation," the party was housed in the large cottage of a former colonel in Washington's army. At this point, the Butler family had been traveling for three full days and two nights, and the next morning, weary and barely washed, they took the overheated train to the point where they boarded the first of two steamboats that would take them to Georgia.

Kemble thought Charleston moderately pleasing, a little like Southampton in England with its narrow streets and brick houses, and although she considered the "colored" servants at their hotel stupid and lazy, she was pleased and surprised to find them so unconquerably good-humored. She was startled to hear at nine o'clock in the evening the sound of bells tolling and drums beating: the curfew for "colored" people to return home, a sound she had always associated with the dread of foreign invasion, not with the threat of "domestic insurrection." After a few days in Charleston, they boarded the steamship to Savannah, stopping on the way at Edisto (famous at the time for producing the finest American cotton), where they inspected a ginning house and saw how the cotton was freed from the seed. At last, Kemble clutching Sarah, the baby nurse holding Fan (who, incidentally, Kemble had breastfed throughout the journey, often huddled in the corner of the railroad carriage), and Pierce Butler superintending their baggage, they arrived at the mouth of the Altamaha River that led to the small town of Darien. As their boat grazed the side of the wharf it seemed to Kemble "as if we had touched the outer bound of civilized creation." The strangeness of this scene, the savage woods beyond the wharf, and the "singular contrasts" in her life sharply apparent to her at this moment brought on a flood of tears.

Kemble, of course, was no Victorian explorer journeying into the wilderness, yet the imagery of desolation, decay, and savagery that characterizes her landscape descriptions often resembles the writing of men and women who undertook perilous and discomfiting journeys. As their boat neared Butler Island, passing by banks covered in giant, straggling cypress trees with branches covered in gray moss, the helmsman sounded out their approach on a huge conch shell; when landed, they were thronged "like a swarm of bees," seized, pulled, pushed, carried, and all but lifted in the air by the clamorous multitude of slaves. As soon as she could, Kemble ventured out for a short walk, something desperately needed after ten days of hellish travel, and she was immediately surrounded by what she described to Harriet as a "cloud of these dingy dependents," eager to touch her velvet pelisse. She was in the midst of people whose labor sustained her existence.

The arrival on Butler Island prompted hysterical tears similar to those she had shed when she arrived in New York, as well as a sense of shame at the sight of the slaves, which she had never before experienced. But what shocked her to the roots of her already fragile emotional being were the rapid changes in her life. Here she was, an ocean's distance away from London and fifteen hundred miles from Philadelphia, doubly dislocated from where she had grown up and where she had been trying, with little success, to shape a new life. Now, she seemed to have gone back in time. Everything was so wild, so peculiar, so full of alligators and snakes that she almost expected to see the "canoes of the red man shoot from the banks, which were so lately the possession of his race alone."[49] Rather than the noise of London carriages rattling through the streets or the brisk canter of her horse down Walnut Street in Philadelphia, she heard the perpetual noise of two steam engines working the rice mills. Each morning she was astonished by the contrast between what was around her and her former life. The most dreadfully different thing was that she was surrounded by her own property, by slaves eager to please but repellent to her in their ignorance, dirt, and stupidity.

Kemble arrived in Georgia knowing full well that she was powerless to alter the economic system that kept the slaves in bondage and the Butler family in wealth, but she had always hoped she might improve their conditions. Initially, this seemed impossible, but as time went on she did manage to achieve a great deal. Pierce had taunted her with his belief that when she actually saw the slaves she would change her views, would see that although they were, in fact, slaves, they

were not constantly flogged, were reasonably well fed, and were happy in their ser-
vitude. Her *Journal of a Residence on a Georgian Plantation* proved him wrong. She
had indeed "touched the outer bound of civilized creation," as she put it to Harriet
St. Leger at the end of the long letter that describes her journey to Georgia. How
was she to live in this perilous place, to endure the inescapable sense of futility, to
live with a man who daily justified an economic system she found deeply immoral
and profoundly uncivilized? To remain sane, she would need to balance her identities as Butler wife, mother, and slave owner, as well as her implacable opposition to
the system that literally put food on her table. Mustering her theatrical technique
to manage the dramatic nature of what she witnessed, she creates a theater of
slavery, played out in the journal she began to keep of her time on the plantations
during 1838–39. Consciously or not, she writes a powerful and withering rejoinder
to the *Quarterly Review*'s refusal in 1835 to grant her no other identity than that of
former actress unable to discard the trappings of jostling, forwardness, and vulgarity. In the writing of her *Journal*, she may be said to recuperate the identity of role-
player assigned to her by reviewers, a moralizing public, and a hostile society: she
rewrites this identity in such a way that role-playing becomes a modus vivendi, a
refutation of roles written for her by a patronizing patriarchal culture and a means
of articulating one of the most harrowing critiques of slavery found in American
literature.

A Dreary Lesson of Human Suffering

I do wonder, as I walk among them, well-fed, well-clothed, young, strong, idle, doing nothing but ride and drive about all day, a woman, a creature like themselves, who have borne children too, what sort of feeling they have toward me. I wonder it is not one of murderous hate—that they should lie here almost dying with unrepaid labor for me.
—Fanny Kemble, *Journal of a Residence on a Georgian Plantation*

A Theater of Slavery

Fanny Kemble's experience in Georgia was far removed from romanticized notions that exist in the popular imagination of prebellum life on a Southern plantation. Rather than being a colonnaded white mansion, the plain brick Butler house consisted of three rooms and an attached outside kitchen; rather than being protected by smiling in-house black servants, Kemble was confronted daily by hundreds of female slaves who worked long hours in the fields and expected her to intercede on their behalf with the master; and instead of living with an indulgent father or adoring husband, she shared a home with Pierce Butler, a man she no longer respected, and for whom her glamorous appeal had long faded and her tearful intercessions were to become intolerable. From the elegant gentleman-farmer's residence outside Philadelphia that she had furnished to resemble a small English country house, staffed by six servants and three gardeners, after a ten-day

journey by train, coach, and steamer, Kemble was deposited on an island populated by nearly eight hundred African slaves. She entered a house furnished with un-
varnished pine tables and chairs; she was served by giggling girls chattering in the
Gullah dialect; and her food was prepared by a gang of cooks who slaughtered the
wild ducks, geese, turkeys, and venison that formed the centerpiece of the plantation house diet. The largest room in the house, sixteen by fifteen feet, was used for
sitting and eating, the second was the Butler bedroom, and the third, immediately
over the downstairs bedroom, housed Sarah, Fan, and Margery O'Brien, the baby
nurse. Pierce's dressing room and office was just off the Butler bedroom, and it
was there, Kemble noted drily, that he "gives audiences to the Negroes, redresses
grievances, distributes red woolen caps (a singular gratification to a slave), shaves
himself, and performs the other offices of his toilet."[1] On his first visit to the large
plantations jointly inherited with his brother, John, from their aunt Frances, the
daughter of Major Pierce Butler, Pierce was in his element. The estate was located
on three islands in the estuary of the Altamaha River, the principal of which was
Butler Island, a tract of about two thousand acres devoted almost exclusively to
the cultivation of rice; next were tracts on St. Simons and Little St. Simons islands, upon which cotton and rice, respectively, were raised.[2]

The only part of the house that Kemble could almost call her own was a rough-
hewn table covered with a green baize cloth that stood at one end of the main
room. In that spot, almost every evening, she sat and wrote many letters to Elizabeth Sedgwick, sister-in-law of Catharine Sedgwick; the letters were based on her
journal entries and on random notes of what she had observed on that particular
day.[3] Elizabeth ran a girls' school called the "Hive" situated in Lenox, and Kemble
had been deeply influenced by her dedicated abolitionism as, indeed, she had been
by the moral and political values of the entire Sedgwick family. It was natural,
therefore, that Elizabeth should be her principal correspondent when she was on
the plantation, and the many letters that she wrote to her became her Georgian
Journal, modeled on the text published in 1834 that Mathew Lewis (known always as "Monk" Lewis after the sensational success of his gothic novel *The Monk*
published in 1796) kept on a visit to his Jamaican estate. When Kemble returned
to Philadelphia she made a fair copy of the letters, shaped her notes into a coher-
ent narrative, and then put the whole thing away. Her public position was that it
would be a "breach of confidence" for her to expose the Butler estate to open condemnation. In actuality, Pierce threatened to deny her access to the children if she
published one word of her impressions of life on Butler and St. Simons islands.
It was not until May 1863, when they had been long divorced and Sarah and Fan
had reached their majority, that Kemble allowed the *Journal* to appear. Distressed

by the "ignorant and mischievous nonsense" that was being bandied about by her English friends, she published in the hope that her eyewitness account of plantation life would discourage English intervention in the American Civil War on the side of the South.[4] How far she succeeded in this aim is difficult to judge, but we do know that the *Journal* went into a second printing and that excerpts were circulated in pamphlet form.[5]

In an extraordinary winter that dramatized as nothing had before the amazing alteration of her position from celebrated actress courted by London society to alienated wife of a slave owner on the sea islands of Georgia, Kemble produced the most graphic and moving of all her published writing. The *Journal* records the harrowing conditions in which the Butler slaves lived and worked; it evokes the lush, beautiful, and exotic scenery of the islands; and it documents Kemble's growing disgust for her husband.[6]

Writing was Kemble's salvation while she was on the plantations. Through the imaginative creation of a scene, she found a way if not to accept what she witnessed then at least to endure it; and theatrical distance gave her the means to negotiate her complex moral position. As the wife of a slave owner, she was also a slave owner, and she was married to a man who had little interest in her anguished efforts to improve conditions on the plantations. As Kemble describes his views in the *Journal*, the slaves were not too badly treated, things had always been that way, and his wife was a hysterical embarrassment to his authority. Casting herself in the part of Englishwoman in America, assuming rhetorical stances derived from her theatrical attitudes, and appropriating for her own ends the imposition of proper roles for the plantation wife, Kemble sat down every evening and produced a sad account of what was happening to her. In the process of creating her textual theater of slavery and abolition, she began to see the way out of her difficulties. When she left Georgia, her letters finished, her supervision of renovating the infirmary over, her tearful pleadings with Pierce at an end, she knew that she would never return and that her future would be away from him, somewhere she might recover her moral and political self-respect and build on the controversial success she had achieved with the publication of her American *Journal*. Writing at her desk in the evenings about her complicity in the harrowing practices of slavery forced her to examine the circumstances and decisions that had brought her there. It also enabled her to see a world elsewhere, to consider seriously, without the usual hysteria or depression that accompanied examination of her marriage, what she might do if she were to leave Pierce. The following long description of the common pattern of her evenings shows her at the crucial work of writing, which probably saved her from impotent despair when she was in Georgia.

The Calibanish wonderment of all my visitors at the exceedingly coarse
and simple furniture and rustic means of comfort of my abode is very
droll. I have never inhabited any apartment so perfectly devoid of what
we would consider the common decencies of life; but to them, my rude
chintz-covered sofa and common pine-wood table, with its green baize
cloth, seem the adornings of a palace; and often in the evening, when my
bairns are asleep, and M [Margery] upstairs keeping watch over them,
and I sit writing this daily history for your edification, the door of the
great barnlike room is opened stealthily, and one after another, men and
women come trooping silently in, their naked feet falling all but inaudibly
on the bare boards as they betake themselves to the hearth, where they
squat down on their hams in a circle, the bright blaze from the huge pine
logs, which is the only light of this half of the room, shining on their
sooty limbs and faces, and making them look like a ring of ebony idols
surrounding my domestic hearth. I have had as many as fourteen at a
time squatting silently there for nearly half an hour, watching me writing
at the other end of the room. The candles on my table give only light
enough for my own occupation, the firelight illuminates the rest of the
apartment; and you cannot imagine anything stranger than the effect of
all these glassy whites of eyes and grinning white teeth turned toward me,
and shining in the flickering light. I very often take no notice of them at
all, and they seem perfectly absorbed in contemplating me. My evening
dress probably excites their wonder and admiration no less than my rapid
and continuous writing, for which they have sometimes expressed compassion, as if they thought it must be more laborious than hoeing ... they
troop out as noiselessly as they entered, like a procession of sable dreams,
and I go off in search, if possible, of whiter ones.[7]

A white European woman on an island sits and writes, and illiterate African slaves squat and watch. It is no wonder that Kemble evoked *The Tempest* (the
Shakespeare play she loved above all others) as her principal literary reference,
as she cast herself as a kind of female Prospero performing magic writing before
enslaved "Calibanish" dependents.[8] *The Tempest* had been engraved in her memory
when Bellina Grimani told her the story of the exiled father and daughter, and
for many years she had wistfully imagined herself as Miranda to her father's Prospero. When she had seen the painting of Prospero and Miranda, she had wept
for the pain of the exiled father; now she began to weep for the Butler slaves—
tears of supplication as she pleaded with Pierce for relief of their harsh working
conditions, and tears of frustration as he maintained an adamantine resistance

to her entreaties. Her memories of slavery haunted her for many years after she left Georgia: Anne Thackeray Ritchie, Thackeray's daughter, recalls that Kemble "would sometimes start to her feet in agitation and passionate declamation; she who with streaming eyes and wrung heart had walked about the plantations. . . . To her free and ruling nature every hour of bondage must have seemed nothing short of torture."[9]

The "Calibanish" wonderment of her slaves is not Kemble's only reference to *The Tempest* in her Georgian letters. She wryly observed to Elizabeth Sedgwick that until she arrived, the island was as innocent of "bribery, corruption, and pauperism . . . as Prospero's isle of refuge," but now she was bribing the slave children to wash their faces.[10] She says that the slaves' virtually incomprehensible speech— "a Negro mode of talking"—is just like that of Caliban, whom she describes in her essay on *The Tempest* as a "gross and uncouth powerful savage,"[11] and that the foul smell of an old female slave reminds her of Trinculo's soliloquy over Caliban, an allusion to Trinculo's observation that Caliban seems neither man nor fish, neither dead nor alive, yet exudes "a very ancient and fishlike smell."[12] And the contorted, witchlike form of Caliban's mother, Sycorax ("with age and envy" grown into a "hoop"), lurks in Kemble's descriptions of the scarred female slaves who petition her for longer release from field labor after childbirth. To be sure, these pitiful, broken women possess none of Sycorax's destructive magic, yet the "savage vehemence" with which one of them suddenly tears up her scanty clothing and exhibits a spectacle with which Kemble was "inconceivably shocked and sickened" conjures up Sycorax's deformed female body. This particular slave displayed to her owner genitals deformed by incessant childbearing and field labor, a "beautiful and wonderful structure," Kemble lamented, "made the victim of ignorance, folly, and wickedness."[13]

If Kemble casts herself as Prospero and her squatting slaves as Caliban, then her Ariel was Jack, a slave appointed by Pierce to be her special guardian and attendant. Jack was a man of "very extraordinary intelligence and faithfulness," intensely curious about the world beyond the islands, and eager to talk as he accompanied Kemble on her exploration of the inlets in a rowboat, crewed by two oarsmen and a steersman.[14] She spent more time with Jack than she did with Pierce—fishing, rowing, riding a fine stallion normally deployed as a plow horse— and she did so without the fear that she knew haunted most Southern women: "every Southern *woman* to whom I have spoken on the subject has admitted to me that they live in terror of their slaves."[15] Trusting her instincts and relying on his intelligence, Kemble felt no need for "white companionship and supervision" when she was with Jack: as a reward for his companionship and fidelity, he was granted the privilege of keeping a pig when Fanny and Pierce left the plantations.

In the vivid description that she fashioned for Elizabeth of the slave owner mistress at her writing table, Kemble creates a tableau in which the placement of the furniture, the lighting, and the movement of the actors are carefully arranged. In creating an offstage melodrama, she may be said to rely on models of "highly charged emotion" and the personification of "absolutes like good and evil" that Elaine Hadley identifies as a sign of the prevalence of the rhetoric of nineteenth-century melodrama in narratives of political dissent.[16] Kemble wanted Elizabeth, a woman to whom slavery was an abhorrent practice but not a felt reality, to visualize the shape of the barnlike room, the writing table at one end and the blazing hearth at the other. She wanted her to hear the tentative, stealthy opening of the door, the barely audible sound of black feet on the bare pine floor, and the shifting of weary black bodies as they settled before the fire; she wanted her to see the squatting slaves, their "sooty limbs and faces" gleaming in such a way that they resembled a ring of ebony idols; and she wanted her to see them as the slave flesh that they were, the means of privileged existence for the woman who was writing at the other end of the room. Kemble wanted them to be felt by Elizabeth as *bodies*, their stark, frightening, and almost comically bizarre corporal reality signaled in "the glassy whites of eyes and grinning white teeth." The elegantly dressed abolitionist wife sits in the house of the plantation master, doing her "rapid and continuous writing," but at the same time she distances herself from the scene in the process of presenting it. Constructing the tableau in which she is a performing writer, she occupies a moral and cultural space between complicity in the practice of slavery and its literary representation.

The one role in Georgia that Kemble seemed less to appropriate than to inflect with her own identity was more wrenching than any she had undertaken onstage: that of plantation mistress. Confronted daily by the custom that required her to entertain pleas, particularly from the women, for alleviation of their burdens, she listened sympathetically, almost always in tears, unable to distance herself from the disclosure of unspeakable conditions in the slave quarters, in the infirmary, and in the fields.[17] Kemble had never disguised her distaste for the vulgarity of the theatrical profession, but when she sought to fulfill her responsibilities on the plantations, her former life seemed dignified, even magnificent, when compared to her present position of being supported by the unpaid labor of these suffering people. On the journey to Georgia, she had imagined herself in the role of an Englishwoman in a strange land, the curious Victorian woman traveling into the uncivilized scrub of North and South Carolina.[18] On her arrival, rather than recuperating a socially prescribed role for subversive ends, as she had done in Philadelphia, she immersed herself as completely as she was able into the part of plantation mistress, flavoring her performance in that role with her own English identity. Her setting was islands that seemed otherworldly in their vegetation, their climate, and their population of slaves who, because of the isolation of the islands and minimal contact with their white owners and overseers, had retained through generations the customs of the Congolese, Ibo, and Gabon tribes from which they had been snatched. What she brought to this part was her ingrained sense of being a civilized Englishwoman in a barbaric place, witnessing barbaric customs, with the telling difference that the barbarians were white slave owners and overseers, not black, colonized peoples.

To Elizabeth Sedgwick, she wondered how slaves fared on plantations where there was no "crazy Englishwoman to weep, and entreat, and implore, and upbraid for them, and no master willing to listen to such appeals."[19] As things turned out, Pierce grew bored with her weeping and impatient with her upbraiding and was relieved to take her back to Philadelphia, but not before the "general theoretic abhorrence of an Englishwoman" with which she had come to Georgia became a furious cry in the face of raw reality. In the dreamy walks along the canals and in her visits to the hellhole of the slave infirmary, she discovered that Butler and St. Simons islands were places of "material beauty and moral degradation."[20] When writing to Elizabeth about the discrepancy between the ideals of a nation founded on individual liberty and its practice of buying and selling human bodies, she distanced herself from America by referring to it as this "land of yours," and when she wonders how "my own people in that blessed England of my birth would marvel if they could suddenly have a vision" of her receiving petitions from her husband's female slaves, she cast those English friends as an audience who might view the spectacle of Kemble performing her role as plantation mistress. And when she relates the story of a female slave who has had sixteen children (of whom only two are living) and who was repeatedly flogged when she was pregnant, she concludes, "And to all this I listen—I, an Englishwoman, the wife of the man who owns these wretches."[21] To listen to such stories and then to reconcile her politics and her practice demanded from Kemble an emotional and intellectual equilibrium that under the best of circumstances was often difficult for her to summon.

Defending himself against his wife's humiliating tirades (she would become hysterical in front of the overseers), Pierce evaded culpability by attributing Kemble's behavior either to her unstable personality or to an aggressive sense of national identity. Charging, in his divorce statement, that she had come to America "with a prejudice amounting to hatred" and that everything that she found different from what she was accustomed to she pronounced to be inferior and wrong,[22] he insisted her feminist ideas and her abolitionist views about his potential source of considerable wealth had never been conveyed to him before they were married, which seems highly unlikely given Kemble's temperamental incompatibility for dissembling. Skilled in theatrical technique and adept in the appropriation and performance of roles to suit her own moral and political purposes, Kemble was not disingenuous in matters of her own beliefs and opinions. Pierce was correct, however, in his comprehension of Kemble's participation in the political critique of hypocrisy that was common to virtually all nineteenth-century English writing about America. After she had seen firsthand the number of racially mixed children on the Butler plantations, Kemble ridiculed those who speak of a "natural repugnance in all whites to any alliance with the black race," and she found it almost comically ironic that Americans enacted laws against racial mixing as they simultaneously termed such mixing "abhorrent to nature." If racial mixing were so fundamentally repugnant, then there would be no need to make it illegal.[23]

When she landed on Butler Island, Kemble was besieged by slave women wanting help for their sick children, and as soon as she was settled into her rustic quarters she set off to visit the slave cabins and the slave infirmary. She never forgot what she saw. The one-room cabins were twelve by fifteen feet, divided by rough wooden partitions, and housed two families sometimes as many as ten in number. Most of the cabins had a rude bedstead, with gray moss for a mattress and "filthy, pestilential-looking blankets for covering." A wide ditch ran immediately behind the cabins, which was filled and emptied daily by the tide. Fowl and ducks traveled in and out through the door left open to the ditch for human waste. Squatting round the dismal wood fire were small children from four to ten years old, too young to work and delegated as babysitters; their job was to carry the babies to their mothers for breastfeeding in the fields. These sights led Kemble to recognize that her particular "corner of work" must be to teach habits of cleanliness, beginning with the penny bribes for a clean baby's face, since she could do nothing about the institution that had created these conditions. She knew, for example, that improving the slave diet or lessening their hours of work was out of the question: the Butler slaves were herded into the fields at daybreak, allowed to eat the first of their meals at noon (cornmeal), and allowed to cook their second (cornmeal again) when they returned from the fields in the evening, after at least six hours of afternoon labor. At the very least slaves worked close to eleven hours a day harvesting rice and picking cotton.

Kemble's first visit to the infirmary seemed, quite literally, a descent into hell, a demonic "spectacle" she recounted as shock theater to Elizabeth Sedgwick. Dying women were prostate on the floor, without bed, mattress, or pillow, buried in tattered and filthy blankets, and Kemble stood in the midst of these women, unable to speak, the tears pouring from her eyes, pierced with the knowledge that they had spent all their health and strength in "unrequited labor" for the Butler family.

At the moment she stood there, she knew that the husbands, fathers, brothers, and sons of these women were "sweating over the earth, whose produce was to buy for us all the luxuries which health can revel in, all the comforts which can alleviate sickness."[24] The women died from complications of childbirth; their mothers were bent with rheumatism; their babies, if they lived, suffered from lockjaw; and their older children were riddled with pleurisy, peri-pneumonia, and a disease that rotted the joints and led to loss of toes and fingers. Kemble brings down the curtain on this scene with the savage remark that Elizabeth should take notice that "this is the hospital of an estate where the owners are supposed to be humane, the overseer efficient and kind, and the Negroes remarkably well cared for and comfortable."[25] When she returned from the infirmary, she vented her shock and indignation to Pierce and his overseer; the latter responded that when he had taken over nineteen years earlier, the hospital had seemed to be in need of "reform," but, receiving no encouragement from the former manager, Roswell King, Jr., Pierce Butler, or John Butler, he had left it as he found it.

Early in 1839, Roswell King, Jr., arrived at Butler Island for a visit. Given the fact that for nineteen years he had directly governed and abused hundreds of slaves scattered over the two plantations, Kemble was not inclined to like him, but she admitted that she was impressed by his energetic intelligence. King's calmly reasoned view of a brutal system reveals itself in a long letter he wrote to the *Southern Agriculturalist* on September 13, 1828. He argues that most of the injustices perpetrated on the slaves came from the drivers; punishing them out of "private pique" rather than concern about neglect of duty, the drivers refused to believe the slaves could be taught right and wrong or learn the advantages of industry. King believed that "no Negro, with a well stocked poultry house, a small crop advancing, [and] a canoe partly finished" would ever run away.[26] To King, flogging was a last resort; he preferred other methods of discipline such as digging stumps, clearing away trash, or confinement to the plantation for six months, which prohibited "slaves from going to town on Sundays to sell their eggs, poultry, coopers' wares, canoes, and so on. If King is to be believed and if Kemble's account of the slaves having only two meals a day is accurate, then conditions on the Butler plantations would seem to have deteriorated between 1828 and 1838. King describes the slaves' diet in great detail: the cornmeal to which Kemble refers, supplemented by mackerel, beef, pork, and molasses, with the occasional allotment of rum and okra soup with pork for the "little Negroes." King's regime, allowing for the transparent difference between overseer and abolitionist, is not that different from what Kemble would have implemented had she been in a position to run the plantations. Both King and Kemble advocated teaching the slaves industry, perseverance, and cleanliness, and both believed in the power of rewards. Knowing she could not emancipate them, Kemble tried to teach the slaves habits of industrious self-reliance so that they might, with her help, achieve some small improvement in their conditions.

When Kemble's *Journal* was published in 1863, some readers found it difficult to reconcile her seemingly racist judgments of slave habits with her devastating indictment of the institution: how to explain the disjunction, say, between a comment that slaves live more filthily than animals in their lairs and an impassioned attack on their masters? What's more, Kemble often referred to the woolly heads and white grinders of the slaves; their laziness, filthiness, and inconceivable stupidity (as she put it) drove her to distraction, and she railed against the begrimed ignorant "untrained savages" who stumbled around the Butler family.[27] She admired the smooth skin of most of the slaves, a "compensation for the coarse woolly hair," and she liked the faces of the babies since they had not yet developed the nose and mouth "so peculiarly displeasing in their conformation in the face of a Negro man or woman."[28] She bluntly reveals her surprise that one of the boatmen, a splendid basso *profundo*, could speak, let alone sing, given his physical similarity to an ape, orangutan, chimpanzee, or gorilla: "Such stupendous long thin hands, and long flat feet, I did never see off a large quadruped of the ape species."[29] On the other hand, she was much taken by the physical appearance of a slave named Morris who came to request permission to be baptized. Jet black, tall, and straight, with a perfectly oval face and high forehead, he came, she asserted, from an African tribe famous for supplying the West Indian slave market that does "not at all present the ignoble and ugly Negro type, so much more commonly seen here." Thinking about Morris's noble bearing, she speculated that Othello might have come from the same tribe and that if certain Shakespeare critics who were determined to see Othello as a Moor knew of Morris, they would accept Othello as a dignified African hero rather than a Moorish one.

In the context, however, of English nineteenth-century writings about race (which is something different from English writings about slavery), Kemble's dislike of woolly hair and flat noses was not anomalous. Although many Victorian writers and travelers to America assented to the brilliant attack on slavery articulated by Dickens in his *American Notes*,[30] fewer believed that Africans were capable of lifting themselves from the bottom rung of a spurious ladder of civilization. Isabella Bird, the intrepid Englishwoman who rode alone across the stormy Rocky Mountains in the early 1850s, announced that providence had "not endowed the negro with intellectual powers of the highest order."[31] Another Englishwoman, Amelia Murray, a lady-in-waiting to Queen Victoria, traveled through South Carolina in January 1855 and wrote to her court friends back in England that her prejudices and national feelings had been opposed to slavery, but now she was

beginning to change her views: "My compassionate feelings are rapidly changing sides," she confided; the more she saw of slaves, the more she deemed them
"grown-up children. . . . Music, nursing, washing, and cooking are their peculiar
talents, and cheerfulness their special virtue." They would perish if freed and placed
in competition with their former masters: logically, it was in their best interest to
maintain the institution.[32] Kemble's old admirer, William Thackeray, on a visit to
Richmond, Virginia, in 1853, was almost comically offended by the sheer waste of
labor he saw being expended on a plantation: fifteen slaves do the work a London
cook and housemaid do perfectly comfortably on their own, and these "niggers"
are the pick of some eighty or ninety who do nothing but lie around pretending to
be sick. Why, Thackeray asks, wish for a score of Bengal elephants when a single
stout horse is all you need to pull your brougham?[33] In the early 1860s, Anthony
Trollope announced that American "Negroes" have become "a race happier" than
their "still untamed kinsmen in Africa"; inferior to white men "through laws of
nature," they are like children (a common assessment), and none possesses the
capacity for self-maintenance and self-control. Trollope allowed the slim possibility that American "Negroes" might one day, far in the future, become responsible,
hardworking, independent citizens, but given the founding fathers' error in omit-
ting to provide some means for the gradual extinction of slavery, he is not sanguine about this prospect.[34] In the context of much Victorian writing about race,
Kemble's sentiments appear relatively mild and moderately conventional.

Fanny's Islands

Kemble's wanderings through the woods and explorations of the beautiful shal-
low canals that emptied into the Atlantic were a relief after visits to the infirmary
and confrontations with Pierce. With Jack by her side, she delighted in the discovery of shades of green in the shrubbery that she had never seen in England;
she identified profuse wild myrtle, magnificent magnolia bushes, and spiked palmetto; the saffron brightness of the morning sky was unlike anything in England;
and the golden splendor of the sunsets outdid anything she had seen in New York.
Enormous hawks and great turkey buzzards swooped down into the sedges where
the alligators and snakes of the Altamaha River had their "secret bower" and the
glittering evergreens were covered in streaming garlands of fragrant golden cups.
Butler Island was not only her *Tempest* island of exile, it was also the magical forest of *A Midsummer Night's Dream* through which she flitted, Titania-like, admiring mauve flowers that would have done duty as "Oberon's banqueting service."
An exquisite curtain of yellow jasmine seemed to drape the entire island.

A favorite walk took her along the canal dug through the island to transport rice to the grinding mills, and as she marveled at the lushness of the evergreen thickets that lined the canal, she was struck by the immense expense entailed in procuring these very same shrubs for English parks.[35] In Georgia they were used for firewood. She was also amazed by the depth of her emotional and physical calm in the midst of such disturbing sights as slaves sunk up to their knees in the rice fields. As she walked around the islands and was rowed up and down the Altahama River, she was almost tranquilized by the "wild savage loneliness," and the quiet monotony of her days seemed to calm her excitable temperament. Early in her friendship with Harriet St. Leger she had confessed she suffered from a "tendency to imaginary terrors, and I have always felt sure that a determined exercise of self-control would effectually keep them from having the dominion over me." This tendency was exacerbated, she believed, by "certain electrical conditions of the atmosphere."[36] It is possible that the humid somnolence of the islands calmed her when she saw the slaves at work and Pierce exercising his sovereignty as their master. She also believed that one secret of her ability to suffer as acutely as she did, without being made either ill or absolutely miserable, was "the sort of ecstacy which any beautiful thing gives me." Like a Victorian botanist, she knelt at the side of the coral-bordered roads and peered intently into the undergrowth, seeking new, unnamed flora; she lay down in the reeds by the canals and studied the capers of crabs and the variegated colors of the mosses; as she rode her stallion under a canopy of gnarled oaks and mottled vines, she reached up her hand to feel the slippery texture of the leaves. This tranquil immersion in the landscape also prompted her to think about the use of the land, and she concluded that it was going to waste through careless management and proliferation of easy slave labor.

It seemed to her that the vast tracts of sandy soil that supported the luxuriant gardenia bushes, the gnarled oaks, and the fine bay myrtle could also be cultivated to produce olive trees, mulberry bushes, and grapevines: "I cannot help believing that silk, and wine, and oil, may, and will, hereafter become with the present solitary cotton crop, joint possessors of all this now but half-reclaimed wilderness."[37] Kemble not only proposed ways in which the Butler land could be cultivated beyond rice and cotton so that it might resemble something more lushly biblical (Lebanon, say), she also predicted that unless the estate shifted its entire production to rice it would sink financially under the exhaustion of the land through the cultivation of sea-island cotton. In 1838, cotton had been seriously devalued to a shilling a pound (now approximately three English pounds sterling) from a price of half a guinea a pound (thirty pounds English sterling) that it had fetched on the Liverpool exchange in the time of Pierce's grandfather. Southern estate owners, spoiled by the natural abundance of their plantations and the easy availability of slave labor, were letting their land go to ruin, and Kemble was not surprised. Bristling with an air of Northern rectitude and sounding like the English middle-class advocates of hard work who had jostled into Parliament at the time of the Reform Bill in 1832 (as she saw it), she declared to Elizabeth that Southerners were "cursed with indolence, with recklessness, with the sleepy slothfulness" that satisfied an "animal existence."[38]

In the letters evoking an intelligent interest in her surroundings, whether it was to watch, fascinated, as snakes slid into the Altamaha River or to speculate about the possibility of planting olive trees, Kemble found a distraction from writing about slavery. She also found solace in reading. Despite her characteristic confessions of intellectual laziness, she actually read a great deal when she was in Georgia. When she was not writing at her desk, she was reading newspapers and periodicals, keeping herself informed about a Northern world that seemed a million miles away in terms of culture, vegetation, and climate. For example, she read all the congressional speeches that were part of a heated debate on the question of the people's right to petition their representatives for the abolition of slavery in the District of Columbia: she particularly admired a speech delivered by Kentucky senator Henry Clay on February 7, 1839. Clay, an unsuccessful candidate for president in 1824, 1832, and 1844, systematically denounced the abolition movement since it perpetuated the erosion of states' rights. Although Kemble disagreed with Clay's anti-abolition politics, she was committed to the right of individual states to determine their own positions on slavery, a view she did not relinquish until the Civil War. Kemble also much admired another political speech that she read while being rowed up and down the Altamaha River, the stroke of the oars accompanied by the chants of the boatmen, delivered by Congressman Ely Moore of New York on February 4, 1839, and part of the District of Columbia slavery debate. She believed Moore's argument to be the only defensible one yet advanced, which suggests her views were not in total accord with the antislavery majority and that her political positions were sometimes complex, even contradictory. She knew that the Sedgwick family felt differently, but she strongly advocated Moore's position: a believer in autonomy for individual states, he argued that slavery in the District was a local concern and not a matter for the American people as a whole.

Reclining in her boat, reading congressional speeches, and listening to the chants of Gullah-speaking oarsmen, she could not have been more distant or dislocated from Covent Garden, Paris, Niagara Falls, or Philadelphia. As a trained singer, she was especially attentive to the way the chorus, composed entirely of high tenors, would strike in between each phrase of the melody chanted by a single voice. She thought this was "very curious and effective," and wished that some great musical composer could "hear these semisavage performances . . . one or two barbaric chants and choruses might be evoked from them that would make the fortune of an opera."[39] But the "semisavage" lyrics were not always to her liking: a chant that consisted only of the sentiment "God made man, and man makes money!" she thought worthy, but she was troubled by a song that announced "twenty-six black girls not make mulatto yellow girl." She thought it dreadful the slaves would "despise and undervalue their own race and color, which is one of the very worst results of their abject condition."[40]

After almost three months at the rice plantation on Butler Island, Fanny, Pierce, and the children moved to St. Simons, where the cotton plantations were situated. They boarded a strange hybrid vessel named the *Lily*, for Kemble something like a soldier's baggage wagon and an emigrant transport combined, and she wrote to Elizabeth that "all in the blue unclouded weather" they were rowed for fifteen miles down the huge stream by eight oarsmen chanting in tune with their strokes. Kemble often quoted Tennyson in her letters and "The Lady of Shallot" was a special favorite, a poem she evokes in her memoirs when she describes feeling "cursed" by the news that Covent Garden was to be sold; as the strange barge is rowed to St. Simons, she is the "Lady" after she has forsaken her loom, entered her boat, and begun to drift down to her destiny at Camelot. When Fanny and Pierce arrived, they moved into a place even more rustic than the plantation residence on Butler Island: an old, half-decayed, and rattling farmhouse, it demanded all of Kemble's ingenuity to become habitable. Once settled, however, her spirits picked up since St. Simons was more inhabited than Butler, and the isolation she had felt at the rice plantation was remedied somewhat by going to the island church and being invited to dine with her planter neighbors. With Jack by her side, she explored St. Simons, admiring its lushness as much as she had delighted in the vegetation of the rice canals. She also broke the law in undertaking to teach one of the slaves to read, a sixteen-year-old waiter named Aleck; since she was a married woman, Pierce would be charged with the offense were she found out, which gave her some secret satisfaction. Doing this small act of kindness for just one of the slaves caused her to write to Elizabeth that some good must be done when there is "the brain and heart of one human being in contact with another." She added that everyone is answerable for "incalculable opportunities of good and evil in our daily intercourse with every soul with whom we have to deal; every meeting, every parting, every chance greeting, and every appointed encounter, are occasions open to us for which we are to account."[41] Kemble always felt herself accountable. In Georgia, beset by depression and anguished by the incompatibility between Pierce and herself, she never deviated from doing what she thought was her moral duty, and, quite simply and directly, she did try to grasp, every day, every opportunity for doing "good." The best she could hope for on the plantations was that she would have some "influence," although one week of reading lessons for an illiterate slave was nothing in terms of contesting the "evil" in which she was immersed. All who knew Kemble were aware of what Anne Thackeray Ritchie called "her great and fervent piety,"[42] and in Georgia, her religious faith both sustained her in her misery and compelled her to take action.

Late one afternoon, idling in her canoe, a "sort of dreamy stillness" creeping over her, she saw a huge cotton barge making its way down the Altamaha River and felt a barely perceptible heaving of the water, a tilting of the canoe against the wharf. She heard the sound of a "melancholy, monotonous boat horn" from upstream and presently into sight floated a "huge, shapeless, black" form, dark against the sky. As Kemble writes about this moment, she creates a scene of imaginative guilt. The barge assumes a mysterious, menacing, unknowable quality, and she felt it was bearing down upon her in an act of punishment for her transgressions. But she soon realized it was nothing but "a monstrous square box, made of rough planks, put together in the roughest manner possible . . . upon this great tray are piled the swollen, apoplectic-looking cotton bags."[43] Still, that great, dark, looming, monstrous vessel, loaded with cotton picked by the Butler slaves (her own property), came, moving slowly and inexorably down the river to jolt her boat against the wharf, to remind her (as if she needed reminding) of what it was that enabled her privilege.

Pierce Degraded

Although the vegetation on St. Simons was different from that on Butler Island and Kemble's days were enlivened by conversation with her neighbors, one thing remained unchanged: performance in the role of plantation mistress, bound to listen to pleas from women who picked cotton rather than sifted rice. Since the sole means by which Kemble could alleviate the suffering of female slaves was to appeal to her husband, on St. Simons, her distressing ineffectiveness was unchanged. Constantly besieged by "innumerable petitioners," her sympathy intensified by the knowledge that their nakedness clothed her and that their heavy labor maintained her in idleness, she became incrementally disgusted with Pierce as he refused to budge from the cruel codes of slave master. One evening when he was asked to listen to a complaint of overwork from a gang of pregnant women, the feelings of distaste and disrespect she had harbored almost from the start of her marriage reached a boiling point, and this moment signaled the beginning of the end of it, not merely because she and Pierce were so at odds over slavery but because his behavior crystallized, in her eyes, his moral dishonesty.

Mr. [Butler] seemed positively degraded in my eyes as he stood enforcing upon these women the necessity of their fulfilling their appointed tasks. How honorable he would have appeared to me begrimed with the sweat and soil of the coarsest manual labor, to what he then seemed, setting forth to these wretched, ignorant women, as a duty, their unpaid exacted labor! I turned away in bitter disgust. I hope this sojourn among Mr. [Butler]'s slaves may not lessen my respect for him, but I fear it; for the details of slaveholding are so unmanly letting alone every other consideration, that I know not how anyone with a spirit of a man can condescend to them.[44]

For a woman whose emotional equilibrium depended on some form of work—whether conquering the London stage, landscaping Butler Place, cleaning up the infirmary on Butler Island, or writing every evening to Elizabeth—Pierce's laziness and inflexibility made him a "degraded" and emasculated being. When she married, she did not know that his indolence and profligacy were notorious in Philadelphia, and although she had wondered how he could follow her around when she was touring the Northeast, she had assumed that after their marriage he would settle down to some sort of work. But hearing him now, privileged and wealthy, lecturing to wretched enslaved women about their moral "duty" to work, was repellent to her: he was dishonorable, disgusting, and he lacked "the spirit of a man." However many attempts at reconciliation that occurred after this time, and however much Kemble tried to overcome her feelings of repugnance for Pierce's indifference to suffering, she never forgot this moment when she lost all respect for him.

The story of two slaves, Psyche and Joe, took her to a point of no return. Psyche was a mulatto slave who had become a sort of under-nursemaid to Margery; Joe, as Kemble learned, was her "husband" with whom she had several children. Once the property of Roswell King, Jr., Psyche was uncertain about the identity of her master since she had lived on Butler Island since the time King had left to start his own slave plantation some years before. She timidly asked Margery, who in turn asked Kemble, if it would be possible for Pierce to buy her if it turned out that she really belonged to King. He would probably wish to take her with him when he returned to his Alabama plantation, forcing her to abandon Joe and her children. Determined to help her, Kemble discovered that King was, in fact, *not* her owner; Psyche was the property of the overseer to whom she had been sold by King. Delighted, Fanny was sure that Pierce would agree to buy Psyche and allow the family to stay together.

The next morning she witnessed a heartrending scene (and she described it as such in a long letter to Elizabeth) as Joe, having learned that he had been given by the overseer as a parting present to Roswell King, begged Pierce to intervene. Pierce leaned nonchalantly against a table with his arms folded, murmuring that the sobbing Joe should cease fretting since nothing could be done. Kemble immediately appealed to her husband "not to commit so great a cruelty" as to separate Psyche and Joe, and Joe's agony was hardly greater than hers as she argued with her husband about "this bitter piece of inhumanity." Silent and sullen, Pierce declined to reply and refused to speak to Kemble throughout the next day. She, in the meantime, learned from the overseer that Roswell King had decided not to take Joe with him—he did not wish to be bothered with troublesome "niggers"— and all that remained was for Pierce to buy Psyche from the overseer. Fearing that her husband would remain intractable, Kemble began to make an inventory of her jewelry, and as she calculated how much money she might muster, realizing it would be insufficient to buy a female slave and her children, she was struck with a significant insight into her history and her present position: "then the great power and privilege I had foregone of earning money by my own labor occurred to me, and I think, for the first time in my life, my past profession assumed an aspect that arrested my thoughts most seriously. For the last four years of my life that preceded my marriage, I had literally coined money, and never until this moment, I think, did I reflect on the great means of good, to myself and others, that I so gladly agreed to give up forever for a maintenance by the unpaid labor of slaves."[45] Inasmuch as one can say so, the story ended happily: Pierce bought Psyche and her children from the overseer, though he sadistically declined to tell Kemble what he had done, bored, she suspected, by her "unmeasured upbraidings." Kemble now realized the severity of her subjugated condition: she was without money of her own and she had exhausted the female Victorian leverage of moral appeal and anguished tears. As Lydia Maria Child reported to a friend on December 5, 1838, after hearing from Kemble in Georgia, "she keeps tugging at her husband's conscience all the time, about his slaves. One day he begged her to spare him—saying 'You know, Fanny, we don't feel alike on the subject. If I objected to it in my conscience, as you do, I would emancipate them all.'"[46] However, she neither gave up nor gave in. The flogging of female slaves became the next subject of petitions to her husband.

Kemble knew he neither cared about such practices nor wished to change them. Pierce maintained that the flogging of female slaves was not a hardship; it was merely established custom on the plantations and the slaves themselves never complained. He told Kemble that her presence in Georgia must not be allowed to "overthrow the whole system of discipline established to secure the labor and obedience of slaves."[47] It was a methodical arrangement of measured punishments in which each driver of a gang was allowed to inflict a dozen lashes upon any disobedient slave in the field at the time of the offense; if the slave continued to be recalcitrant, then the driver reported him or her either to the head driver or to the overseer, and the former was allowed to inflict up to three dozen lashes; the latter could deliver up to fifty. The master had limitless authority to inflict as many lashes as he wished. Just before they were about to return to Philadelphia, Kemble learned a terrible story from a female slave named Die, who had had sixteen children and four miscarriages, one caused from having her arms strained up to be lashed. Pregnant, her clothes rolled down to her waist, she had been flogged by a driver with a cowhide whip.

The "weight of horror and depression" occasioned by such testimony almost quenched Kemble's rebellious spirit and ameliorative efforts. Moreover, after the "benevolence" he displayed in the Psyche and Joe incident, Pierce refused to hear any more petitions from his wife, weary, she knew, "of hearing what he has never heard before, the voice of passionate expostulation and importunate pleadings against wrongs that he will not even acknowledge."[48] In the middle of February 1839, after two months on St. Simons, she realized she would be relieved to return to the North; impotent to alter the wretchedness she saw all around her, she knew she was seen as a danger to the "institution." But she also knew she could not return alone since if she left her children with Pierce, he would, in all likelihood, find legal means to prohibit her from ever seeing them again. She wrote to Elizabeth that she had no choice but to stay "and learn this dreary lesson of human suffering to the end."[49] Still, shortly after hearing the story of Die's flogging, she ran away and managed to get herself to the small town of Darien at the mouth of the Altamaha, where she hoped to get a boat north. The desperation of this move must be attributed to a manic fantasy of surviving alone since she had insufficient money even to leave Darien, let alone find transportation out of Georgia. Pierce followed and demanded that she return, threatening to bar access to the children and leave her penniless if she refused. She had no choice but to comply.

In mid-April 1839, Kemble stood and watched the slowly revolving light that warned the ships away from a dangerous bar at the mouth of the Altamaha; as she heard the measured pulse of the great Atlantic waters on the beach, she tried to think no more of slavery, knowing that they would soon be leaving. She never returned to Georgia, never saw again nor heard anything of the "poor people" with whom she had lived for four months, save Jack. After becoming ill, his "owners," as Kemble termed Pierce and her brother-in-law, brought him to Philadelphia, and in an ironic ending to his story, Jack was confined to a high upper room of a large empty house lest he learn from some "philanthropic abolitionist" that he was now free under the provisions of the Fugitive Slave Bill, passed in 1850. Kemble was allowed to see him shortly before he died—theoretically freed from slavery but literally imprisoned by the Butler family. By then she was divorced from Pierce but she had known as she stood at the edge of the Atlantic in April 1839 that her marriage was over. It was merely a matter of how much longer it might officially endure, and also how much financial and emotional capital she could muster for a break from Butler. It was only after four more years of quarrels, reconciliations, travel in Europe, and humiliating efforts to accommodate herself to Pierce's domestic despotism for the sake of her children that her own "dreary lesson of human suffering" came to an end. Writing had been her salvation on the islands, both as eyewitness testimony to human suffering and a means to live with her own complicity in what she recorded. *Journal of a Residence on a Georgian Plantation* testifies primarily, of course, to the horror of slavery, but it also documents the fortitude and spirit of its author.

8

"A Woful Ruin"

Weep'st thou to see the ruin and decay
Which Time doth wreak upon earth's mighty things?
Temples of gods, and palaces of kings,
Weep'st thou to see them crumbling all away?
Oh I could show thee such a woful ruin
As doth surpass the worst of Time's undoing,
A fortress strong of life, not wrecked by years,
But overthrown by sighs, and sapped with tears;
A noble mansion, wherein youth did dwell,
To which this palace were a lowly cell;
A goodly temple, in whose holiest shrine,
Love had a worship like himself divine;
And all these fabrics fair deserted be—
A weed-grown heap, shunned even by memory.
    —Fanny Kemble, "Sonnet: Written Among the Ruins
       of the Castle at Heidelberg," 1841

Fanny's "Excitable Machine"

On May 26, 1843, John Barlow, a clergyman and honorary secretary of the Royal Institution of Great Britain, delivered a lecture at the institution titled "On Man's Power over Himself to Prevent or Control Insanity." Shortly thereafter, Barlow published the lecture, and in 1849, under the same title, the prolific London publisher and bookseller William Pickering issued a second edition. Today, in the Special Collections Library of the University of Virginia one can find an annotated and underlined copy of the Pickering edition inscribed with Fanny Kemble's name: the name and the annotations are all in Kemble's handwriting and it is safe to assume that she also underlined this copy. Given Kemble's unreserved admission in her memoirs that she experienced periods of deep depression and frantic energy, her interest in the subject of insanity and methods of its prevention and control is particularly telling, as are the annotated and underlined passages in Barlow's book. Moreover, Barlow's moral prescription of a life of moderation and exercise of the will as a remedy for emotional illness is one that Kemble advocated and followed.

It is difficult to know exactly when Kemble might have first read, annotated, and underlined *On Man's Power over Himself to Prevent or Control Insanity*: she spent all of 1849 in America, negotiating the terms of her divorce from Pierce Butler and performing her Shakespeare readings in Boston and New York, and she did not return to London until the spring of 1850. While in America, she may have had it sent to her, or she may have first read it when she returned to London, but more important than the date of her reading is her emphasis on "domestic troubles" as the cause of emotional instability, on its remedy through attention to "physical well-being," and on the particular vulnerability of "artists of all kinds" to mental illness.[1]

The first underlined passage explores differences between insanity in England and in France. According to Barlow's unsubstantiated and Francophobic claim, there are more cases in the latter country than in the former, something he attributes to religion no longer bringing "consolation and hope" and to a society, both in France and in England, where there seems to be "no more domestic affection, nor respect, nor love, nor authority, nor reciprocal dependencies." Given that her mother was French, that she spent five years in France when she was a young girl, and that her marriage to Pierce Butler (certainly as she viewed it after their divorce in 1849) lacked domestic affection, love, and reciprocal dependency, it is not surprising Kemble would find this passage of interest. Thérèse Kemble's bewildering volatility and Pierce Butler's imperious domestic rule both exacerbated Kemble's fragile temperament *and* created her determination to become neither like her mother nor the tamed and docile wife Pierce had in mind when they married. Kemble next underlined a section advocating physical exercise as a cure for depression: Barlow claims that "whatever relates to the moral well-being of man, has always a most intimate connection with his physical well-being, and the preservation of his health." Finally, it is easy to imagine Kemble has herself in mind when she includes the following marginalia next to Barlow's assertion

Fig. 25. *Fanny Kemble Butler*, by Henry Inman, ca. 1840s. Kemble's serene appearance belies the tumultuous state of her marriage in the 1840s. Photography Collection, Miriam and Ira D. Wallach Division of Art, Prints, and Photographs, New York Public Library, Astor, Lenox and Tilden Foundations.

that an artistic sensibility makes one vulnerable to emotional illness: "artists of all kinds and poets have generally in the organisation which determines their choice of occupation a more delicate and excitable machine to deal with than others."[2] Fathoming the ways in which Kemble dealt with the "more delicate and excitable machine" that was her temperament, as she describes those ways in her memoirs, discloses to the reader a further aspect of the valiant personality that battled Pierce

Butler when they were on the plantations. Declared "diseased" in her mind by her husband, after she returned from Georgia, and seen as doomed by her friends by virtue of the "morbid tendencies" they declared she had inherited from her mother, Kemble struggled for seven years after her return to find release from her emotional distress, to attain financial independence from Pierce, and, most of all, to discover a way to leave him.

Lacking her own money and bullied by Pierce's demand for obedience, Kemble did not have many choices. She could appeal to her American friends for help while devising some means of support, she could return to England and her family, or she could remain where she was in the hope that something would happen to improve her situation. Going to the Sedgwicks, say, perhaps helping Elizabeth Sedgwick at her school, would mean she could stay in America and thus retain a slim chance of seeing her children; going home to her father would mean a return to the stage, given his reduced income and selfish concern for his own comforts, and such a move would also subject her to legal charges of desertion. Staying put promised only more unhappiness. For the moment, she decided to stay, and quickly began to displace the misery and frustration into renewed complaints about Butler Place and Philadelphia: the rooms were too small for someone of Pierce's fortune, the grounds were too arid for her English flower gardens, and the neighbors were dull, unfriendly snobs. Visitors to Butler Place saw things differently. Many admired the graceful proportion of the rooms and the elegant furniture with which Fanny had improved things, and the Butlers appeared to the world as a composed if ill-matched couple. When Sidney George Fisher, the Philadelphian diarist who chronicled many impressions of Kemble, visited in October 1839, he noted that the "very rich" Butlers lived in "grand style" and that their house was surrounded by fine trees and superbly kept grounds. Unlike many Philadelphians who had ridiculed Pierce for marrying an actress in 1834 and turned a frosty shoulder when Kemble appeared, Fisher reported to his social circle that Pierce was "extremely gentlemanly in manner" and Kemble "a very gifted person ... her qualities of heart and character are as excellent as her intellect."[3]

It would seem that Kemble dissembled skillfully before Fisher. But even if she donned the mask of satisfied wife in a stable marriage, her family life enriched by Sarah and Fan, and her comfortable existence secured by her husband's wealth, in the five years since their wedding, Kemble had tried at least five times to leave her husband, she had threatened suicide, and she had narrated a saga of neglect and isolation to English and American friends. After Georgia, Pierce was irreparably diminished in her moral eyes and in May of the very year that Sidney Fisher found them reigning over Butler Place, she had accused him of sleeping with other women when he spent time in Philadelphia. In his turn, Pierce was bored with

Kemble's constant complaining about her social isolation and incensed by her refusal to obey his wishes, and he had lost interest in the fiery glamor that had drawn
him to her in the first place. In light of his reputation as a sexual adventurer before
his marriage and the fact that he was accused a few years later of being in bed with
someone else's wife at the Astor Hotel in New York, Kemble's accusations about
his philandering were probably well founded.

For almost six years Kemble patched the crumbling facade of her marriage, but
in September 1845, drained by months of bitter quarrels, with no prospect of seeing
her daughters for some years to come, and only a faded reputation on the theatrical and social scene to sustain her, Kemble set about building a new life. During
this period—from her return from Georgia in April 1839 to the anguished departure for England in September 1845—she battled the most serious oscillation she
was ever again to experience between despair and elation. The prospect of being a
mother separated by the Atlantic from her daughters, of being a thirty-year-old
financially dependent daughter, and of being a social cipher after a decade of fame
and wealth was, at the very least, not encouraging—but neither was the prospect
of remaining with Pierce. As she evokes this period in her memoirs, she describes
moments of fiery resistance to his will as well as moments of deep inertia: the
"delicate and excitable machine" that was her "organisation" almost became irreparably damaged. But this was also the time when Kemble, with valiant zest and
defiance, breathed life into the feminist ambitions for professional and financial
independence that had been stifled by the seductive wealth and sexual appeal of
her husband. Eventually victorious in her valiant battle against emotional illness,
she shook off the role of Butler wife and became, once more, Fanny Kemble.

In a household dominated by the unpredictable mood swings of Thérèse Kemble, Charles had coped by living apart from her during the week when he was in
London and by undertaking lengthy acting tours in the provinces and on the Continent when he was still performing. Her children had no choice but to suffer as
best they could Thérèse's restlessness, hysteria, and anger. As a child, Fanny knew
she resembled her mother—impetuous and amusing but also angry and morose—
and as she grew older she was haunted by memories of Thérèse's erratic behavior.
Like Thérèse, she was frequently overcome by debilitating languor when no work
seemed possible and then charged by a frantic energy when nothing seemed out
of bounds. Knowing her vulnerability and her hypersensitivity to her surroundings
(those "electrical conditions of the atmosphere" that made her very nervous), she
crafted for herself a modus vivendi of rules and regulations to govern her daily life,
anticipating, in this regimen, some of the prescriptions offered by John Barlow in
1843 for the prevention and control of insanity. As a schoolgirl at Mrs. Rowden's
in Paris, she had followed carefully the highly disciplined curriculum, and she had

been an outstanding student; during her Edinburgh year, she had read copiously and listened attentively to the stimulating talk at Harriet Siddons's house; and when she became an actress, she followed a strict regimen of eating and resting at specific times of the day. Obsessively, and much to the alarmed amusement of her friends, she established a lifelong habit of rotating her dresses by color throughout the week; regardless of the weather and the occasion, she wore whatever color dress was designated for that particular day. Being fearless in her riding, indefatigable in her walking, and sensible in her eating kept Kemble on an even keel.

When she returned from Georgia none of the carefully calibrated schemes of exercise, study, and diet assuaged her rage and misery. The Sedgwick family was about to go to Europe, her sister, Adelaide, now sixteen, was garnering critical applause for her singing, and Pierce had taken to spending several nights a week in Philadelphia at the house of his brother, John. On the evening of May 28, 1839, Pierce failed to return to Butler Place for his daughters' joint birthday, and Kemble became distraught. In a long letter Pierce included in the *Statement* that he published after the divorce, Kemble wrote to him on this night demanding release from her "intolerable life" of loneliness and oppression and swearing that she would no longer remain in America to be his housekeeper, his children's nurse, or, even worse, what he made her, something "still more degrading and revolting."[4]

What he "made" her, of course, was his sexual slave when he felt like doing so, although this is not something that appears in any of the letters Kemble included in her own published writings. Her excision of his name from all of her memoirs, journals, and letters is complete and telling, and the anguished letter she wrote to Pierce on May 28, 1839, begging for release is quoted in part from several that *he* offered as exhibits in his exculpatory *Statement*. He offered as evidence of her "inherent" morbidity that she had obsessively tried to leave him and their children (as he saw it, entirely without cause) and had accused him of "making" her his sexual chattel. She had a "diseased" mind, as he declared was evident from a letter she wrote to him three months after the birth of Sarah in 1835 in which she announced she was "weary" of her "useless existence" and wished to return to England; she declared that if he procured "a healthy nurse for the baby she will not suffer; and, provided she is fed, she will not fret after me."[5] Over a period of six years, Pierce assembled documentary evidence of what he saw as his wife's virtual insanity. In his *Statement*, he argues that no "sane" woman would wish to leave her infant to the care of strangers.[6]

When Kemble declared she was ready to leave her three-month-old baby, it is possible she was suffering from postpartum depression, but the extreme despair was also symptomatic of a masochistic self-destructiveness she displayed when at her most unhappy. There is no evidence that Kemble consulted a physician or that

Pierce insisted she do so, but had this happened (through a visit to the specialist S. Weir Mitchell, for example) it is probable she would have been diagnosed as "hysterical." As Carroll Smith-Rosenberg argues, hysteria emerged "as an endemic disease among bourgeois American women" in the mid-nineteenth century, "a disease related, as well, to the role changes and conflicts bourgeois matrons experienced between the 1840s and 1890s."[7] Hardly a "bourgeois matron," Kemble was nevertheless expected by her husband to act in compliance with a wish that was in extreme conflict with one of her own: he demanded obedience and she desired equality. Given what Pierce has to say about Kemble's behavior in his *Statement*, he would, without question, have concurred in the diagnosis of Fanny as "hysterical": as Smith-Rosenberg notes, mid-nineteenth-century American physicians diagnosed hysteria from the symptoms of women who "were highly labile, their moods changing, suddenly, dramatically, and for seeming inconsequential reasons. ... Doctors complained that the hysterical woman was egocentric in the extreme."[8] The hysterical woman was often also termed suicidal.

In the letters to Pierce, which he quotes at length in his *Statement*, Kemble speaks openly about her suicidal tendencies, threatening that she would be led "to the most fatal results" if he agreed to neither a permanent separation nor a definitive reconciliation. But suicidal thoughts were something that Kemble had learned to manage; she denied them neither to herself nor to the world at large, and in the divorce hearings she defended herself against Pierce's charges of malicious desertion by claiming that she had no choice but to leave him since she had become suicidal as a result of paroxysms of depression "which arise in great part in physical causes not under my control."[9] In her memoirs she recounts an exchange with a girl working at a provincial theater who told her she was so tired she was ready to kill herself. Don't do it, cautioned Kemble, for you will be called to account in "another world." The girl replied that she had never thought of that, to which Kemble responded, "But I have, very often."[10] Realizing that she had inherited an emotional illness from Thérèse originating in "physical causes" *not* under her control helped her live with that illness, just as relying on her faith in an afterlife helped her not to commit suicide when she was at her most deeply depressed.

Ironically, the only people in America to whom Kemble felt she could confide her troubles, the Sedgwick family, not only were recruited by Pierce as his allies but cautioned *her* in very strong terms about her inheritance of emotional instability and the dangers of her self-destructive temperament. On May 31, 1839, after receiving Kemble's letter accusing him of paternal neglect, chronic infidelity, and tyrannical demands for sexual compliance, Pierce wrote to Elizabeth Sedgwick. This was either a calculated move to enlist Kemble's allies on his side or a sincere appeal for help to the Americans who knew Kemble better than anyone else. Declaring that Elizabeth Sedgwick was the *only* person to whom he could write of his misery and his domestic sorrows, he confided that he was utterly distraught: when they argued, Kemble would get into such a state that "reason" left her; five or six times since their marriage, she had run away and been retrieved; and at least twice she had tried to sell her jewelry in Philadelphia in order to get money for the passage to England. He was convinced she was unbalanced. The constant gloom and weeping, the sick and unnatural thoughts, and the readiness to abandon her children could only indicate one thing: she had a "diseased mind." Elizabeth Sedgwick's response, which he quotes in his *Statement*, confirmed his belief that Kemble was seriously unbalanced. She recommended that he treat her "soothingly and compassionately, as you would do if she were sick with an ordinary malady."[11]

Almost immediately after writing to Pierce, Elizabeth Sedgwick, the woman to whom Kemble had poured out her indignation about slavery and her misery about Pierce, sent her a most remarkable and frank letter. Pierce included this letter in his *Statement*. Dated June 7, 1839, it articulates without reserve the view of Kemble's closest American friends that she was self-destructive, hysterical, and suffered from an inherited emotional illness. Elizabeth Sedgwick began by spelling out what she believed Kemble must see as the indisputable blessings of her life: she was affluent, she had a husband whose love could not be questioned, she was gifted with robust and healthy children, and she possessed "rare gifts of mind and heart." Apart from the assertion that Pierce's love was unquestionable, this was all very true, as was Elizabeth's painful diagnosis of Kemble's condition: "you inherit, undoubtedly from your mother, those morbid tendencies which poison and spoil all; and if, instead of manfully resisting them, of calling in the aid of religion, and of that moral and intellectual strength for which you are remarkable, you yield to them, let them obtain this complete triumph over you, I very much fear they will forever have the mastery."[12] Outlining a battle between inherited morbidity and willed resistance strengthened by religious faith, moral strength, and intellectual power, Elizabeth exhorts her dear friend and correspondent to vanquish the destructive legacy Thérèse Kemble had bestowed upon her daughter. Should she fail, she would be forever at the mercy of her "morbid tendencies." When Kemble received this letter, Pierce wrote to Elizabeth Sedgwick that he was amazed the "sad example" of Thérèse Kemble had not been "shunned" by Fanny.

Neither Pierce's insistence that her misery was caused by mental illness and not his neglect nor Elizabeth Sedgwick's warning that if she did not rally she would be irreparably defeated by inherited morbidity appears in Kemble's memoirs. Rather, this tormented period in her life is signaled through a symptomatic and familiar recitation of isolation, loneliness, and longing for England, as well as through pessimistic declarations to her friends that *nothing* she ever said or did had any influence on the Butler family. The explicit nature of Pierce's correspondence with Elizabeth and the implicit disclosures in Kemble's public writings reveal her valiant battle with depression, which she never entirely vanquished. The depression also robbed her, some of the time, of the strategy of resistance she had developed against stifling gender codes and unsatisfied desires for recognition as a woman intellectual: performance of self-scripted roles. In 1839, she was temporarily depleted, and that she lived so heroically in the shadow of her mother's illness and, within that shadow, eventually achieved so much as an independent woman is remarkable.

In the winter of 1839, Pierce and John Butler returned to Butler and St. Simons islands, and just before he left, Kemble wrote to Harriet St. Leger that her life was "externally *nothing*." She listed the familiar complaints: no intellectual companions, exiled from her English friends, forced to live with a frivolous sister-in-law while Pierce and John Butler were in Georgia, her sole exercise restricted to lonely rides through the icy streets of Philadelphia. Just as the exaggerated cries heard early in her marriage that she read nothing were contradicted by her actual study of Milton and Thomas Carlyle, so the "nothingness" of her life this winter was contravened by her accounts of reading Gibbon's *Decline and Fall of the Roman Empire*. Even if Kemble's depression usually plunged her into inertia, she rarely lost her intelligent curiosity and her intellectual ambition, and there were few periods in her life when she was not writing something—letters, obviously, but also journal entries, poetry, essays, and even plays. Just before leaving for Georgia she had finished *An English Tragedy*, which she had begun in England in the summer and autumn of 1837, and which she always regarded as the only worthwhile thing she had ever written, with great ease and rapidity, almost "*currente calamo*," as she wrote to Harriet. Hopeful it would be staged in London, she had sent it to William Charles Macready, who, despite his distaste for the Kemble "teapot" style, noted in his *Journal* that he thought it "one of the most powerful of the modern plays I have seen—most painful, almost shocking, but full of power, poetry, and pathos. She is one of the most remarkable women of the present day."[13] But despite his admiration for both Kemble and her play, Macready decided it could not be produced as it would be greeted as a moral outrage by critics and audiences alike, and would bring her only disrepute. She had based it on a contemporary London scandal involving gambling, cheating, and adultery, the details of which had been related to her by Charles Kemble.

Initially she wrote *An English Tragedy* as a mere dramatic figment, but she later realized it might become a full-length play. The plot traces the tragic story of an aristocratic woman named Anne who marries a wealthy older man when her family loses its money and reputation. Shortly after her marriage, Lord Alford, a former admirer, reappears on the scene and they enter into a passionate affair, whose sexual urgency Kemble evokes with remarkable skill. Revealed as a philandering cad and notorious gambler, and desperate for money to pay his debts, the lover blackmails Anne into getting seven hundred pounds from her husband and forces her to accept the attentions of his friend John Forrester, who has fallen in love with her picture. Rather than taking advantage of her, John urges that she confess all to her husband and then delivers a speech about woman's virtue and national morality.

> Not in her stormy girdle of proud waves,
> Not in the rugged ramparts of her rocks,
> Not in the winged fleets that fly around her,
> Guarding her watery gates, lies the defence
> of our dear country; but within her homes,
> The virtue and the truth upgarner'd there,
> Lives the right strength of England. Let but once
> Rottenness creep to this, the inward core
> Of all true bravery, and we are nothing.[14]

Woman's moral virtue is England's national strength and by the same token it was the moral virtue of the Kemble dynasty: its women, although actresses, embodied virtue and truthfulness. At the end of the play, Lord Alford kills John Forrester after a gambling disagreement and Anne dies in the arms of the husband who had wished to throw her out like "some foul rag" to haunt the common streets. The play is pure melodrama: the heroine is forced into legalized selling of herself in marriage to a rich and older man; the villain is an aristocratic gambler; and the hero an insufferable prig whose principal function is to declaim the power of woman's virtue. What is remarkable about *An English Tragedy* is the strong sexual excitement felt by Anne and her lover, inspired, perhaps, by Kemble's reunion with Pierce in Liverpool in the autumn of 1837 after ten months apart. The play also offers a warning about the dangerous consequences for women if they succumb to sexual desire.[15]

When Kemble received the news in wintry Philadelphia from Macready that performance was out of the question, she impetuously tore up a copy of the play, assured herself that she cared no more about it, and settled down to read Gibbon, which she was studying with the aid of a classical atlas, Bayle's historical dictionary, and an encyclopedia. *An English Tragedy* was eventually published in London in 1863, but in the winter of 1839, believing that all her compositions were "impromptus," inspired by the changing vicissitudes of her life, and dispirited by the news from Macready, she assessed her existence as so ordinary that not only could she write nothing, she had nothing to write *about*. It seems that after the emotional upheavals of the previous year and the warning from Elizabeth Sedgwick that unless she struggled against her depression she would go under, she opted for quietude. Reading Gibbon, planting tulips, and supervising the baby nurse kept her passions in check, as did the hope of a visit to England that Pierce had promised for the following September.

In July 1840 Pierce went to Hot Springs, Virginia, in hopes of alleviating his rheumatism, and in August Kemble and the children went to Lenox to be with the two women she felt were "sisters" to her in a strange land: Elizabeth and Catharine Sedgwick. In response to a query from Harriet St. Leger about how far Hot Springs might be from Lenox, Kemble responded indifferently that she had absolutely no idea. She was glad to be with the Sedgwicks and away from Pierce: her only worries were that she was getting fat, that Pierce vacillated about the journey to England, and that Adelaide was taking risks in agreeing to sing in such dangerous places as Constantinople. When Pierce returned to Philadelphia from Hot Springs in the autumn, he confirmed what she had feared: since Charles and Adelaide would be traveling on the Continent until the spring of 1841 while Adelaide took lessons from different teachers, Kemble and the children were to stay at Butler Place while he returned, once more, to the plantations. She was distraught: she would be trapped indoors by severe weather where, as she put it to Harriet, "the absolute solitude is a terrible trial to my nerves and spirits."[16]

One bright spot in the autumn of 1840 was a suggestion from the abolitionist Lucretia Mott that her Georgian journal should be published. When she broached this possibility to Pierce (it is difficult to believe she imagined he would assent), he was appalled, and John Butler ruled shortly thereafter that she must never be allowed to return to Georgia. As she put it in her memoirs, the Butler brothers believed that such a journey would be a "source of distress to myself, annoyance to others, and danger to the property," a view she did not regard as unreasonable given her undisguised hatred of slavery. Worried about the forthcoming winter to be spent alone at Butler Place and lacking encouragement or praise, she felt herself once more falling into "absolute intellectual solitude," sliding into the severe depression she had been struggling to vanquish during the previous fifteen months.[17] The forthcoming presidential election in November 1840 was of interest to her only because she was sympathetic to the politics "of the man I belong to," which had become her sarcastic way of referring to Pierce. At this point in their marriage, probably the only thing they had in common, besides their children, was support of the Republican Party.

Arrangements for the winter were suddenly altered by news in mid-November that Charles Kemble had returned unexpectedly to England from the Continent, seriously ill (probably with pneumonia) and not expected to live. On December 1, 1840, the Butler family sailed for Liverpool, learning on arrival that Charles might not survive beyond the next twenty-four hours. But he rallied and recovered, so cadaverous, however, that when he arrived at the house on Clarges Street, just off Piccadilly, that Pierce had rented for their London stay, he seemed to Kemble as if returned from the dead. When William Macready visited to inquire after his fellow actor, he was shocked by Charles's "wasted, old, decrepit" appearance, but Fanny he found to be "frank" and "genuine," someone he had rarely been so taken with.[18] Fanny and Pierce knew they would be joined by Adelaide on her return from Italy, and when Harriet St. Leger came over from Ireland to join the group for a short visit, Kemble felt as happy as she believed she could be, given the still frail condition of Charles and the circumstances of her marriage. She was with her convalescent father, her grown-up and gifted sister would soon be with her, and her dearest friend of thirteen years was in London.

A Musical Maelstrom

Early in 1841 Charles Kemble returned to health, and Fanny resumed the scintillating London social round she had enjoyed when last in England in 1837, this time with a feverish intensity prompted probably by the previous months of depression. In a significant alteration of their roles while in Philadelphia, she was now the powerful, sought-after figure and Pierce was the attendant spouse: in Philadelphia his wealth granted him social currency; in England, her Kemble credentials opened most social doors. They went out all the time. She adored the opera, although she disliked sitting in the stalls where she felt the unwelcome press of other bodies; she delighted in the dinner parties where they mingled with politicians, musicians, and literary figures; and she relished weekend visits to the country houses of her aristocratic friends. Pierce was tolerated since he was her rich husband, but she was adored because she was witty and entertaining. The letters Kemble wrote during these heady winter months in London tickled Harriet with descriptions of figures such as the wife of George Grote, distinguished historian and Member of Parliament from 1832 to 1841. Mrs. Grote liked to wear a man's hat and a coachman's box coat over her petticoats when she was at her country house and scarlet dresses with white satin hats when she was in town. A Victorian character, she was very tall, square built, and high shouldered, with the face of a clever man, and she reminded Kemble of no one so much as her companion from the trip to Niagara, Edward Trelawny, who reappeared in her life when she returned to London. Mrs. Grote's appearance was so masculine, according to a delighted Kemble, that the wife of Henry Chorley, the music critic for the *Atheneum*, asked her husband, "Henry, my dear, who is the gentleman in the white muslin gown?"[19]

Old friends and acquaintances such as Thomas Macaulay, Tom Moore, Samuel Rogers, and Caroline Norton—these were the people with whom the Butlers spent their time, she at the attentive center listening to discussions of "great questions of European policy, and the important movements of foreign governments, or our own, in matters tending to affect the general welfare and progress

Fig. 26. *Adelaide Kemble*, by Alfred Edward Chalon, 1830. © National Portrait Gallery, London.

of humanity" and he, bemused by his wife's dazzling social success, wondering how soon he might escape to one of the London clubs to which he had been introduced.[20] Adelaide's return to London in April 1841, fresh from her acclaimed performances at La Fenice in Venice and La Scala in Milan, prompted even more invitations for the Butlers. Kemble, however, was presented with a fresh and unexpected difficulty. Her depression lifted by a return to London society and her marital unhappiness shunted aside by a packed social calendar, she was displaced from a starring role in the Kemble family by the accomplished and famous sister whom she had not seen for four years.

Kemble dearly loved Adelaide and felt in her bones that their way of perceiving and being affected by things and people was often identical. She was moved to sobs by her sweet singing (so overcome when she first heard her sing in public that she hid behind a pillar lest others see her tears), yet Adelaide's arrival at the house on Clarges Street was disruptive. Kemble confided to Harriet that Adelaide had grown "very large" and had begun to resemble Thérèse, something that alarmed Fanny since she was worried about her own weight, to say nothing of her own emotional, if not physical, resemblance to her mother. According to Charles Dickens, by 1856 Adelaide had grown so big that he feared inviting her to dinner at his apartment on the Champs-Elysées: he wrote to Wilkie Collins that he worried that she would "not be able to get in at the dining room door. I *think* (am not sure) the dining room would hold her, if she could be once pressed in."[21] Bothered also by the fact that Adelaide seemed to need constant social excitement, Kemble thought she talked rather too much about the "dulness of our mode of life here as intolerable and oppressive to the last degree," a complaint that recalled for Fanny the dreariness of Philadelphia.[22]

She also expressed some reservations to Harriet about Adelaide's voice, which did not stem from annoyance or jealousy of her sister but from her own experience of celebrity. Conscious of the ways in which artistic fame can lead to the dependence on adulation that Fanny had seen in her aunt Siddons, she feared that with the aim of creating a sensation for the public, Adelaide's voice was being pushed unnaturally by her teachers into a higher range. Her true voice was a high mezzo-soprano and it was being stretched to the higher pitch of soprano-*assoluto*; after seeing her sister perform a "hotchpotch" of roles in three different operas, she became convinced that Adelaide was increasingly nervous, that her performances were becoming feeble, and that she was, perhaps, a better actress than she was an opera singer. What she feared most, however, was that Adelaide would be spoiled by celebrity.

When Adelaide arrived in London in the spring of 1841, Kemble found herself in the midst of a "musical Maelstrom." The house was filled from morning to night with people coming to sing with, or listen to, Adelaide, and Fanny felt they were all "enveloped in a golden cloud of fashionable hard work, which rather delights my father; which my sister lends herself to, complaining a little of the trouble, fatigue, and late hours; but thinking it for the interest of her future public career."[23] The problem with all this hard work was that it prevented Kemble from following the domestic rules that kept her own "delicate and excitable machine" in balance. Some of the excitement was undeniably splendid. The occasion for Adelaide's London debut was a morning benefit for Polish refugees at Stafford House, and after a reading from the French actress Rachel and a recital by Franz Liszt (both of them the rage of London at the time), Adelaide astounded them all with the power and sweetness of her voice. Kemble loved the scene at Stafford House that morning: the galleries were filled with brilliantly dressed women, the staircases were lined with pyramids of perfect flowers, and the drawing rooms were decorated with china vases stolen from the Arabian Nights. She was as enchanted with this scene as she had been with the Blackheath drawing room she visited as a girl, at the age of thirty-two as intoxicated by the color and fragrance of a splendid London mansion as she had been at the age of six by a plush red carpet and jars of potpourri. But back on Clarges Street, she was bewildered by the tumult caused by Adelaide's success, irritated by the incessant music, and annoyed by the riotous behavior of her children.

Since the spring of 1839, when Elizabeth Sedgwick had warned her she must fight against her inherited "disease," she had tried to stabilize the erratic swings between despair and excitement, helped in part, of course, by the shift from Philadelphia to London, from dull routine without companions to warm embrace by her old and new English friends. Now, the agitation of the household occasioned by Adelaide's celebrity began to wear on her nervous temperament and to prohibit adherence to her schedule. She suffered constant interruptions. The moment she sat down at her writing desk, the door was thrown open to admit a throng of visitors; Adelaide and little Fan (more boisterous than her sister) were constantly romping all over the house; and there was incessant music below late into the night and often "a most stupendous row at the pianoforte." She felt that her brains were being "addled" by the "whirl" of frenetic activity.[24] If Butler Place was too quiet, Clarges Street was a musical bedlam.

In July 1841, it seemed certain the Butler family would stay another year in England. Although from Fanny's skeptical perspective it seemed that Pierce did little but loll around the clubs to which he was invited, while in London he had arranged some profitable sales of the Butler sea-island cotton. He wished to develop the English market even further and Fanny's friends were useful to him; consequently, he rented a house at 81 Harley Street, close to Cavendish Square, where they might entertain on a grand scale. The elegant spaciousness of this house gives an idea of the luxury in which the Butlers lived when they were in London: almost thirty feet wide, graced with a fine spiral staircase and beautifully glazed atrium window at the top, it is now a private medical clinic.

Visits in midsummer to the country houses of Kemble family friends provided, for Fanny, relief from the musical "maelstrom" of Mayfair and the smoggy air of the city, and, for Pierce, an opportunity to cultivate more business for the Butler cotton. She rode in the morning and entertained her fellow houseguests in the evening with readings from Petrarch, Shakespeare, and Wordsworth. Charles Kemble and Adelaide sometimes joined them, although Adelaide was preoccupied with plans for a late summer tour of the Rhineland, where she was to be accompanied by Franz Liszt. What was initially imagined as a small group composed of Fanny, Pierce, and Adelaide grew to include the Butler children, their Irish nurse, Henry Kemble (the younger brother of Fanny and Adelaide), his fiancée, and the fiancée's aunt. In mid-August, a large party sailed for Holland on what was to be Kemble's first visit to the Continent since she had returned in 1825 from Mrs. Rowden's school in Paris.

Kemble never forgot the thirty-year-old Franz Liszt as she heard him play that summer, "in the very perfection of his extraordinary talent." Stunningly handsome and a brilliantly powerful pianist, he displayed a kind of "seven-leagued boot style"; as far as Kemble was concerned, none of his contemporaries—Mendelssohn, Chopin, Sigismond Thalberg—ever produced anything like his volcanic musical effects, "perfect eruptions, earthquakes, tornadoes of sound." But when she returned from the Rhineland and collected her thoughts, which she later incorporated into her memoirs, she concluded that his too easily achieved brilliance offered a cautionary tale for Adelaide. Liszt had become from the start of his career "so immediately a miracle, and then an oracle in the great world of Paris" that he had been allowed too much of his own artistic way. She believed that he achieved fame too early, lacked sobriety, sought too frantically after strange effects in his playing, and covered his "exaggeration and false taste" with musical fireworks. He was doomed by the need to outdo his own acrobatic performance, by a compulsion to create more and more difficulties in his playing so that he might overcome them.[25] Although she never believed Adelaide possessed as extraordinary a talent as that of Liszt, she *did* fear that if her voice were pushed to achieve increasingly sensational effects, she would run the risk of becoming as much a caricature of herself as did Liszt quite early in his career.[26] As things turned out, however, Kemble's fears were not realized; in January 1843 Adelaide married Edward John Sartoris and retired from the stage, but not before temporarily restoring the fortunes of Covent Garden.[27] Just as Fanny's performance as Juliet in October 1829 had revived both the family theater and its finances, Adelaide's triumphant debut in Bellini's *Norma* in November 1841 lifted the theater from its financial doldrums, at least temporarily. Charles Dickens wrote to Angela Burdett-Coutts on November 24 that his "domestic peace" was disturbed and his hearth "rendered so very desolate by the incursions" of those who had heard Adelaide sing that he would have no peace until he took his wife to Covent Garden.[28] But the theater made money only on the nights that Adelaide performed and the rest of the time it was almost empty. It remained a "ruinous concern," Kemble notes in her memoirs.

Excited by her visit to the Continent, Kemble thought Brussels was a cheerful imitation of Paris, the Rhine not as beautiful as the Hudson, and Wiesbaden less appealing than Lenox and Stockbridge. At Heidelberg she composed the sonnet that is the epigraph to this chapter, a poem that aligns metaphorically the ruins of a castle destroyed by time and the ruins of a love ravished by sighs, tears, and betrayal. The reader should not waste tears on the ruin wrought by "Time"; rather, the speaker urges, consider the "woful ruin" of a "fortress" where once the "Love" that was worshiped there has become a "weed-grown heap." The "fortress strong of life, not wrecked by years" overthrown by sorrow suggests Fanny Kemble herself, her body still strong but her spirit infected by the "weed-grown" rankness of her marriage. After Heidelberg, they traveled to Coblentz, which Fanny thought glorious with its view from the Ehrenbreitstein fort over the confluence of the Rhine and Moselle rivers below. It was there, standing alone at the edge of a parapet as she had stood on the edge of a ruined fort at West Point, that Kemble envisioned the future she wanted for herself.

In fine physical fettle and buoyed by the conviviality of the trip along the Rhine, she clambered alone to the highest point of the fortress walls. No one in the party shared her "zeal" for climbing and few were as robust: Adelaide had grown too fat to do much exercise, Pierce preferred to sit and smoke a cigar, and her brother and his fiancée were preoccupied with each other. Alone, she reached the last gates that guarded the top of the fort, only to be stopped by a sentinel on duty. Her exchange with him, as she relates it in her memoirs, was strange and revealing: "'Oh *do* let me in,' cried I in very emphatic English. . . . 'Where is your father?' quoth he in German, as I made imploring and impatient gestures, significant of my despair at the idea of having had that stupendous climb all for nothing. 'I have none,' cried I, in English and French. . . . He gravely shook his head. 'Where is your husband?' quoth he in German, to which I replied in German—oh, such German!—that 'I had none, that I was a woman, only a woman, an Englishwoman.'"[29] Feeling her power as the vibrant social performer that she was, when not laid low by depression, in her memoirs Kemble scripts a dramatic scene: center stage is Fanny Kemble Butler, flushed with exercise and fumbling her charming way through a conversation with the bemused sentry. Exhilarated by her solitary climb, Kemble impetuously expresses a wish to have no encumbering identity as the daughter of Charles Kemble or as the wife of Pierce Butler, to be free, paradoxically in terms of her theatrical reconstruction of the moment, of role-playing. But even to be "a woman, only a woman, an Englishwoman" would entail either the acceptance of the established Victorian identities encrypted in those terms or an interrogation of them. In the years that followed this epiphanic moment at the Coblentz fort, as Kemble became increasingly independent and intellectually mature, she chose interrogation.

The sentry relented and allowed her to reach the top of the fort, and as she marveled at the magnificent scene below, her only regret, and it was a slight one, was that she had no companion to whom she could express her pleasure. Yet the loneliness of this moment was very different from the desperate isolation she felt at Butler Place; now, at Coblentz, standing alone, stirred by the glorious sight of the rivers below her, she knew that what she had blurted to the German sentry was her *desire* to have one strong identity as an independent woman. Even if she presents herself as the vibrant performer in a mini-drama in her recollection of the moment, she had spoken what she knew to be the truth: she neither needed nor wanted the cloak of Kemble identity, and she no longer wished to be married. Her displacement by Adelaide as the charismatic center of the Kemble family precipitated an assessment of her position, and the desire to be free of Pierce that she had felt as she stood at the edge of the Atlantic just before leaving Georgia was clarified as she stood at the fort. In the months that followed Kemble's moment at Coblentz, the interest in the sexual and gender politics of her time that she had temporarily abandoned in the heady social whirl of a return to England became the frame for her preoccupation with her own perilous financial situation.

At the Clarendon Hotel

After her marriage, Kemble's opinions about social class and the subjugated position of women in Anglo-American culture, most of which found their way into her American *Journal* despite Pierce's censorship, were either voluntarily suppressed or muffled by the political conservatism of the Butler family. Just at the moment when she was beginning to articulate thoughtful views about social class and sexual politics, and to sense her place in the world as an independent woman, the comfort of not working after five years on the stage, combined with Pierce's strict demands for her compliance with all his wishes, rendered dormant her emerging feminist politics. While on the plantations she had not been silent, but when she got back to Philadelphia she subsided once more into a kind of intellectual and political doze. It was not until the galvanizing moment at Coblentz that she began to consider her own peculiarly privileged and yet subjugated position as a wealthy woman under the patriarchal governance of her husband.

On a cold December morning in 1841, on a weekend visit to Bowood, the home of Lord Lansdowne that had been designed by Robert Adam and landscaped by Capability Brown, she rode with her host over to Heaton Hall, near Manchester. This was the country house where she had dazzled the dinner table back in 1830 dressed in black velvet ready to go onstage as Julia in *The Hunchback*. The day was dark, dismal, and foggy, and Kemble thought it was made even more miserable by the "Manchester smoke" coming down with the penetrating cold drizzle, "like the defilement and weeping of irretrievable shame, and sin, and sorrow." She had seen this smoke before, of course, and back in 1830 she had tried to imagine conditions in the factories she could see from Heaton as she galloped with Lord Wilton across his land. But in 1841 she saw these factories with a knowledge few people could have brought to the scene, and the whole aspect struck her with terrible dismay.[30] No more was Heaton Hall the sumptuous country house where she had charmed everyone with her fame and wit: it was shrouded by a literal and moral miasma that came from the nearby factories, where ill-housed and ill-fed workers were spinning cotton that could well have been picked by slaves on the Butler plantation. As Pierce's wife, she was the legal owner of those slaves and this moment revealed a social and political web of responsibilities and consequences. The sight of what John Ruskin in 1884 was to term the "storm-cloud of the nineteenth century" (he meant it both literally and metaphorically in terms of pollution and moral confusion)[31] led her, when she returned to Bowood after her ride, to write to Harriet St. Leger and inveigh against the insidious power of inherited wealth and privilege, something she enjoyed both as the wife of a man who had inherited a considerable fortune and as the guest of wealthy Victorian landowners. Just as the sight of the Butler slaves disclosed the unrequited labor that sustained her comfortable life, the sight of the Manchester smoke signaled the factories where English working-class "hands" were laboring in conditions as dreadful in their way as those in Georgia. She wrote, "The accumulation of enormous wealth in the hands of individuals who transmit it to their eldest sons, who inherit it without either mental or physical exertion of theirs, is an inevitable source of moral evil."[32] Kemble created in this letter to Harriet a web of political connections between a dismal December fog, polluting smoke from the factory chimneys, American cotton, and inherited wealth that resembled, in its own imaginative way, the writing about industrialization being produced by many social investigators and politicians at the time.

Kemble's complex response to the factory smoke had some of its origin in a fight with Pierce that had occurred just before they left their London house on Harley Street. In October, she had received a letter from Lydia Maria Child asking if her antislavery newspaper, the *National Anti-Slavery Standard*, published weekly by the American Anti-Slavery Society, could publish all or parts of the Georgian journal. Pierce claimed later that he used "entreaty and remonstrance" to induce Kemble to disregard the request but she ignored him and wrote to Lydia Child on November 2, "I do not feel at liberty to give that to the public, or I should have done so long ago."[33] Instead, she offered to send the four or five long letters containing her account of the journey from Philadelphia to Georgia, and she regretted that it was not in her power to do more. Extraordinary as it seems, Fanny gave all her outgoing letters to Pierce for sealing and forwarding; it is clear that he read them all, and this one, he later admitted, he did not send but threw into a drawer of his writing table, where Fanny found it just before they left to travel to Bowood. She promptly posted the letter, and Pierce flew into a tremendous rage and swore, as Kemble recounted in a letter she wrote to Katherine Sedgwick Minot (daughter of Theodore Sedgwick) on March 2, 1842, that "my sending that letter to Mrs. Child put an end to our living together and that henceforth we were parted as man and wife." In this letter, she also declared that under no circumstances can she allow herself to "be maintained by a man who casts me off from him as wife . . . the only prospect before me is to return to the stage for a year."[34] Her complicity in slavery was very much on her mind as she looked at the smoke from factories weaving cotton that could well have come from her own fields, picked by her own slaves.

When Kemble returned to London from the "Manchester smoke," she resumed work on her poetry and began to take serious interest in the increasingly perilous nature of the American economy caused, in her view, by an undue extension of the credit system.[35] At least Pierce could not censor her reading, even if he censored her correspondence. It seemed to her a "pernicious system" of trading on fictitious capital had led to economic crisis, despite the inexhaustible real sources of credit. Admitting to Harriet St. Leger that in the past she had not mastered the difficult details of finance, despite the study of double-entry bookkeeping she had taken up at Butler Place as a way of not falling asleep on the sofa in the afternoon, she announced she was now better informed about the individual merits of paper money and coin currency. The former was a mere "financial expedient, the substitution of an appearance or makeshift for the real thing," and she argued there would be economic chaos when a demand arose for the "real article." These are not penetrating insights about fictitious capital and real money, but they reveal how attentively she was listening to the talk about finance, politics, and art that swirled

around her: in addition to Pierce and Fanny, the Bowood guests had included
Samuel Rogers, Tom Moore, Thomas Macaulay, and Charles Greville, and various
pretty and intelligent women like herself. She was delighted to be in the midst of
so much serious and witty talk and would slip into the drawing room after dinner
to listen to the heated political argument, often to see Macaulay holding forth in
his full and sonorous voice on the hearth rug, always in the same spot and always
engaged in answering everybody's questions, as Kemble put it, "about everything."
Charles Greville, however, who had known Fanny from the time of her debut in
1829, thought her a tragic figure; he wrote in his diary on December 8, 1842, that he
had been seeing a lot of "Mrs. Butler, whose history is a melancholy one, a domestic tragedy without any tragical events."[36]

Visits to country houses continued throughout the winter, but early in May
1842 Kemble told Harriet she was less inclined "to fly at all quarry" than she had
been the year before. What she does not disclose is that for at least a month she
had been desperately trying to get back to America, where she believed she stood
a better chance than she would in England of resuscitating her theatrical career. In
March she had written to Katherine Minot asking her to find out the price of land
in Lenox, should she choose to be there "at a future time." Early in April, after a
dreadful quarrel in which she voiced her suspicions that Pierce was sleeping with
the governess, Amelia Hall (described to Harriet St. Leger as a "fat, pampered
porpoise" by Kemble),[37] and he countered with taunts about her "diseased" mind,
she gathered up Sarah and Fan, left the Harley Street house, and traveled to Liverpool with the aim of catching the next transatlantic steamer. She left a letter in
which she expressed her hope he would provide for her and the children. Pierce
followed her to Liverpool, persuaded her to return, and talked her into a reconciliation. Three months later, on July 4, she again absconded, this time getting as far as
Kingston in Surrey, just outside London, and leaving a letter asking for his financial support until she could resume her acting career in September. Pierce tracked
her down, again prevailed, and after three days she returned to the Harley Street
house. He told their worried friends there was nothing wrong with their marriage
except Kemble's peculiar idea that it should be companionship and partnership on
equal terms, but he also said his love for her had been almost entirely consumed in
his fight against her wish that he be "an automaton of 'companionship, friendship,
and love'" without any rights to guide and rule his own family as he thought fit.[38]

After the Liverpool episode and a brief reconciliation, Pierce felt victorious:
Kemble was acting in a spirit of "compliance" and there was no need for him to
"claim obedience." Within weeks, however, she was frantic. From his perspective,
she was driven by a demon of resistance, and from hers, he was obsessed with
obtaining her compliance with his will and ridiculing her conscience. As far as he

was concerned, there was only one matter of contention between them that could involve her values and beliefs and that was slavery, but since she had willingly married a slave owner and acquiesced in the reality that her support was derived from slave labor, she had no grounds, he argued, to bewail matters of conscience. To their friends, they presented their battle as a fight about differing moral values and the right of husbands to demand obedience from their wives, but there were two other matters that neither of them tackled in public documents they prepared at the time of their divorce. The matter of money concerned the issue of how much support Kemble could rightfully expect should they separate, given the manner in which she had supported herself before marriage, and the matter of sex concerned the question of Pierce's rumored philandering, in particular his alleged affair with the governess, Amelia Hall, who had joined the family when they arrived in London and accompanied them when they returned to America.

When asked by Harriet St. Leger in May 1842 whether it is a blessing or a curse not to provide one's own means of subsistence, Kemble responded that it was a "great blessing" to be able to do so. Before she married she had earned large sums of money and this "very much destroyed" her liking for any other means of support. To others, perhaps, her present position in which she was supported by a wealthy husband might seem preferable; in her view, it was not. When she heard Adelaide sing *Norma* in her farewell performance at Covent Garden, she cried bitter tears, in part because Adelaide's singing and acting were as perfect as she had heard or seen them, but also because she was worried about Adelaide's future if her marriage should turn out to be unsuccessful—perhaps not as dreadful as her own, but of a nature to cause her to wish to be financially independent of her husband. Adelaide was leaving a path "where the sure harvest of her labor is independent fortune, and a not dishonorable distinction . . . for a life where, if she does not find happiness, what will atone to her for all that she will have left?"[39]

Kemble knew what it was to have no atonement for what a woman might leave when she marries. Just as she had wished to buy the slave Psyche from Roswell King and had rued her loss of financial independence, now, when she was desperate to leave Pierce, she was trapped by her lack of funds. She told her friends that being in "want of money" to pay a large millinery bill of £97, she was translating a French play, *Mademoiselle de Belle Isle*; if she could earn £200 by it, she would be glad (the fact that today the millinery bill would amount to approximately £6,000 indicates Kemble's privileged standard of living in 1842). She wrote a review of Victor Hugo's novels for the *British Quarterly Review* for the sum of sixteen guineas and, defying Pierce's wishes, offered the opening scenes of the Georgian journal to Richard Bentley, the publisher. The thought of returning to Butler Place was more than she could bear to contemplate. The contrast between her English life in the summer of 1842, riven as it was by fighting and reconciliation, and what awaited her on a return to America was chilling. She wrote to Harriet that the thought of being "placed for years day after day together out of the reach of all society; to be left day after day to the solitude of an absolutely lonely life; to be deprived of all stimulus from without; to hear no music; to see no works of art; to hear no intellectually brilliant or even tolerably cultivated or interesting conversation" was a frightening prospect for a woman accustomed to the eloquent talk of people like Thomas Macaulay.[40] At least in London she attended dinner parties where the conversation was so dazzling its details were reported to Elizabeth Barrett, who, in turn, reported them to Mary Russell Mitford: at the house of a Mr. Harness in late December 1842, Fanny, Adelaide, and their respective spouses, Elizabeth Barrett announced, all "talked fireworks and catherine wheels."[41] Barrett also reported to Mitford that Anna Jameson had declared to her that "Adelaide was the cleverest of the sisters. . . . She was speaking of their comic powers in conversation—drawing a general inference which the premises I heard of, seemed to disclaim."[42]

By October 1842, Pierce and Fanny had become entirely estranged, and as her defense in the divorce proceedings made clear, they no longer slept together: by the summer of that year, she painfully admitted, her husband "had ceased to entertain or manifest towards me any sentiment or sign of conjugal affection or personal respect. He neglected me, absented himself from my society, left me alone and otherwise testified by his whole deportment, absolute indifference and estrangement."[43] But Pierce still wavered between a definitive separation and yet one more reconciliation: first he thought they should return immediately to America, then he decided they should wait six months, and then he decided they should all move into the luxurious Clarendon Hotel on New Bond Street. His uncertainty tried Kemble's nerves to the extreme. Charges and countercharges continued to fly, in private and in public—of neglect and infidelity, of irrational behavior and refusal to comply with reasonable requests—and at one point Fanny moved in with Adelaide and her husband, Edward Sartoris, at their house on Chapel Street. After a few days she returned to the Clarendon Hotel in the middle of the night to rent separate apartments with the aim of retaining access to her children. The letters that she wrote to Pierce during their weeks living apart at the Clarendon resemble a script for the theatrical staging of the final act of their marriage.

Some of these letters were included by Kemble in the narrative she prepared in response to Pierce's charges of malicious desertion. He sarcastically termed them "remarkable compositions," containing "as much real feeling" as "beautiful writing," and he thought it singular that copies should have been made at the time of writing since he possessed the originals. Kemble did, indeed, keep copies since she knew at the time she wrote these letters, often in hysterical tears at the Clarendon

Hotel in 1842, that she would need every means of evidence against Pierce if he were to try to divorce her. He did try, and succeeded, but not before she had her hearing through her creation of a domestic melodrama, in which she cast herself as the loving, erratic wife and Pierce as a faithless, demanding tyrant. In the letters she gives one of her most riveting offstage performances. She raised the curtain on this melodrama by assuming the role of repentant offender, entreating his pardon for all past offenses but wondering why her repeated appeals for his affection, compassion, justice, and humanity had been ineffective. In a soaring admission of her love for him, in which she assumes an epistolary expression of her tragic attitudes (especially "supplication"), she declares that she gave him her entire life, made him the center of all her hopes of happiness, and that she had never loved any other human being as she had loved him. Then, enacting the role of passionate lover, she cries that her body still answers to his voice, her blood to his footsteps, and that he has no compassion for someone "endowed by nature with a temperament" unfit to deal with such tumultuous feelings. She is on the rack as she wrestles with "perpetual pain, sudden, violent, intense, almost intolerable pain."[44]

When Pierce got to have his say in the divorce documents, he offered fragments from his responses to these melodramatic letters written from an adjacent room in the Clarendon Hotel: he wrote to her that all her pain was self-imposed and the result of her refusal to acknowledge "the pledged acquiescence of a wife to marital control." The root cause of the failure of their marriage was her peculiar view that marriage was companionship on equal terms and her delusion that "she had a husband who was not a husband."[45] During these extraordinary weeks, Kemble became convinced that Pierce was sleeping with Amelia Hall. When they returned to America, she began to hear what she termed "painful rumors affecting her husband," which came from letters she received from English friends, although she admitted through her counsel in the divorce proceedings that "of the truth of those rumors she had no proof, but she spoke of them to her husband and felt assured by the circumstances that there was no further hope of regaining his affection."[46] As refutation of these charges, Pierce went so far as to include in his exculpatory *Statement* a letter written to him by Amelia Hall on June 22, 1845, saying she had received a letter from her sister passing on scandalous reports of an affair with her employer; she declares that it is a duty to her character that "Mrs. Butler should explicitly, and in writing, either deny what she has said, or state her motives for propagating such a falsehood."[47] Kemble did neither.

Extraordinary as it may seem, just one month later there was yet one more patched-together reconciliation, brought about by concerned friends and an unspecified illness on Pierce's part. We now see Kemble performing the role of contrite wife, promising to do her duty henceforward in a better manner than in the past, and Pierce promising to have more patience with the nervous excitement outside her control. She affirmed her undying love for him, her misery at his illness, and her promise not to annoy or irritate him. By this time their marital battles had become the regular subject of London gossip, even to the extent that news reached Theodore Sedgwick of their troubles. Kemble wrote to him on April 17, 1843, with an outright declaration: "As for people's comments on me or my actions, I have not lived on the stage to be cowardly as well as bold; and being decidedly bold, 'I thank God,' as Audrey might say [a reference to the character in *As You Like It*] that I am not cowardly, which is my only answer to the suggestion of 'people saying,' etc."[48]

His business transactions in England concluded, Pierce decided they would all be better off back in Philadelphia, and Kemble realized she had no choice but to go with him if she were to retain any claim on their children. They gave two large and lavish farewell parties in mid-April, entertaining a total of four hundred people until two in the morning. Fanny and Adelaide sang, there were six policemen at the door, and everyone was fed by Gunters, a fashionable Mayfair caterer. Even if his marriage was the subject of transatlantic gossip, Pierce did not scrimp on entertaining the hundreds of people who had welcomed him into London society for the previous eighteen months. Amelia Hall attended the party in an elegant black satin dress with her hair curled in profuse ringlets all over her head, which Kemble thought most unbecoming. They sailed from Liverpool on May 4, 1843, and, after a stormy voyage, arrived in Boston fifteen days later. Kemble was seriously seasick all the way and consumed only small glasses of calves'-foot jelly to sustain her. In Boston she made a pilgrimage to Mt. Auburn cemetery, the site of Dall's grave and the place where she and Pierce had strolled, ridden, and fallen in love in 1833, and she lay full length upon the stones, exhausted and mourning her beloved aunt and the picked-over corpse of her marriage. There were eighteen more months of fighting, scandals, and patched-up reconciliations before Kemble found the emotional strength and financial wherewithal to rescue herself from being "the woful ruin" of the sonnet she wrote while in Germany to become what she had unconsciously admitted to a bewildered sentry at Coblentz—"only a woman," even if she was known thereafter to all the world as Fanny Kemble.

The Havoc of a Single Life

Oh! Rome, tremendous, who, beholding thee,
Shall not forget the bitterest private grief
That e'er made havoc of a single life?
—Fanny Kemble, "Verses on Rome"

Fanny Fights Back, and Loses

Philadelphia in early June 1843 was hot and humid, weather Kemble found unbearable, and the heavy atmosphere seemed to be conspiring with Pierce's aim to make her life so miserable she would have no choice but to leave him. But even if the oppressive weather was deepening Kemble's melancholy, she was determined to fight Pierce with all she had, which, admittedly, was not much beyond a rebellious spirit. The best she could hope for was that he would become so weary of her inconvenient presence and so exasperated by her refusal to fade away into the dubious moral shadows of the stage that he would agree to a financial settlement and arrangements for custody of the children. She decided to soldier on and wage a guerilla campaign.

Pierce's first move in the battle was to announce, without warning or consultation, that he had rented Butler Place and that they were to move into Mrs. McPherson's boardinghouse on 111 South Sixth Street, on Washington Square in the center of Philadelphia, where they were to occupy separate quarters. Kemble wrote to Sarah Perkins Cleveland in July that the disquiet and anguish that had begun to "invade" her life had become a flood and had torn apart the "fabric" of her marriage, that she had been ousted from the only home she had ever had in America, and that she possessed nothing of her own: "how could I imagine such a fabric could stand—its very foundations from the very first were rotten and bitter and terrible as this wreck has been to me. I have been forced to acknowledge that it was as inevitable as written."[1] Pierce justified the move by saying that he could no longer afford to maintain Butler Place. Although it was certainly true that English imports of American cotton slackened during the 1842–43 depression, described by many economic historians as the worst of the nineteenth century,[2] it is unlikely that renting Butler Place would have made a substantial difference in the family finances. It is more likely Pierce wanted to make Kemble's life as dismal as possible by depositing her in a boardinghouse, with the advantage that he would be free to come and go as he wished.

To Kemble, boardinghouse life was detestable. Like many English people in America, she was appalled by meals served "family style," repulsed by American table manners, and disdainful of the enforced sociability that led to unwelcome intrusions into one's private life. It was abominable, an offense to her sense of propriety and the meticulously designed regimens essential for her emotional equilibrium. In addition, since she and Pierce occupied separate rooms, it was also public proof that her husband no longer found her desirable, even if at this point she wanted nothing to do with him. She had never been conventionally beautiful, but she had always been vibrantly attractive to men (and to women), and although there was no acceptable alternative to separate rooms at Mrs. McPherson's, it was still an advertised blow to her sexual appeal. She also worried about getting fat on the boardinghouse diet and ruefully declared in her memoirs that the only benefit from the anxious summer of 1843 was that she did not become as wide as her mother had been at the age of thirty-three.

From the time she married in 1832, Kemble had lived in too many places for her domestic serenity. First had been her brother-in-law's townhouse in Philadelphia while the residence in Branchtown was decorated for the newly married Butlers; on the return to England in 1836, she had lived with her parents for six months; then she was back at Butler Place for a year before traveling south to the rough-hewn plantation houses in Georgia. In London with Pierce and the children from December 1840 to April 1843, living in elegant houses on Harley Street and Upper Grosvenor Street as well as in the Clarendon Hotel, Kemble had felt dislocated and adrift. As she wrote to Sarah Cleveland at the time, Pierce was out in search of "amusement" from morning to night; they hardly spoke to one another; and they found distraction from their problems by spending three or four days a week at the houses of friends in the country: "I see very little of him and day after day passes by without exchanging chosen words. . . . Our so called *home* is in London."[3] The boardinghouse was the last straw, a place, she noted drily to Harriet St. Leger, that her "acquaintances" (by this time she had ceased to refer to Pierce and his brother by name) assured her was "very comfortable."[4]

Feeling exiled from her country but determined not to return, Kemble wandered through the steamy Philadelphia streets much as she had tramped through the rocky countryside around Butler Place. Pierce tormented her with his quixotic indecision about everything: their future, his social engagements, her financial security, at what hour they would eat dinner with the children. She, mustering some spirited feminist defiance, ridiculed him at every opportunity in a campaign to undermine his patriarchal rule. In a gesture of public disobedience, she regularly attended the First Unitarian Church where the Rev. William Henry Furness was preaching abolitionist sermons, an action that not only defied Pierce's wishes but also antagonized even further his pro-slavery Philadelphia friends. Cross-dressed for fishing in the Schuylkill, she devised a theatrical exhibition of her contempt for male ideas of appropriate clothing for women. Wearing a frock coat, pantaloons, and a man's hat (to one observer possessing "every outward appearance of a male" and violating "the accustomed laws of female decorum"), she shattered the image of feminine and subservient wife.[5] Ridiculing conventional nineteenth-century codes for female behavior became a defensive weapon against Pierce's plan to oust her, unprotected, from his life: whether riding alone down Walnut Street, superbly dressed in elegant English male riding clothes, or sparring with the male guests in witty dinner party conversation that left Pierce in a fumble, this was when she came alive. Six years earlier, she had asked "upon what grounds" he could presume to exercise control over her: derisively, she queried, "Is it because you are better than myself? . . . Is it because you are more enlightened, more intellectual? You know, that is not so, for your opportunities have not been the same."[6] In the battle with Pierce to gain autonomy, she never hesitated to deride his cultural inferiority, and this confident belief in her own intellectual supremacy both contributed to her contempt for him *and* fueled her resistance. In 1843, to Philadelphians who had been reluctant to admit her into their company and who stayed loyal to Pierce, her unconventional behavior signaled her shoddy identity as a former actress. They attributed all the Butler troubles to Kemble's volatile temperament, theatrical vulgarity, and naive abolitionist politics.

As she struggled to make her grimly furnished bedroom at Mrs. McPherson's look like a cozy sitting room, the dispiriting difference between this makeshift existence and her former luxury was painful to behold. Even if Adelaide's singing and stream of admirers had unsettled her in London, at least there she had lived elegantly. As she confided to Harriet, at Mrs. McPherson's the messy disarray taxed her self-confessed "morbid love of order, system, and regularity" and "positive delight in the decencies and elegancies of civilized life."[7] Some relief came when Pierce decided that the Philadelphia summer was too much even for Fanny, and he arranged for his wife and children to escape to a rundown spa in the Pennsylvania countryside, Yellow Springs. Beautifully situated in a cool valley near a spring of mineral waters and composed of several rambling farmhouses, Yellow Springs brought relief after steamy Philadelphia. Every day, Fanny and the children bathed in the icy water of the springs, but the landscape, the weather, and her children were the only pleasures. Receiving gossip from Philadelphia that Pierce was spending time with other women, she could barely speak to him when he made his languid appearances on the weekend to spend time with Sarah and Fan. She was thirty-three years old, as physically robust as ever, yet she was worn out by unhappiness. Once again, she was suicidal.

To Theodore Sedgwick, brother of Catharine and brother-in-law of Elizabeth, she wrote that when in "sheer weariness of spirit" she sometimes longed for death, she would check her rashness with reminders of work to be done, of duties to be fulfilled. But now, emotionally exhausted, she wondered whether it might not be better to lie down in her grave and become a "clod," to relinquish her "immortal birthright simply for rest."[8] Within days she somehow rallied, or perhaps the nature of her emotional illness launched her into a period of frantic activity, and she rode furiously in the summer heat, spent hours obsessively fishing as her mother had at Weybridge, walked for miles around Yellow Springs, and wrote late into the night at a rickety desk she had set up in the living room. She worked on a review of Tennyson's recently published verse that she planned to send to the editor of the *Knickerbocker*,[9] and she struggled with her own poems, one of which, published many years later and titled "Lines After a Summer's Walk," deploys imagery of the crystal clear water in which she was bathing every day. The poem expresses profound melancholy and despair and addresses an unworthy, disloyal lover.

Kemble relies on the conventions of sentimental verse to express the stormy feelings that, for reasons of privacy and self-esteem, she did not wish to express elsewhere, except in the most private letters to her most intimate friends, particularly Harriet St. Leger. Even these letters, of course, are carefully edited, and there is no extant correspondence that provides as revealing a picture of Kemble's feelings about Pierce as do her poems. It is not so much that she put into verse details of her life that were undisclosed elsewhere but that the formal demands of poetic composition licensed her to express more fully and without embarrassment the pain that she tended to gloss with irony in her letters. In the Yellow Springs poem, the speaker recalls a "sweet summer day" when the image of her companion cast a shadow over a clear spring; the clear water grows "turbid" yet she sees no "cloud" upon the person's brow: "Say could it mirror, thinkest thou, / Some evil hid within thy breast? / Were they lips guileless, thy heart true, / When by the fairy well they bent?" And just as the speaker's hidden duplicity has stirred the waters of the spring, so, too, has it cast a shade over the surface of the speaker's soul: "And stirred beyond my own control / The depths, that makes myself afraid."[10] It is a poem about the insidious power of betrayal to create a turbulence in the betrayed that matches the turbulence of the spring.

In the middle of August, Pierce commanded a return to the city as punishment for Kemble's reputed misbehavior at Yellow Springs. Regulations for bathing at the spa called for women and children to leave the baths at noon so that the men might occupy them from twelve until two o'clock. As appalled by the prospect of bathing with other women as she was offended by eating at a boardinghouse table, Kemble defied the rules and arrived every day right before noon. She would then refuse to leave, relishing a small female victory as the men were forced to wait until she decided it was time to depart. The men had complained to Pierce, and he took it, rightly it would seem, as a further sign of Kemble's insubordination, evidence of a chronic refusal to cooperate with anyone or anything that interfered with the way she wished to run things. He announced it was this attitude that had ruined their marriage, and he obtained a letter from the manager of the Yellow Springs resort complaining about Kemble's behavior, which he threatened to use against her when it suited him. Her victory was a small and short-lived one, and she paid dearly for it in discomfort when Pierce dictated a return to the city, although he relented quickly at the sight of his wilting children in the sultry city streets and packed them off to a farm. Their mother was confined, once more, to Mrs. McPherson's.

Kemble managed to survive August, and in mid-September she persuaded Pierce to allow her to go to New York to see William Macready, at the opening of an American tour, playing *Macbeth*: Macready noted in his journal, "Saw Mrs. *Butler*, whom I dared not ask after her husband."[11] On September 30 he had an opportunity to see Pierce firsthand when he dined with the Butlers and Henry and Fanny Longfellow in New York, and he was astonished by Kemble's forwardness at the dinner table. Admitting that she spoke admirably well, he added that if *he* been her husband, he would have been deeply offended by the manner in which she carried on "quite like a man." By now, Kemble was not only cross-dressing for riding and fishing, she was also assuming social roles conventionally allotted to men. Women did not assert themselves at the dinner table and the fact that she did it so well, with such style and wit, complicated male responses to her performance. She could not be dismissed outright as a silly and pretentious woman who wanted to show off. Macready acknowledged that she was a woman of "most extraordinary mind" and that she spoke the "stern truth" about all things, but he was troubled by her withering derogation of Pierce; he noted that even if she spoke the truth, she spoke "what in the true spirit of charity should not have been said in the presence of one who was obliged to listen to it. Alas!" At this dinner, Kemble probably voiced moral contempt for Pierce's indifference to the suffering of his slaves and to the institution of slavery itself, or she ridiculed his notorious philandering, or possibly both.[12] If Pierce tormented her with Mrs. McPherson's, a refusal to agree to terms for a separation, his indifference to slavery, and his involvement with other women, she retaliated with her cultural superiority, her irony, and her by now well-developed defiance of his orders.

When Macready saw her again on November 6, however, at the start of an engagement in Philadelphia, she behaved very differently. No longer the scintillating talker who reduced her husband to conversational mincemeat, she was subdued, downcast, and tearful. Hoping to cheer her up, Macready assured her that she was highly gifted, that in addition to writing such powerful plays as *An English Tragedy* she could become an important cultural influence in transatlantic society. But this articulation of her potential to become what she had longed to be from the time she met Harriet St. Leger—a respected intellectual woman, perhaps a published poet—painfully hit home and she burst into tremendous tears. What Macready did not know was that on her return to Philadelphia from New York she had discovered and opened a packet of sealed letters written to Pierce by a woman whose name is not revealed in Kemble's correspondence or in Pierce's papers: confronted by accusations of infidelity, Pierce denied an affair with this particular person, but, weary of Kemble's incessant accusations and suspicions, he admitted to adultery earlier in their marriage. Devastated by confirmation of what she suspected but also elated by possession of some evidence against him, on October 27 she wrote to Pierce that as a consequence of his ill treatment, she planned to seek a legal separation and financial support. In response, Pierce offered the following: he would provide £2,500 a year for her support (now roughly $55,000–$60,000), they would continue to live under the same roof but in separate apartments, and she would be allowed unfettered access to the children. The offer came with three conditions: she must not return to the stage, she must not advocate in print the cause of abolition, and she must not publish anything he had not approved. Desperate to stay close to Sarah and Fan, Fanny agreed to the conditions on November 6, 1843, the very day that Macready called at Mrs. McPherson's in Philadelphia and told Kemble she was wasting her intellectual gifts.[13] It is not surprising that she burst into tears.

In his divorce *Statement*, Pierce offered his version of these events. He charged that the Sedgwick family constantly interfered in his marriage, and that despite their sympathy for him back in 1839, when Fanny was reminded by Elizabeth Sedgwick of the inheritance of her mother's emotional illness, they accepted her exaggerations and distortions without question. Feeling wounded and miscast in the role of villainous husband, he angrily stated that none of the Sedgwicks made any effort to listen to his side of the story. As evidence of the family's malicious interference in his marriage, he quoted a letter written to him by Elizabeth Sedgwick on November 5, 1843, the day before Fanny signed the separation agreement: the letter charges him with profligacy, with deep and deliberate injury to a cherished friend of the Sedgwick family, and with lying in the spring of 1842 when he swore he had not "sinned" against his wife in any way.[14] He charged that Fanny had constructed a melodrama saturated in "angry invectives and suspicions," with her performing self at the suffering center and her husband relegated to the role of treacherous and philandering villain. Her tales were squalid fantasy, invented and performed for the Sedgwicks, her sympathetic and gullible audience.

In his *Statement*, he also claimed that Elizabeth Sedgwick had sunk so low as to interrogate the Butler nursemaid about his behavior in London the year before. Elizabeth's unscrupulous manipulation led the nursemaid to allege that not only was Butler's dissipation a regular topic of downstairs gossip, he had also made an attempt upon her virtue. Dismissing this allegation as irresponsible, untrue, and malicious, he found it as insupportable as Kemble's claim that her discovery of letters from an unknown woman "gave her sufficient reason for insisting on an instant separation." The truth, he claimed, was that while dishonorably going through his papers, Kemble had found two letters with unbroken seals, broken them and read the letters, and waved them triumphantly as evidence of his adultery. He swore they were no such thing: these "violated letters, never read by me, are absolutely all that she and her allies, the Sedgwicks, have ever been able to conjure up in support of their oft repeated charges of infidelity."[15] Kemble was the mistress of the arts of "ingenuity, perversion, and pretence," and, rather than suffering as an imperiled heroine betrayed by the cupidity of a villainous husband, she was vaunting her imagined moral superiority and ignoring the symptoms of her inherited emotional illness.

The Butler marital melodrama that had long been the gossip of Philadelphia society became a public sensation with the charge by a Philadelphia businessman, James Schott, that on March 9, 1844, he had discovered his wife and Pierce Butler in a New York hotel room in compromising circumstances. Like Pierce, Schott published a self-vindicating narrative that provided an account of the events leading to *his* divorce in the summer of 1844. Claiming that he suffered the divorce to be decreed by default from motives of delicacy, he stated that he now wished to explain his silence and defend himself against the "knavish craft" with which Pierce was spreading his own version of events. Schott's wife, Ellen, and her sister had decided to accompany the two men to New York on a business trip; Ellen Schott wanted to go to the opera and she also asked for her own room at the Astor Hotel. At midnight on March 9 Schott claimed "a circumstance occurred" to which he desired to give no publicity: either there was a comic misunderstanding or a scandalous moment of in flagrante delicto. Pierce swore, "on the oath of a Christian and the honor of a gentleman," that there had been no impropriety; Ellen Schott made a sworn statement that her husband was a violent brute and frequently threatened to shoot her; and Schott demanded a duel, which took place on April 15 at Bladensburg, Maryland. He withdrew after the second fire on account of a swollen foot, which he claimed interfered with his ability to shoot, and he contented himself with a proclamation of the "infamy of Pierce Butler, who, under the mask of friendship, ruined the peace and happiness of an unoffending family, and then sought to escape the consequences by resorting to the meanest artifices, the most cowardly subterfuges, and the most despicable falsehoods."[16]

Philadelphia society was galvanized by these sensational events, "thrown into a state of great excitement by a flare-up of a very sad character," as Sidney Fisher noted in his dairy on April 7. Fisher added that everyone believed the charge against Ellen Schott to be "totally false" and agreed that Pierce had behaved "with great propriety throughout."[17] Fisher's recollections of riding with Kemble in May 1844 indicate his sympathies in most things tended to be with Pierce, even if he had pronounced her a woman of great discrimination and character back in October 1839. Now, he felt, she lacked "delicacy and refinement . . . the reverse of feminine in her manners and conversation. She is also guilty of the imprudence and bad taste of alluding constantly to her domestic troubles, which I believe are brought about by her own want of tact and temper."[18] Fisher's opinion confirms if not Kemble's success in securing what she wanted from Pierce, at least the visibility of her resistance to his will. Philadelphia society's irritation with Kemble's refusal to conform to conventional codes for feminine behavior had begun, of course, well before her retaliation against Pierce's punitive maneuvers. In 1835 Pierce's friends had dismissed her American *Journal* as, at best, the misguided sympathies of a naive Englishwoman in America and, at worst, as the ungrateful ravings of a hysterical former actress. Now her defiance of almost every rule for proper feminine conduct became disturbing to a larger group of people: cross-dressing, demolishing fools with her saber wit in dinner party conversations, riding alone every day, refusing to defend Pierce against malicious charges of infidelity—all this gained her no sympathy.

The volatile political atmosphere in Philadelphia in 1844 offered an unsettling background to the Butler troubles. In May, working-class Protestant mobs, incited by fear and hatred of "Popery," set fire to Catholic churches and to various private houses; the city was, as Kemble reported, "lighted from river to river with the glare of these conflagrations," and she was "accosted in the streets as Papist, because of the little iron crucifix, that badge of the universal religion of sorrow" that she always wore around her neck.[19] Kemble's "badge" of sorrow was an apt symbol for her feelings as Philadelphia was going up in flames. Her world was falling apart. At Mrs. McPherson's, Fan fell over the banister and broke her arm; Pierce wrote to Kemble's advocate, the Rev. William Furness, that she neglected her children; and Pierce punished her at every opportunity for the Sedgwicks' interference. When they charged him with something of "even a more serious character" than infidelity and "soiled" their own lips with terrible "calumnies," he declared it would be savage of him to name the charges. Since he had already admitted to adultery early in the marriage, had been charged with sleeping with the governess and molesting the upstairs maids, and allegedly been found in a compromising position in Ellen Schott's bedroom at the Astor Hotel in New York, it is likely that the Sedgwicks accused him of sleeping with his female slaves, which would hardly have been surprising, given plantation practices. Whatever the "conduct," the charges convinced Fanny she must escape before her emotional and physical reserves were exhausted. That she might be contemplating such a move and that the prospect of financial support from her father was not promising is indicated by a letter written by Sydney Smith to Lady Grey (both old friends of the Kemble family) on March 9, 1844, in which he notes that "Poor Charles Kemble (utterly ruined by American Stocks) is putting about a subscription of 5 guineas for public readings. . . . Mrs. Butler I believe will be soon in England and I conjecture will reappear on the stage."[20]

Three mornings a week, between seven and eight o'clock, Kemble walked with the children around Washington Square, onto which Mrs. McPherson's Sixth Street establishment faced; on other mornings, she took them to the market to buy fruit and flowers. The children spent the rest of each day with the governess, and Kemble spent the morning and afternoon studying German, doing her correspondence, and riding out to the Schuylkill. At six-thirty, she was allowed by Pierce to take the children out for another walk. When the Philadelphia heat became intolerable, Pierce decided to take Sarah and Fan to Newport, Rhode Island, and he allowed Kemble to visit the Sedgwicks at Lenox. Just before she left Philadelphia, Kemble wrote to Sarah Perkins Cleveland that her life was one of "trial and perpetual irritation as well as deep and fatal disappointment," and that "every conceivable measure" was being deployed to keep her children from her.[21] A legitimation of the self-fashioned performance as injured wife that she crafted in her letters was becoming clear through Pierce's vindictive maneuvers.

At Lenox, Kemble was a tragic figure. Pierce had just purchased a new house at 424 Walnut Street; she knew he was preparing a revised agreement that would settle her future; and she suspected one of the conditions would be a complete prohibition of contact with the Sedgwick family. Charles Sumner, the Boston lawyer and abolitionist, was a visitor to Lenox that summer, and he wrote to Sarah Perkins Cleveland that Kemble was entrancing but sorrowful, "a wife without a husband, a mother, without her children." He thought her genius and character matchless, her griefs unutterably touching, and her talent for reading Shakespeare superb, but he was also troubled by a "prevailing intensity," for him "the attendance of genius and too often the fore-runner of unhappiness."[22] As the time neared for her return to Philadelphia, Kemble wrote to Kate Minot that she was trembling at the "near approach of her martyrdom" and she needed to marshal all her emotional forces to meet the onslaught.

What awaited her was the new agreement, in essence not that different from the arrangements concluded the previous November, but with new conditions so punitive they testify to the unmitigated dislike with which Pierce now regarded her: she was to live separately from him in the new Walnut Street house with full access to the children, provided she agreed never to communicate in any way with any member of the Sedgwick family, never to speak of the past or of anything that might occur in Pierce's household, to any person whomsoever, and never to return to the stage. Ten years earlier, Fanny Kemble had come to Philadelphia as a brilliant young actress and Pierce had been her slavish admirer: now he had her boxed in. After several months of wretched indecision about validating something cast so entirely in Pierce's favor, Kemble signed the agreement in mid-February 1845. For the rest of her life she nursed the rage that accompanied this acquiescence, which was essential, at the time, if she were to see her daughters. Thirty-four years later she was relieved to be unable to attend the christening of Fan's son since he was to be named Pierce Butler; she wrote to Anne Thackeray Ritchie, "I cannot be present to hear the child so baptized and can only pray God to avert from it the evil omen of such a name."[23]

After six months, she knew that the bargain she had struck with Pierce for access to her children and financial support for herself was the coup de grace in the scheme to get rid of her. She was under constant surveillance by Pierce's servants, ridiculed by friends of the Butler family, and tortured by cruel indignities such as being prevented from attending her children's birthday party. She had no choice but to return to her father's lodgings in London and to a stage career, if she still possessed any professional currency, which would provide Pierce with the grounds for divorce: desertion from her household and her children, and resumption of a career prohibited by their agreement. As she weighed her choice, she was consoled by the fact that the bulk of her father's income was derived from her own labor: as she put it candidly in mid-August to Samuel Gray Ward, a Boston lawyer and friend of the Sedgwicks, her father's present funds were "the fruit" of her former work, and distasteful as she might find it to live in his house, she would, in truth, "be subsisting upon my own means." In this same letter, she also confided that she was now certain that for the previous three years Pierce had only one object at which he had "aimed so steadily . . . his getting rid of me."[24]

On October 16, 1845, she gratified that aim and sailed for England, her fare furnished by an unidentified "friend," in all probability the wealthy Samuel Gray Ward to whom she confided details of the financial arrangements with her father. A closing scene for the melodrama of her marriage is found in a bitter poem titled "A Promise" that appeared in her book of verse published in 1844. The poem is addressed to a faithless lover.

> I'll come to thee in all youth's brightest power,
> As on the day thy faith to mine was plighted,
> And then I'll tell thee weary hour by hour,
> How that spring's early promise had been blighted,
> I'll tell thee of the long, long, dreary years,
> That have passed o'er me hopeless, objectless;
> My loathsome days, my nights of burning tears,
> My wild despair, my utter loneliness,
> My heart-sick dreams upon my feverish bed,
> My fearful longing to be with the dead;
> In the dark lonely night,
> When sleep and silence keep their watch o'er men
> False love! in thy despite,
> We two shall meet again![25]

Resemblances between a speaker whose love has been "blighted" by "long, long, dreary years" of unhappiness and Fanny Butler did not go unnoticed by Philadelphia society: Sidney Fisher concludes that too many poems in Kemble's 1844 volume contained "allusions to her position and conjugal unhappiness that had better have been omitted."[26]

To Italy

When she arrived at Liverpool, Kemble was met by Harriet St. Leger and they went together to Bannisters, the country home of Emily Fitzhugh, an old friend of the Kemble family. After visiting her brother John at the Weybridge house he had inherited from Thérèse, Fanny arrived at 44 Mortimer Street, where she was to live with her father, who, at the age of seventy, was vigorously pursuing his new and lucrative career as a reader of Shakespeare's plays. Within days, she wrote to Harriet, she was overwhelmed with invitations, and her life was an "amazing contrast" to the "idiotic" existence in America (an ironic understatement of her recent experience and characteristic of the way she sometimes glossed over what was painful and humiliating). After the enervating dullness of Mrs. McPherson's and the exhaustion of combating Pierce's malevolence, Kemble was intoxicated and dizzied by brilliant London talk, but she was also overstimulated by an abundance of what she loved most—lively, informed conversation about literary, social, and political topics—and she feared she might be entering one of her unmanageably active phases. After the enforced inertia in America, the shift in setting and intellectual excitement proved too radical, and she felt her "nervous temperament" was being stimulated to an extreme state. She began to blame herself, to feel she was being "seduced" by the power, skill, and dexterity of her scintillating friends who performed extraordinary intellectual feats on a "low moral level," practiced a sophistry that she both admired for its theatrical skill but distrusted because of its suspect moral nature.[27] In this ambivalent reaction to thrilling London talk after depressing Philadelphia silence, Kemble is both vibrant performer and troubled critic of her own performance.

In early December, while staying with her close friends, Lord and Lady Dacre at their house, the Hoo, she sang out her love of life and pleasure in the world: "What a delightful thing good writing is! What a delightful thing good talking is! How much delight there is in the exercise and perfection of our faculties! How *full* a thing, and admirable, and wonderful is this nature of ours!" she wrote to Harriet.[28] Back in London, the dinner guests at a party given by the Proctors (parents of the poet Adelaide Proctor) created an amazed awareness of the transformation in her life: she sat down with the art critic Henry Chorley, an old friend; John Kenyon, patron of the arts and friend of Elizabeth Barrett; Richard Monckton Milnes, the poet and close friend of her brother John (they had been fellow Apostles at Cambridge); and Robert Browning, by now deeply in love with Elizabeth Barrett after having met her in May 1845. In her account of this dinner, in her memoirs, Kemble mentions no women guests, a significant omission since men tended to be her chosen sparring partners in dinner party conversation; either there were no other women present (besides her hostess) or she was insufficiently interested to mention their names. In some ways, she was as ferocious as Thomas Macaulay, said to be a "lion" at conversational parties, and when she left the Proctors, she wrote playfully to Harriet that after such a party it was hard to tolerate "poor pitiful *prose people*" like her dear old friend.[29]

Ten days later she was a neurasthenic mess, bursting into sobs at the slightest noise, suffering a constant pain in her heart, and sometimes passing the whole morning sitting on the floor in tears. She now believed that her "late experiences" had completely shattered and broken her nervous equanimity, and she longed for the peace of her "beloved" Lenox in the Berkshire hills. But when Adelaide and Edward Sartoris invited her to visit them in Italy, where they now resided, she eagerly accepted; she had not seen her sister for two and a half years, and with the irrepressible enthusiasm that always surfaced after depression, she began to read up on Italian art. She quickly formed some severe moral objections about Renaissance depictions of the female body, in particular to an etching of Eve made by Raphael about which her old friend Anna Jameson was ecstatic. This Eve was far too mature, voluptuous, and self-aware for her taste; her preference was for Eve figured as an eager, inquisitive, greedy child, a "sensual, self-willed, ignorant savage, who saw something beautiful, that smelt good, and looked as if it tasted good and so tasted it."[30] Kemble confided to Harriet St. Leger that her ideal of womanly beauty was that of an antique Diana as she draws an arrow from her quiver, an evocative image that nicely recalls Harriet herself as she appeared to Kemble some eighteen years earlier: slim, tall, austere.

Lack of money preoccupied Kemble as she prepared for the Italian journey. The time had not yet arrived, either in England or America, when married women were allowed to possess, in their own right, money they had earned or inherited. As Kemble observes in an interpolated comment in *Records of Later Life* (writing in the late 1870s and referring to the 1870 Married Women's Property Act), "How infinite a relief from bitter injustice and hardship has been legislation that has enabled women to hold and own independently property left to them by kindred or friends, or earned by their own industry and exertions."[31] Her financial situation in 1845 was precarious, a grating reminder of the unavoidable reliance of Victorian women on their fathers, husbands, and male relatives for support. She had left America with no secure financial future, and her father was unwilling to consign the interest on the money she had earned on her American tour; he provided nothing more than lodging—comfortable, to be sure, but still under his aegis. What was especially galling was the financial success of his Shakespeare readings. His reading of *Cymbeline* for Queen Victoria in 1844 had launched a lucrative career; he earned twenty guineas per performance (often three times per week), and other than complaining of the odd rheumatic twinge, he showed no sign of slowing down. Hopping down to Brighton or nipping up to Highgate from Cavendish Square seemed to make him sprightlier than ever. Kemble was glad of this, but the financial situation with Pierce was precarious: her aunt Victoire had left her a small legacy but she was unable to claim it without his consent, and negotiations through her lawyers back in Philadelphia for an annuity had stalled. Possessing only one resource, a risky return to the stage, she was relieved in December 1845 to know that she would be staying with her sister and brother-in-law for a year. She vowed to put Pierce and her embarrassing financial reliance on her relatives at the back of her mind, although there was hardly a moment when she did not think of ten-year-old Sarah and seven-year-old Fan, now under the complete control of their father.[32] Thirty-six years old, missing her children and ruing her financial dependency, Kemble felt bereft and despondent during the few weeks before she left for Italy.

Happier to advise his daughter about her travel plans than share the income from the capital that she had earned and that enabled his own comfort (he never seemed able to do more than offer the odd ten-pound note), Charles Kemble planned her taxing journey to Italy, to be undertaken at a terrible time of year: diligence from Havre to Rouen, railway from Rouen to Paris, coach from Paris to Marseilles, steamboat to Civita Vecchia, and then carriage to Rome. He managed to do even this begrudgingly, driving Kemble to distraction by saying nothing to her about her "means of subsistence" while she would be abroad.[33] Accompanied by her maid, Hayes, and advised by the Kemble family physician that there was no cure for her physical symptoms of pains in the heart, the side, and the head since they could all be traced to "mental causes," Kemble left Southampton on December 20, 1845. In her memoirs, she relates how the night before she sailed she reviewed her unhappy history. She had been a transatlantic celebrity, a promising author, and a financially secure wife and mother: now, she was an almost forgotten Kemble, a sporadic writer of reviews, an abandoned wife, and a dependent daughter. Perhaps as a way of enduring her misery, she began to perform the role of martyr and presented herself to her friends in a theatrical attitude of acquiescence to her fate: declaring it was hopeless to wonder why certain individuals were selected for sorrow, she wrote to Harriet St. Leger, "all trial is the positive result of or has been incurred by error or sin . . . sent to teach us better things than we knew, or than we did, before." Her Christian faith, now tinged with a kind of melancholic masochism, was stronger than ever and she believed that her sorrows must be accepted and that she deserved her trials: "They are appointed to me because they are best for me, and whatever my apparent impatience under them, this is, in deed and truth, my abiding faith."[34] The Fanny Kemble who poked fun at American prudishness, lacerated her husband for his indifference to the suffering of his slaves, and told a German sentry she had neither father nor husband and was just "a woman" became, at this low point in her life, masochistically resigned to her unhappy fate. A martyr to her own failings, she implies that all her misery may be traced to her own "error" or "sin," her self-reliance and irrepressible buoyancy given to her precisely in proportion to her sorrows. This was the mood in which she set off for Italy.

It was a hellish journey. The channel in winter surpassed anything on the Atlantic, and crossing the snowy mountains in a coach to Rouen involved being insulated by vast amounts of hay, which seemed to her like being stuffed into a manger. Passing through France was a trial of cold, dirt, bad food, and grasping landlords; traveling through Italy, she suffered neglect and impertinence. A veteran of touring the English provinces and sailing the gusty Atlantic, she wondered whether it was all worth it.

When she arrived in Rome on January 9, 1846, the warm weather, the roses and the lemon blossoms, and the rides out into the countryside restored her health and spirits, but it was a bittersweet joy to hold Adelaide's baby girl; she had not seen her own daughters for almost three months and she had no idea when she would see them again. Her sadness was registered in a sonnet interpolated into *A Year of Consolation*, the travel narrative that she published in 1847. The speaker of the poem is a mother who warns a child, "They [one assumes adults in charge of the child] have not taught thee yet / That hapless mother's image to forget," but that these guardians believe the coming years, full of the grand pageant of life, "shall brush that waning form away." The speaker, bereft of her own child, knows her *own* experience will be the reverse: "All other images" will be chased away by the "blessed, lovely vision" of the child from whom she has been separated.

Aside from this interpolated poem about a mother's wrenching separation from her child, *A Year of Consolation*, dedicated with great affection to Edward Sartoris for his "kindness and indulgence" in having her stay for a year, offers little in terms of Kemble's feelings. She fashioned it as a travel narrative from which she hoped to earn some money (although, legally, her earnings would have belonged to Pierce), and she devoted at least two-thirds to descriptions of churches, paintings, sculpture, and local vegetables. The reviews of *A Year of Consolation* refused to forget she was an actress and patronized her intellect. The *Spectator*, for example, praised Kemble for finding a tone "greatly superior to that of the volumes she published a dozen years ago—more sober, and much less flippant," but warned its readers that "neither her mind nor her education renders her a trustworthy guide on large and complex subjects." The *Examiner* announced that what "would have made her writing better, would doubtless have also made her life happier—something less of this predominance of self. . . . We cannot but think of the theatre."[35] Demeaning what can only be interpreted as a woman's education (incapable of tackling "large and complex subjects") and impertinently suggesting that Kemble's life would have been "happier" had she not been an actress and thus less narcissistic, these reviews suggest some of the unabated animosity that Kemble encountered throughout her life.

For one month, she spent two hours a day in the Vatican and felt that she
was living on Olympus—to see the paintings of the great Italian masters was to
leave the world of mere mortals, although she found Raphael's *Fornarina* a little
too louche for her English taste. The painting of a half-naked woman wearing a
splendid turban suggested nakedness for display rather than art. When she viewed
the illumination of St. Peter's at Easter, she was excited by the rare sight of streams
of people pouring into the piazza from every street and alley, controlled by mounted police whose drawn sabers glittered in the illuminations; the sight of nuns
washing the feet of peasants moved her to tears; and the chattering of oafish English tourists offended her national pride. In the summer of 1846, when Rome became almost as unbearable as Philadelphia and Fanny was bilious from the sirocco
winds that seemed to come directly from hell, they all went to a villa in Frascati,
rented by Edward from the Borghese family, where they were joined frequently
by friends such as Frederic Leighton, who had become devoted to Adelaide, and
Harriet Hosmer, the American sculptor. This was an idyllic summer, filled with
picnics, music, and singing, and she felt that to have had such a perfect time was "a
miracle."[36] The exquisitely clustered stone farmhouses, their tiled roofs glittering
in the Italian sun, contrasted brilliantly with what she always evoked as the ugly
stiff-staring villages of the Pennsylvania countryside and she commemorated this
summer in a poem, "Close of Our Summer at Frascati."

> The end is come; the golden links are parting,
> That in one chain of happy circumstance,
> And gentle, friendly, human fellowship,
> Bound many hearts for many a day together.
> . . .
> Our sun of pleasure hastens towards the west,
> But the green freshness of fair memories
> Lives over these bright days for evermore.[37]

When they returned to Rome in the autumn, the "fellowship" was enlarged
by visits from English travelers such as William Thackeray and his daughter, who
remembers being taken by her father to the Sartoris villa. The drawing room was
dominated by a large piano, the stone floors were covered in soft carpets, huge logs
burned in an enormous fireplace, and Adelaide, now grown quite large, received in
a kind of gray satin caftan. Kemble was wearing the dress she had designated for
that particular day of the week since she obsessively wore her clothes in rotation,
partly as an economy and partly as a means of keeping her life in order. Regardless of whether she were attending the opera or going on a picnic, she wore the

dress that was set aside for that day—if a black gown chanced to fall on a gala day she wore it, if the pale silk gown fell on a working day, she wore it. As Adelaide Sartoris recalls, Americans were horrified to see Kemble tramping through the Pamphili Gardens, "the delicate folds of a white silk embroidered with flowers . . . sweeping over the anemones."[38] When Thackeray took his daughter to visit the newly married Elizabeth Barrett and Robert Browning, they found Elizabeth "dim in her dusky gown unrelieved" and Kemble "upright and magnificent, robed on this occasion like some Roman empress in stately crimson edged with gold." It was her red dress day, and she wore it.[39] Kemble now knew that she could not live if she did not live by rule: when in Rome, she sat with her watch open before her as she read, wrote, and did needlework, and every evening she played an appointed number of games of Patience. Conscious of the dangers of deviation from her rules, she shaped her diurnal existence to a recurring pattern: no scheduled activity was allowed to run over its allotted time; no unscheduled event was given space on her disciplinary calendar.

That the Italians took a more relaxed view of things was the mildest of the criticisms she eventually leveled against their nation during this consoling year with Adelaide and Edward. However glorious their past and however lovely their present, the Italians were, from Kemble's Protestant perspective, irreparably damaged by the prevalence of "women without chastity, and men without integrity, and a whole country without religion."[40] Italy was priest-ridden, its people ignorant, superstitious, and lazy. In addition, for someone highly sensitive to changes in atmospheric conditions, the weather was sometimes oppressive and exhausting. After the first glorious Roman spring, the sirocco winds gave her headaches and the air that was like a blast from an oven steeped her in perspiration before breakfast. Nevertheless, it was a restorative year, one that gave her much to write about. On the Georgia plantations, she had established some distance from her conflicted position as slave owner and abolitionist by assuming the role of performing writer, and here she did something similar: she took many notes, she wrote almost every day without fail, and when she returned to England, she had a record of this year of consolation. Just as she had presented herself as an Englishwoman in Georgia, appalled by what she witnessed, now she was an Englishwoman in Italy but, of course, with a significant difference: apart from her distaste for Catholicism and all its rituals, she loved being in Italy and always remained deeply grateful to Adelaide and Edward for suffering her sadness and idiosyncrasies for as long as they did. It was to Adelaide, especially, that she paid special tribute in a poem titled "A Summons," inspired by a late autumn moment when they stood on a sunny hillside and saw a snow-capped mountain in the distance.

O thou beloved, by whom I stand,
Straining in mine thy kindred hand,
Farewell!—on yonder mountain's brow
I see a beckoning hand of snow;
Stern winter dares no nearer come,
But waves me towards his northern home.[41]

On December 7, 1846, as she knelt on the edge of the fountain of Trevi on a dark, gloomy day in the pouring rain, she said goodbye to Rome and realized that when she returned to England she would be faced with some serious questions about her financial future. Kemble not only found answers to those questions but she triumphed spectacularly over the unhappiness of the previous ten years.

Fanny Redux

Soon after her return, deciding to risk Pierce's vengeance by returning to the stage, Kemble eagerly accepted an offer from a Manchester theater manager. Although she was allowed to appear in plays and roles of her own choosing, she was not sanguine about her success; disadvantageously altered, as she put it, she assessed herself as stout, middle-aged, not particularly good-looking, and professionally rusty after thirteen years away from the boards. At the age of thirty-seven, she had assumed some of the fleshiness of her aunt Siddons (particularly in profile), although she lacked the statuesque height that balanced Siddons's bulk. With no manager and no assistance beyond that provided by her faithful Hayes, for the next year she negotiated all her engagements, revisited many of the provincial theaters she had toured with her father in the early 1830s, and earned on average £54 a night (now, close to £3,000, which was considerable compared to the paltry support Pierce had been prepared to offer before she left America). The schedule was often grueling—in one week in January 1847 she acted on a Friday and Saturday in Norwich, on Monday, Tuesday, and Wednesday in Kings Lynn, and on Thursday in Cambridge—but Kemble was tough and determined, and the income allowed her to rent a small house just off Portman Square in London and to amass without difficulty the £3,000 she decided was needed to return to America for reclamation of her children, news of whom was sent by American friends. She invested her money in English funds, beyond the reach of American laws of coverture and Pierce Butler, and vowed to act in St. Petersburg, if necessary, "where one tyranny will protect me from another."[42] The initial anxiety about exposing herself to a curious, perhaps unfriendly theatergoing public was alleviated by the prospect of earning money, and the mood of martyred victim with which she had set off for Italy a little more than a year before shifted to one of triumphant satisfaction.

Invigorated by her return to acting (despite an unabated distaste for the profession), she wrote jubilantly to Harriet St. Leger, "Oh, my dear, what a world is this! Or, rather what an unlucky experience mine has been—in some respects—yes, in *some* respects! For while I write this, images of the good, and true, and excellent people I have known and loved, rise like a cloud of witnesses to shut out the ugly vision of the moral deformity of some of those with whom my fate has been interwoven."[43] Yet the "ugly vision" of Pierce Butler, in her eyes the most morally deformed of those with whom her fate had been entangled, loomed close to her when she began rehearsals in Manchester in early 1847 for a return to the stage after thirteen years away from acting. She was very nervous, even in approaching her most famous role, Julia in *The Hunchback*; distressful moments in the play made her shudder from head to foot and she was so sensitive to noise that she dreaded the applause she knew would greet her first appearance. But she vanquished her nerves, weathered the applause, and during the next year traveled widely in the English provinces and in Scotland. Her success defied many predictions to the contrary, particularly those voiced by William Macready. When he had seen her in 1843 in Philadelphia, he noted that although she was literally wretched and her husband's feeling toward her "was absolute aversion," it "*would not do*" for her to return to acting. Seeing Kemble perform in an amateur production of Victor Hugo's *Hernani* in May 1847 (the play performed in the country house theatricals where she had met Augustus Craven in 1831) was painful for him—she was affected, monotonous, and ignorant of the "very first rudiments of her art."[44] Hearing of her plans for the Manchester engagement, he declared that even if she was "a woman of unquestionable genius," her judgment was deficient and she would be spoken of harshly. She was not. The actors in the Manchester company were courteous and respected her ideas; her greatest asset before the public—the physical power of voice and delivery—was undiminished; and her self-possession onstage was greater than it had ever been, something she attributed to her trials with Pierce. After all she had endured, she told herself, it would be impossible to feel any apprehension about performing before an enthusiastic audience.

On February 17, 1847, the *Manchester Courier* reviewed her return to the stage in rapturous terms: welcomed by much applause and cheering when she entered, she showed the audience that her voice had lost "none of its exquisite music" and that her "attitudes and action" were still graceful and picturesque.[45] From Manchester she moved on to Liverpool, and a contemporary account by an actor in the company shows Kemble at her courageous best. Lacking an advance agent, a press agent, or an actor-manager, she walked onstage alone and unattended. Expecting the arrival of a demanding tragedy queen, the company saw instead "a quiet, unassuming lady of middle age and middle height, simply attired in a black silk dress. Her pale, classic features were irradiated by a pair of dark, lustrous eyes, which wore an eerie expression—imperious one moment, pleading the next—and which showed forth in vivid contrast to the glory of her abundant hair, even then slightly streaked with grey at the temples." In elegant recognition of the simultaneous baring of heads "to the last of the Kembles" on the part of company, Kemble made a simple curtsey, and the rehearsal began. This actor, fifty years later, swore he never saw the equal of her "grace, beauty, tragic fire, and perfect majesty."[46] After Manchester, Liverpool, and Birmingham, she toured Bath, Bristol, and Plymouth and then went to Scotland. Three weeks in Edinburgh were bittersweet since everywhere she looked she was reminded of her year with Harriet Siddons in 1827, "the happiest of my existence hitherto," she wrote to Harriet St. Leger.[47]

Riding in Hyde Park on December 11, 1847, Kemble met William Macready and told him that she particularly wished to act with him, which suggests she had heard nothing of his strong reservations about her return to the stage. For reasons that remain unfathomable except that he had a canny eye on the box office, Macready jumped at the offer and proposed she perform with him in the roles of Desdemona, Cordelia, Ophelia, Lady Macbeth, and Queen Katherine. Given his dim view of her work onstage and the sharp difference in their acting styles, his shaped by the emerging Victorian interest in revising the rules and hers by early nineteenth-century mastery of the stylized assumption of attitudes and exaggerated verbal delivery, this engagement could only lead to difficulty—and it did. As Alan Downer observes, "The nineteenth century actor, like his predecessor, was the repository of the accumulated conventions of the stage, and, while adhering to them, was continually in revolt against them."[48] What had been planned as a four-week run, to be extended if successful, ended after only three weeks, and at the end of it Kemble bore the scars of some serious verbal abuse and physical injury. A serious collision of acting styles, temperaments, and reputations, the engagement was a monumental disaster.

In rehearsals, Macready did not disguise his disgust with what he saw as Kemble's posturing and haughty behavior; never having seen anyone "so unnatural, so affected, so conceited," he declared her to be a self-deluded "monstrous pretender to theatrical art," carrying on as if *"en grande reine."* He maliciously noted that during a performance of *Henry VIII*, Charles Kemble, sitting majestically in the stalls, knocked so loudly and so often with his stick upon the floor whenever Fanny appeared that people called for him to be removed from the theater. Kemble, in turn, was shocked by the sheer physicality of working with Macready: at the end of the day she was bruised from being so knocked about. She was not the first actress to

Fig. 27. William Macready as Macbeth, 1821. Macready acted in this role with Kemble in 1847. V&A Images/Theatre Museum.

feel the force of Macready's emotional and physical intensity. Helena Faucit (1817–1898), who joined the Drury Lane Company in 1842 (then under Macready's direction), recalled that when she acted with him in *The Winter's Tale* (as Hermione), his "passionate joy at finding Hermione really alive seemed beyond control. Now he was prostrate at her feet, then enfolding her in his arms. . . . The hair, which came unbound, and fell on my shoulders, was reverently kissed and caressed. The whole change was so sudden, so overwhelming, that I suppose I cried out hysterically, for he whispered to me, 'Don't be frightened, my child! Don't be frightened! Control yourself.'"[49] When Macready delivered Macbeth's fervent instruction to Kemble's Lady Macbeth to "Bring forth men-children only; / For thy undaunted mettle should compose / Nothing but males," he seized her so ferociously by the wrist, she reported, that she was compelled to execute the most remarkable pirouette that a "lady did surely never perform before, under the influence of her husband's admiration."[50]

Initially Kemble did not think Macready as uncivil as she had been led to believe, although she soon dismissed him as ill-bred, inconsiderate, and irritable. There was no fire in her dressing room at the Princess's Theatre, he remained seated when she was standing and talking to him, he violated all the cues, he interrupted when she was in the middle of a soliloquy, and he prowled around the back of the stage like a tiger, snarling and grumbling, so that she had no idea where he was and when he would pounce upon her. Struggling in her memoirs to be fair, Kemble praises him for his talent for creating dramatic spectacle and for his vigorous performances in colorful roles such as Rob Roy, in an adaptation of Scott's novel, but she was appalled by his shoddy declamation of blank verse. What admirers called his natural style of delivery was to her simply chopping blank verse up into prose with no understanding of the artificial construction and rules of rhythm and measure.[51] Always considerate to her fellow actors, even when she was secretly laughing at them, Kemble was appalled by Macready's selfishness onstage. In performing *Macbeth*, for example, she was accustomed to the convention, established by her uncle and aunt, John Philip Kemble and Sarah Siddons, of having the royal dais and throne with steps at the middle stage with two long tables on either side, which allowed Lady Macbeth to descend from the dais and return for repeated expostulation with her husband: as Joseph Donohue notes, during this scene, Siddons remained mostly immobile raised above the other actors, her unease and terror visible to the audience—her descent downstage was dramatically highlighted by the immobility.[52] Macready had a long table set at the foot of the dais, which prevented Kemble's descent and secured the center stage for himself.

It is possible that Macready's rough-and-ready realism and his brusque disregard of decades of theatrical tradition compelled Kemble, in a strategy of retaliation, to exaggerate her already mannered style and to polish her displays of Kemble hauteur. In a further instance of the fluid performances that had previously flouted Pierce's domestic tyranny and derided Philadelphia prescriptions for appropriate feminine behavior, she may have deliberately overplayed the style Macready despised and the customs he considered redundant to show up his coarseness of acting style and social manners. In addition, her concept of the character of Lady Macbeth was very different from what Macready had in mind: where he wanted a Lady Macbeth who remained literally and metaphorically at the back of the stage, Kemble believed that this character was "a masculine woman" who belonged down front. In her writings about Shakespeare's characters, she declares, "Lady Macbeth was this; she possessed qualities which generally characterise men and not women—energy, decision, daring, unscrupulousness; a deficiency of imagination, a great preponderance of the positive and practical mental elements; a powerful and rapid appreciation of what each exigency of circumstance demanded, and the coolness and resolution necessary for its immediate execution. Lady Macbeth's character has more of the essentially manly nature in it than that of Macbeth."[53] In sum, Lady Macbeth, at her best, was very much like Kemble herself when she, too, was at her best: energetic, cool, resolved—more like a man than a woman in terms of Victorian prescriptions for male and female behavior. This is how Kemble attempted to play the part, but on Macready's stage there was room only for one character with an "essentially manly nature," and that was Macbeth, played by himself.

Subversive or not, Kemble's behavior did not change his view of her acting: he thought her Desdemona well enough conceived, but for him she never *was* Desdemona—it was all affected voice, a leaning back of the head, exaggerated walking across the stage. In sum, it was *so* theatrical, formal, contrived, and external that there was no trace of dramatic feeling left in the performance. For Kemble, the only thing that pleased her about playing Desdemona to Macready's Othello was her costumes, which she described to Harriet St. Leger as "beautiful and correct": contrary to the custom of English actresses to dress in white satin for this role, Kemble insisted on black and gold, "the only habit of the noble Venetian ladies." That Kemble's performances with Macready might have failed to match her reputation is suggested by a tactfully ambiguous note from Dickens, written on February 10, 1848: he makes no reference to the play he had just seen but refers instead to a recent encounter—"I do not easily forget any meeting with one for whose genius I have so great and sincere an esteem as I entertain for yours."[54]

Kemble labored on to the end of her engagement, preoccupied with her professional future. While touring the provinces the previous winter she had offered the occasional Shakespeare reading, prompted, in part, by her father's decision to retire (for example, she read *Coriolanus* in Hull in early December 1847). Now, smarting from the blows to her esteem, and to her body, caused by Macready's behavior, she decided it was time to pursue a second career. On March 25, 1848, she gave her first London Shakespeare reading, at Highgate. Two weeks later, early in the morning of the day of the large meeting of Chartists, April 10, she drove to Westminster Bridge. The shops were shut, the streets were deserted, and everything appeared quiet and orderly. For Kemble, as she proceeded peacefully down Whitehall, nothing suggested the dread that had induced people to pack up their valuables and prepare for instant flight. As things turned out, England remained relatively calm: the workers presented their charter to Parliament, were summarily dismissed, and then trudged back to their factories and workshops. As Kemble had forecast to Theodore Sedgwick in March 1848, there was no revolution: "Alone of all the thrones in Europe, that of our excellent queen and her admirable consort stands unshaken; alone of all the political constitutions, that of the country they govern is threatened with no fatal convulsion."[55] Kemble experienced this momentous day, so disappointing for the English working class, as one of great relief. If she felt any sympathy for the plight of the Chartists (and she may well have, given the strong condemnation of the indifference of Manchester manufacturers to the suffering of their workers that she had articulated in 1832), she did not express it, although three isolated acts of kindness and political intervention on her part that occurred in late 1847 suggest a sympathetic awareness of lower-class suffering.

On November 18, 1847, Kemble wrote to Harriet St. Leger to relate the outcome of her action in removing from the hands of the police a pregnant, homeless girl she had discovered sleeping in Hyde Park. Having paid the expenses for the girl to return to Bristol, to her "poor young sister, only a year older than herself, who earns her scanty support by sewing" and also providing some money to get her through "the first difficulties of her return," Kemble lamented the insistence of the workhouse authorities that the girl go back to "whence she came, no doubt to go through a similar experience as soon as possible again."[56] On December 4, 1847, again to Harriet St. Leger, Kemble writes that as she was taking her daily exercise by walking around the "magnificent" Hull railway station (shaped like a horseshoe, broad pavement, skylight all around), she almost tripped over a bundle of rags: a homeless, starving boy, whom Kemble promptly took to the workhouse in a cab. In "a succession of convulsions of rage and crying," once she received assurance that he would either go to sea or be apprenticed, she pledged one of the readings for the purposes of "outfit or entrance-fee."[57] In Southampton, on December 16, 1847, she saw a five-year-old boy staring into a pastry cook's window: he wanted baked apples for his sick baby brother. In a scene that anticipates the visit of Esther Summerson and Ada Clare to the brick makers in *Bleak House*, Kemble relates that she "went to see his people, and found them poor and ill, in much distress; and the mother, looking at her youngest child, a sickly, wasted, miserable little object, lamented bitterly that she did not belong to such associations [a burial society], for then, if it should please God to take the child, she would have five pounds to bury it."[58] What is notable about these three incidents is that Kemble does more than offer money to the suffering and the sick: she forcefully insists that the pregnant girl be removed from the park; she takes the "bundle of rags" that is a homeless boy in a cab to the workhouse; and she visits the miserable home of the five-year-old who wants the baked apples for his sick brother. These acts of intervention cannot, of course, be read as evidence of a sustained political commitment to alleviating poverty and distress, but they do suggest how Kemble was influenced by the prevalent Victorian encouragement of moral sympathy if charity were to become more than perfunctory duty.

In the middle of her acting engagement with Macready, Kemble wrote to Anne Lynch (later Botta), an intellectual young woman who was a poet and a teacher at a girls' academy in Brooklyn, to thank her for a sonnet she had sent: "its poetical merit is great, its moral value even greater; and it is very comfortable to me, dear Anne, who am walking along a rough and thorny path and carrying at my heart the burden of an irreparable loss, which, however, I take it, is lighter than an evil deed."[59] However, even as she suffered the "irreparable loss" of her children, Kemble was able still to derive satisfaction (and justifiably so) in what she had achieved since she left Philadelphia in 1845. She had mastered her depression through travel and hard work, she had accumulated a healthy bank balance, and she had made a successful start to her Shakespeare readings. She was the legal wife of Pierce Butler, but his betrayals and petty cruelties could no longer touch her, and what had begun as a guerilla campaign of defiance of his tyranny and manipulation was ending now in her professional triumphs and financial independence.

Fanny's Master

Oft, when my lips I open to rehearse
Thy wondrous spells of wisdom, and of power,
And that my voice, and thy immortal verse,
On listening ears, and hearts, I mingled pour,
I shrink dismayed—and awful doth appear
The vain presumption of my own weak deed;
Thy glorious spirit seems to mine so near,
That suddenly I tremble as I read—
Thee an invisible auditor I fear:
Oh, if it might be so, my master dear!
With what beseeching would I pray to thee,
To make me equal to my noble task,
Succor from thee, how humbly would I ask,
Thy worthiest works to utter worthily.
          —Fanny Kemble, "To Shakespeare"

Reading Shakespeare

As she performed her Shakespeare readings, Fanny Kemble was not only judged
by her listeners as supremely equal to the "noble task" she feared might defeat her;
she was, in the words of Henry James, "saturated" in the language of her "master."
According to James, she made Shakespeare "the air she lived in, an air that stirred
with his words whenever she herself was moved, whenever she was agitated or

impressed, reminded or challenged. He was indeed her utterance, the language she spoke when she spoke most from herself."[1] Having attempted with varying degrees of success up until the moment when she began the readings to rewrite the various roles to which she had been assigned, Kemble now assumed a form of directorial autonomy over her work and over her life. Rather than performing as Kemble daughter and Kemble actress or, with considerably more resistance, assuming the roles of Butler wife and plantation mistress, she became a sovereign figure, subject to no authority but that dictated by the "master" who gave her, as James observed, "the language she spoke when she spoke most from herself."[2]

For the readings, Kemble sat behind a large rectangular reading desk, its top usually covered with a green velvet cloth, some carefully piled-up books, and candelabra at each end. The bookstand on the desk would hold the 1820 Clarendon Press Shakespeare given to her by Charles Kemble, and she followed almost exactly his abridgments, designed to fit a play into a two-hour period. A red screen placed behind the table framed her luxuriant dark hair (tinged now with a little

Fig. 28. *Frances Anne Kemble*, by Peter Frederick Rothermel, 1849. © National Portrait Gallery, London.

Fig. 29. Butler House, northwest corner of Eighth and Chestnut streets, 1851. The house was occupied in the 1850s by John Butler and purchased in the mid-1860s by Pierce Butler from his brother's widow. Historical Society of Pennsylvania, Philadelphia.

gray) and whichever of her magnificent dresses she had chosen for the evening. From the time of her first Covent Garden season, Kemble had loved designing her theater costumes, and for the Shakespeare readings she wore black or red velvet for the tragedies, white or pastel satin for the comedies, and dark green or blue brocade for the history plays. Making a brief curtsey before opening her book, Kemble compelled her audience before she had spoken a word of the play, and she arranged this scene as a prelude to an event in which she read all the parts, was bothered by no other actors, and gave the finest performances of her career. Always having aimed to control the setting, the audience, and the text before her, whether enchanting audiences at Covent Garden or tolerating awed and bumbling actors in dingy provincial theaters, now, in the readings, she was in complete charge as she enthralled her listeners with the range and vitality of her impersonations. Whereas before she had appropriated and subverted her allotted roles, she now undertook the autonomous creation of a part that she performed for the rest of her working life. Relying on her cultural capital as an Englishwoman in America as well as on the authority embedded in that role as a woman intimate with Shakespeare's language, she traded on what Henry James characterized as her "rich old-English quality, which always counted double beyond the seas."[3] At the same time, as she impersonated both male and female characters, she revised conventional expectations regarding female performance.

Ironically, the itinerant nature of Kemble's readings recalled the vagabond life of her grandparents, Roger and Sarah Kemble. However, through the superior education of the Kemble children and the stately presence of Charles Kemble in English cultural life, Fanny's parents had ensured a respectability for the family untainted by the green-room. Moreover, Kemble was so majestic in her manner, in her appearance, and in her voice that none could suggest she was merely a touring actress. She seemed to move through English provincial towns and American cities as if on a regal progress, delighting her audiences with an arch Rosalind in *As You Like It*, terrorizing them with the appalling hags in *Macbeth*, or calling so loudly for a horse in *Richard III* that one alarmed little boy in Philadelphia jumped "like a pea on a trencher."[4] A virtual embodiment of Shakespeare and a consummate Victorian performer, Kemble reconciled, in a sense, the conflict that Nina Auerbach identifies in her exploration of what she terms "a Victorian fear of performance": Auerbach claims that Shakespeare "came to stand for human inviolateness" and that the theater, "that alluring pariah within Victorian culture, came to stand for all the dangerous potential of theatricality to invade the authenticity of the best self."[5]

For twenty years after her first London reading, Kemble ruled her audience, brought together Shakespeare, theatricality, and a vibrant "self" in her readings, and discovered a pleasing reconciliation of her flair for dramatic fireworks and her desire for theatrical control. Channeling her tremendous powers of vocal and visual impersonation into a tightly governed structure, she gained sovereignty over the terms in which she would appear before the public. As time went on, her autocratic impatience sometimes offended those who paved the way for her appearances, particularly in America, where, although managers remained obsequious and audiences enthralled, people resented her undisguised impatience with inefficiency and fools. Through her imperious presence, inherited from two generations of performance at Covent Garden and polished in the elegant drawing rooms of London's social elite, she announced that although she had been an actress, she was a Kemble—an identity that transcended the grubbiness of the career she despised and had left behind her.

When Kemble began the readings, she followed a family tradition established by her aunt Siddons. After her spectacular debut at Covent Garden as Juliet in 1829, critics hailed Kemble as the new Siddons, but where Sarah was tall, Fanny was short, and where Sarah's expression was said to be "peculiarly happy . . . and never for an instant seeming overcharged . . . nor coarse and unfeminine under whatever impulse," Fanny's face was thought too fierce for a feminine woman.[6] So forbidding did she appear in later years that Frederic Leighton used her as the model for a defiant Jezebel in his 1863 painting *Jezebel and Ahab, Met by Elijah*;

with her brilliant black eyes and withering sidelong glance, Kemble is a terrifying figure, a brilliant incarnation of Jezebel's vindictive energy.[7] Conveying a smoldering anger, Jezebel's expression evokes Kemble's perennial struggle to curb a volatile temperament that was very different from her aunt's more serene personality and mode of performance: Siddons's Lady Macbeth, for instance, moved audiences to hysterical tears but at the same time reassured them by showing the womanly art that produced their intense response. According to one contemporary critic, she applied "the formulas of the passions" so as to make them accessible to the public, not to keep them shrouded in theatrical mystery.[8] Jonathan Bate, in his examination of the conjunction of Shakespeare, politics, and criticism between 1730 and 1830, finds it "striking" that William Hazlitt responded to Siddons entirely in emotional terms and that he adored her Lady Macbeth precisely because she betrayed her womanly vulnerability. Bate's claim that "it is a mark of the spirit of the age that women, even though they appear on the public stage, are confined to the private sphere"[9] is confounded in an interesting way by Fanny Kemble in her Shakespeare readings: as she sat upon her dais in brightly lit assembly rooms, impersonating male and female characters, she moved beyond the portrayal on-stage of women only, and broke down the barrier between darkened audience and lamp-lit stage.

Sarah Siddons began her readings when she was in her late fifties. Wearing spectacles and dressed always in white, she stood alongside a desk, moved around as she declaimed, and despite her formidable reputation as the greatest tragic actress of her age, appeared warm and welcoming. She was a kind of dignified grandmother, unsettling in her tragic moments and calming by virtue of her genial presence. In contrast, Kemble sat bolt upright, moved only her arms, sported nothing as endearing as spectacles perched on the end of her nose, and maintained a severity broken only by her rendition, through her voice and expression, of comic characters. The almost mesmerizing control she maintained over her audience is indicated by a contemporary account of how she not only "enchained" them but compelled "an unconscious imitation of her looks in those of her hearers." So magnetic was the power of her presence for this particular critic that he found himself "responding to her expression or copying with my own features the varying emotions depicted on her mobile countenance."[10] What truly stunned her audiences was the limpid switch from one character to another, a versatility so amazing that people became almost disoriented, uncertain as to whether they were in a theater or an assembly hall.

Equally mobile and charismatic, Sarah Siddons, however, appeared more interested in entertaining and charming her audience than in "enchaining" them,

Fig. 30. Fanny Kemble: a study for *Jezebel and Ahab*. Frederic Leighton, 1862, chalk on paper. Leighton's use of Kemble as model for a study of the male head of Elijah in his 1863 painting *Jezebel and Ahab* complements the masculinity of her image as Jezebel in that painting. © Tate, London 2006.

and while Kemble devoted herself entirely and obsessively to her readings, Siddons conducted hers as a part-time career. In common with William Macready, Henry Irving, and Ellen Terry, she read as a kind of sideline; it assuaged the loneliness and desire for audience adoration that she felt painfully after she retired. She read for the applause, whereas Kemble initially read for the money and later for the pleasure of managing every aspect of her performance. Her bank account was healthy after the year of acting, to be sure, but she was receiving nothing from Pierce and was realistic enough to know that her chances for sustained financial success were better on the assembly hall dais than on the stage. Planning her tours with rigorous care, she entertained no deviation from the master scheme, regardless of where she read or what her audiences might have wished to hear. It was a formidable operation.

Kemble's old friend Henry Greville was the first to suggest the readings, in early February 1848; he urged her to become an entrepreneur—hire her own rooms, send out the advertisements, and so on—but she was reluctant initially to jeopardize the capital she had earned from her return to acting, and Mr. Mitchell, her theatrical manager whom she described as "general undertaker of pleasures and amusements for the fashionable great world of London"[11] and whom she could now afford to retain, was not too sanguine about her prospects. Moreover, despite the bravura success of her return to the stage and the informal Shakespeare readings that had delighted Tom Moore and other friends back in 1841, she was apprehensive about exposing herself so intimately to the public. Charming a drawing room full of adoring admirers kept her safe, as did the physical and formal distance between stage and audience in the provincial theaters, but there was a kind of threatening proximity in the smaller assembly hall full of strangers. On one level, she loved the promised theatricality of it all, but on another, feared she would be unsettled by the nearness of her audience. This fear had prompted her, early in 1848, to refuse an invitation to read *Antigone* at Buckingham Palace before Queen Victoria, to the accompaniment of Mendelssohn's music. She was chided in the newspapers as ungrateful and disloyal, but as she explained to Harriet St. Leger, her sorrow at the recent death of Mendelssohn (in November 1847) was so painful that grief compounded by "natural nervousness" brought the risk of "breaking down in an uncontrollable paroxysm of distress, and perhaps being unable to finish my performance."[12] She was worried now that she might collapse not from grief but from nerves.

Before embarking on the new venture, Kemble needed to secure a bulwark against her anxiety, and it came with the agreement of Mr. Mitchell to manage her new career and his reassurance that she could set the ground rules. On a March night in 1848 she read at the Highgate Institute for the small sum of ten guineas, encouraged by the presence of many of her London friends who had been rounded up by Henry Greville for the occasion. Even if she had adopted her father's abridgments of the plays, she made the readings all her own. What so astonished, and in some cases alarmed, her audience was that she not only followed in her father's performing footsteps, she outdid him in impersonation of Shakespeare's male characters. She was Othello, Iago, Prospero, and, most implausibly of all, a devastatingly funny Falstaff. A drama critic of the time vividly evokes the way in which the audience "laughed itself almost faint" over her interpretation: the performance of a "middle-aged Englishwoman," reading out of a big book from an "ungarnished platform," remained, for him, unmatched, even by Beerbohm Tree's performance, executed in full costume and with supporting cast, some thirty years later. With nothing but her voice and her expressive face, Kemble had them rolling in the aisles. Tree could barely evoke a chuckle.[13] Licensed and reassured by the disciplined form of her readings, Kemble infused her expression of the strong passions embodied in these male characters with some of the turbulent emotions that lurked beneath her regal presence, despite her tremendous success. The fluid, stunning readings drew on the emotional seesaw that had been her life: exhilaration, disappointment, rage, bittersweet reconciliation to loss, and deep pleasure in her renewed fame.

Before a public reading of any play, she studied it very carefully, comparing her own ideas for abridgment with those that had been adopted by her father and that were available to her in the edition of Shakespeare he had given her, with a graceful reassurance that he had renounced all thought of ever again reading in public. She generally followed his abridgments, which she judged wise and appropriate, and when she did not, it was to excise certain things she thought offensive, usually to be found in the racy dialogue of lower-class characters (the drunken exchanges of Trinculo and Stefano in *The Tempest* were particularly troubling; all the talk about "horse-piss" had to go). Her repertoire was composed of twenty-four of the plays, roughly two-thirds of the total number, and mainly what was left out were the farces, which she found uncongenial for public reading given their physical rather than verbal appeal.[14] Contrary to the wishes of her patient manager, Mr. Mitchell, that she read only the plays most popular with her audiences (*Hamlet, Romeo and Juliet*, and *The Merchant of Venice*) and abandon those less favored (*Richard III* and *Measure for Measure*), she insisted on a rotating repertoire of her selected twenty-four. And although they both knew that she could command full rooms for six days a week, she was adamant about performing for no more than four. She was determined to preserve the "inestimable value" to her of the readings, something that went beyond the money she was making, that was symbolic of her triumph over depression and over Pierce, and something that provided a perfect resolution of the dilemma she had always faced in her acting career (she adored being *on* the stage but loathed the profession). Refusing to run the risk of becoming hackneyed in her delivery, she put together a meticulously arranged program: a week that mixed comedy and tragedy would be followed by a week that offered history and comedy, and familiar plays were mingled during the week with the less familiar. The readings generally took place in assembly halls commonly used for lectures on science, literature, and social issues, and the average size of her audience, whether in London or the provinces, was seventy-five people.

Always, she strove to convey her deep pleasure in the plays as poetic wholes, something she believed was often lost in a theatrical production when the scenery, the costumes, or the power or weakness of particular actors tended to distract the attention of the audience from the poetic text. Her sonnet to Shakespeare—really a prayer—that is the epigraph to this chapter expresses her powerful love for his verse, and she sought, above all things, to express that love to her listeners. In her poem, as a vain, presumptuous, and dismayed speaker of Shakespeare's lines,

she trembles as she fears and yet hopes for the presence of an "invisible auditor"—were Shakespeare to be with her as she rehearsed her readings, he would
provide "succor," comfort, and reassurance that she was equal to her "noble task."
Bruised from the battle to resist Pierce's unjustifiable mastery, Kemble found in
Shakespeare the "master dear" who sustained and taught her through the years to
come. Feeling no compulsion to perform *for* Shakespeare, as the obedient "theatrical" daughter she had been to her father from the moment of her audition in the
darkened Covent Garden Theatre, now she wished to be a performing mediator
between Shakespeare's sublime texts and her enraptured audiences.

Before beginning her readings, however, she was often lonely and despondent in the small house off Portman Square. In February 1848, she read Charlotte
Brontë's recently published *Jane Eyre* and was unsettled by a correspondence between Jane's loneliness and her own, and by a dissonance between Rochester's
intense love for Jane and Pierce's betrayal and dislike: she wrote to Harriet St.
Leger that Jane Eyre's "safest course would have been to have left Thornfield without meeting her lover's despair."[15] The Highgate debut was followed by a short
tour, and she opened in London with tremendous success at Willis's Rooms, King
Street, St. James, a considerable achievement since Willis's elegant ballroom,
beautifully mirrored, decorated with gilt columns and pilasters, and lit with gas in
cut-glass lusters, measured one hundred by forty feet and could seat three hundred
people. But as she ate her solitary dinner in February 1848, she felt as she had at
Butler Place with a book propped in front of her, wondering when Pierce would
return from amusing himself in Philadelphia. It was oppressive, she wrote to Harriet, and on the evenings when she was not reading, she would dine early and go to
bed at ten, trying desperately "not to rejoice when each day ends."[16]

The loneliness was strangely heightened by a frenzy of political alarm that
whirled around her in the streets and in the houses of her friends, caused by the
1848 overthrow of the Orleanist monarchy in France and the proclamation of the
Second Republic. She was not sympathetic to the dire predictions of her conservative friends that British liberals such as Richard Cobden and John Bright were
leading the country to similar upheavals, and she abhorred the exaggerations of the
bawling paper vendors who shrieked that revolution and bloodshed were on their
way to English shores. Kemble put her faith in English good sense, devotion to
duty, and a gentry class whose preferred mode of social change was advantageous
marriage. That, she believed, would ensure the continued stability of English society.
When the country calmed itself in March, she wrote to Harriet, "The last month in
Europe has been like the breathless reading of the most exciting novel."[17]

If events in a restless Europe were like an exciting novel, then developments
in her marriage were becoming the material of sensational fiction. In mid-April

she received a summons from Philadelphia to return to answer a divorce suit filed by Pierce's lawyers on the grounds of desertion. Technically, she *had* deserted him as a last, desperate resort; now she was branded as a wife who had wantonly abandoned her husband and as a mother who was unfit to care for her children. She quickly made plans to sail from Liverpool to New York on the *Hibernia*, wrote frantic letters to America begging for legal advice, and canceled her social and professional engagements. Macready noted in his diary on April 26 that he had just received a letter from "Mrs. P. Butler" informing him that she would be unable to act on the Siddons Monument night (presumably a tribute scheduled to memorialize the date of Siddons's death on June 8, 1831) because she had to sail for America to answer Pierce's charges of desertion. Macready added, "I was truly sorry to hear it. Faults on both sides would have made mutual forgiveness wisest, discreetest, best."[18] At the beginning of May she was at the Adelphi Hotel in Liverpool, dreading the ordeal ahead and angry that she was about to forego the £470 she would have earned from engagements contracted for June. She took £1,500 with her to America, money she knew would be eaten up in the "bitter process" of her defense. As she wrote to Elizabeth Sedgwick just before she sailed, she could think of nothing "more full of loss, vexation, annoyance, and torment, than this proceeding of Mr. Butler's." Yet her newly won independence and self-protective acumen color this last letter from Liverpool: after facing the "tribunal," she declares she would stay in America for a year and tour with her Shakespeare readings, replenishing the capital eroded by her legal defense against Pierce's charges; she also begs Elizabeth to forward immediately to Theodore Sedgwick "my Journal and letters written during my last stay in Mr. Butler's house, also whatever letters of mine you or any members of your family have preserved, written at any period *subsequent* to my *last return* to the United States."[19] Kemble knew Pierce would seize any document to cause her pain and humiliation, but, invigorated by professional acclaim and financial success, she no longer feared him, nor was she willing to perform the roles prescribed for her by an oppressive culture.

Divorce

Sidney Fisher, the indefatigable chronicler of Philadelphia gossip, noted in his diary on May 28, 1848, that Kemble had returned to the city to defend herself against Pierce's divorce action. Given that Fisher was no real friend of Kemble's—her vigorous personality was too much for his fastidious taste—his observation that it was "quite notorious" that Pierce had driven her from the house through "his own barbarous treatment" is telling.[20] By now, Pierce's womanizing, gambling, and contempt for his wife were the common talk of Philadelphia: Rebecca Gratz, for instance, wrote to her sister-in-law that her friend Mrs. Butler had been forced by her "persecuting husband" to defend herself, "tho' it is well known he drove her out from her privileges of Mother and wife."[21] But people still waited eagerly for revelations in the most sensational marital battle in a long time. There was an initial disappointment, however, when the first hearing of the case in the Philadelphia Court of Common Pleas produced no judgment, although the charges and countercharges promised riveting disclosures. Kemble was accused of having "wilfully and maliciously deserted and absented herself" from her husband, and she, in return, claimed that for a long time previously, Pierce had "separated himself" from her as a husband, had engaged in "wrongful and unlawful conduct," and had heaped "cruel treatment" and "personal indignities" upon her.[22]

The venomous nature of the charges brought against Kemble by the Butler lawyers is astonishing. They quoted letters from Pierce in which he claimed his wife was blind to "all the vices of her nature, whose reason is sophistry, and whose religion is cant, and whose unbounded self esteem renders her happy and satisfied in all her wrong doings." They proffered a self-serving narrative of wounded pride in which a wealthy man rescues an attractive woman from a profession she despises, and she, in return, does nothing but berate him "in the spirit of untamed rebellion, which could not be soothed." As evidence of Kemble's allegedly hypocritical character, they submitted two letters from reputedly upstanding Philadelphia residents: one expresses surprise that she would seek liberal support from someone whose income is derived from slavery and declares her to be in a lamentably contemptible situation; the other addresses her as follows: "Madam, you disgrace your country and your sex, and all right minded Americans think so, although some weak-minded ones still appear your friends, more from pity than from any true feeling" (the latter opinion clearly a low blow aimed at the Sedgwick family). Kemble's defense against this barrage alleging hypocrisy, cant, and maternal neglect was to emphasize the cruel behavior that forced her, in October 1845, to leave Pierce and resume "the exercise of the laborious and distasteful profession" of her youth: namely, his notorious adultery, his refusal to let her see her children, his insistence she speak to no one about her marriage, and his sadistic command that she never communicate with anyone in the Sedgwick family. The records of this hearing tell a miserable story, one that Kemble had struggled valiantly to put behind her when she returned to England in 1845, and one that had, for the moment, neither a happy nor unhappy ending. In the absence of a judgment, further hearings were postponed until September.

When they resumed, Kemble was determined to win a public vindication of her actions and restoration of her reputation. On October 7, 1848, she submitted

a formal plea for a trial by jury, a procedure that would entail wider public exposure of Pierce's alleged profligacy than had occurred in the Court of Common
Pleas, signaling to Pierce's lawyers her intention to fight. Worried, moreover, by
rumors of his dwindling finances, she had written to William Minot, the husband
of Katherine Sedgwick Minot, in September that she had heard an "incredible
tale of ruin" from one of Pierce's creditors. Gambling on the stock exchange and
waging astronomical bets in poker games, Pierce was said to be $500,000 in debt
(today, close to $116 million). According to Kemble, in a long interview she had
obtained with "one of Mr. Butler's assignees," she had learned that they were "daily
finding new claims upon the estate, the southern property is mortgaged, [and]
he has cheated his sisters each of a large sum of money": he had mortgaged the
plantations and so devastated the Butler fortunes that his daughters were likely to
receive no more than $40,000 upon his death. In England, Kemble declared in her
letter to William Minot, such financial recklessness would have been grounds for
a "statute of lunacy" to be taken out against him.[23] What she does not record anywhere in her memoirs is a report in Philadelphia that Pierce planned to remarry;
to whom one does not know, although Rebecca Gratz hoped the second Mrs.
Butler would not be shouldered with the "sad care and charge" of Sarah and Fan,
reputedly difficult children damaged by the absence of "domestic control for three
or four years."[24] As things turned out, Pierce never remarried.

The trial by jury was set for April 16, 1849. Determined to omit nothing from
his arsenal in the battle to come, Pierce immediately retained an extraordinarily
powerful legal team composed of George Mifflin Dallas, former mayor of Philadelphia, and at this time the vice president of the United States in the Democratic
administration of James K. Polk, and the most famous lawyer in America, Daniel
Webster. Kemble's lineup, although less celebrated in the public eye, was also notably strong: William M. Meredith and Benjamin Gerhard in Philadelphia, and
in Boston, her close friends Theodore and Charles Sedgwick, and Samuel Gray
Ward. She also asked Charles Sumner, who had been an admirer and supporter
since they met in Lenox, to be the trustee for the settlement of a mortgage on Butler Place, whose provision her lawyers were demanding from Pierce. The phalanx
of competing lawyers on either side was awesome, and Pierce was so desperate to
win this last battle with Kemble that he had retained Daniel Webster when he
heard a rumor that Webster was about to join Kemble's defense team. Admitting
to friends that although he had no particular wish to employ Webster in the jury
trial, he would be "sorry" to have his power against him.

By 1848, the divorce rate in America had risen steadily from the beginning of
the century, and in 1816 Pennsylvania had been the first state to make changes that
permitted its routine availability under the direction of the bench, not the legisla-

ture.[25] But it was not until the end of the century that traditional paternal custody and guardianship rights were superseded, and Kemble's lawyers knew that even if Fanny were to win the trial by jury, Pierce would still be awarded custody of their daughters. For that reason, the two months that she was permitted to spend with them in Lenox in the summer of 1848 were particularly precious; in July she wrote to her old friend Sarah Perkins Cleveland that she was at last with her "chickens" (now thirteen and ten), adding that the holiday had been brought about by labor far more full of agony than that which had accompanied their birth. After giving Cleveland a lengthy account of the proceedings in the Court of Common Pleas, she revealed that she would be willing to withdraw her insistence on a trial by jury in return for an agreement from Pierce to give her a mortgage on Butler Place and the right to be with her children for two months every summer: she believed that the interest on the mortgage would provide her with an allowance of $2,000 a year and the eventual ownership of Butler Place. These were the terms that were eventually agreed upon, although the distressing uncertainty about the outcome of negotiations being conducted by her lawyers with Pierce's legal army made for a bittersweet summer. She was reunited with her daughters, living among her dearest American friends and supporters, but her nerves, she wrote, were "in a most wretched state of irritation and excitement."[26] As things turned out, the negotiations were successful, the trial never took place, and the divorce was eventually granted to Pierce on September 22, 1849.[27] Kemble was able to leave Butler Place to her daughters when she died in 1893. Apart from the official court records, two extraordinary documents emerged from this sensational episode in Kemble's life: her "Narrative," composed in the summer of 1848, and Pierce Butler's *Statement* published in 1850.

Kemble's "Narrative" was submitted to the Court of Common Pleas as part of her petition for a trial by jury, and it is in the form of four long letters written to Pierce that record her passionate love for him, her pleas for reconciliation after their numerous separations, and her admissions of guilt for past offenses. This document was first made known to the public through the opinion of the Court of Common Pleas delivered on January 20, 1849, which set the trial by jury for April 16, 1849, and decided the "Narrative" should be stricken from the record since it was devoid of any written evidence to support the claims of Kemble's letters. Pierce refers to the "Narrative" in great detail in his self-vindicating *Statement*. He dismisses it as a craftily assembled work of fiction, and it does, indeed, read this way; the four letters are placed together as if no others intervened—as if he had never answered and as if Kemble wrote no other letters to him at the time. Pierce concludes with the sarcastic observation that when these four letters were presented to the court in the form of a "Narrative," it struck many people as singular that copies would have been made at the time they were composed, particularly one written while they were in London in 1843, living in the same house but in separate quarters. Part of this letter reads as follows: "I hear with great pain that you are ill. I dare not come to you for fear of annoying and irritating you; but I implore you to let me come to you and be with you while you are suffering and helpless. Oh, Pierce, I love you dearly, pray let me come and nurse you, and do anything in the world I can for you. I am miserable to hear of your illness; only send me word that I may come—pray, pray, do, dear Pierce."[28] Kemble must have made copies of the letters since Pierce retained the originals, and in all likelihood she did so as a matter of understandable self-preservation. But she also seized the opportunity to present herself in this sensational melodrama as both the writer of the script and the principal actor on the stage. She copied letters written in a throbbing prose that resembled the assumption of dramatic attitudes of supplication, fidelity, and despair. They were heartrending pleas for Pierce's love and forgiveness. Both spontaneous and studied, the letters were then copied for use against the person to whom they were written. Kemble's theatrical talents positioned her as the principal performer at the tragic center of an epistolary drama, and the letters emerge as a demonstration of theatrical technique, attitudes to be exhibited for the audience in the pit or, in this case, in the courtroom.

The time between Kemble's return to America and the granting of the divorce (early summer 1848 to September 1849) was not, on her part, devoted entirely to clever scheming to outwit Pierce. Secure now in her mastery of the Shakespeare readings and glad to be making money on her own account, she decided to take advantage of her celebrity and begin readings in America, something she was planning to do anyway before the arrival of Pierce's summons to Philadelphia. She began the American readings in Boston early in 1849 with *The Tempest*, the play that had fascinated her from the time she saw the painting of Prospero and Miranda in the house at Blackheath when she was six years old. Reading with a particular intensity in Boston, the scene of Pierce's ardent wooing in 1833, the home of the Sedgwicks, and a hub for the antislavery political movements Pierce despised and feared, she performed Prospero with a melancholy power that evoked her own painful narrative of exile, despair, and triumphant return to her friends. The *Evening Herald* on February 22 noted that her choice of play was appropriate "considering the strong ordeal she has recently passed through."[29]

Fanny Appleton Longfellow was also deeply moved by the resonances running between the Boston performances and Kemble's recent trials. For her, Kemble had always had a "geyser-like soul," erupting without warning in passionate feeling, barely controllable, and she felt the *King Lear* reading was "astonishing proof" of her power and pathos; her Constance in *King John* was beautifully por-

trayed and her Catherine most touching, "so much her own story, a stranger resisting her husband's divorce and pleading for her daughter." She was amazed by
Kemble's witches in *Macbeth*, enchanted by her Portia, and astounded by what
she achieved in *Richard II*: that Fanny Longfellow was stunned by the masculine
intensity of Kemble's reading testifies to the manner in which Kemble, by now,
had thoroughly revised the expectations attached to female performance.[30] The
key was her voice. Sonorous, sweet, and chilling, her voice superbly impersonated
male and female characters; according to her old friend Edward FitzGerald, who
declared her a "noble-hearted and noble-souled woman, however wayward," she
seemed "to do the men and the soldiers best."[31] Henry Longfellow was as thrilled
as his wife to hear Kemble read, and in his jubilant sonnet written to commemo-
rate the occasion, he recalls, "How our hearts glowed and trembled as she read, /
Interpreting by tones the wondrous pages / Of the great poet who foreruns the
ages, / Anticipating all that shall be said!" The sonnet ends, "O happy Poet! By no
critic vext! / How must thy listening spirit now rejoice / To be interpreted by such
a voice!" Kemble's voice enthralled not only the enraptured listeners but, imaginatively, Shakespeare himself, Kemble's "master dear," from whom she shrinks in
her sonnet, as she mingles her voice with his verse. A year later she paid homage to
Longfellow by reading his long poem "The Building of the Ship" at the Mercantile
Library Association of Boston. An allegory of building America's ship of state, the
Union, the poem was read so powerfully by a trembling and weeping Kemble that
Henry Longfellow, together with the rest of the audience, was reduced to tears.[32]

Readings in New York almost immediately followed the Boston engagement
where, Kemble's old friend Philip Hone recorded in his diary, Kemble had taken
the city by storm. She read three evenings a week and once on Mondays at noon
at the Stuyvesant Institution, a room that held seven hundred people. She had no
problem filling it since, as Hone noted, "the *elite* of the world of fashion: delicate
women, grave gentlemen, belles, beaux, and critics, flock to the doors of entrance,
and rush into such places as they can find, two or three hours before the time of
the lady's appearance."[33] For this labor, Hone calculated, Kemble earned approximately $500 per reading (by her own admission, she could command a minimum
of $500 in New York and Boston and about $300 in a smaller town), which produced an annual income of over $30,000, calculated on the basis of reading three
or four times a week for about six months out of the year. When she was reading in
Philadelphia in October 1849, Sidney Fisher noted in his diary that she was making "money rapidly by these exhibitions, having already invested from her profits
$20,000"; he also noted the impending purchase of land in Lenox, "among the
Sedgwicks, who were one cause, I think, of her domestic troubles, for Butler hated
them, not without reason, and she would not give them up."[34] That Kemble was

working so industriously and raking in such a good income just after the second hearing in the Court of Common Pleas is testimony to the resilience under pressure that she had developed over the previous few years.[35] In the past, she probably would have collapsed under the barrage of vicious invective aimed at her by Pierce's lawyers, but now, anticipating definitive termination of her association with him, she flourished.

Her ebullience was noted drily by the *New York Herald* on March 10, 1850: "We begin to think that divorce and popularity must go hand in hand these ecstatic days." New York's "intellectual classes" must marvel, the paper observes, at the way Kemble is "followed, admired, complimented, and adored, including the dollars, in all quarters. . . . The same enthusiasm originating in the notoriety produced by the divorce, attends her footsteps wherever she goes."[36] Kemble's notoriety as the divorced wife of Pierce Butler and as a mesmerizing reader of Shakespeare provided fodder for gossip, envy, and grudging admiration. Her longtime foe (at least on stage), William Macready, neither admired nor envied her when she was in New York. He noted in his diary on April 28, 1850: "Dined with the Coldens. Went with them afterwards to Mrs. Butler's Reading of *King Henry VIII*, which was *too bad—I could not stay*."[37] All of Macready's principles for acting were offended by the sonorous clangor of her voice, the exaggerated delivery, and the imperious presence. He found it unbearable to hear and to watch. But in October of the same year, Philadelphians adored Kemble's *As You Like It;* rather than lampooning her as a grasping adventuress as they had before her marriage, they delighted in the tributes paid by the *Pennsylvanian* to the "indescribable charm that lingered" in her voice.[38]

During the spring of 1849, her income secured by the promise of engagements in the autumn, Kemble had bought land in Lenox, Massachusetts, and started making plans to build a cottage. She immediately endeared herself to Lenox by giving a reading in the courthouse for the purpose of endowing the villagers with a clock. Her pleasure was marred only by a brief visit from Pierce to discuss the forthcoming visit of Sarah and Fan to their mother: it left her feeling bitterly annoyed. But she recovered quickly, buoyed by the wonderful riding and proximity of interesting neighbors such as Nathaniel Hawthorne, whose son, Julian, she would take on gallops across the countryside. In his recollection of this event, Julian Hawthorne says that Kemble would ride up to the door "on her strong, black horse [ask] the smallest of the party whether he would like to have a ride; and on his answering emphatically in the affirmative, she swung him astride the pommel of her saddle, and galloped off with him. The wild delight of that gallop will never be forgotten by him who experienced it." On their return, Kemble reined in her horse with one hand and, grasping her "cavalier" with the other, held him out at arm's length, exclaiming, "'Take your boy! Julian the Apostate!'"[39]

Herman Melville felt less warmly about her than did Julian Hawthorne and his father. Early in 1849, Melville spent some ten weeks in Boston, where his wife had gone to give birth to their first child. He sent the following unguarded impression to a New York friend: "Mrs. Butler too I have heard at her Readings. She makes a glorious Lady Macbeth but her Desdemona seems like a boarding school miss. She's so unfemininely masculine that had she not, on unimpeachable authority, borne children, I should be curious to learn the result of a surgical examination of her person in private. The Lord help Butler. . . . I marvel not he seeks being amputated off from his maternal half."[40] The charge that Kemble was unfemininely "masculine" was neither new nor surprising but the sheer nastiness of Melville's comment that he would like a "surgical examination" to determine her true sex anticipates the caustic criticism of her "masculine" behavior that she was to receive in the next few years.

The two months that Sarah and Fan spent with their mother in Lenox in the summer of 1849 were not easy. Kemble had not seen her children for nearly four years: Sarah was now fourteen, Fan was eleven, and they had been strongly influenced by Pierce and by the governesses he had employed to take care of them. Strangely enough, this four-year absence from her daughters almost exactly rep-

Fig. 31. Kemble Street, Lenox, Massachusetts. Photography Collection, Miriam and Ira D. Wallach Division of Art, Prints, and Photographs, New York Public Library, Astor, Lenox and Tilden Foundations.

licates the four-year absence from her own mother that Kemble had experienced between the ages of twelve and sixteen when she was at school in Paris. During the holidays, she had not returned to England and her great pleasure had been visits from her father. To her own daughters, now, she was as strange as Thérèse Kemble had been to her when she tumbled out of the coach in 1825 at Weybridge that brought her back from France, and she felt this resemblance to Thérèse. At the age of forty, Kemble was still dynamically attractive with the noble profile, flashing eyes, and luxuriant dark hair that created a resemblance to her father, but she had become stout and matronly, and although she was not behaving like Thérèse, her growing girth was troubling evidence of her physical inheritance.

When Kemble visited Philadelphia in the autumn, Sidney Fisher thought she looked well but older, and he found her reading of *As You Like It* less theatrically exaggerated than he had feared it might be. But despite her financial security, the long-anticipated reunion with her daughters, and the purchase of land in Lenox for her cottage, she was faced, Fisher believed, with a life of unhappy solitude, given all her grief and her vehement, restless temperament. Fisher was right about the temperament but he was wrong about her future. The more she read Shakespeare, the more she loved it, feeling almost guilty that she was paid for reading the poetry of that "glorious spirit" who had guided her as Juliet when she was twenty and nourished her now, twenty years later. The divorce led to solitude, to be sure, but, paradoxically, it propelled her into a career that she almost certainly would never have assumed had she stayed with Pierce under his withering conditions. She relished her new, if lonely, life.

Fanny Cracks the Whip

If in physical appearance Kemble had begun more and more to resemble her mother, in her clothing and her manners, she was perceived by many as becoming more masculine. In actuality, however, her persona was increasingly androgynous; as she sat swathed in white satin, her low, commanding voice and regal manner expressed an authority conventionally associated with men. A journalist for the *Cleveland Democrat* who saw her perform in the spring of 1849 declared forthrightly, "She is masculine, very, in mind and body. Her figure is not majestic, or commanding, or elegant. . . . Her person is short and massive; she has nothing of the light and graceful in her form. You can read in her face, that she was born to command, never to obey." The *Worcester Aegis*, reporting on the habits of the new and famous resident of Lenox, provided full details of the attention she drew to herself with her masculine costume and of her "management of a fleet steed, or in driving a pair of fast trotters." The fondness for male riding clothes had affronted Philadelphia when she was first married, and her general haughtiness, deep voice, and social assertiveness had been judged (not without foundation) as unfeminine derision directed at her languid husband. When she returned to Philadelphia for the divorce and shortly thereafter for the successful readings of *As You Like It*, a local newspaper recorded that she was "witching the world of Chestnut Street" with her dashing horsemanship and her masculine style of dress: "Her hat, cravat, shirt-bosom, tight-fitting spencer, and all except the flowing skirts, were similar to the attire of the ruder sex." Provocatively cross-dressed, Kemble emerged after her divorce as an androgynous figure in a gender-confusing masquerade.[41]

Kemble's cross-dressing, however, was undertaken with a different purpose and produced a different effect from that engaged in by her mother when she performed Macheath in *The Beggar's Opera* at the end of the eighteenth century. In 1862, Edward FitzGerald, writing to an old friend, refers to a portfolio of old theatrical prints in which he discovered a sketch, "and a very clever one, of Mrs. C. Kemble in *very tight Men's Clothes*. . . . I have not dared to buy it: but I almost think it *should* be bought up . . . one certainly would not wish one's Mother to be so represented."[42] On Thérèse Kemble, men's clothing served to reveal her voluptuous female body, whereas on her daughter, it served either to disguise her sex or to present her as a sexually ambiguous figure. That Kemble was on a horse embellished the image of masculine swagger. As a child she had been a fearless but untutored rider, and when she became wealthy after the Covent Garden debut she intimidated the future Queen Victoria at Captain Fozzard's Riding Academy with her flamboyant horsemanship. Much of her time alone with Pierce before they married had been spent on horseback, riding out into the Pennsylvania countryside or around Boston, especially out to Mt. Auburn cemetery where Pierce proposed and where her beloved Dall was buried. In her memoirs, she tells a thrilling story of riding through the Massachusetts countryside with Pierce on a winter's night about six months before their marriage. After acting for a week in Boston, she was due to take the one o'clock coach to New York, from the small town of Dedham. It was seventeen degrees below zero, a brilliant and exhilarating night, and so cold that Fanny's veil froze on her lips. In a racy adventure that suggests their mutual sexual attraction, Fanny and Pierce rode "hard and fast and silently," side by side, through the bright, profound stillness of the night, and never drew rein until they reached Dedham. Still fearless at forty, she could sit sidesaddle without reins or stirrups and was ready to gallop across the countryside as fast as any man. She rarely took a tumble.

At all the country houses where she had been an entertaining guest before and after her marriage, she had ridden out with the men, impeccably dressed, a small, alert, and sprightly figure in the saddle. In London she had been a major attraction on Rotten Row as she galloped with Lord John Russell, her habit flying (women had not yet adopted jodhpurs) and her red waistcoat and brown velvet jacket making her look like a jaunty robin, as she put it. At the lowest point in Philadelphia when she was living in the same house as Pierce, close to her children, but apart from him as a husband, she had taken her earnings from the publication of the 1844 poems to buy and maintain her horse, Forrester. Riding was a lifelong pleasure, a means of escape on some occasions and on others a chance to perform before delighted audiences. Carriages often contained other passengers and one was at the mercy of the driver; horses allowed her to parade her independence, crack the whip, and put on a show.

The show was dazzling enough for the *International Magazine of Literature, Art, and Science* to make it the focus of an article in October 1851 about her recent readings in London, to which she returned in the spring of that year. With the knowing declaration that the history of the Butler-Kemble marriage was sufficiently notorious not to require rehearsal, the article announces that "of all her sex" Kemble was "the most ill-fitted by nature" for marriage. By virtue of her being "a woman of masculine abilities, tastes, and energies; fitted better for the camp than for the drawing-room, and often evincing a degree of discontent that she is not a man," Kemble is caricatured as a kind of cross-dressed cowboy. The animosity of the article assumes the conventional Victorian cloak of an attack on Kemble's femininity, which raises the question of the significance of a woman being termed "masculine" in the Victorian period.[43]

George Eliot was said to have a man's brain in a woman's body: her body and her gentle, maternal demeanor signaled an unquestionable femininity that enabled cultural acceptance of an intellect that outsmarted most of her fellow Victorian sages, most of whom were men. Fanny Kemble also had a man's brain in her stout, not too feminine body, but her demeanor was anything but feminine, especially when on a horse. Whether the writer of the *International Magazine* article evoked Kemble's "masculine tastes" in order to signal her homoerotic interests or was reaching for the handy Victorian dismissal of authoritative women (not sufficiently "feminine") is hard to determine: whatever the case, the October 1851 article resonates with the conventional Victorian linking of female aggressiveness with mastery of a horse. Obsessed with what is termed Kemble's "equestrian exhibitions," the writer announces they illustrate her "masculine aspirations." Apparently, every day at the same time in New York, "so that a crowd might assemble to look upon her performance, her horse was brought to the front of the hotel, and when mounted, with affected difficulty, made to rear and pitch as if he never before had felt the saddle or bit, and then to dash off as if upon a race-course or to escape an avalanche."[44] Ironically, whether the writer of this article knew so or not, he was positioned precisely where Kemble would have wished him to be: as an enthralled spectator of her performance. Trouncing her as an exhibitionist who courted the "wondering admiration of country bumpkins by unsexing herself for feats of horsemanship" and making a show of her "heart" as a laughable defense against the protestations of a "gentleman whom she had treated with every species of contempt, obloquy, and insult," the *International Magazine* affirms the celebrity she both enjoyed and scorned. That Pierce Butler is pitied as the public victim of Kemble's "contempt, obloquy, and insult" verifies the success of her resistance to his sadistic treatment.

Fanny Kemble was by no means the only nineteenth-century theatrical celebrity to face charges of being "unfeminine" by virtue of her fondness for male attire and her adoption of assertive social manners conventionally associated with male behavior. One of the best known of this group, the American actress Charlotte Cushman (1816–1876), shares certain similarities with Kemble, although there are crucial differences between them. As Lillian Faderman observes, Cushman (who begins her memoirs with the sentence "I was born a tomboy") "early developed what were considered 'masculine' tastes but what were in reality those that any intelligent young person would prefer if allowed to grow without intimating restraints."[45] Claudia Johnson makes the interesting point that early in her career Cushman modeled herself on William Macready: "She imitated his movements, his gestures and inflections. Her voice, it was reported, was already, in her late twenties, as deep as his. Furthermore many observers thought that Charlotte even looked like Macready."[46] Certainly, Fanny Kemble's bright intelligence and interrogation of dominant sexual and gender politics make her somewhat similar to Cushman, but, unlike Cushman, she was attracted to men as well as to women (Edward Trelawny and Harriet St. Leger obviously come to mind here). Cushman never married; rather, she entered into a number of passionate relationships with women, the most enduring with her biographer, Emma Stebbins.[47] Also, unlike Kemble, Cushman played a number of male roles on stage ("breeches parts"), including Hamlet, Romeo to the Juliet of her younger sister Susan (with an "ardor" that shocked some audiences), and Oberon in *A Midsummer Night's Dream*. Finally, what might distinguish the sexist animosity that was directed both at Kemble and Cushman is the presence and defiance of certain cultural expectations in Kemble's public life: her "masculine" behavior violated popular ideas embedded in the roles of Kemble daughter and Butler wife. Less encumbered, perhaps, by associations attached to specifically allotted roles, Charlotte Cushman was both freer to express her sexuality (within the context, of course, of confining mid-nineteenth-century prescriptions for women's behavior) and less subject to shocked response to a violation of expectations.

One of the most virulent attacks on Kemble's reputation was offered by Eliza Lynn (after her marriage, better known as Eliza Lynn Linton) in her novel *Realities*, published in the late 1840s. Kemble read it in December 1847 and wrote to Harriet that she had just got through it "with unbounded amazement." It was "realities with a vengeance."[48] Readers were astonished by Eliza Lynn's inclusion of a character named Lucretia Kemble, a down-at-the-heels vagabond actress who befriends and encourages the heroine, Clara. Lucretia is a vicious parody of Kemble, a devastating image of what she might have been in an improbable situation where the readings failed, the paltry alimony from Pierce disappeared, and all her friends deserted her. Lucretia Kemble is given to flinging back her head affectedly and declaiming in a voice "to which no words can do justice, and nothing but Astley's or the Surrey represent [music halls catering to the popular audience]." She has haggard, well-chiseled features, a voice harsh and strained, although it may once have been full and sonorous; her clothes are stylish but made of poor materials and tawdrily arranged, and her manners "those of a queen on a fifth-rate stage."[49] In actuality, Kemble's patrician features were much admired; her voice was pleasantly melodious; she always adored her clothes and spent a great deal of money on them; and her manners were exquisite. The lowest blow comes in the narrator's genteel contempt for the figure of the "strolling actress," a phrase that evokes the common association of acting with prostitution in the first part of the nineteenth century. Bold, ill dressed, and affected, Lucretia Kemble is no lady. Moreover, she is a poor actress, never "having understood more in her profession than the coarsest technical business and the most parrot-like imitation of conventional models—of the vivid delight that rushed through heart and brain when pit, boxes, and gallery applaud."[50] At worst, Lucretia Kemble is a vulgar, pretentious, and morally suspect faded actress who has strolled her way around provincial theaters; at best, underneath her tawdry clothing, she is a "good woman at heart" who seeks to protect the imperiled heroine of the novel from the lascivious attentions of a lustful theater manager.

Lucretia Kemble is not Eliza Lynn's only attack on Fanny Kemble. In *The Autobiography of Christopher Kirkland*, published in 1885 (Lynn Linton's disguised autobiography), the male narrator describes his meeting in Paris with "one who had been in her day the most famous of our tragic actresses, till she married and made herself the most miserable of wives, and her husband as wretched as herself."[51] Again, Lynn Linton goes for the theatrical jugular: this once famous actress has a deep voice, a stage-stateliness of manner, and a tremendous talent for assuming "attitudes," particularly that of dominance. She levels her "big black eyes" at the narrator and "crushes" him flat. But this time Linton adds the suggestions of masculinity that framed so many attacks on Kemble after the divorce, which is ironic at the very least, given Linton's assumption of a male persona to narrate her own life; the nameless faded actress is so brutal, sarcastic, and contemptuous that quivering Christopher feels a "shuddering horror for her, such as I fancy a man would feel for one who had flayed him in the market-place."[52] Equipped with the whip that taunts the horse into rearing disobedience so that she may perform as its master, as the *International Magazine of Literature, Art, and Science* would have it, here Kemble is reviled as a mannish bully, very different from her sister, Christopher adds gratefully (presumably Lynn Linton means Adelaide, preferred by most people by virtue of a gentle nature that differed from Kemble's more brusque manner). Womanly where the actress is vile, sweet and sympathetic where she is insolent and inhuman, this "more gifted sister" is a delight. Lynn Linton rounds off her parody by saying that the obsessive and compulsive regulation of the wardrobe of this famous actress was infamous, and that all of English and Roman society knew that "her method of expressing order"—numbering all her dresses, hanging them in rows, and wearing them regardless of the occasion—was "the germ of all she was and did, and the cause of all she suffered and made others suffer."[53]

The exaggerations of Eliza Lynn in her novel and in the fictionalized auto-biography written some thirty years later, like most parody, have some truth in them: liberated, finally, from the demands of playing the roles of Kemble daughter and Butler wife, Fanny's manner in the years following her divorce did, indeed, become even more assertive than it had been in the years of her Covent Garden celebrity. She wrote and directed herself in the role of financially independent, professionally acclaimed, and sexually ambiguous Victorian woman. But to term her assertiveness "masculine" is, of course, to characterize her behavior in terms of what was conventionally prescribed for men during the mid-Victorian period. Codes of what constituted appropriately feminine and masculine behavior were, and remain, matters of social consensus and construction. Whether Kemble was putting on a "masculine" masquerade as a means of asserting authority in a male-dominated culture or expressing, consciously or not, a preference for homosexuality in her female friendships remains unknown. But that she may have preferred the comradeship or bodies (or both) of women is suggested in one of her poems that expresses through a gender-neutral speaker a powerful erotic attraction to a woman. Just as the feelings of loss, rejection, and disappointment about Pierce that are not expressed in her published memoirs are licensed and encouraged by poetic form, indeed given shape by that form, homoerotic attractions never mentioned in the memoirs are given voice in verse as well.

What might have surprised readers of Kemble's memoirs goes unnoticed in a poem titled "By the Seaside." It is noon and the sun beats down with "piercing fervid heat" upon a sandy beach. "Come in" calls the speaker to an unnamed female companion, into a cool cave where she can dip her feet, "Gleaming like rose-hued pearls below the wave," into the glassy, icy pools. As the speaker lies beside the female object of desire, he or she gazes on her and finds her fairer than Aphrodite "smiling in her rosy sleep" and more enticing than Leda, "the shuddering girl, / Whose wide distended eyes, / Glassy, with dread surprise, / Saw the huge billow curl, Foaming and bristling, with its grisly freight; / While, twinkling from afar, / With iris-feathered heels, and falchion bright / From the blue cope of heaven's amazing height, / Her lover swooped, a flashing noon-tide star." The eroticism of the poem is sustained through the final stanza.

> Sleep my beloved! While the sultry spell
> Of silent noon o'er sea and earth doth dwell:
> Stoop thy fair graceful head upon my breast,
> With its thick rolls of golden hair opprest,
> My lily!—and my breathing shall not sob
> With one tumultuous sigh—nor my heart throb
> With one irregular bound—that I may keep
> With tenderest watch, the treasure of thy sleep.
> Droop gently down, in slumb'rous, slow eclipse,
> Fair fringed lids! Beneath my sealing lips.[54]

The gentleness in this poem is rarely heard in the public voice of Fanny Kemble. The fervent wish for the breathing not to sob and sigh, for the heart not to beat too loudly so that the beloved may sleep untroubled, lulled to rest by the sense of her lover's lips upon her eyelids: all this bespeaks a private, offstage desire rarely expressed in the letters, essays, and memoirs.[55]

After she returned to England in 1850 upon news that her father was seriously ill, Kemble, then, mingled masculine bravura and feminine tenderness into an androgynous persona. These were years marked by transatlantic travel, the marriages of her daughters, and the successful Shakespeare readings that fused the dramatic fire of her mother with the theatrical discipline of her father. One of Kemble's old friends, Samuel Rogers, records Sarah Siddons's ironic aside, delivered on the occasion of a "grand public dinner" being given in honor of John Philip Kemble on his leaving the stage: "Well perhaps in the next world women will be more valued than they are in this."[56] Fanny Kemble's private and public success in her later years (despite the carping about her "masculinity") proved that women could, indeed, be valued in the present world.

Mothers and Daughters

The two nations, mother and daughter though they be, can no more understand each other than I and my children can.
—Fanny Kemble to Henry Lee, 1864

Choosing Sides

When Fanny Kemble wrote about America in September 1832, she had readily adopted a metaphor common to much nineteenth-century British writing about its lost colonies: that of mother country and rebellious child. Although she was sure the new nation would perpetuate the English language and English virtues, she regretted that when the American colonies became politically restless in the late eighteenth century, England had not adopted "a more maternal course of conduct." When she was in Georgia, she spoke frequently in her letters to Elizabeth Sedgwick about her national identity as a principled Englishwoman in the midst of immoral slavery and cultural stagnation, a strategy that distanced her from complicity in the misery before her and provided a rhetorical perch from which she could survey, judge, and rewrite the allotted role of Butler plantation wife. During the 1850s and 1860s, political upheaval in America prompted, once more, an assertion of Kemble's national identity, and as America headed for civil strife, she recorded her dismay in regard to the heedless materialism and political recklessness she perceived all around her. At the same time, a looming decision about which side of the Atlantic should become her permanent home was complicated by her national loyalties. If, until this moment, she had boldly appropriated and rewritten the cultural and social roles to which she had been assigned, now she was somewhat at a loss. Confident in displaying what were termed her "masculine" qualities, delighted with her successful career, and fashioning an androgynous persona for Victorian society, she wondered how she might play the role of English mother to American daughters—or whether, indeed, this was actually in any sense a role to be played and, in the playing of it, to be rewritten.

In her early forties, Kemble was clearly a different Englishwoman from the actress who arrived in 1832 and the young married woman who traveled to Georgia in 1838. She recognized her complicated position as the mother of two daughters from whom she had been separated for four years after leaving America in 1845, and with whom she had spent two months a year, at most, since their reunion. It was not until Sarah and Fan reached their majorities in 1856 and 1859, respectively, that Kemble had unfettered access to her children, since after the divorce, in addition to reneging on his financial obligations, Pierce had persisted in presenting obstacles to them spending their allotted time each summer with Kemble. At a moment in America's history when the nation seemed less and less affiliated with the mother country and more and more headed for disaster, Fanny Kemble was preoccupied with the challenge of being in almost normal contact with her children as they neared the age when they would be free to spend as much time with their mother as they wished. Literal and symbolic motherhood, her relationship with her grown-up daughters, to which transatlantic nation she owed allegiance: these were the issues that challenged Kemble in the 1850s.

From the moment she burst into tears as the *Pacific* entered New York harbor, Kemble's Englishness was a significant aspect of her transatlantic celebrity, and she had deployed this identity for cultural authority when she launched her sprightly critique of American society. Twenty years later, however, America hardly resembled the nation she had written about in her journal in 1832 to 1834 or in her letters from Georgia in 1838–39. The child colonies that she had saluted in terms of their cultural heritage from the mother country were moving beyond grateful adolescence to a distanced maturity. Surprisingly, this was not the case in Kemble's domestic life since Sarah and Fan, the American children of an English mother, did not seem to harbor resentment of her powerful personality—what Sidney Fisher called "too much will and vitality and force of character." As young women, they went their own way, seasoned in the unhappy business of being pawns in their parents' fighting. Kemble, however, had barely shaped their education, their moral values, or their political opinions. Painfully aware that they were the children of their father's culture, Kemble felt they were, and were not, strangers to her, bound by blood but separated by national identification. In her memoirs Kemble effaced almost all mention of the pain she felt at being separated from Sarah and Fan,

Fig. 32. Fanny Kemble in middle age. Hulton Archive/Getty Images.

wishing, she claimed, to shield her daughters from the "bitter heartsick yearning" of those years, but when they were all free to be together, she knew she would have to live in America if she wished to see them.[1] It was not a place she wished to be.

Having long enjoyed transatlantic celebrity as the Kemble actress who married an American and wrote two journals that criticized American manners and American slavery, Kemble had been identified as an Englishwoman in America for a good while. But the demands on her loyalties during the 1850s and 1860s necessitated fresh ways to negotiate the difficulties created by contesting affiliations. During these years of American political unrest, Kemble affirmed the strength of her English national identity in "On the Stage," an essay that appeared in *Cornhill Magazine* in 1863. For a long time, her determination to have the "theatrical," associated with her father, quell the disruptive material of the "dramatic," associated with her mother, had governed her private life, and she talked about this often in her writings and with her friends. What she discussed less frequently, probably because it only became significant as her daughters neared their majorities and America headed for civil war, was her analysis in this essay of national characteristics, although, in 1842, she had written to Theodore Sedgwick that she had come to "consider the difference of nationality a broader, stronger, and deeper difference" than that of dissimilarities of individual character.[2]

In "On the Stage" Kemble writes, "Both nations and individuals in whom the dramatic temperament preponderates are rather remarkable for a certain simplicity of nature, which produces sincerity and vehemence of emotion and expression, but is entirely without *consciousness*, which is never absent from the theatrical element."[3] Talking first about the individual, she ventures that children are innately dramatic but become theatrical when they know themselves to be observed. Kemble may be said to anticipate Freud's familiar distinction between the pleasure and reality principles: unaware of the subduing strictures of social organization, children abandon themselves to the pleasurable (in Kemble's terms, the dramatic, "the simplest portion of our composition, after our mere instincts"); when the reality principle arrives in the form of discipline and sublimation, they become self-aware (in Kemble's terms, a condition "never absent from the theatrical element"). Moving from individual to national characteristics, Kemble states bluntly that the Italians are unquenchably dramatic, the French haughtily theatrical, and the English neither one nor the other since they have succeeded in achieving a reconciliation of both. Politically stable while the Continent was thrown into revolution in the late 1840s and commercially unmatched because of a vigorous middle class, vast imperial possessions, and a stable monarchy, England knows how to harness its energies into a disciplined and magnificent supremacy. In discussing America, Kemble argues that the political and financial turbulence in the 1850s and the civil strife of the 1860s signal a turn to the theatrical in a love of speeches, oratory, celebrations, and bellicose declarations. But, simultaneously, America is also regressing to the brawling, passionate, selfish, indeed childish, world of the dramatic, the world of rebellion and struggle for autonomy that had given it birth. Kemble's assertion that only English national identity reconciles the dramatic and theatrical elements suggests, perhaps, that she believed she had finally achieved such a reconciliation in her private life.

This reconciliation came after Kemble had amassed an impressive record of travel, both in Europe and America. By the age of forty, she crossed the Atlantic eight times, been to Georgia, traversed the wintry Continent to stay with her sister in Italy, and toured the English provinces as actress and reader. The decade that followed her divorce was equally nomadic: four more Atlantic crossings; overland to Rome, Frascati, and the Amalfi coast with Adelaide and Edward; to the Berkshires every summer where she built her cottage in Lenox; and to Detroit, Chicago, St. Louis, and Milwaukee with her Shakespeare readings. When she was in London, she moved from one comfortable lodging to another, unable or unwilling to stay put, and arriving with little more than her books, her pictures, her considerable wardrobe, and her maid. No wonder she wrote in 1854 to Arthur Malkin, an old friend and fellow Cambridge Apostle of her brother John, that she was leading a wandering, "stay-nowhere" sort of life. Attributing this vagabond existence to a "villainous propensity I have of living entirely and greedily and with all my might in the present,"[4] she provides an apt description of the vital immediacy that characterized her personality.

During these itinerant years, Fanny Kemble's father died in 1854 and her two brothers, John Mitchell and Henry, died in 1857. In 1852, Fanny and Adelaide had undertaken the care and education of Henry Kemble's three-year-old illegitimate son, Harry, born while he was in Ireland on military duty; his aunts plucked him from a poverty-stricken life in Dublin with his actress mother, Adelaide taking him to live with her family and Kemble paying for his support and education. He grew up to be an actor and traveling companion for his aunt Fanny in her old age, who thought him unusually amiable in his manner, gifted with a particularly sweet temper, good common sense, and touchingly like his father and grandfather in appearance. She acknowledged, however, that her "abrupt and brusque manner and quick, sudden strong transitions of feeling" must have proved difficult for him, something he admitted after her death when he recalled that his aunt Adelaide he loved entirely but his aunt Fanny he always found rather frightening.[5]

After the divorce in 1849, Fanny Kemble had quickly returned to England to resume her Shakespeare readings. In the summer of 1850, she gave a thrilling performance at the St. James's Theatre of *The Tempest* that ruled out any of the "weariness or *ennui*" Henry Greville believed was entailed in listening to this particular play. In 1851, Anne Thackeray accompanied her father to the Southampton Assembly Rooms and they were enthralled by the way Kemble, in her Falstaff impersonation, would suddenly lift her voice in comic, jolly moments and point outward with open hands. Thackeray had first fallen in love with her when she was Juliet in 1829: then a slip of a thing, now she was just past forty and well on her way to getting fat—yet, according to his daughter, she still entranced him, as she did Edward FitzGerald, a fellow Apostle of her brother John at Cambridge, who had known her from childhood.[6] FitzGerald, an accomplished translator of Greek tragedy, was said to have intended his *Agamemnon* as a tribute to Kemble's talents and achievements; to Kemble he was a dear, eccentric, and brilliantly gifted old friend. She treasured his "most kind heart and fine taste." When she came to read *Richard III* in Woodbridge (the Suffolk town where FitzGerald lived with his companion, Aldis Wright) and made her formal curtsey to her audience before commencing, FitzGerald got up and bowed to her, a gesture of homage immediately copied by the audience. He noted afterward in a letter to a friend, dated October 20, 1852, that *Richard III* would not have been his choice of play but it had fallen to them in Kemble's routine, and she brooked no interference with her schedule: she is "really a noble woman, much bothered," he added, to whom he would have been happy to give money had she not read at all.[7] He does not say "much bothered" by what, but since Kemble was making good money, was free of Pierce and reunited with her daughters, and was honored wherever she went, it is possible she displayed signs of the erratic mood swings that she never entirely conquered. At the best of times, and this was certainly one of them as she made her triumphant progress through England, she was subject to her "blue devils."

The distress was apparent to sixteen-year-old Anne Thackeray when she met Kemble again in Adelaide's magnificent drawing room on the Via Bocca di Lione in Rome in 1853, where Kemble had joined the Sartoris family for the summer. In her memoirs, Anne Thackeray recalls, "It was at a very hard and difficult hour of her life, so I have heard her say, a time when she needed all her courage to endure her daily portion of suffering."[8] What that daily portion of suffering might have been is difficult to determine, given that Kemble was welcomed by her sister's family and was warmly applauded when she read Shakespeare in the evenings to Adelaide's friends. Frederic Leighton, for example, who had become Adelaide's adoring cavalier, wrote to his brother from Rome that Kemble's readings were "unapproachable," her women pathetic and touching, and her men absolutely extraordinary: "it is *too* good and it seems discrepant to hear male harsh sounds coming from the mouth of a woman."[9] Moreover, Kemble was surrounded by intellectually interesting people such as Elizabeth and Robert Browning, who lived nearby on the Via Bocca di Lione, the sculptor Harriet Hosmer, the son-in-law of Walter Scott, and, of course, Leighton, people with whom she went on elegant picnics into the Roman countryside (three carriages-full of people, champagne, and English tea, Elizabeth Barrett Browning gleefully reported to her sister).[10] Yet she openly announced this was a "very hard and difficult hour." Being with Adelaide undoubtedly exacerbated her chronic sense of homelessness, a sad recognition that even though she relished her "stay-nowhere" existence, she had no settled home, no children around her, no brilliant Italian villa where she might be the sparkling magnet for writers and artists. Seeing Adelaide with her children, admiring the brilliance with which she presided over her elegant house filled with gorgeous flowers and the rare and beautiful objects she was so fond of collecting, Kemble felt left out and bereft of the rules that kept her sane. As Henry James said after her death, "If she had not lived by rule, she would have lived infallibly by riot."[11] With Adelaide and Edward, she was not writing the rules, and a certain melancholia seems to have dampened the hard-won achievements of the late 1840s: victory over Pierce, a brilliant second career, financial independence. Courageously having written a new role for herself, she could not, it would seem, erase entirely the inheritance of depressed spirits from her mother.

This second visit to Rome also prompted painful memories of her arrival there in 1846, bruised from the battles with Pierce and distraught by the separation from her children. The flowering acacia trees on Adelaide's terrace were a sad reminder to Kemble of a poem about maternal sorrow she had composed in 1846 in which she had expressed the bittersweet sorrow of giving birth to Sarah, "the first blossom of my spring."

> And as I lay, panting from the fierce strife
> With death and agony that won thy life,
> Their snowy clusters hung on their brown bough,
> E'en as upon my breast, my May-bud, thou.

In the poem, a bereft mother "sits lamenting" on a distant shore when she sees the acacia blossoms that "crowned" the May mornings when her daughters were born, just as Kemble mourned the loss of Sarah and Fan in the Roman May of 1846.[12] It is also possible that in 1853 Kemble, at the age of forty-three, was entering early menopause, which could have deepened her misery. When Anne Thackeray saw Adelaide and Kemble in Rome, one sister wafting regally in her satin robes through her drawing room and the other moodily sequestered by the smoldering wood fire, she thought them, in some ways, "unfit" for the world, and she wondered about the temperamental clashes in this "most stormy family" with its "highly-wrought home atmosphere."[13]

Back in England, on February 10, 1855, Kemble filled Exeter Hall on the Strand with a performance of *A Midsummer Night's Dream*, accompanied by Mendelssohn's music; this was no small achievement since Exeter Hall's smallest room could hold 800 people and its largest, 2,500 (she probably read in the smaller of the two). No longer afraid that she would break down if she listened to Mendelssohn (as she had been when asked to read for the queen in February 1848), she was a tremendous success, especially praised for bringing out the "womanly" nature of Helena.[14] Two days later she was in Brighton, reading *Romeo and Juliet*, a performance witnessed by Henry Crabb Robinson who declared it "instructive" and "exciting": "In her glass Shakespeare is a philosopher. I know her, and honor her for her truthfulness amidst all trials."[15] Ridiculed by the *New York Herald* five years earlier as a discarded divorcée cashing in on her celebrity ("we begin to think that divorce and popularity must go hand in hand these ecstatic days"), now she was feted in England for the moving gravity born of well-known sadness with which she infused her readings. Also, her reading of *Romeo and Juliet*, the play in which Charles Kemble had played Mercutio and Romeo to her Juliet, might have moved her more deeply than any other at this moment since her father had died just three months previously.

Sarah and Fan

In the spring of 1856, Fanny Kemble returned to America, excited and anxious about the forthcoming reunion with her children, particularly Sarah, who would turn twenty-one on May 28.[16] Kemble always laughed about the fact that she gave birth to her two daughters on the same day of the year (it was a sign of her insistence on regular habits, she would say), and she also spoke proudly about the ease with which she brought them into the world. When Sarah was just two weeks old, Kemble wrote to Sarah Perkins Cleveland that she was "perfectly well and up and about as if nothing had happened. My health and strength seem to amaze everybody here"; and she added that Sarah was "a very fine, strong baby, with dark *blue* eyes and a luxuriant head of hair."[17] Up until the seventh month of her pregnancy with Fan, Kemble rode every day and made no secret of her contempt for the way American women and their young children were so coddled and stuffed with sweet foods that their complexions were pasty, their digestive systems a mess, and their constitutions feeble. Until she left America in 1845, and the care of her daughters to a succession of nurses and governesses, Kemble ensured that they consumed a healthy diet full of fruits and vegetables and that they spent a lot of time outdoors, whether playing in the gardens at Butler Place, splashing in the icy pool at Yellow Springs, or walking with her to the Ninth Street market when they lived at the awful Mrs. McPherson's. They grew up to be physically robust young women.

The cost to their emotional health is difficult to determine. It cannot have been easy to hear their parents quarreling about Pierce's financial recklessness and sexual exploits, Kemble's rugged refusal to conform to conventional American notions of wifely obedience, the fundamental immorality of slavery, how often they might be permitted to see their mother, and whether their governesses were in league against her, maybe even sleeping with their father. There were some devastating moments of confrontation and humiliation for Kemble in the months before she finally left Philadelphia in September 1845, most of them witnessed by Sarah and Fan: being prohibited from attending their joint birthday party in 1844 (too many in the carriage, decreed Pierce, as they set off for Butler Place from Washington Square); restricted to seven hours a week of visits under the punitive terms of Pierce's agreement to support her while they lived apart at Mrs. McPherson's; prevented by their governess from speaking to them when she approached them on the Philadelphia streets. For four years, they knew their mother only through letters, and when they were reunited in the summer of 1849 it was with a woman who had been vilified by their father in the divorce hearings as vain, hypocritical, unstable, and heartless. It is unlikely, of course, that they were familiar with the intimate details of the divorce, but it is difficult to imagine that during the four years under the sole guardianship of their father they had not heard unpleasant talk about Kemble. Pierce monitored very carefully the correspondence between mother and daughters, and Adelaide confided to friends that she believed he held back certain letters from Sarah and Fan if he deemed them unsuitable. They must have had an awareness of themselves not just as Butler children but as descendants of the most famous theatrical family in England. In a symbolic sense, Sarah and Fan's inheritance was analogous with that of America itself: blood daughters of the mother country born in the former colonies and grown to adulthood in a new and independent nation. To her credit, Kemble succeeded in establishing a lasting bond with her daughters when they were reunited, although initially it was not easy. After she had been with Sarah for a few weeks, she wrote to Henry Greville about her plans for reading in the West in such a way that he reported to Frederic Leighton he suspected it would "answer better to her than the girl's society!"[18]

As soon as she arrived in America in May 1856, Kemble whisked Sarah and her sister up to Lenox for a two-month holiday. It was a tense reunion, and when

Adelaide Sartoris heard of the difficulties that Kemble was having with Sarah, she admitted to a friend, "it is a painful business—a strong feeling of duty on my niece's side, and a strong mother's yearning on my sister's, draws them together, but they do not agree."[19] Their temperaments were similar in the sense that Sarah suffered from a melancholia bordering on depression; unfortunately she possessed none of the vitality, wit, and spontaneity that saved her mother from a life of self-recriminating disappointment. Kemble struggled to make the best of it and she wrote to Arthur Malkin saying she would love to show him Sarah since "she is so handsome and so clever." By all accounts she *was* good-looking—taller than her mother, with long chestnut hair and vivid blue eyes, and looking, in most ways, nothing like a Kemble. Kemble had hoped Sarah would return with her to Europe to see England, France, and Italy through her seasoned eyes, but she declined, having fallen in love with Owen Wister, whom she married in October 1859. Ten years older than Sarah, Owen Wister was an established physician with a successful practice in Branchtown, not far from Butler Place. According to Rebecca Gratz, who was very close to the Butler daughters, Owen Wister was not Sarah's first love: she had confided to Gratz three years before she married Wister that she was engaged to a Mr. Sandford of New York (about whom we know nothing); Pierce had approved but the engagement must have been broken off.[20] In her memoirs, Kemble makes no mention of this Mr. Sandford, probably because she was so fond of Owen Wister. When Sarah gave birth to Owen Wister, Jr., in July 1860, Kemble arrived for a prolonged grandmotherly visit of some nine months, eager to spoil the baby and pass along to his mother her prescriptions for healthy childrearing, but even more delighted at the prospect of spending time with the baby's father.

Despite the pleasure she took in Sarah's family, however, by this time Kemble had begun to find living in America "very, very irksome," and when she considered that her home for the rest of her life must certainly be in America, she felt sadder than she knew she ought to be.[21] As early as September 9, 1856, she wrote to Henry Greville, "The whole state of this country, moral, social and political, makes one's hair stand on end with amazement and apprehension. . . . Everything is horribly distasteful to me here."[22] She had been cheered by Fan Butler's willingness, when she turned twenty-one in May 1859, to accompany her mother to Europe; jollier than Sarah and more resilient, Fan had a splendid time shopping in Paris, tramping through the Highlands as her mother had in 1827, and spending time with her cousins, Greville and May Sartoris. Surprisingly confident for her years, when she met the Prince of Wales in New York in 1860, she termed him a nice little fellow who moved well.[23] That Kemble, in the latter years of her life, spent much time living with one of her daughters is witness to the fact that the three of them managed to devise a modus vivendi. After seeing Kemble seemingly at ease with Sarah and

Owen Wister in Philadelphia in August 1860, happy in her daughter's marriage and delighted with the one-month-old Owen Jr., Sidney Fisher noted, "Her manners and conversation this evening are more quiet than they used to be and she was very cordial, easy and pleasant."[24] Sarah Wister, however, did not always feel as comfortable as she might appear when her mother was staying with her; a few months before Sidney Fisher's impression of family happiness, she wrote in her diary that after Kemble had made arrangements to leave Butler Place the following day, "Owen in a moment of insanity begged Mother to prolong her visit. . . . Of course there was a scene. She said she would stay if I wished, as long as I wished, & of course I was placed by my silence in the agreeable posture of declining a further visit."[25] In general, however, Kemble proved to be an amiable mother-in-law for Owen Wister and the Hon. James Leigh (who married Fan Butler in June 1871) and an adoring grandmother to Owen Wister, Jr., and Alice Leigh.

The 1850s and 1860s were less happy for Pierce Butler. His long-term addiction to gambling on the stock exchange brought his complete financial ruin in the notorious Panic of 1857. The panic began with the sinking of a sailing vessel carrying gold to American banks; investors in the market and in the railroads made a frantic run on the banks to withdraw their money, and the banks began to collapse, starting with the New York branch of the Ohio Life Insurance and Trust Company. By December, Pierce faced bankruptcy and was forced to hand over his remaining assets to trustees, a disgrace that prompted Kemble to complain bitterly to her friends that Pierce's "insane gambling in the stocks" had ruined her "girls' worldly prospects." Pierce had paid her no alimony for seven years, and her only consolation in December 1857 was that Butler Place would not be sold since she held a mortgage on it, from which she was supposed to have received her income. However, Philadelphia society, in the predictable person of Sidney Fisher, spread unfounded rumors that the Butler property was to be cut up in lots, although Fisher was correct in judging the utter recklessness of Pierce's gambling: he recorded in his diary on August 7, 1857, when he heard of Pierce's ruin, "What a result—an hereditary fortune of $700,000 lost by sheer folly and infatuation."[26]

The 1857 panic led to a severe economic depression that lasted for nearly three years, and in early 1859 Pierce had no choice but to sell 436 Butler slaves to settle debts rumored to be as much as $500,000. At the time of the sale, the overall holdings of the Butler family included 900 slaves; the holdings were divided—450 went to the estate of John Butler, 20 were left on the cotton plantation, and, on two rainy days in early March 1859, the remainder were sold to settle Pierce's debts. None of the slaves had been sold before and most had lived on the two plantations since they were born. Brought to a race course in Savannah, Georgia, and housed in stables, for two days they were inspected by prospective buyers. According to

Mortimer Thomson (who wrote a popular column for the *New York Tribune* under the pseudonym "Q. K. Doesticks"), "There were no light mulattoes in the whole of the Butler stock, and but very few that were even a shade removed from the original Congo blackness."[27] At the end of the second day, as the last family stepped down from the auction block, the rain stopped, and, according to Thomson, Pierce "appeared among his people, speaking to each one, and being recognized with seeming pleasure by all. The men obsequiously pulled off their hats.... Occasionally to a very old or favorite servant, Mr. Butler would extend his gloved hand."[28] The sale brought in close to $304,000, by early twenty-first-century calculations, $6 million. Almost immediately Pierce left for Europe to escape the notoriety of his financial ruin and the humiliation of having decimated the Butler family fortunes. But within months, however, he was back in Philadelphia, fired by talk of secession of the Southern states, eager to buy arms with the remnants of his fortune, and determined to join the Southern army.

During these same months, in late 1859 and early 1860, Kemble began to write to her English friends about settling near her children, most probably in Lenox where she had experienced her happiest American days and where they would be able to visit her. She knew that she needed to return to England to make arrangements in regard to Harry, her brother's son, and to look into the small inheritance left by Charles Kemble to herself and Adelaide, but she did not relish the prospect of gathering together her scattered property—books, pictures, silver plate, and so on—and she kept delaying her departure, dreading not her arrival but the leaving of England. In November 1858 she had written to Arthur Malkin that "it is certain that I must look to America henceforward as my abiding place, for I have utterly given up all hope and expectation of my children ever settling anywhere else, and it is better so, in spite of all my wishes and all my regrets."[29] Although the reunion with her daughters was deeply gratifying, she did not wish to live permanently in the country that housed Pierce Butler; she also regretted that America, in the midst of the economic depression that lingered beyond the Panic of 1857, was able to neither recover financially nor settle the furious disputes about slavery. She wrote to her dear old friend Henry Greville (whose four-volume diary is richly enlivened by the letters Kemble sent him from America) that the "terrible and inevitable Slavery question is beginning to weigh like an incubus upon the whole country, pressing, every day, nearer and nearer to some solution, which threatens to be a hideous catastrophe."[30] To Kemble, it seemed as if America was bent on a great national trial, the people besotted by material prosperity, the government despicable and despised, and the whole country retrogressing to national disaster.

Kemble never pretended, in her social and cultural commentary, to be anything other than an intelligent and astute spectator on the transatlantic scene. Neither a historian nor a political essayist, she sensibly kept her commentary at the level of on-the-spot observation, but it is worth remembering that her social circle before she came to America was not restricted to the world of the theater. From the ages of twenty to twenty-three, she dined out with an English cultural elite composed of politicians, essayists, novelists, and poets, and in the years to come she maintained her correspondence with many of these people, and with new and influential friends. What she reported to her English friends about American life in the years leading to the outbreak of war on April 12, 1861, delineates a nation bent on folly, feverish from financial speculation, and, from her despairing perspective, destroyed by an addiction to gambling and a thirst for excitement. None of this was startlingly new, and from a modern historical perspective it seems commonplace, but she wrote about what she saw with notable intelligence and in vivid prose. One of the surprising things about her views of the forthcoming disaster is that she believed it might be the salvation of the nation, a check to "insolent forwardness . . . an unripe rottenness, decay without duration,"[31] an image virtually identical to that deployed by her old friend Tom Moore in his poems written from Washington in 1803. Recurring frequently in much British writing about America in the first half of the nineteenth century, this image evokes the disappointed mother country admonishing the rebellious colonies for having fled the empire too soon, moved too fast, and wasted their energies—with the result that the nation has unnaturally decayed.

In November 1860, the visit of the light-footed Prince of Wales "to his grandfather's rebellious provinces" prompted Kemble to write to Henry Greville that she hoped he had received a pleasing impression and retained a cordial feeling toward America; although America does not need England "otherwise than commercially," England must collaborate with "her vigorous offspring" to avert the looming civil strife that will seriously test moral values.[32] Unsaid here is the fear expressed by many people besides Kemble that demand for American cotton would propel England into support for the slave states, and in December 1860, she wrote again to Greville that she blessed providence for having dealt an ambiguously beneficial blow to her children. The loss of their property through their father's unprincipled extravagance meant they had been saved from inflicting injustice and oppression as slave owners and that they would be spared the "impending retribution."[33]

By January 1861, as the prospect of the secession of the Southern states loomed closer, she declared her bitter hope that they would be utterly destroyed, reduced to a kind of wilderness of fertile land, which the North might then reconquer, cultivate, and re-form into a free and flourishing part of the Union. In May (a few weeks after the outbreak of the war), Greville noted in his diary Kemble's latest bulletin about Pierce: she wrote to Greville that Pierce has "gone off to swear his allegiance to the Southern Confederacy, taking in spite of her own and her sister's entreaties, and the remonstrances of all his friends, Fanny with him, his purpose, I understand, being to establish himself on his plantation again, buying a new force of slaves instead of those he sold two years ago, and thus become a resident Georgian slaveholder."[34] That Pierce set off for the South with his younger daughter a few weeks after the beginning of the Civil War says a great deal about his reckless fidelity to the social order of slavery that had long sustained his privilege, as well as something about the almost obsessive devotion of Fan Butler to her father and, after his death, to his memory. Fan's eager departure with Pierce for Georgia demonstrates her loyalty not only to Pierce and sympathy for the Southern cause but, ironically, also how much she was like her mother in sticking to her political principles. They never agreed about the South. Kemble remained implacable in her indictment of brutality, hypocrisy, and political self-delusion; Fan desperately wanted to restore a workable agrarian economy, unsupported by slavery but still grounded in the Southern gentry values that were exemplified in her father (even though he was raised in Philadelphia). After the war, still devoted to her father, Fan accompanied him every winter until his death in 1867 on his increasingly hopeless journeys to the plantations that had been wrecked by Union troops. She worked with him to restore the rice and cotton fields, with the help of freed slaves still willing to work for the Butler family, but, devastated by neglect, war, and a diminished black labor force, the plantations never again flourished.

On May 7, 1861, about a month after her precipitous departure for Georgia with Pierce, an exhausted and disheveled Fan Butler arrived unannounced at her sister's house in Branchtown; Sarah noted in her diary that Fan had come "by Kentucky, Tennessee and had not changed her clothes for six days, till this morning, and has not been in bed for six nights. Nevertheless she looks fat and fresh."[35] Pierce's whereabouts were unknown since nothing had been heard from him since he returned to Georgia after bringing Fan to Cincinnati. But five months after leaving with Fan to return to the South, he reappeared in Philadelphia and a few weeks later was arrested by special order of the secretary of war on charges of high treason: he had refused to take an oath of allegiance to the government of President Lincoln and was charged with having bought arms to be transported to Georgia. Interned at Fort Hamilton in New York harbor on August 3, 1861, he was released after five weeks, having been visited by his daughters through the special permission of the president. Sarah and Owen Wister (and Fan) had successfully persuaded family friends to intervene on their behalf so that they might see their father; these family connections, combined with the fact that the government had been unable to discover sufficiently incriminating evidence, led to Pierce's release on September 21, 1861. Sidney Fisher thought Pierce had gone completely mad, but admired "the knightly spirit these southern men are displaying. They rush recklessly on fearful odds and fearful dangers and talk like men insane."[36] Just before Pierce was released from Fort Hamilton, Kemble had written to Arthur Malkin, somewhat hopefully one imagines, that Pierce would "be detained until the conclusion of the war, as he is not likely to accept any oath of allegiance tendered to him by this government, being a determined democrat and inimical, both on public and private grounds, to Mr. Lincoln and his ministers."[37] His financial and political humiliations having already destroyed her daughters' prospects (to say nothing of the devastating wreck he had made of her own, younger life), Kemble would have been delighted to have him incarcerated throughout the war, and beyond. For the most part, though, Pierce spent the remainder of the war living either in Branchtown or at his sister-in-law's house in Philadelphia.

Writing About the War

For Henry Greville, Kemble provided a vivid description of Philadelphia shortly after the official opening of hostilities with the firing of Confederate artillery on Fort Sumter on April 12, 1861: troops were pouring into the city day and night, the Stars and Stripes was flying from every house, and the newspaper offices were thronged with men, women, and children in search of news. Pitying the Northern states for an ignorance of the South born of their own insulating material prosperity, Kemble believed they were "wholly unprepared" for the ferocity with which the South would defend itself. But, elated by Ulysses Grant's capture of Confederate strongholds in western Tennessee in February 1862, she wrote to Henry Greville that she thought the war would soon be over. Hopefully but incorrectly, she believed that the graduate encroachment of Northern forces into the South would bring a quick end, and Sidney Fisher records that on February 18 he found her "as usual exuberant and animated, a little theatrical, very clever and somewhat dictatorial. . . . She is very enthusiastic about the war and predicts from it the destruction of slavery."[38] Writing to Henry Greville after a train journey from Philadelphia to Washington, immediately after Fisher saw her, she describes a scene of strings of camps and military stations along the line, of tents pitched along the railroad embankments, and eager requests for newspapers at every stop along the way by soldiers desperate for news. At this moment, she thought deliverance of the slaves was near, and she was reminded of her walks along the shores of the Altamaha River twenty-three years earlier. With the roar of the Atlantic in her ears and an awareness of the West Indies not far away, she had hoped that the abolition of slavery that had been enacted there in 1833 would soon come to Georgia, but it had not, and the Butler slaves, "sold and dispersed to pay their owners' debts," were now, in April 1862, "scattered into a more hopeless and miserable slavery still."[39]

In the summer of 1862, still hopeful that the war might be nearing its end, Kemble took Fan to Europe with the aim of distracting her from her fierce loyalty to the South and to her father. Henry Greville reported they were both in good health and spirits when he saw them in London, though Kemble was reluctant to speak of the conflict, which he regarded as "lucky, as she would find but little sympathy with her opinions." She delivered lacerating indictments of the moral hypocrisy she believed was shared by American Northerners and English liberals: in America, Northerners talked abolition and became cotton spinners; in England, liberal factory owners fed their looms with the produce of slavery. Now, American men were dying for the North and South, and English workers were starving "in deplorable inactivity; the countless hands that wrought from morn til night the wealth that was a world's wonder are stretched unwillingly to beg their bread."[40]

By December, Greville found her in "great distress" about the defeat of the North at Fredericksburg, Virginia, on the thirteenth of that month, but despite his sympathy for her distress, he and his friends were as ignorant of the South as the North had been at the beginning of the war. A month after Kemble read *Henry V* on April 23, 1863, in London, the publication of the Georgian *Journal* did a great deal to rectify the ignorance of her friends, not just about the South but about the American Civil War in general, although they had certainly been aware of the mass meetings organized by working-class leaders in London in 1863 proclaiming support for the North. Some of Kemble's ruling-class acquaintances, whose sympathies favored gentlemanly Southern plantation owners, were shocked and alarmed by these developments. What Kemble hoped to achieve through publication was their education in the graphic practices of slavery and, in her own small way, a speedy end to the conflict. They needed to know that Southern slaveholders were very different from Manchester manufacturers or Massachusetts merchants, not because they were more "gentlemanly" but because they were a remnant of barbarism and feudalism. Her old friend Edward FitzGerald, however, reacted somewhat ambiguously to the Georgian *Journal*, writing to a friend on June 23, 1864, "Did you not like Mrs. Kemble's book? A very honest, courageous, and eloquent one I thought. I really am tempted to side against the North."[41]

Publication of the Georgian *Journal* in 1863 was a work of political action, perhaps in part a way of signaling Kemble's agreement in May 1853 with the "Affectionate and Christian Address of Many Thousand Women of Great Britain and Ireland to Their Sisters the Women of the United States of America."[42] Many wondered why Kemble had not signed this petition, a protest against slavery's "outrages on the Christian family" on behalf of half a million women, which had been presented to Harriet Beecher Stowe at Stafford House during her triumphant visit to England after the publication of *Uncle Tom's Cabin*.[43] Kemble, however, was on her way to Rome in the spring of 1853 and it may have been inconvenient, even impossible, for her to sign. What is more important is that Kemble's publication of the *Journal* probably had greater influence than adding her signature to those of half a million other women. As she wrote in a letter to *The Times* that was appended to the first English edition, "I have seen what few Englishmen can see—the working of the system in the midst of it."[44]

When she had returned from Georgia in 1839, she had made a fair copy of the letters to Elizabeth Sedgwick and over the years, until the time of publication, she made certain revisions to her original text and shared some of it in readings for her closest friends, although the sheer immediacy of her perceptions suggests that whatever changes she made were minor. A deft writer with a telling sense of detail, she probably added and subtracted a few things here and there, but it is doubtful that the brilliant sense of place that she brings to the *Journal* was tacked on in later years. Sidney Fisher, always eager to have the latest gossip and to read about his fellow Philadelphians, obtained a copy of the *New York Tribune* in July 1863 in order to be one of the first to read parts of the *Journal* before it was published in book form by Harper Brothers. For him, it revealed "terrible secrets of the prison house. Filth, squalor, cruelty, and wretchedness are painted in very strong colors. . . . I remember hearing at the time that her conduct at the plantation had enraged Butler and the overseers and caused much dissatisfaction among neighboring gentlemen as she put dangerous notions into the minds of the slaves."[45] He added that he had just spoken to Mrs. John Butler (Kemble's former sister-in-law), who confirmed to him that Kemble's account of the conditions of the Butler slaves was indisputable, "and she ought to know as she owns half the property, or did before the war, and has frequently resided on the estate."[46] When the *Journal* was published in England in May 1863, it was praised for its disturbing power: "A more startling and fearful narrative on a well-worn subject was never laid before readers," declared the *Atheneum*. As Catherine Clinton notes, passages were read aloud on the floor of the House of Commons and to cotton workers in Manchester.[47] Fan Butler, however, loathed the book and upbraided her mother for allowing it to be published, indeed for publishing anything at all about her life. In 1881, when Kemble was preparing the second volume of her memoirs, Fan angrily wrote to her about the bitter distress she had caused her children by publishing the Georgian

Journal—"Nothing would ever induce me to have it in the house. . . . You have said over and over again that you thought people most unjustified in writing personal reminiscences of others which turn out to be painful to their relations and friends. . . . Does being their mother give you the right to wound and distress them?"[48]

When General Lee surrendered at Appomattox Court House on April 9, 1865, Kemble was in London, again with Fan—they both wept over the news, Kemble with happiness and Fan with despair. Fan returned immediately to America to be with her father, who, with the aim of making a permanent home in Philadelphia for himself and his younger daughter, had bought the Philadelphia mansion owned by Gabriella Butler, the widow of his brother, John. Kemble followed shortly thereafter and by the end of April she was in New York; in a long letter to Arthur Malkin she ruminates on the challenges and preoccupations of the previous fifteen years or so. In perceptive detail, she explores her feelings about being an Englishwoman in America and about being a mother to her American daughters. That the nation was prosperous and thriving, she was entirely confident, and the check received to its material progress by the Civil War seemed only to have accelerated "its vigorous action now that the people's energies have returned to their accustomed channels." But what impressed her most deeply, right after the war, was that the country was no longer English, no longer a place that resembled a remote part of England inhabited by some very "queer English people" as it had when she arrived thirty-four years before. Now, she declared, there was not a trace of British origin in the Americans she met, except in their speech. Having come through civil strife, America was on the cusp of becoming a "real nation" bearing fewer and fewer resemblances to its mother country. In fact, she believed that the character and culture of the postbellum nation would become increasingly German. Paradoxically, however, her own identity as "an elderly English woman" (she was fifty-five) gained a certain force as she wondered about her place in this surging nation. Realizing that she was no longer a symbolic representative of the mother country since America seemed to have no cultural need for such a figure, she affirmed her less vexed identity as a literal mother.

On a note that perfectly evokes the victory of her struggle to regain her daughters' affection, eroded over the years through Pierce's malign influence, she concludes, "My children are Americans, and the gain to my happiness and peace of mind, in no longer being divided from them by the Atlantic, is indescribable."[49] Sarah Butler Wister and Fan Butler, and Kemble herself, arrived at maturity at the end of the Civil War—all of them battered and bruised in different ways but looking to a more settled, peaceful future. The lonely death of Pierce Butler in August 1867 on the Georgia plantation, at the age of fifty-six from what was probably malaria, troubling as it was for Kemble since it triggered memories of their stormy connection, seemed to seal the end of civil and private conflict. On his death, Sidney Fisher had this to say about Pierce: "He was a man of strongly marked character with some good qualities and many faults. He led a very unsatisfactory life and threw away great advantage. He was handsome, clever, most gentlemanlike in his manners, but uneducated, obstinate, prejudiced and passionate."[50] Kemble could now settle down to being an indulgent grandmother, to a resumption of her Shakespeare readings, and to the bittersweet experience of losing many dear old friends through death, and gaining some new ones through her writings and her travels.

The Unfurling Sea

Good-bye, my dearest Harriet. God bless you. The sea unfurling on the shore sings of you to me.
— Fanny Kemble to Harriet St. Leger

A Story Without an End, or Fanny's Memoirs

Harriet St. Leger died a few weeks after Fanny Kemble wrote to her from Switzerland with the promise that she would soon be in Ireland, called by the moving song of a friendship that had lasted fifty years. During the last year of Harriet's life, Kemble had visited her beloved old friend and was prepared for her death—when she traveled to England in 1877 after three years away from Europe, she got off the steamer at Queenstown and rushed to her side—but the loss of Harriet was still a sad blow. In the following summer of 1879, she was also in Switzerland when Adelaide died at her English country house from complications from diabetes. By this time, Kemble was seventy years old and had outlived her three siblings, which probably says something about her robust constitution, sensible diet, and dedication to vigorous exercise. John had died at age fifty, Henry at forty-one, and Adelaide at sixty-five. Kemble was still healthy even if so fat that she had to be carried over the highest Alpine passes by sturdy Swiss guides when she was on her summer walking tours (by her own admission in August 1872, she weighed fourteen stone or one hundred and ninety-six pounds, which is a lot for a sixty-three-year-old woman of just over five feet). But despite her own good health, the deaths of her dearest friend and her sister at the end of the 1870s heightened a piercing awareness of the past and a bittersweet intimation of her own mortality. To see her own face and mannerisms in her daughters, to catch a glimpse of her uncle John Philip Kemble in the serious gaze of her grandson, Owen Wister, at the piano, and to smell a jasmine plant given to her by Pierce that had been nurtured by her Butler Place neighbor, Mary Fox, and returned to her thirty-five years later in a beautiful porcelain planter was to be brought face-to-face with the extraordinarily dramatic spectacle of her life. As Kemble saw Sarah standing on *her* former doorstep at Butler Place, she seemed an "apparition" of her own youth; when she entered her former "house of woe," she was so overwhelmed by memories that she began to doubt her own identity. The jasmine in full bloom brought "a strange flowering again" of the exciting time just before her marriage when Pierce was her ardent follower and she a glittering prize. To live at York Farm, the small cottage just across the road from Butler Place, where she resided intermittently from 1874 to 1877, was to encounter, in the most literal way, her history.

This unfolding pageant of scenes from a past that she now began to shape into her memoirs prompted a rehearsal, as it were, for the last act that was beginning to unfurl, an act that lasted longer than she predicted since she lived until she was two months past her eighty-third birthday. It was a time of deaths, of aging, and of last visits to favorite places, a time when she sometimes seemed so deeply sad that she reminded her grandson, Owen, of Tennyson's Mariana, an insight she admired for its sensitivity but wondered about in terms of how well she might be meeting the challenge of mortality. But as she aged and learned of the death of friends and saw her daughters become mothers, the depression always associated with her own mother became apparent to those who knew her well, despite the fact that she soldiered on, mustering her reserves of religious faith and remarkable vitality. When she sent a photograph of herself in 1875 to Edward FitzGerald, long a dear friend of the Kemble family, he responded that in Fanny's features he saw the "deep current of melancholy" that Thérèse Kemble had covered (when she was able) with a sparkling persona. And just as FitzGerald saw Thérèse in Fanny and Fanny saw her uncle in her grandson, so Fanny also became increasingly aware of the physical and temperamental traces of herself in her daughters. The curtain rose on the last act of her life when she returned with Fan from England at the close of the Civil War in April 1865.

Almost immediately Fan Butler left for Georgia with her father, eager to join him in restoring the plantations after the wartime devastation. She wrote to her sister on March 22, 1866, of the crushed and sad condition of the defeated Southerners—the women had retreated into grief-stricken fixation on their prebellum security and the men seemed only to live in the present, trying, listlessly, to repair their ruined fortunes.[1] Fan's account of her time in Georgia, initially with Pierce, then alone, and, eventually, with her husband, James Leigh, reveals how much she resembled her mother temperamentally and also how much she differed from her in the matter of Southern politics. Like her mother when she was at Butler Place in the early days of her marriage and at the cotton plantation house on Butler Island, Fan set to work making things habitable and pleasant: the desolate shell of a house, shattered by war and neglect, its windows in shards, its plaster falling off the walls, and its furniture consisting of a broken table and two rickety chairs, was rapidly restored with the assistance of former Butler slaves still on the plantation who made her feel, she confided to her sister, like "Robinson Crusoe with three hundred men Fridays."[2] In Darien, the small town at the mouth of the Altamaha River where Kemble, almost thirty years before, had tried to get a boat north, leaving Pierce and abandoning her daughters, Fan bought sturdy new furniture, muslin curtains, and attractive table covers. She set up her writing things in precisely the same place where Kemble had composed her Georgian journal, and behind the writing table she hung a picture of General Lee in a gesture of decorative defiance of her mother's antislavery politics.

But Fan resembled her mother in many ways. She loved the natural beauty of the sea islands, riding along the paths to the post office twice a week through woods of red-trunked pines, oaks, dwarf palmetto, and sweet-smelling bay, and marveling at the gray moss that grew in the trees meeting over her head as she trotted by. It seemed to her like a gossamer veil, and on these rides she met no one, heard nothing but the songs of different birds and the wind in the tall pines, and smelled only the aroma of the pine trees mingled with the sweet salt breezes from the sea. Back at the house, she built a fence to shut out the view of former slave quarters and to enclose the magnificent magnolia and orange trees that, together with the flowers she planted, created a lovely garden (as her mother had done at Butler Place). When she traveled to the cotton plantation on St. Simons, she attacked the wooden overseer's shanty in a similar manner: the house was a marvel to Kemble when she read about it in her daughter's letters—painted, prettily furnished, the spiders and centipedes that had been the bane of her existence swept away. Also, with her mother's fearsome energy, Fan persuaded some of the former slaves to sign work contracts; she set up a school for children during the morning and for young people working in the fields in the evening; and she restored the old hospital, that dreadful place where Kemble witnessed so much suffering. Ironically, she finally achieved for the former slaves what her mother had failed to realize thirty years earlier: reasonably fair working conditions, a simple education, and rudimentary medical care.

Threaded throughout Fan's account of Southern restoration is a redemptive picture of her father that directly contradicts her mother's earlier writings. Where

Kemble had derided him as heartless and emasculated in her Georgian *Journal*, his daughter presents him as beloved and noble. The number of former slaves who greeted Fan and Pierce when they arrived on Butler Island in 1866 is astonishing, given emancipation and the over four hundred who had been sold at the 1859 auction, as is Fan's loyal recital of their avowals of love for the master who had sold their families. She recounts that she shook hands with almost four hundred, nearly all of whom spoke to her of their loyalty to Pierce. An old slave named Bram tells of having been consoled in 1859 by Pierce's promise that, although he was in great financial trouble, he would know where everyone was going and would buy them all back as soon as he could; according to Fan, Bram said that if it would help Pierce for him to be sold, he would be willing, and that now, in 1866, a freed slave, he would work until he died for his "old master." She also recounts the sad story of Pierce's illness and death. Felled by malaria shortly after she returned to the North in late May 1867, he was nursed and buried by the former slaves who put flowers in jam jars by his grave.

At the close of this redemptive narrative, in all but official terms dedicated to the memory of her father, Fan hastens to say that she has not aimed to defend slavery, nor does she pretend that the Butler slaves would willingly return to their former condition "any more than we would have them slaves again." But she insists that they did not "suffer" under slavery, nor did they "regard it with the horror they were supposed to by all the advocates of abolition,"[3] an unambiguous denial of her mother's published opinions. Wisely, she reserved these sentiments for the publication of her book in 1883, choosing in the spring of 1867, when she left Pierce behind in Georgia to return to Philadelphia, to speak rarely of her father and to direct her notable Kemble energy into plans for restoring the rundown Butler Place and the adjacent York cottage to their former comfortable condition. Sarah and Owen Wister were to live permanently in the big house and, since the entire property was entailed upon her grandchildren, Kemble was to rent the cottage from her daughters, occupying it during the summer and whenever Fan and her husband, James Leigh (whom she married in 1871), were not in Philadelphia.

Over the next few years Fan Butler refused to abandon her hope that the plantations would make a profit and thus stand as a recuperative memorial to her father, his besmirched reputation as little more than philandering dilettante erased by her success. Moreover, she married the clergyman she had met in Georgia when he was visiting the south with a group of English friends, and James Leigh became as dedicated as she to the Butler memory. In the main, they made very little money but James managed to become a successful rice planter. Some thought him a rather dim-witted if good-natured parson but Kemble treasured his gentle spirit and tender manners, and she admired his unflagging industry and moral decency.

But she was troubled by Fan's efforts to transform what was, to her, a dreadful history, better buried than revised. While the Leighs remained in Georgia, she waited eagerly for Butler Place and York Farm to be ready, although the bigger house was always her "former purgatory . . . the home of my very sad married life," as she confided to Arthur Malkin in August 1868. From 1867 until she moved into the cottage when it was ready for occupancy in 1874, she resided in rented houses in Philadelphia and London, and stayed with Sarah and Owen Wister for part of the time when they lived in Rome for two years from 1870 to 1872.

Sarah physically resembled her mother far less than did Fan, and although Kemble acknowledged that others saw resemblances between the sisters, to her there was very little likeness between them. Tall, big boned, and auburn haired, Sarah looked more like a Butler, and she seems to have possessed a cooler temperament than either her mother or her sister, whose coloring and stature were similar. In fact, Kemble was almost frightened by an absence of ardent feeling in her elder daughter, expressed, as she described it to Harriet St. Leger, in an alarming lack of maternal affection: Sarah was "as fond of her baby as I think she could be of any creature too nearly resembling a mere animal to excite her intellectual interest, which is pretty much the only interest in infants or adults she seems to me to have."[4] Kemble, who had always spontaneously expressed her physical delight in her daughters and who was eager to talk, to argue, and to be a vibrant performer on the social stage, was puzzled by Sarah's coldness, which she attempted to explain by attributing it to an intensely intellectual nature. But not to feel the vital pleasure of nursing a baby or not to want the love of other adults seemed unnatural to someone who tumbled with her children on the Butler Place lawn and always warmly embraced her friends. Yet, given the passionate nature of her correspondence with Jeannie Field Musgrove that is discussed by Carroll Smith-Rosenberg,[5] it is possible Sarah would have understood the emotional intensity of her mother's attachment to Harriet St. Leger, expressed, for instance, in a letter written in January 1877: hoping to see Harriet before she died and knowing that by now she was entirely blind, Kemble wrote that she had not "the faintest doubt that in spite of your loss of sight you will recognize the human being you have loved so tenderly and constantly, and who has loved you so dearly for so many years."[6] In other letters to Harriet she excuses Sarah's seeming coldness through references to her intellectual labor devoted to writing essays on music and literature, some of which appeared in the *Atlantic Monthly*, without attribution, beginning in the mid-1870s under the encouragement of its editor, William Dean Howells. Interested, also, in women's higher education, Sarah Butler published a small-scale biography of Deborah Logan (1761–1838), the wife of a prominent Philadelphia Quaker and physician. To Frederic Leighton, Kemble wrote that although Sarah had not "a cultivated or educated taste in matters of art," she was a person of "very fine natural perceptions and great imagination and sensibility."[7]

Sarah's granddaughter, Frances Kemble Wister, as she edited the journals and letters written in the West by her father, Owen Wister, Jr., incorporated into her preface some fascinating details of visits to Butler Place at the beginning of the twentieth century when Sarah was a regal old woman. "Very much aware of the fact that she was a personage," she would receive her grandchildren in the square high-ceilinged parlor of Butler Place, which eighty years or so after Kemble arrived there in 1834 was the centerpiece of a gracious country estate whose driveway was lined with maple, oleander, and lemon trees and whose back lawn was distinguished by the most beautiful walnut trees (all of whose planting had been supervised by Kemble in the mid-1830s). In the hallway of Butler Place hung two framed letters from George Washington to Pierce Butler, Sr. (a signer of the Constitution on behalf of South Carolina), and in the elegant dining room, with its dark red painted walls, there were five portraits of the Kemble family, one of which was Thomas Sully's 1834 portrait of Fanny Kemble.[8] Frances Wister notes that these portraits "presided magnificently" over the dining room and that "all the Kembles were beautiful, and we loved them."[9] Regnant over a grandeur that was barely present at Butler Place in the early months of her mother's married life was Sarah Butler Wister herself, her iciness seeming to deny any temperamental inheritance from her mother, but her manner of self-presentation suggesting something of the Kemble talent for theatrical display. She would sweep into Philadelphia's concert halls in dramatic gowns of black velvet and white lace, rather like Fanny mounting the dais for her readings, and, according to one of her granddaughter's informants, wore white gloves to carve at dinner parties. She was unbending, says Frances Wister, a woman "who could not get along with anyone except those in her own walk of life and intellectual bent."[10]

Sarah Butler Wister, then, seems to have resembled her mother in her intellectual ambition and fondness for self-display, but she clearly possessed a cooler emotional barometer. The icy persona, however, masked a struggle with the deep depression that had plagued her mother and grandmother. More explicitly than Frances Wister, Sarah's son, Owen, suggests that she was troubled by much more than people with whom she was not comfortable. On October 14, 1882, when he was traveling in France with his forty-seven-year-old mother, Owen alludes to an unspecified illness and writes to his father that Sarah "has made up her mind she will never be better and has told me so—and to insure the truth of her opinion she seems to be taking the worst steps possible the whole time."[11] For one week during this trip to France, Owen Wister and his mother were joined in Tours by Fanny Kemble and Henry James: Kemble reveals nothing in her memoirs about her daughter's health, but James notes that she was a person of such "a tragic nature, so much worn, physically, that I am sorry for her."[12] Almost immediately, Owen Wister responded to his son's letter in terms that indicate Sarah had suffered for some time from serious emotional difficulties: "She is incapable of believing herself wrong, regards advice of moderation as a manifestation of timidity, and has again and again involved me in very great trouble, of which she is entirely ignorant to protect her from the results of her own unreasonableness." Owen Jr. replied in grave terms. After returning to America, he declares, he will be unable to see his mother for anything other than "short visits"; he believes that her "calm statements about herself are annihilating," and, most alarmingly, he announces that it will be a "relief to herself, and ought to be to all who love her, when Death closes her story. I hope there are not many like it in the world—So utterly out of reach of outside help."[13] That Fanny Kemble, when discussing Sarah in her memoirs, never refers to those "morbid tendencies" she herself was believed to have inherited from Thérèse Kemble discloses how rigorously she censored the letters that are the foundation of her autobiographical writing.[14]

When Kemble returned to Philadelphia in October 1867, after the transatlantic travel of the Civil War years, she was hailed by its indefatigable social chronicler, Sidney Fisher, with ceremonial flourish. If her arrival in 1832 as an outspoken, self-satisfied actress had been scorned and parodied by Philadelphia society, now, Fisher, the spokesman for that society, hailed Kemble as "prosperous, victorious, and triumphant . . . a success fairly achieved by courage, energy, and genius, making determined battle against adverse powers and finally subduing them." Those adverse powers were Pierce's "dogged and iron will" and her own "fiery and impetuous temper."[15] Larding his tribute with extravagant encomia, Fisher admits that even if Kemble is a person of overwhelming force, no one can resist the magnetism of her presence; she is a grand creature, full of intellect and passion, cultivated and accomplished, her faculties strengthened and trained by "the influences of genius, culture, and performance." Carried away by Kemble's middle-aged charisma, Fisher then reminds himself that as a young actress she filled every theater and mesmerized every audience, that she wrote much-admired books, and, more recently, she had won "her daily bread" by Shakespeare readings "unequaled in force and beauty by any artist before or since." Eventually finding his reservoir of praise exhausted by Kemble's talents, Fisher declares, "What a giant is such a woman compared to ladies of ordinary experience."[16]

Here, Kemble was not the private grandmother who allowed Owen Wister to glimpse the sadness covered by determined cheerfulness; rather, she is the public Kemble at her dazzling best. In these late middle years of her life, she was, for the most part, in good spirits, invigorated by a tour to the Great Lakes in 1868 and reassured by the fact that in the six months ending in January 1869 she had made about $4,300 from her Shakespeare readings (by early twenty-first-century standards, over $57,000). Louisa Alcott heard her read *The Merchant of Venice* in Boston on January 15, 1868, and declared she was "a whole stock company in herself." Looking "younger and handsomer than ever before," Kemble was triumphant, although Alcott did wonder how "a short, stout, red woman *could* look like a queen in her purple velvet and point lace."[17]

In the winter and spring of 1874, while a pregnant Fan and James were back on the plantations, this time growing a bumper orange crop and struggling to get a day's work out of a dozen English laborers they had foolishly imported to Georgia, and Sarah and Owen were living at Butler Place and supervising the renovations of the cottage, Kemble took lodgings at 1812 Rittenhouse Square in the center of Philadelphia. The months she spent there were lonely and unhappy, relieved only by visits from Owen Wister, who would come into the city to dine with her, and from Horace Furness, whose father, the Rev. William Furness, had attempted to reconcile Fanny and Pierce back in the mid-1840s; Kemble described him as "her dear and venerated spiritual pastor and master."[18] Much admiring Horace Furness for his work on the American variorum edition of Shakespeare, Kemble presented him with one of her most treasured possessions: a pair of Shakespeare's gloves given to Sarah Siddons by David Garrick, and left to Kemble by Cecilia Siddons Combe, Sarah's daughter, in her will. She offered them "as a token of the *great* pleasure" it gave her to see his name on the variorum edition.[19] In return, he sent her copies of the editions as they were published, together with serendipitous little presents such as a bowl of fresh green beans or a dish of salad.

Apart from a gorgeous view of the sunset from her Rittenhouse Square windows, Kemble hated the tedium of her life in Philadelphia, a city whose only acceptable quality, for her, was its pleasant shady streets. After dinner at six, she played Patience, knitted things for the expected baby, very occasionally went out, and retired early. No longer working, worried about a reduction from 10 to 6 percent interest on her American investments and having no other income but the annuity from the mortgage on Butler Place, she complained obsessively in her letters to English friends about the high cost of living in America. The letters lament the current state of American politics, morals, and manners, almost as if she were producing a kind of sour sequel to the American *Journal* of forty years earlier. Children are irreparably damaged by an absence of early discipline, their parents cowed by their servants; and boys, in particular, are so damaged by the "absence of all effectual authority" that they become dissolute and profligate, a source of "the general want of health in this country."[20] American women are superficial, cold, and physically feeble, and this Kemble attributes to the "intellectual element" predominating over the "emotional and the sensual," which renders them deficient in "softness and sensibility."[21] These are harsh and surprising words from a woman who prided herself on her superior mind and education and who battled to have the "intellectual element" govern her "emotional" volatility. Readily admitting to Harriet St. Leger that she felt miserable, Kemble wrote in February 1874 that the "nervous strain" of her whole life, "all the early excitement, and all the subsequent trouble and sorrow, and all the prolonged exercise of that capacity for superficial emotion" had rendered her subject to "frequent depression."[22]

Kemble's denunciation in 1874 of the unfeeling American woman ("their animal nature is feeble and ill-developed") presents one aspect of the sometimes problematical feminism with which she had taunted Pierce over the years. However, the attack on American women does not dilute her declarations that women must be financially and morally independent of their fathers, brothers, and husbands, nor does it call into question her valiant subversion of Pierce's domestic tyranny. Kemble paid a heavy price for her refusal to "comply" with his sexual and slavery politics, and it is, in part, this unflinching defiance that makes her the feminist heroine of her performed life. Preoccupied, perhaps, with thoughts of the natural cycle of birth and death, she wrote to Harriet St. Leger in January 1875 that rather than fussing about their rights, women should think more about "the natural law, by which women are constituted and constitute themselves the *subjects* of men."[23] Adding that although she would not deny women the right to be politicians, doctors, lawyers, or even soldiers, she believed they needed, first, to get a "better, more thorough education."[24] The "lady physicians" she met always impressed her as clever and intelligent, but what she termed "something especially and essentially womanly—a sort of tenderness, softness, refinement"—had been sacrificed in the acquisition of their profession. In a rueful conclusion to these ruminations on the "woman question," she adds that brilliantly energetic and well-educated women such as Frances Power Cobbe, with whom Kemble became friendly in the 1870s and 1880s and to whom she entrusted all her papers on her death, were misled by supposing that other women were their intellectual and moral equals, something of which Kemble could never said to be guilty.[25] Almost always, she knew she was more intelligent than most women she met, and her moral certainty provided tough armor to meet her many trials.

During the winter months of 1874, Kemble's comments in her letters on American society were as forthright as her views of women's rights and responsibilities. Pitching her political voice as fiercely as when the nation was on the brink of Civil War, she now focused on the corruption in government that had brought America to a state of "absolute prostration"—in her view, collapsed, dishonored, and impotent. Her undiminished interest in the political world around her sounds a positive note in what is otherwise a litany of dyspeptic complaint in the letters to English friends; there is an uncharacteristic bitterness to these letters, a sense that she feels useless and besieged, fearful that the moral change she believed was the essential foundation for decent social change would never come about. She had always believed, and had never hesitated to say so, that national prosperity was as much a moral as a material question. Perhaps because she was feeling old, isolated, and useless at the age of sixty-five after having worked in front of the public since she was twenty years old (apart from the ten years when she was living with Pierce), American life seemed more dismal than ever before. Perhaps, too, because so much of her private and public life had been fired by a spirit of rebellion against allotted roles and conventional codes of gendered behavior, now that there was little for her to reject or rewrite, she was at a loss.

Finally, something lifted her spirits in this dark, lonely winter: the work she began on her memoirs, which she started "scribbling" when she received the several thousand letters she had sent to Harriet St. Leger, and which Harriet, almost blind and nearing eighty, had returned to her. She was stunned by the abundant details of her history, by the immediacy of the personal narrative of transformation from heady celebrity to discarded wife, and by the chronicle of a changing transatlantic culture that was in the letters. Although she initially spoke to no one about the possibility of publication, she began the work of editing and writing commentary initially as much for amusement and occupation as anything else. In addition to being lonely, she had been dreadfully bored. When she first received the letters, she destroyed all that "revived any distressing associations" (as far as one can tell, almost exclusively to do with Pierce) and then began the invigorating labor of editing, commenting, and arranging, which in many ways resembled the work of theatrical production. It was the sort of labor she relished.

Writing the memoirs, or her "Reminiscences" as she liked to call them, rivaled, in its way, the Shakespeare readings, for Kemble was supreme commander of the operation. She worked on the memoirs as if she were performing in repertory: in the mornings she sorted the letters and proofread what had been cleared (by herself) for publication, and in the evenings she wrote her interpolated commentaries. Disturbing material was excised by a disciplined, theatrical hand and what remained was fashioned into a rhetorical spectacle of impressive historical and cultural scope. She claimed that she was "induced" to publish by sudden, serious diminution of her income and this is fair enough, given the fact that she was no longer working, but she insists a little too often that her motives for publication were purely financial. The gratification of working on the memoirs was more than monetary since publication afforded her yet one more brilliant opportunity to perform before the public on her own terms. She began her rehearsals, as it were, in the winter of 1874 and made her debut under the odd billing of an "Old Woman's Gossip" in the *Atlantic Monthly* in August 1875. These monthly pieces were published as *Record of a Girlhood* in England in the autumn of 1878 by Richard Bentley, who initially offered to pay her £200 in cash on the day of publication for the first portion of the roughly 175 pages that appeared in *Atlantic Monthly*. As things turned out, *Record of a Girlhood* ran to more than 400 pages and she eventually received £500 for the two volumes.[26]

When she moved to York Farm in the spring of 1874, working on Harriet's letters had become a sustaining part of her day, and the longest uninterrupted period of time that she lived at York Farm was in the summer of that year. As always, she found the heat and humidity of a Philadelphia summer stifling (Butler Place was little better, nine miles out of the city), and she was so uncomfortable that she had her maid, Ellen, cut off all her hair, which left her, she thought, looking rather like portraits of her Uncle John as Coriolanus. But, sweltering as she was, she appreciated the effort that Fan had made to transform the small cottage into a sunny and bright space for her mother, although when there were lengthy visits from the Leigh family, the shared occupation of the cottage disrupted her diligently guarded routine.

Everything was arranged to Kemble's elegant and demanding taste. The small rooms were decorated in a range of violets and purples, her favorite colors, the greenhouse was full of treasured plants (including the antique jasmine), and a jolly canary kept her company as she followed the meticulous order of her day. In the mornings she sorted and edited Harriet's letters as preparation for the writing she would do in the late evening, sometimes looking up from letters she wrote from Butler Place when she was first married and seeing across the road the trees and garden walks about which she had written to Harriet so long ago. During the second summer at York Farm of working on the memoirs, having edited the letters and prepared her commentary, she was faced with the challenge of copying the whole thing for the printer, a task that proved too much for her. She was able to obtain the assistance of the village grocer, a terribly unfortunate man, she reported, who had traded on credit without capital and gone bankrupt; she paid him five shillings a day for two and a half hours' work every morning to take her dictation. It was a happy arrangement until James Leigh came to stay and discovered that this very grocer owed him money for forty pounds of plantation rice. The grocer went, and Kemble soldiered on until October 1875, when she bought herself a typewriter, "a very ingeniously contrived machine, which is worked merely by striking keys as one plays on a piano," as she wrote to Harriet.[27]

After morning work on the memoirs, she would study her household accounts, practice the piano for an hour (usually Handel), read her Bible, and tidy her plants.

Every day at noon she went for a walk (weather permitting, but given her physical fortitude it was a rare day that she stayed indoors), sometimes accompanied by a beloved Labrador dog that belonged to James Leigh. After a light lunch, she settled down to read: perennial favorites such as Goethe's autobiography (which she read in German), Macaulay's essays, and old copies of the *Spectator*, as well as new things such as Greville's *Memoirs* and the latest edition of the *Nation*, for Kemble the only American newspaper worth reading. She devoured, for example, all the news about the English purchase of the Suez Canal: it seemed a splendid opening to "vistas of progress and improvement" and she declared to her English friend Arthur Malkin that she thought "the whole question of the existence of Turkey and Egypt and the Danubian provinces and their future conditions intensely interesting."[28] She especially loved the afternoons of reading since she had a tiny book room, off the drawing room, and she could see through it to her greenhouse, where she usually had a dazzling show of geraniums. The evenings were devoted to playing the piano (on Saturday night always ending with "God Save the Queen" since she did not play on Sundays), some coarse needlework, and a few games of Patience. Between ten and midnight Kemble wrote her memoirs, mainly, she explained, because she liked to write by candlelight.

But the smallness of the house and the summer heat oppressed her. The day of her granddaughter Alice's christening, August 16, 1874, was particularly trying since it recalled for her with acute vividness memories of her marriage and the christenings of Sarah and Fan. Much as she adored Alice Leigh, who had been born at York Farm in a tremendous thunderstorm in July, she felt battered by the conflicting emotions prompted by the joyful occasion and recollections of her painful past. She was glad to go to Lenox in October of that year and stay with the Sedgwicks, take a look at her old cottage, the Perch, and at the clock on the village church that she had endowed with the revenue from one of her readings. Seeing the pretty area where she had thought she might make a permanent home stirred up anxieties about where she was to settle in her old age, but until James Leigh decided whether to assume a living that had been arranged for him in Stratford-upon-Avon or to continue to divide his time and that of his family between the Georgia plantations and the York cottage, Kemble's future stayed uncertain. Consoled by the fact that the rent she paid Fan for the cottage helped the Leigh family and that she was close to her daughters, Kemble was still concerned that Fan and James were unwilling to give up the plantations. As late as the spring of 1876, Sarah told her mother, after returning from a visit to Butler Island, that Fan was "happier, better, more useful, and more contented on the plantation than she can ever be anywhere else."[29] Moreover, James Leigh was doing admirable work—zealous and indefatigable, he set up Sunday schools and night schools, and preached in the tiny ramshackle church. But Sarah agreed with her mother that he ought to assume his proper place as a country clergyman in his own country. Kemble continued to hope for a return to England, where she planned to live in London: at her age—"a lonely old woman" was how she had begun to describe herself—London was perfect, rich with consoling memories of her heady young womanhood and, quite simply, much more exciting than Philadelphia.

In the middle of the 1870s, Kemble began to complain uncharacteristically about her health. She felt nervous for the first time in her life about traveling, which she found peculiar given the fact that she had spent the previous forty years crossing the Atlantic. Asked to read at the Centennial Exhibition in Philadelphia in 1876, she declined on the grounds of want of strength, want of voice, and want of decent articulation due to the loss of her teeth, although she did visit the exhibition in June and was taken about in a wheelchair by James and Fan, where her interest was momentarily sparked by the "huge, ingenious, *wise* engines" in the machinery department. The silent, swift, and steady labor of an enormous steam engine that was stationed in the middle of a vast hall mesmerized her; this "stupendous creature" reminded her of a steam engine she had seen in a Leeds factory long ago, its power so beautiful, its "shining" arms so hypnotic in their rhythms that she had longed to fling herself into them, "an English victim to an English Juggernaut."[30]

The brief visit of Monckton Milnes, an old friend from Covent Garden days and now very ancient, to York Farm in November 1875 worried her to the point of collapse: she feared the house was too cramped, the small bedroom uncongenial, and that Branchtown society would prove boring. But since Lord Houghton (as he now was) turned out to have even fewer teeth than she, and was even more deaf than she claimed to be, she stopped worrying about a discrepancy between her appearance at sixty-six and her luminous presence at twenty when Milnes had declared she resembled Beatrice in *Much Ado About Nothing*. But after his visit, she found a new cause of anxiety: the pending return to England of her maid, Ellen, who would be taking with her the English cook and the Irish manservant. Everything seemed to be in decline or already vanished—her teeth, her trusted maid, and sustaining literary gossip from England as old friends became ill or died. Her memory was "quite gone," she dramatically announced to Harriet, adding that she muddled up the names of places and people, could not be trusted to tell the truth about anything, and fell asleep as soon as she picked up a book. Cannily, though, she knew what was the matter with her: she was bored, thrown too much on her own resources, and in the absence of mental and physical stimulation, her mind and body were atrophying. In September one of her large front teeth fell out and in the following February she suffered some jarring injuries when Sarah fell on top of her after their sleigh careened out of control. When Fan and James announced in the autumn that at the beginning of the new year (1877) they would all go to England, Kemble was more than ready. Metaphorically, her bags had been packed from the time she left Europe in 1873, and once more work on the memoirs became invigorating. After all, by the same token that prompted her to say to Harriet, since "there was no narrative or sequence of events involved in the publication, it can, of course, be stopped at any moment; a story without an end can end anywhere,"[31] so the writing could begin again, the story, since it had no ending, could continue. When Fanny Kemble returned to Europe in 1877, Henry James became a principal character in this resumed story of her life. She had met him first in Rome in December 1872 and was eager to see him again.

"The First Woman in London"

In the winter of 1872, after having spent several months in Paris, Henry James traveled to Rome: at the beginning of his literary career, he was supporting himself by writing travel pieces for American periodicals and newspapers. Soon after his arrival, he was introduced to Sarah and Owen Wister, who had arrived in 1870 in search of a better climate for Owen's health. James paid little attention to Owen, whom he thought rather dull, but he was taken with Sarah's handsome appearance and intellectual eagerness; she, in turn, was very much taken with James. For a few weeks, she became his Roman cicerone and he her attentive cavalier as they rode out into the countryside. But Sarah's attractions waned, her social possessiveness became grating, and, most important, he became more interested in her mother, who was visiting the Wisters. James wrote to his mother that Sarah Wister was "'intensely conscious,' and lacks a certain repose comfortable to herself and others," but "the terrific Kemble," with her splendidly handsome eyes, nostrils, and mouth, was mesmerizing.[32] It was Kemble's talk that won him, and for the next twenty years, until the moment that he stood at her graveside at Kensal Green Cemetery and thought that she would probably not have liked the flowers, he quite simply adored her. They went to the theater together, traveled together in Europe, and sat for many hours talking about Kemble's rich life and the promise of his fame that was just beginning. She was a sixty-four-year-old sophisticated woman of the world and he a sexually uncertain young man of almost thirty. When James heard about George Eliot's marriage in 1880 to the much younger John Cross he jokingly wrote to his mother that "old women are marrying young men, by the way, all over the place. If you hear next that Mrs. Kemble . . . is to marry *me*, you may know that we have simply conformed to the fashion."[33] His

Fig. 33. Henry James, *Century Magazine*, 1882. Mary Evans Picture Library.

tone was wry and satiric, and it hardly needs saying that there was absolutely no thought of marriage. But Kemble and Henry James made a remarkably compatible couple. She gave him her undying affection, a rich fund of anecdotes that gave him ideas for his fiction,[34] and a candid opinion of his writing; she declared to Anne Thackeray Ritchie in the late 1880s that his books always appeared to her "very clever and not very amusing. . . . He knows exactly what I think of them."[35] He, in turn, gave her what had been missing from her life for several very dull years in America—a rejuvenating flame, an invitation to cosmopolitan adventure, and a reason to relish her declining years beyond the pleasures of her daughters and her grandchildren. It was for Henry James that Kemble put on her final and most dazzling performance, and it was for Kemble that James became a devoted and attentive audience. As Tamara Follini observes, "Kemble exhibited, in her talk, her actions, and her history, the type of spontaneity that James valued most and found most lacking in the world in which he moved."[36]

After Kemble left Rome, where she first met James, she saw him again in 1876 when he visited Butler Place, an occasion made memorable for him by Kemble's reading from Edward FitzGerald's translation of a Calderón play, her spectacles perched on the end of her Kemble nose and her cheeks rosied by the blazing fire. In 1877 they were reunited in London where Kemble took lodgings at 23 Portman Square, a five-minute walk from Newman Street where she had been born; she later took a one-year lease on a house on Connaught Square, after having visited the frail Harriet St. Leger in Dublin. Kemble had disembarked from the *Britannic* leaving Fan, James, baby Alice, Ellen, the English cook, and a young black servant from the plantation whom the Leighs had taken into their household to continue their journeys: Ellen to her mother and the Leighs to Alveston Manor House near Stratford-upon-Avon. It was to this thirteenth-century low and irregular house with pointed gables and strange chimney stacks, with one side fronting the Avon with a stretch of a lawn amounting to an acre and the other side facing a wonderful orchard full of ancient filbert trees, that Henry James arrived for a Christmas visit in 1877: "Our dark-bearded, handsome American friend," as Kemble described him to Harriet. James's account to his sister Alice of this Christmas visit is not kind to his hosts: he dismisses both Fan and James as "not interesting," but then, for him, everyone paled beside Kemble. Fan he found "inferior both to her mother and sister," and he did not warm to her whining; she hated her position in England and she detested the English, "alluding to it insidiously five times a minute, and rubbing it unmercifully into her good-natured husband." James regarded poor hen-pecked James Leigh as slightly redeemed by his decent dedication to his parish but declared he had "the intellect and the manners of a boy of seven." Summing it all up, James noted that Kemble looked on in bemusement and wondered how Fan would make her future in England.[37] That Christmas as they all trimmed the nursery tree, the discerning worldliness of the ironic Henry James and Fanny Kemble contrasting sharply with the vicarage earnestness of the Leigh family.

Revived by England and stimulated by Henry James, Kemble's lassitude and indifference evaporated. The awakening of her quiescent thirst for life was James's greatest gift to his adored companion: she resumed work on the memoirs and went to Queen Victoria's dentist to get her teeth fixed. Mr. Sanders gave her four false front teeth, not, she proudly announced to Harriet, secured by the new and unreliable mode of suction but secured in her mouth with "the best of gold." When she finished the last installment of "Old Woman's Gossip" (soon to be published by Richard Bentley as *Record of a Girlhood*), she threw into the fire the last of her letters to Harriet, happy to be done with those that detailed the misery and anguish of her last year with Pierce. She concluded the installment with her return to England in 1845, not realizing at the time that the popularity and financial success of the memoirs would lead her to write two more volumes: *Records of Later Life* and *Further Records*, published in 1882 and 1891, respectively, the latter volume culled from papers she had entrusted to Frances Power Cobbe in 1879.

Almost every summer until she died fifteen years later, she traveled to Switzerland, often accompanied by Harry Kemble, her brother Henry's illegitimate son who had become a gifted actor. Kemble found him sweet and amiable, courteous and kind to her when she was depressed and grumpy, and a lively companion when she was not. But although she cherished his facial resemblance to his father and grandfather, she thought him rather too thickset for so young a man and not likely to look well on the stage. It seems that the tall and stately Charles Kemble was the only member of the family who did not incline to stockiness, indeed to sheer obesity. In the late 1870s Adelaide and Kemble had themselves weighed together and what Kemble drily referred to as their "united ponderosity" amounted to twenty-seven stone, four ounces, in other words three hundred and eighty-two pounds.

The stunning difference between the empty solitude of Kemble's American life and the breathtaking pulse of her London whirl repeats the pattern of earlier periods of recovery from depression. In 1836, she had returned to London with baby Sarah and was quickly back on her dancing feet after two years of isolation at Butler Place; in 1845, she flung herself into social activity and the resumption of acting after ten dreadful years with Pierce; and in 1877, she was suddenly, again, in London—off to the Oxford Street stores to buy house linen, back to receive her niece May Gordon, up in London for a Bach concert; in the afternoon, a visit to Lady Enfield, Lady Ellesmere's daughter, and in the evening a dinner party for May Gordon and her husband. In the company of Mrs. Richard Greville and the by now truly old and frail Monckton Milnes, she visited Tennyson (exactly Kemble's age, sixty-eight) and living near Guildford; after tea, he entertained them in his sonorous monotone with recitation of his "British Boadicea, on her Roman Enemies" (Kemble noted that the wobbliness of the carriage they hired for the journey was steadied by three portly bodies of considerable weight).[38] On a visit to the eighty-year-old Thomas Carlyle at Cheyne Walk, she sat with him for an hour and sang Scottish ballads remembered from her Edinburgh year. This was the house where, forty years before and much to the astonishment of Jane Carlyle and the housemaid, she had charged into Carlyle's study, riding whip in hand, and engaged in some sprightly intellectual chat. Now, she found him movingly eloquent in his denunciations of the government and alarmingly dismal about England's future. At a party at the home of Hamilton Aidés, bon vivant, man about town, literary critic, and member of the Holland Park set, she talked at length with George Eliot and George Henry Lewes.[39] Kemble felt herself again at the center of a web of Victorian social and literary connections. English life took her breath away.

On this social and cultural round, Henry James was her enchanted companion. To him, she was "the first woman in London" and "one of the consolations" of his life,[40] a woman of whom he never tired and in whom he took the greatest comfort. He loved her for her absolute directness in conversation ("strong meat" he called it) and for her seemingly inexhaustible fund of gossip, which he absorbed and sometimes transformed into fiction. He described her as having no surface; she was "like a straight deep cistern without a cover" into which, in conversation, one tumbled with a splash. In response to a friend who regretted that James's fiction was superficial, that he never went below the surface of things, Kemble declared that his "gift is neither power nor profundity but a very fine and refined delicate and suggestive treatment of surfaces—below which he allows you very well to see depths of pathos."[41] In this shared imagery of depth and surface, James saw her as having no surface and being all depth; she saw him as having a deceptive surface, one that hardly hinted at the depth of artistic imagination underneath.

After he met Adelaide Sartoris, at sixty-two enormously fat, diabetic, and hardly ever coming to London, James began to spend weekends at Warsash, the Sartoris country house. James preferred the older women to all the men: he thought Edward Sartoris as dull as James Leigh, taciturn and a little too ill-mannered until you got to know him; Adelaide's son Algy he dismissed as "blowsy" and his wife, Nelly (President Grant's daughter who had married Algy in a splendid White House ceremony to which Kemble either was not invited or chose not to go), as sweet-natured but a bore. According to James, she sat speechless on the sofa, understanding nothing of her aunts' sparkling talk and "exciting one's compassion for her incongruous lot in life."[42] Adelaide he found most agreeable, and he wrote to his sister after one weekend at Warsash that it was one of the best things in the world to sit and talk with the two sisters, "for the talk of each is first rate," although he did not think Adelaide had the magnificent integrity of his "sublime Fanny— but she plays round her sister's rugged *mefiance* like a musical thunder-storm."[43] For James, Fanny was always supreme: she took a sharp interest in what he called his "productions" and discussed everything with him intelligently, honestly, and earnestly. Best of all, she recited Shakespeare apropos of everything, and one night treated him to "some of the most beautiful speeches in *Measure for Measure*." He especially loved her "great fund of old British philistinism . . . mixed up in the strangest way with a freedom of judgment which is as great as any I ever knew."[44]

When the restored Kemble was not in London or at the Leighs' house in Stratford-upon-Avon or at Adelaide's country house, she was in Switzerland, and never missing America. She did, however, miss Henry James, as he did her: he wrote to Sarah Butler Wister while he was in Venice in 1887 that when they were apart, he felt the dreadful effects of the distance between himself and her mother—"I am so attached to her, and my periodical visits to her, of an evening, have become after so many years, so much a part of my life—that the interruption of them really operates as a great drawback and loss to me, whenever I come abroad. I think of her constantly—I miss her—I worry about her—and I think she misses me."[45] (He ended a charming letter to her from Marseilles dated February 24, 1881, as follows: "I am afraid you miss me, because I miss you.") During this time, Kemble was working on the next volume of her memoirs, which was published as *Records of Later Life* in 1882. When the first volume had been published in 1879, she had charmingly offered it at a time in her life she described as "the idle end of autumn days": it is astonishing that after this late autumnal period she displayed an appetite for work and pleasure that defied all her gloomy expectations of old age. The English drawing room and the pages of her published memoirs were the stage for the closing years of her performed life, and Henry James was the most enthralled and faithful member of her audience.

The Last Act

When Henry Wadsworth Longfellow died in March 1882, Kemble felt that the world was fast emptying of the friends whose "goodness and wisdom" had brightened it for her through her long life (she was now nearly seventy-three). She believed she would not long remain behind them, but, as was often the case when she was particularly despondent (and the death of Longfellow, together with that of Emerson, made her feel the curtain had descended on the best part of her American experience), she exaggerated the case. Kemble lived for ten more years, increasingly hobbled by circulatory problems but her mind as razor sharp as ever and her intolerance of fools undiminished. During these years, she became friendly with Frances Power Cobbe, the prominent Victorian intellectual and feminist, vigorous campaigner for emancipation for women, and passionate antivivisectionist. She rented the London house of Cobbe's companion, Mary Lloyd, in Hereford Square, and she entrusted her papers to Cobbe upon her death. Cobbe's correspondence with Sarah Wister, to whom she was actually closer than to Kemble, provides some charming impressions of how well Kemble was, and was not, coping with age. In March 1880, she reported that she saw Kemble often, and that she was looking remarkably well despite "occasional little infirmities of lameness"; as the years passed she seemed "constantly to grow softer and more tolerant in character while her *verve*—and wit and brilliancy never pale."[46] In May 1884, she wrote Sarah about a six-day visit Kemble paid them in Wales, where they had moved a month earlier: Kemble's two days on the road each way, despite her "infirmities of lameness," worried Cobbe a little but she was touched that she made such an effort to visit them. Looking very well and in wonderful spirits, Kemble entertained Frances Cobbe and Mary Lloyd for three terribly wet days and one dry one, occasionally resting on her bedroom sofa. She loved the Welsh landscape and the Cobbe garden, sitting under the cherry trees in full blossom with the rooks and the herons cawing over their nests in the woods around them. Cobbe reported to Sarah Wister that her mother's powers of walking were much diminished and that she felt her heart a good deal even when going very quietly. Despite these infirmities, Kemble refused to entertain the possibility she might not go to Switzerland for the summer.

In October, after her return from Switzerland, Kemble wrote to thank them both for the lovely plants that filled the house at 28 Hereford Square in South Kensington when she returned, for the repair of a garden wall that had been in need of attention, and for a "magnificent cheese." Kemble's spirits were still good, although she did write in April 1885 to Horace Furness that she was "getting old and weary of *myself* rather than of any one or any thing else—but one is apt to grow tiresome to oneself at last."[47] In the winter of the following year she seemed to be finding London's weather a trial, and she fled to the Granville Hotel in Ramsgate where she could breathe the fresh, if very chilly, sea air and be away from the poisonous and dense fog that stank in her nostrils. In May 1887, when she was seventy-seven, she complained that gout and varicose veins rendered her unable to walk very far, and she procured a bath chair in which she was wheeled to nearby Kensington Gardens (she called it a "human dog cart"). She was still going to Switzerland in the summers, where she was carried over the mountains in a kind of open sedan chair by six men who relayed each other two at a time every half hour. When she returned from her summer journey in September 1888, she had said her "farewell to the High Alps" since, as she wrote to Anne Thackeray Ritchie in August from Lago Maggiore where she had gone with Henry James, she had great difficulty in breathing at six thousand feet above sea level. Her sadness in saying farewell to Switzerland signaled another ending[48] at a time when only Arthur Malkin and Tennyson remained of the "very able band of spirits" with whom she started in life. "What fine friends I have had!" she exclaimed to Ritchie.[49]

But in October 1888 she was once more entertaining Frances Cobbe with a fund of good stories and reminiscences, doing it all "with an unwonted flow and fun." And she was also writing her novel, *Far Away and Long Ago*, published in 1889. A simple tale of two sisters, daughters of an English immigrant to New England, who meet highly melodramatic ends, the novel suffers from wooden characterizations and awkward plotting. Nowhere do we experience the vital urgency, the vivid detail, and the exuberance of observation found in so much of Kemble's nonfiction writing, despite the fact, of course, that virtually everything she allowed into print had undergone careful review and editing. The merit of *Far Away and Long Ago* lies in the excellent landscape descriptions, which makes one think Kemble would have made a skillful botanical writer; she is as good at describing the flower-filled thickets of the Berkshires as she is in evoking the myrtle and palmetto of Georgia. The narrative frame for the novel presents the manuscript of a Miss Selbourne, whose father is a state legislator and whose brothers are lawyers; the manuscript is to be published sixty years after her death. That the novel is set in a countryside remarkably like that around Lenox makes it difficult to believe the Selbournes are not the Sedgwicks and that the cry of one of the female characters that she longed to go down to the turbulent river "and float away, where it deepens to dark-green round the rocks, and so on to the thirty-feet foaming fall at Watertown, and be carried out to sea—far, far from everything and everybody!" is not the cry of Kemble at her most desperate, as we hear it in some of her poems. In "Lines, on Reading with Difficulty Some of Schiller's Early Love Poems," for example, the speaker feels deeply within herself Schiller's evocation of agonized despair.

> The sharp cry of pain—the bitter moan
> Of trust deceived—the horrible despair
> Of hope and love for ever overthrown—
> These strains of thine need no interpreter.
> Ah 'tis my native tongue![50]

That "native tongue" of pain that Kemble tends to mute in her memoirs and letters is voiced, as we know, in many of her poems and, strangely enough, in her one effort at writing fiction, at the age of eighty-one.

By February 1890 London's fog and chill became unbearable and Kemble left Hereford Square to go to Bournemouth, again to find some fresher air that would help her breathing. Frances Cobbe, however, took this departure very personally and wrote to Sarah Wister that her mother seemed to have taken a dislike to the house. Cobbe was also disappointed that Kemble had not thanked her for the improvements in the garden; rather, she complained that the staircase ceilings were smeared with leaks, that water was pouring into the conservatory, and that there were drain problems in the downstairs bathroom. A certain builder—the "wretched Hancock," according to Frances Cobbe—played a large part in this drain fiasco since when Kemble demanded that the kitchen floor be ripped up and the drains investigated he was delighted to agree, and submitted an elaborate estimate for an entirely new system of drainage for the house. Kemble sent the estimate to Mary Lloyd with the ultimatum that if she would not accept it, she would leave. By the time Lloyd had agreed to the repairs, Kemble had departed. Frances Cobbe related all this to Sarah Wister, explaining that Kemble's age probably made her "continually dissatisfied and restless" and indicating they were sorry to lose her as a tenant.[51] When she returned to London, Kemble moved in with Fan and James Leigh at 89 Gloucester Place.

During the last year of her life, Kemble continued to read but writing became difficult. In April 1892, nine months before her death, she wrote to Horace Furness thanking him for sending the latest volume in the Variorum Shakespeare, *The Tempest*, her favorite play, and she confided that she now wrote letters only to her daughter Sarah and to her old friend Mary Fox. She no longer sat at a table but in a large armchair propped up by cushions, her inkstand on a low table by the side of the chair; her letter paper was on a blotting book held in her left hand, two fingers and the thumb of which had become severely arthritic. But she soldiered on, gripping her pen in her right hand and failing to govern it as she wished. In the last months of her life she was visited by Anne Thackeray Ritchie, who described her as "stately, upright, ruddy and brown of complexion, almost to the very last; mobile and expressive in feature, reproachful, mocking, and humorous, heroic, uplifted in turn. This was no old woman, feeling the throb of life with an intensity far beyond that of younger people, splendid in expression, vehement, and yet at times tender with a tenderness such as is very rare."[52] On January 20, 1893, as the faithful Ellen was helping her into bed, she dropped her head upon Ellen's shoulder and died.

The first person the Rev. James Leigh sent for was Henry James, who rushed to the house as best he could since he was suffering from a severe attack of gout. No biographer can equal the moving tribute that he paid to his brilliant Fanny: in his memorial essay, he writes, "She had, in two hemispheres, seen every one and known every one, had assisted at the social comedy of her age," and in her talk, especially with him, she "reanimated the old drawing-rooms, relighted the old lamps, retuned the old pianos." For James, she was "indomitably, incorruptibly superb." He also reveals his understanding of the meaning for Kemble of the dramatic and the theatrical: even after she left the theater, James wrote, she never entirely governed her instincts, her passions: this "kept her dramatic long after she ceased to be theatrical."[53] James knew of her valiant struggle not to allow instinctive feeling to govern her life, yet he also knew that she never succeeded entirely in establishing the theatrical as sovereign. That the theatrical ultimately failed to take supreme command, that Kemble retained the vital essence of her mother's dramatic personality, must account, in part, for the charismatic valor with which she performed her existence in the world and the spark that fired her feminist refusal to remain merely a Kemble daughter or a Butler wife.

Within weeks after Kemble's death, after having ascertained with the assistance of Mary Lloyd that there was nothing objectionable in them, Frances Power Cobbe sent to Bentley some sixty-four letters from Edward FitzGerald, for which Bentley paid fifty guineas; the letters were printed in *Temple Bar* in eight installments and later published by Bentley in 1895 under the title *Letters of Edward FitzGerald to Fanny Kemble, 1871–1883*, edited by FitzGerald's close friend W. Aldis Wright. Cobbe then returned packets of letters to those she believed would want to have them. There are no surprises on the list: friends from Kemble's youth such as William Bodham Donne, a classical scholar and fellow Apostle with John Mitchell Kemble at Cambridge, Charles and Henry Greville, women with whom she exchanged letters over many years such as Anna Jameson and Anne Thackeray Ritchie, and close male friends and companions such as Frederic Leighton—and, of course, her beloved Henry James.

After consulting Sarah Wister and Henry James, Cobbe decided to assemble several autograph albums of Kemble's correspondence, but she quickly assured Richard Bentley that she had no intention of editing these letters. In all likelihood, this album was sent to Sarah Wister, and apart from the occasional and often innocuous letters scattered around various British libraries, very little remains of Fanny Kemble's papers that provides anything beyond what she wished us to know. Cobbe's scrupulous fidelity to Kemble's wishes in terms of what might and might not be made public has ensured that her life remains a carefully managed performance before the public. And Henry James, in the most exquisitely tactful way, declined Cobbe's invitation to look over his correspondence with Kemble with a view to possible publication; while excited by the prospect, he feared publication might cause embarrassment to Sarah and Fan, given the highly "private and personal" nature of Kemble's later years.[54] As James wrote to Sarah Wister after the funeral, he felt "the great beneficence and good fortune of your mother's instantaneous and painless extinction. Everything of the condition, at the last, that she had longed for was there—and nothing that she dreaded was."[55] This was a life performed so elegantly that even the death was as she willed it to be:

quick, painless, no mess. James also shied away from editing the letters they had exchanged since he did not wish to assume Kemble's role as censor of her life. That he knew she had fought bravely on several fronts was sufficient: against symptoms of Thérèse Kemble's irrationality; against confinement to the role of Kemble daughter; against claustrophobic mandates regarding the limited rights of women; and against the horrors of slavery. In one way or another, Fanny Kemble valiantly defied her antagonists through rewriting the roles to which she was assigned, through appropriating and subverting nineteenth-century cultural and social prescriptions for women's lives.

On a soft, kind, balmy day as he described it, a gout-stricken James hobbled to Kensal Green Cemetery for Kemble's burial. Sarah and Fan were in America, and the only members of her family by the simple graveside were James Leigh and his daughter, Alice. Fanny Kemble was buried in the same earth as Charles Kemble, and today, on the gravestone that marks the spot, one can barely make out their names carved in the limestone; the stone is covered in moss and the names have been eroded by London's smog and rain. Kensal Green Cemetery is surrounded by the industrial and commercial scenery of West London—gas tanks, plumbers' outfitters, and curry houses are right up against the red brick walls. Here, there is no theatrical arrangement of a life that has ended, nothing more than other neglected, mossy headstones. It is a strange place for the commemorative marker of this extraordinary nineteenth-century woman who lived so much in the public eye, braving her way through private and public difficulties to become the brilliant performer of her own life.

Kemble Genealogy

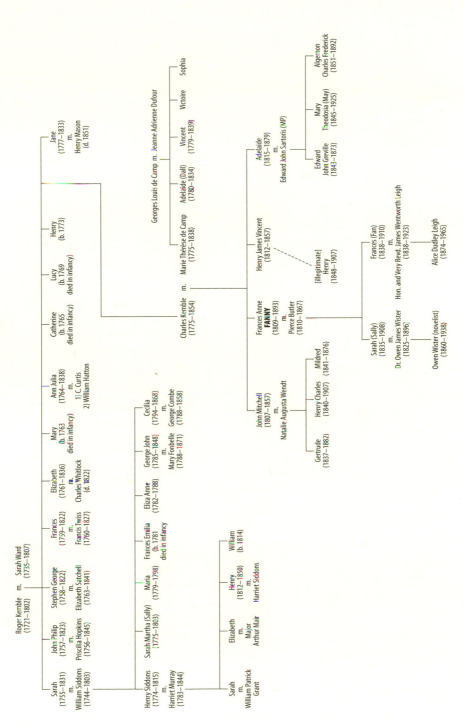

Notes

Prologue: Before the Curtain

Note to epigraph: Reprinted in James, *Henry James: Literary Criticism.*

1. Throughout this study, I shall refer to Fanny Kemble as "Kemble," except in the context of reference to other members of the Kemble family, where such reference would be confusing.

2. Charles Young's memory of Sarah Kemble is recounted by Henry Greville. He notes in his diary on September 1, 1871, that Adelaide Sartoris (Fanny Kemble's sister) told him "to-day" that Young believed Sarah Kemble "was one of the greatest actresses that ever lived" (*Leaves from the Diary of Henry Greville*, 4:346).

3. In her analysis of the economic structures of the British stage in the nineteenth century, Davis notes that these families "ran distinct businesses while the extended family cooperated by hosting each other at their theatres . . . and by not undercutting each other's offers as prospective lessees when they sought to expand their domain" (*The Economics of the British Stage*, 142–43). Bratton observes that the "theatre is an extreme example of a professional group for whom family, very broadly understood, is a central structure of feeling and support" (*New Readings in Theatre History*, 196).

4. Bate, *Shakespearean Constitutions*, 64. Placing such management of crowd scenes—marshaling and disciplining the players—within the historical and political context of post-Revolutionary France, Bate makes the interesting point that Kemble's theatrical sovereignty over the crowd "served as an image of control, a proclamation that London would not go the way of Paris."

5. Ann Julia Kemble Curtis Hatton (as she was variously known) is an unacknowledged and scandalous presence in Fanny Kemble's life. I discuss her raffish career in Chapter 2.

6. In her biographical narrative of the first thirty years of Kemble's life, Jenkins argues that the key to understanding Kemble "lies in the complexity of her family inheritance. . . . The significance attached to the Kemble name was an inescapable element throughout Fanny's life. . . . The family image-makers of the previous generation were so successful in marketing their renown to posterity that the Kemble fame was debatably more potent as myth than in its contemporary reality" (*Fanny Kemble*, 7–8). Jenkins's well-researched exploration of the potency of the Kemble name is persuasive and important, and it has proved helpful for my more elaborate examination of Kemble's life. (Jenkins essentially ends her narrative with Kemble's departure from Georgia in 1839; my aim has been to provide as full and as complete a coverage of the life as possible—from 1809 to 1893.)

7. Kemble, *Further Records*, 1:187.

8. Corbett, *Representing Femininity*, 114. Corbett also argues that the way actresses define themselves in their writings "becomes less contingent on the 'facts' of their private lives, and more on how well they can publicly imitate and reproduce the signs and attitudes that mark individuals as belonging to a certain class and gender" (108). I have tended to place more emphasis on gender than on social class than does Corbett.

9. Kemble, *Journal*, 1:12–13. Throughout the book references are to the English edition of this work. I also refer to it as the American *Journal* to avoid confusion with *Journal of a Residence on a Georgian Plantation, 1838–1839*. An American edition of the 1835 *Journal* is to be found in the Rare Book and Manuscript Library, Columbia University; this copy was annotated in approximately 1860 by Fanny Kemble and given to Charles B. Sedgwick. It was donated to the Brander Matthew Dramatic Museum at Columbia in 1926.

10. Sedgwick, *The Power of Her Sympathy*, 132.

11. Burr, *Weir Mitchell*, 131–32.

12. In addition to assuming that what Kemble says about her life in her memoirs constitutes the "facts," most of her biographers to date have also tended to isolate certain aspects of this rich and varied existence. Armstrong's *Fanny Kemble: A Passionate Victorian* (1939) limits itself to a historical approach; Wright's *Fanny Kemble and the Lovely Land* (1972) focuses on Kemble's time in America. More recently, Clinton's impressively researched *Fanny Kemble's Civil Wars* (2000) focuses on the related strife of Kemble's marriage and the American conflict, and Blainey's *Fanny and Adelaide: The Lives of the Remarkable Kemble Sisters* (2001) usefully explores the relationship between Kemble and her sister. Driver's *Fanny Kemble* (1933) provides excellent bibliographies of Kemble's published writings and of published material about her. Furnas's study, *Fanny Kemble: Leading Lady of the Nineteenth-Century Stage* (1982), emphasizes Kemble's theatrical career and is an invaluable source on theater history. All of Kemble's biographers (including this one) lack a rich archive of manuscript material. No original copies of her diaries exist, except for a few pages held by the Folger Shakespeare Library, where one can also find fifty-three letters from Kemble addressed to Harriet St. Leger, many of them incomplete; almost all of these letters appear in the autobiographical writings. The Library of Congress holds the manuscript of the American *Journal* sent to the printer by Kemble, including her cuts and changes; the British Library holds fragments of an early autobiographical manuscript that deals with her debut and subsequent celebrity. The manuscript of the *Journal of a Residence on a Georgian Plantation* was reputedly circulated among abolitionists for twenty years before its publication in 1863, but it has never been found.

13. Postlewait, "Autobiography and Theatre History," 252. Postlewait notes that Kemble's memoirs "were written and received as scrupulous reports on her activities and the social conditions of her age," yet they reveal "a calculated literary style, a creative shaping of narrative voice. We need to ask to what extent these autobiographies exist not only as historical records but as epistolary fictions" (253–54).

14. Kemble, *Journal*, 2:25.

15. In her study of Victorian women's autobiography, Sanders argues that Kemble persistently sets out to "entertain" and thereby evades "a full investigation of her developing

self," a point that is similar to my emphasis on Kemble's management of various conflicts through the tropes of performance (*The Private Lives of Victorian Women*, 115). From a different perspective, Jelinek claims that the style of women's autobiography may often begin as a chronological narrative but quickly gives way to interruptions, insertions of letters, and so on: "That has been women's autobiographical history from earliest times because chronological order does not seem to be sustainable in narratives with selves that are weak in focus, feeling ambivalent, or are intent on portraying various and often conflicting roles" (*The Tradition of Women's Autobiography*, 188). Since I do not view Kemble's "self" as weak, I am not inclined to agree with this view, although her ambivalence about many aspects of her life is undeniable.

16. In a thoughtful essay that explores what she sees as Kemble's usurpation of her father's textual authority, Booth observes, "Conflicts, however disturbing and illegible they may have been in actual life, are what we look for when we focus the lens of biographical interpretation on historical women; we readily dramatize ideological strains as antagonistic motives within the famous woman's personality" ("From Miranda to Prospero," 247). In my analysis of conflict in Kemble's life, it has not, I think, been necessary to dramatize what is already presented to the reader in dramatic terms.

17. Martineau, *Autobiography*, 1:366; Mowbray Morris to Anne Thackeray Ritchie, May 31, 1893, Eton College Library; Henry Kemble to Anne Thackeray Ritchie, July 29, 1902, Eton College Library.

18. Roberts, *Samuel Rogers and His Circle*, 106.

19. Kemble, "On the Stage," republished as introduction to *Notes upon Some of Shakespeare's Plays*, 1:17.

20. "On the Stage," 1:18.

21. Oxberry, *Dramatic Biography and Histrionic Anecdotes*, 9.

22. Kemble's dislike of the acting profession resembles, in a way, the nineteenth-century recognition identified by Barish "that the actor, or imposter, practices a perilous art, and tempts other men to do the same." As Barish describes it, this is the art of "mutability" (*The Antitheatrical Prejudice*, 317).

23. Bratton's claim that Kemble was as "a lamb to the slaughter" when she went onstage is somewhat undermined, I believe, by Kemble's energetic resistance, although Bratton's claim that Kemble is an "immensely important marginal figure in several histories" is certainly apt ("Working in the Margin," 131).

24. Henry James, review of *Records of a Girlhood*, by Fanny Kemble, *Nation*, December 12, 1878, reprinted in James, *Henry James: Literary Criticism*, 1069–71.

Chapter 1. The Green-Room

Note to epigraph: John Keats to Fanny Keats, August 28, 1819, *Letters of John Keats*, 2:148.

1. Dickens, *Bleak House*, 189.

2. Hunt, *Dramatic Essays*, 105.

3. Baker, *The London Stage*, 138.

4. Hunt, *Autobiography*, 1:250–51.

5. Boswell, *London Journal*, 215.

6. Thomas Gillilard, *Elbow Room* (1804), quoted in Baer, *Theatre and Disorder*, 207.

7. Thackeray, *Vanity Fair*, 20.

8. Vandenhoff, *Dramatic Reminiscences*, 47.

9. Boswell, *Life of Johnson*, 143.

10. Fanny Kemble to Harriet St. Leger, January 15, 1848, *Records of Later Life*, 601. A few weeks after this letter, Kemble relates to St. Leger a charming story of inadvertently calming Thackeray's nerves when he was about to lecture on the English essayists at the Willis Rooms in London. Reaching up to a reading table placed on a platform where he had placed his lecture, she knocks it to the floor. Putting the lecture back together, Kemble reports, helped settle him down. Kemble, *Records of Later Life*, 601.

11. According to Bratton, the "genius" of the Kemble dynasty originates in Sarah Ward Kemble. This interesting claim is made less persuasive by Bratton's reliance on somewhat suspect evidence: the testimony of the black sheep in the Kemble family, Ann Julia Kemble Hatton, whose scandalous life is discussed in Chapter 2. Bratton's evidence is taken from a letter written by Ann Julia Kemble Hatton to John Payne Collier, located in the Folger Shakespeare Library, Y.c.923 (1–4). See Bratton, *New Readings in Theatre History*, 190–91.

12. *Monthly Visitor*, November 15, 1797, quoted in Coleman, *Fifty Years of an Actor's Life*, 1:3, 15.

13. See Donohue, *Dramatic Character in the English Romantic Age*, 246–49. John Philip Kemble's intellectual approach to acting was saluted in some "Valedictory Stanzas" composed by Thomas Campbell in June 1817. The penultimate stanza reads: "Fair as some classic dome, / Robust and richly graced, / Your Kemble spirit was the home / Of genius and of taste— / Taste like the silent dial's power, / That, when supernal light is given, / Can measure inspiration's hour / And tell its height in heaven. / At once ennobled and correct, / His mind surveyed the tragic page, / And what the actor could effect / The scholar could presage" (*The Complete Poetical Works of Thomas Campbell*, edited with notes by J. Logie Robertson [London: Oxford University Press, 1907]).

14. Hunt, *Autobiography*, 1:244.

15. Bate discusses, in particular, a carton depicting John Philip Kemble as Hamlet with the grave diggers: they snigger that he looks like a ninepin dressed in a blanket, to which he responds, "Ye Num sculls, be silent how dare ye presume To find fault with my Dress tis your Danish costume" (*Shakespearean Constitutions*, 36). William Macready witnessed one of Kemble's last performances (as Cato) and wrote that "imagination could not supply a grander or more noble presence. In face and form, he realised the most perfect ideal that ever enriched the sculptor's or the painter's fancy, and his deportment was in accord with all of outward dignity and grace that history attributes to the *patres conscripti* . . . his attitudes were stately and picturesque, but evidently prepared; even the care he took in the disposition of his mantle was distinctly observable" (*Macready's Reminiscences*, 135–36).

16. Hunt, *Autobiography*, 1:292.

17. Downer discusses the "teapot" style in "Players and Painted Stage," 528–29. For his discussion of John Philip Kemble's "teapot" delivery, Downer quotes from James Boaden, *Mrs. Sarah Siddons* (Grolier Society, n.d.), 1:259.

18. Hunt *Autobiography*, 1:244.

19. Doran, *Annals of the English Stage*, 2:390.

20. Hunt, *Dramatic Essays*, 108.

21. *Spectator* 11 (1829): 330.

22. Byrne, *Gossip of the Century*, 1:346.

23. Covent Garden Playbills, Special Collections, Van Pelt Rare Book and Mss. Furness Collection, Library of the University of Pennsylvania, Philadelphia.

24. *The Girlhood of Queen Victoria*, 1:147.

25. Oxberry, *Dramatic Biography and Histrionic Anecdotes*, 1:9. Jenkins quotes J. R. Planché as saying, "It was 'jolly' enough to dine with Kean at the Black Jack Tavern, or sup with him and a few more 'choice spirits' at Offleys; but the retrospection was more gratifying after a quiet little family dinner with Mr. and Mrs. Charles Kemble" (*Fanny Kemble*, 125).

26. Quoted in Highfill, Burnim, and Langhans, *Biographical Dictionary*, 8:326–27.

27. Original letters of dramatic performers, collected and arranged by Charles Britiffe Smith, Garrick Club Library, London.

28. Bratton, *New Readings in Theatre History*, 193.

29. Kemble, *Record of a Girlhood*, 1:2–3. Most Kemble biographers fail to note the discrepancy between the British and American titles of this text. *Record of a Girlhood*, published in London by Richard Bentley in 1878, was published in America as *Records of a Girlhood* by Henry Holt in 1879. All my references are to the British edition.

30. Kemble, "On the Stage," 15.

31. See Tomalin's excellent *Mrs. Jordan's Profession* for a study of this relationship.

32. See Kelly, *The Kemble Era*, 161–65.

33. Altick, *The Shows of London*, 176.

34. Baker, *The London Stage*, 1:95.

35. Kemble, *Record of a Girlhood*, 2:253.

36. Kemble, *Records of Later Life*, 3:330.

37. Quoted in Baker, *The London Stage*, 1:162. It would be a mistake to imagine there was nothing between Sarah Siddons and gaudy farce. John Keats, for instance, went to the pantomime at Covent Garden in early January 1818 and found it "a very nice one" despite "a middling Harlequin, a bad Pantaloon, a worse Clown and a shocking Columbine" (*Letters of John Keats*, 1:199).

38. See Davis, *The Economics of the British Stage*, 150.

39. Sheppard, *London*, 245.

40. Baer, *Theater and Disorder*, 19.

41. As Davis notes, the total cost of rebuilding was £127,000; only £76,000 had been raised by selling shares (*The Economics of the British Stage*, 165).

42. Bate argues that the Old Price Riots were motivated, in part, by a political appropriation of Shakespeare by John Philip Kemble, on the one hand, and by political resentment

of such appropriation by lower-class audiences, on the other. Bate sees the riots "as a battle for the possession of Shakespeare. To remove cheap gallery seats and replace them with secluded boxes was to make Shakespeare less widely available, more exclusive—to appropriate him for the elite." The pit audience intuitively realized that they were being excluded, even if they might have preferred something livelier than Kemble's notoriously slow and labored performance of Hamlet. See Bate, *Shakespearean Constitutions*, 50.

43. Quoted in Jenkins, *Fanny Kemble*, 44.

44. Baer, *Theater and Disorder*, 44.

45. Pope-Hennessy believes that the prominent Kemble features suggest "Jewish ancestry," something for which I have uncovered no evidence. See *Three English Women in America*, 114.

46. Kemble, "On the Stage," 123–25. Booth discusses the importance of this painting for Fanny Kemble in "From Miranda to Prospero."

47. Kemble, *Record of a Girlhood*, 1:26.

48. Ibid., 1:15.

49. Ibid., 1:53.

50. Ibid., 1:71.

51. Ibid., 1:104.

52. Ibid., 1:113.

53. Ibid., 1:134.

54. Ibid., 1:139.

55. Ibid., 1:138.

56. Ibid., 1:152.

Chapter 2. *The Gaze of Every Eye*

Note to epigraph: Dickens, *David Copperfield*, ch. XIX, p. 286.

1. Faderman terms the romantic friendship between Eleanor Butler and Sarah Ponsonby "a great 'success story'" (*Surpassing the Love of Men*, 120–25, passim).

2. Cobbe, *Life of Frances Power Cobbe*, 197–98.

3. Ibid., 198.

4. Robert Bernard Martin notes that Fanny's letters to Harriet often mention her flirtations with older men but that she never refers to Harriet's private life; Martin adds, "The truth probably is that when they met, Harriet was uninvolved but within a year or two met the woman who was to share her home and her affections until she died [Dorothy Wilson]. . . . On May 18 1827 Harriet seems to have written about her feelings on meeting Dorothy, to which Fanny responded with a mixture of rueful joking and real worry that she was being replaced in her friend's affection: 'I am glad you like Miss WB, but take care not to like her better than me'" (Martin, unpublished manuscript, quoting from Kemble, *Record of a Girlhood*, 1:178).

5. Kemble, *Record of a Girlhood*, 2:99.

6. Describing Harriet's eccentricities, Cobbe says, "I imagine she must have afforded a somewhat singular contrast to her ever magnificent, not to say gorgeous friend Fanny

Kemble, when at the great Exhibition of 1851, they were observed of observers, sitting for a long time side by side close to the crystal fountain" (*Life of Frances Power Cobbe*, 198).

7. Kemble, *Record of a Girlhood*, 1:220. The Christ Church, Philadelphia, records at the Historical Society of Pennsylvania indicate that the marriage took place on June 17, 1832, clearly an error since Fanny Kemble had not yet arrived in the United States. According to the Historical Society, the notation "1832" could have been entered at any time and by anyone. I am grateful to Fran L. Lassiter for research assistance in tracking down these records.

8. Jenkins justly criticizes *Francis the First* for having too many characters and implausible switches on their part "from love to violent hate"; she adds that the play shows the Kemble family's "theatrical flare rather than literary genius" (*Fanny Kemble*, 158–59).

9. Kemble, *Record of a Girlhood*, 1:227.

10. Martineau, *Autobiography*, 1:366.

11. In Chapter 8, I discuss more Fanny Kemble's emotional illness. Elizabeth Sedgwick's letter to her of June 7, 1839, warning her about her inherited "morbid tendencies" is quoted in Butler, Statement, 33–39.

12. Kemble, *Record of a Girlhood*, 1:230–31.

13. Ibid., 1:258.

14. Ibid., 1:261.

15. Ibid., 1:271.

16. Ibid., 1:276.

17. Davis, *The Economics of the British Stage*, 4. Davis examines in impressive detail "the relationship of economics to aesthetic representation, interested rhetorics, and business functioning. . . . Culture, broadly wrought, permeates all business decisions, just as business matters permeate all pertaining to culture, more narrowly defined" (7).

18. The destructive nature of Chancery suits is brilliantly satirized, of course, in Dickens's *Bleak House*. Whatever financial gain might have been awarded to the litigants in the notorious case of *Jarndyce vs. Jarndyce* is consumed entirely by the legal costs involved in its lengthy pursuit.

19. Kemble, *Record of a Girlhood*, 1:225.

20. Ibid., 2:5.

21. Ibid., 2:16.

22. British Library Department of Manuscripts, Add. MS. 55048, Macmillan Archive.

23. *The Secret History of the Green Room*, viii–iv.

24. Ibid., 19.

25. Wordsworth, in the seventh book of *The Prelude*, places James Graham's image among the string of "allegorical shapes" advertising "the string of dazzling wares" to be found on the London streets; Graham is figured as "the attractive head / Of some quack-doctor, famous in his day" (7:166–67). I am grateful to Stephen Gill for drawing this reference to my attention.

26. For details of James Graham and his Temple of Health and Hymen, see Otto, "The Regeneration of the Body," and Altick, *The Shows of London*.

27. Quoted in Altick, *The Shows of London*, 82.

28. Full details of this appeal are in Kennard, *Mrs. Siddons,* 193–94.

29. Quoted in Highfill, Burnim, and Langhans, *Biographical Dictionary,* 7:172.

30. As Davis observes, "The popular association of actresses and prostitutes is not a straightforward issue of class and gender, for neither actresses nor prostitutes represented a single class of women who uniformly broke specific cultural taboos. Among actresses, a vast range of incomes, and grades of 'respectability,' arising out of social background, training, talent, [and] luck, are involved" (*Actresses as Working Women,* 77).

31. Dunlap, *History of the American Theatre,* 200.

32. Review of *Chronicles of an Illustrius House: or, The Peer, the Lawyer, and the Hunchback; a Novel,* by Ann Julia Hatton, *Monthly Review* 79, n.s. (1816): 438.

33. Jenkins notes that Fanny Kemble was not exactly unprepared for the stage, having grown up among the leading proponents of tragedy; she also knew how to project her voice from singing, and dancing lessons had taught her how to move—in short, she was "better equipped than most *ingenues*" (*Fanny Kemble,* 198).

34. In *Characteristics of Women: Moral, Poetical, and Historical,* Anna Jameson observes that in Portia "there is nothing of the passionate self-abandonment of Juliet, nor of the artless simplicity of Miranda" (65). Jameson dedicated her analysis of Shakespeare's women characters to Fanny Kemble and presented her with a newly published copy just before Charles and Fanny left for America in August 1832.

35. Kemble, *Record of a Girlhood,* 2:6.

36. Ibid., 2:8.

37. Ibid., 2:61.

38. "Sonnet: On Mrs. Kemble's Readings from Shakespeare," in H. Longfellow, *Poetical Works,* 158–59.

39. Kemble's cousin, the deceased husband of Harriet Siddons, was the author of a study of the "positions": *Practical Illustrations of Rhetorical Gesture and Action.* Robert Bernard Martin quotes from the impressions of Charles and Mary Cowden Clarke of Fanny Kemble's Juliet: "Fanny Kemble's acting was marked by much originality of thought and grace of execution. Some of the positions she assumed were strikingly new and appropriate, suggestive as they were of the state of feeling and peculiar situation in which the character she was playing happened to be" (unpublished manuscript).

40. Jenkins, *Fanny Kemble,* 207.

41. Kemble, American *Journal,* 1:183–84.

42. *Spectator* 2 (1829): 792, quoted by Downer, "Players and Painted Stage," 528.

43. *Spectator* 3 (1830): 846, quoted by Downer, "Players and Painted Stage," 531.

44. Donohue, *Dramatic Character in the English Romantic Age,* 244.

45. Kemble, *Record of a Girlhood,* 2:60.

46. Quoted in Agate, *These Were Actors,* 12.

47. Quoted in Matthews and Hutton, *Actors and Actresses of Great Britain and the United States,* 250.

48. This letter is quoted by Robert Bernard Martin in his unpublished manuscript.

49. Quoted in Matthews and Hutton, *Actors and Actresses of Great Britain and the United States,* 150–51.

50. C. Greville, *The Greville Memoirs*, 2:129–30.

51. Quoted in Matthews and Hutton, *Actors and Actresses of Great Britain and the United States*, 252–53.

52. Baker, *The London Stage*, 1:158.

53. According to an "Original Memoir" (signed S. D. L.) that prefaces an 1833 edition of *Francis the First*, Kemble's success slaughtered the competition: "So entirely had the extraordinary talents of this wondrous girl centred dramatic taste in Covent Garden, that the rival Theatre was thrown completely into the shade, and even the Italian Opera and Astley's had lost their charms. So that on the opening of the new season Drury Lane had to resort to the unprecedented novelty of bringing wild beasts upon the stage, to secure some share of the patronage so liberally awarded to its rival" (10).

54. During her almost five years of acting from October 1829 to June 1834, Fanny Kemble's principal roles were the following: Juliet; Isabella in *The Fatal Marriage*; Portia in *The Merchant of Venice*; Lady Macbeth; Constance in *King John*; Belvidera in *Venice Preserv'd*; Euphrasia in *The Grecian Daughter*; Mrs. Beverley in *The Gamester*; Bianca in *Fazio*; Julia in *The Hunchback*; Lady Teazle in *A School for Scandal*; and Lady Townley in *The Provoked Husband*.

55. Moore, *Journal*, 3:146.

56. Ibid., 3:126.

57. Hallam, *Letters*, 348–50.

58. Kolb, "Arthur Hallam and Emily Tennyson," 39.

59. Quoted in Hallam, *Letters*, 350.

60. Kemble, *Record of a Girlhood*, 2:108–9.

61. Ibid., 2:71.

62. Furnas, *Fanny Kemble*, 40.

63. Kemble, *Record of a Girlhood*, 1:220.

64. Ibid., 1:220.

65. *Literary Chronicle* 379 (August 19, 1826): 518–19, quoted in Wu, *Romanticism*, 991.

66. Quoted in Wu, *Romanticism*, 991–92.

67. Kemble, *Record of a Girlhood*, 1:223.

68. Ibid., 1:221.

69. Kemble, *Francis the First*, 4.

70. *The Nation*, December 12, 1878, quoted in James, *Henry James: Literary Criticism*.

71. Kemble, *Record of a Girlhood*, 3:69.

72. Davis's study of the life and work of nineteenth-century actresses has proved very helpful in my understanding of Fanny Kemble's views of the profession. See *Actresses as Working Women*, particularly pages 41–42.

73. Quoted in Davis, *Actresses as Working Women*, 41–42.

74. Donohue, *Dramatic Character in the English Romantic Age*, 5.

75. Covent Garden Playbills, Van Pelt Rare Book and Mss. Furness Collection, Library of the University of Pennsylvania, Philadelphia.

76. Kemble, "On the Stage," *Notes upon Some of Shakespeare's Plays*, 14.

77. Kemble, *Record of a Girlhood*, 2:327.

Chapter 3. Reform and Romance

Note to epigraph: Quoted in Vicinus, *The Industrial Muse*, 45.

1. As Clark observes, "In the first quarter of the nineteenth century, it was becoming increasingly clear that what was politically, socially, intellectually and spiritually a new society was growing up in England for which neither the institutions, nor the ideas, that had been inherited from the eighteenth century would suffice" (*The Making of Victorian England*, 39–40). For a discussion of the European political unrest that formed a background for discussion about parliamentary reform in England, see Cole and Postgate, *The British People*, 244–57.

2. Quoted in Jenkins, *Fanny Kemble*, 256.

3. Kemble, *Record of a Girlhood*, 2:148. In a poem interpolated into her American *Journal* immediately after a letter to Harriet St. Leger dated December 28, 1832, and almost certainly addressed to her, Kemble recalls the joy of lying beside her "beneath the brake": "Oh, friend! my heart is sad: 'tis strange, / As I sit musing on the change / That has cover o'er my fate, and cast / A longing look upon the past, / That pleasantest time comes back again / So freshly to my heart and brain, / That I half think the things I see / Are but a dream, and I shall be / Lying beside you, when I wake, / Upon the lawn beneath the brake. / With the hazel copses behind my head, / And all the new-mown fields before me spread" (*Journal*, 78–79).

4. See Courtney, *The Adventurous Thirties*, 244–45. According to Samuel Rogers's biographer, R. Ellis Roberts, "Women did not frequent Holland House, and women, as might be expected, had no love for its mistress; and the virtual ostracism she suffered from many of her own sex, and the angry resentment she aroused in those younger than herself, probably added to the bitterness of character that so often showed itself in rudeness of behavior and vehemence of speech" (*Samuel Rogers and His Circle*, 232). Clearly, Lady Holland (who had left her first husband and eloped with Henry Holland) made an exception for Fanny Kemble, for whom she seems to have harbored no recorded resentment.

5. Kemble, *Record of a Girlhood*, 2:164.

6. Cole and Postgate, *The British People*, 142.

7. Kemble, *Record of a Girlhood*, 2:190.

8. Ibid., 2:197.

9. Ibid., 2:215.

10. Ibid., 3:7.

11. Ibid., 3:36.

12. The familiar history of Chartism (its origins and eventual defeat) has been well documented by many historians. Cole and Postgate provide a particularly detailed and lucid analysis in *The British People*, 272–91.

13. Kemble, *Record of a Girlhood*, 2:244.

14. Burroughs, "'A Reasonable Woman's Desire,'" 266.

15. Austen, *Mansfield Park*, 121–22.

16. Ibid., 124.

17. Fitzgerald, *The Kembles*, 2:62.

18. See Braudy, *The Frenzy of Renown*, particularly chapter 5. Braudy argues that figures such as Napoleon and Byron are created, in part, by an audience no longer willing "to watch and passively take in the self-constructions of its society's great men. Its gaze now creates and shapes those who move before it, forcing greatness to occupy a certain space in its eye" (398). It would be foolish to claim this kind of greatness and visibility in the public eye for Fanny Kemble, but it is reasonable to assume she performed as much on the small stages of aristocratic English country life as did enormously public figures such as Napoleon and Byron on the stages of continental war and the literary marketplace.

19. See Kemble's autobiographical fragment, British Library Department of Manuscripts, Add. MS. 55048, Macmillan Archive.

20. Burroughs notes, "Between 1780 and 1805 Elizabeth Berkeley Craven either composed, translated, or altered nineteen plays. As Lady Craven she organized and appeared in private performances in Warwickshire, and upon relocating with her second husband from Germany to England, as the Margravine of Anspach, she supervised the building and operation of a private theater in the 1790s at Brandenburgh House in Hammersmith. Here she alternatively performed the functions of actress, playwright, producer, translator, musician, and singer" ("'A Reasonable Woman's Desire,'" 268).

21. Kemble, *Record of a Girlhood*, 3:130.

22. Some of Kemble's biographers have no doubt that she was seriously in love with Augustus Craven and that there was a definite engagement. Robert Bernard Martin, in his unpublished manuscript, declares that "it is no wonder that the arch-romantic Fanny fell in love with this paradigm of the Byronic hero," which is how he describes Craven; Blainey claims that in a letter written by Adelaide Sartoris ("just discovered"), Fanny's sister was less discreet: "Fanny, she wrote, was in love with Augustus Craven, and they were engaged to be married" (*Fanny and Adelaide*, 63). Since Blainey provides no source for this letter and does not quote it directly, the claim cannot be taken as proof. Jenkins argues, "The evidence is that the love between Augustus and Fanny was mutual and sincere" (*Fanny Kemble*, 317).

23. British Library Department of Manuscripts, Add. MS. 55048, Macmillan Archive.

24. Robert Bernard Martin quotes from a letter Kemble wrote to William Dean Howells fifty years after the Craven episode; discussing the publication of her memoirs, she declares, "I was engaged to be married and I came with my father to America for two years—my engagement was broken and I married Mr. Butler—and that is the whole story." The letter is in Houghton bMS AM 1784 (268).

25. Royal Academy LAW 5/383. Letter from Kemble to Lawrence, undated but late 1829.

26. Moore, *Journal*, 3:1271, 1261. The well-known playwright Joanna Baillie was also in the audience for this performance and wrote to Thomas Lawrence to thank him for arranging a box: "I have admired your young friend already so much in the character of Juliet that I long mightily to see her in that Belvidera which I think will suit her particularly well; one of the few faults she has (in my opinion at least)—a little over-acting, will not be so obvious in that character" (Royal Academy LAW 5/409).

27. Kemble, *Record of a Girlhood*, 2:43.

28. Royal Academy LAW 5/413.

29. Kemble, *Record of a Girlhood*, 2:43.

30. Kemble, *Records of Later Life*, 3:90.

31. Kemble, *Record of a Girlhood*, 2:54.

32. Ibid., 2:54.

33. Ibid., 3:121. Kemble expresses similar sentiments, and in similar language, when she notes in the autobiographical fragment that on July 15, 1831, she had "a long talk this morning with dear Dall about my dislike to the stage—I do not think it is the acting itself that is so disagreeable to me but the public personal exhibition the violence done (as it seems to me) to womanly dignity and decorum in thus becoming the gaze of every eye and thence of every tongue—if my audience was reduced to my intimates and associates I should not mind it so much—I think—but I am not quite sure I should like it then" (British Library Department of Manuscripts, Add. MS. 55048, Macmillan Archive).

34. Browning and Browning, *Correspondence*, 3:241.

35. Ibid., 3:35–36. Richard Hengist Horne found *Francis the First* "inexcusably bad throughout. . . . It was a weak subject, weakly treated, and passed through fourteen editions in a short time" (*Exposition of the False Medium and Barriers Excluding Men of Genius from the Public* [London: E. Wilson, 1833]). After reading Horne's comments, Elizabeth Barrett remarked to Mary Russell Mitford, "even women of genius pass silently" (Browning and Browning, *The Brownings' Correspondence*, 3:102).

36. Kemble, *Journal*, 2:155–56.

37. Kemble, *Record of a Girlhood*, 3:230.

38. Ibid.

Chapter 4. Seeing the World

Note to epigraph: Fanny Kemble reports Washington Irving's congratulatory sentiments to Harriet St. Leger in a letter dated April 16, 1833. Fanny also reports that Irving told her "when with fame you have acquired independence and retire from these labors, you will begin another and a brighter course with matured powers" (*Record of a Girlhood*, 3:293). It was not until 1848, when Kemble had retired from the stage and began her Shakespeare readings, that she may be said to have embarked on this course.

1. My reading of the *Journal* is taken from the British edition of the 1835 American publication. Gough's *Fanny Kemble: Journal of a Young Actress* (New York: Columbia University Press, 1990) is based on her reading of the 1835 American edition in the Rare Book and Manuscript Library of Columbia University. I have found Gough's editing unreliable. Although she usefully fills in names that were indicated by initials in the original publication (by following Kemble's annotations on the Columbia copy), Gough seems to have edited out certain parts of the 1835 edition.

2. See Erickson, *Leaving England*. Erickson's figures are taken from N. H. Carrier and J. R. Jeffery, *External Migration: A Study of the Available Statistics, 1815–1950*, General Register Office, Studies on Medical and Population Subjects, no. 6 (London: HMSO, 1953), 95.

3. Dickens, *American Notes*, 1–2.

4. Moore's book about Byron, *Thomas Moore's Letters and Journals of Lord Byron*, was published in 1830 (New York: J. & J. Harper).

5. Kemble, *Records of Later Life*, 1:4–5.

6. Martineau, *Autobiography*, 1:364.

7. For the full description of how Martineau felt about the Kembles, see *Autobiography*, 1:364–66. Of all the Kembles, Martineau much preferred Adelaide Kemble, finding her "morally of a far higher order," her only wish being that Adelaide "had not been a Kemble."

8. Kemble, *Journal*, 1:228.

9. Ibid., 1:158.

10. Ibid., 1:50.

11. Moore, *Poetical Works*, 325–26.

12. Ibid., 361.

13. Ibid., 375.

14. C. Greville, *The Greville Memoirs*, 3:260.

15. Cobbett, *A Year's Residence*, 194.

16. Kemble, *Journal*, 2:156.

17. Ibid., 1:213.

18. Cobbett, *A Year's Residence*, 312.

19. Kemble, *Journal*, 1:97.

20. Ibid., 2:13.

21. Hamilton, *Men and Manners in America*, 174.

22. Ibid., xviii, 63. Rebecca Gratz, a socially prominent resident of Philadelphia, noted that she had been reading Hamilton's book and that she was "quite provoked" by his misrepresentations; she added, "No English traveller can speak the truth of us" (*Letters*, 186).

23. Kemble, *Journal*, 2:105–6.

24. F. Trollope, *Domestic Manners of the Americans*, 404.

25. Ibid., 18–19, 222. The preface to the American edition of *Domestic Manners of the Americans*, "A Brief Inquiry into the Real Name and Character of the Author of This Book, by the American Editor," argues that "a total want of delicacy in style and sentiment; a coarse disregard of all those nice decorums which are sacred in the eyes of a well-bred lady; a flippant ignorance of genteel life; and above all a daring reckless meddling with scenes and topics" precludes the possibility that the book was written by an English lady. The editor wittily suggests that the book must have been written by Basil Hall, a prolific travel writer who visited North America in the late 1820s.

26. F. Trollope, *Domestic Manners of the Americans*, 157.

27. Burke, *Two Speeches on Conciliation with America*, 113.

28. A. Trollope, *Autobiography*, 22.

29. A. Trollope, *North America*, 1:9.

30. Ibid., 1:106.

31. Kemble, *Journal*, 1:237–38.

32. Ibid., 2:184.

33. Ibid., 1:59.

34. Hone, *Diary*, 1:75–77.

35. On September 20 Philip Hone noted in his diary, "The distresses of the lower classes in England and Ireland have caused emigration to America in numbers so great as to cause serious alarm.... They have brought the cholera this year and they will always bring wretchedness and want. The boast that our country is the asylum for the oppressed in other parts of the world is very philanthropic and sentimental, but I fear that we shall before long derive little comfort from being made the almshouse and place of refuge for the poor of other countries" (*Diary*, 1:78).

36. Hone, *Diary*, 1:77–78. Hone misspells the name of Eliza O'Neill, reputed by English critics to be the greatest Juliet of the first quarter of the nineteenth century and to whom Fanny Kemble was often (favorably) compared.

37. Odell, *Annals of the New York Stage*, 3:606.

38. Wister, *Fanny the American Kemble*, 86–87.

39. Odell, *Annals of the New York Stage*, 3:608.

40. Hone, *Diary*, 1:78–79.

41. Odell, *Annals of the New York Stage*, 3:607.

42. Whitman, *Complete Poetry and Collected Prose*, 704.

43. Odell, *Annals of the New York Stage*, 3:608.

44. Hone, *Diary*, 1:79.

45. Kemble, *Journal*, 2:26.

46. Ibid., 1:192.

47. Henry Fitzharding Berkeley to Pierce Butler, September 23, 1832, Wister Family Papers, Historical Society of Pennsylvania, Philadelphia. Robert Bernard Martin, in his unpublished manuscript, speculates about Pierce Butler's relationship with Emily Chapman, a member of a family close to the Butlers. Martin believes that at the time Pierce was wooing Kemble, Chapman was pregnant with his child, something impossible to confirm despite various letters in the Wister Family Papers that refer to Pierce's sexual promiscuity.

48. Henry Fitzharding Berkeley to Pierce Butler, October 3, 1832, Wister Family Papers, Historical Society of Pennsylvania, Philadelphia.

49. In Chapter 9, I discuss Kemble's sexual attraction to Butler, as expressed in letters produced as evidence during their divorce proceedings.

50. For S. Weir Mitchell's views of Butler, see the quotations from his autobiography in Burr, *Weir Mitchell*, 131. For Butler as a "well-bred fox," see Furnas, *Fanny Kemble*, 122.

51. Kemble, *Journal*, 1:221–89, 2:66.

52. Ibid., 1:72–73.

53. Ibid., 1:100.

54. Ibid., 1:61.

55. Ibid., 1:99–101.

56. Ibid., 1:273–74.

57. F. Trollope, *Domestic Manners of the Americans*, 69, 75.

58. Kemble, *Journal*, 2:165–66.

59. Ibid., 1:175.

60. Ibid., 2:131.

Chapter 5. On the Brink

Note to epigraphs: Kemble, *Records of Later Life*, 1:115. The passage in the second epigraph is underlined in pencil in a copy of *The Married State, Its Obligations and Duties*, originally part of Pierce Butler's library. The book is inscribed with his name and is found in Special Collections at the Library of the University of Virginia, Charlottesville.

1. Quoted in Armstrong, *Five Generations*, 211.

2. Kemble, *Journal*, 1:167–68.

3. Strong as she was, Kemble could not have matched Trelawny's amazingly powerful constitution. According to the entry on Trelawny in the Oxford Dictionary of National Biography (written by Peter Cochran), Trelawny endured the extraction of a bullet from his knee "with all the equanimity of a man having his hair cut."

4. Quoted in Wister, *Fanny the American Kemble*, 137.

5. Quoted in Blainey, *Fanny and Adelaide*, 100.

6. Kemble, *Journal*, 2:215, 237–38.

7. James, *Henry James: Literary Criticism*, 1089–90.

8. Kemble, *Journal*, 2:235.

9. See Howe, *The Articulate Sisters*, 107–8.

10. Ibid., 209–10.

11. Ibid., 223–24.

12. Kemble, American *Journal*, 2:256–57.

13. Ibid., 2:254.

14. Weld, *Travels Through the States of North America*, 2:128.

15. Barbauld, *Eighteen Hundred and Eleven*, ll. 95–96.

16. Martineau, *Society in America*, 1:211.

17. Kemble, American *Journal*, 2:286–87.

18. The letter to Claire Clairmont is taken from Trelawny's *Letters*, edited by Buxton Forman (190–91) and is quoted in Crane, *Lord Byron's Jackal*, 309. Anna Quincy reports in her journal that in August 1833 Trelawny was in Saratoga Springs: "the lion of the moment at the Springs is Trelawney [sic] . . . [he] has now wandered over to America to seek that peace which he certainly does not merit. . . . All the ladies are quite frantic, of course, about this gallant Rover, who, by the by, can be no chicken if he went thro' all these adventures" (*The Articulate Sisters*, 240–41).

19. Quoted in Armstrong, *Five Generations*, 217.

20. Quoted in Poirier, *Trying It Out in America*, 140.

21. *Narrative of the Capture and Subsequent Sufferings of Mrs. Rachel Plummer, During a Captivity of Twenty-One Months Among the Cumanche Indians*, in *Held Captive by Indians*, 360.

22. Hall, *Travels in Canada and the United States*, 466.

23. F. Trollope, *Domestic Manners of the Americans*, 222.

24. Dickens, *American Notes*, 142, 166.

25. Kemble, American *Journal*, 2:126.

26. Ibid., 2:214.

27. Ibid., 1:129.

28. Ibid.

29. Theodore Sedgwick to Catharine Sedgwick, Sedgwick Papers, Massachusetts Historical Society, and quoted by Robert Bernard Martin, unpublished manuscript.

30. Sedgwick, *The Power of Her Sympathy*, 132.

31. Adams, *Diary*, 438.

32. Kemble, *Record of a Girlhood*, 3:76.

33. Ibid., 3:174–75.

34. Kemble, American *Journal*, 1:67–68, 2:26.

35. Kemble, *Record of a Girlhood*, 3:304.

36. Ibid., 3:315.

37. I discuss the documents relating to the Butler divorce more fully in Chapter 9.

38. Butler, *Statement*, 28.

39. In an undated letter from Kemble to her financial advisor, William Minot, she says that Charles Kemble insisted that on his death the money should be left "to me under Trustee . . . to save it from Mr. Butler or his creditors." Sedgwick Papers, Massachusetts Historical Society, quoted in Robert Bernard Martin, unpublished manuscript.

40. Gratz, *Letters*, 205.

41. Fanny Kemble to Sarah Perkins Cleveland, May 31, 1834, the Berg Collection, New York Public Library.

42. For the report of Kemble weeping after she left Philadelphia, see Gratz, *Letters*, 205.

43. Before actually seeing Kemble onstage, Anna Mowatt had read "critiques upon her acting in the papers, and heard her talked of as a most devoted daughter and truly excellent woman" (*Autobiography of an Actress*, 38–39).

44. Sidney Fisher dismisses John Butler as "a mere idler, with a large fortune, blasé, with no intellectual resources and tired to death of a life of ennui" (*Philadelphia Perspective*, 197). Fisher was slightly more positive in his assessment of John's wife, Ella, who came from a rich Southern family: some seven years after Kemble began to live in Philadelphia, Fisher described Ella Butler as still "one of the most beautiful women in the world and her charms are enhanced by exquisite taste in taste. . . . Tho she has no mind, she has the ease and high breeding of the southern aristocracy" (110, 113).

45. F. Longfellow, *Selected Letters and Journals*, 14.

46. The house was sold in 1916 by the descendants of Fanny and Pierce for $800,000. It was torn down in 1925 to make way for five hundred row houses. All that remains of Kemble's presence in Branchtown is the Fanny Kemble Park at Olney Avenue and 17th Street in Germantown.

47. Martineau, *Autobiography*, 1:364–66.

48. Kemble, *Records of Later Life*, 3:25.

49. Kemble, *Poems*, 31. The 1866 edition contains many poems from the 1844 edition of verse published in Philadelphia under the name Fanny Kemble Butler.

Chapter 6. The Outer Bound of Civilized Creation

Note to epigraph: *The Girlhood of Queen Victoria*, 1:129.

1. Clinton, *Fanny Kemble's Civil Wars*, 84.

2. *Quarterly Review*, 39–40. The periodical was established by John Murray in 1809 as a Tory rival to the Whig-inclined *Edinburgh Review* and was not favorable to authors advocating parliamentary reform. Although Kemble's *Journal* is sympathetic to the working classes in both England and the United States, she was, of course, also forthright in her dislike of ambitious merchants (as she saw them) elbowing their way into Parliament as a result of the 1832 Reform Bill. Ironically, Murray was the publisher of the English edition of the *Journal* and had also paid her a healthy sum of money in March 1832 to publish *Francis the First*. The moralizing sentiments expressed by the *Quarterly Review* were commonly propagated by the American clergy: Timothy Dwight, president of Yale College and a nationally known theologian, wrote in 1824 that theater people are "a nuisance in the earth, the very offal of society" (*An Essay on the Stage*, 101; quoted in Johnson, *American Actress*, 7).

3. *Quarterly Review*, 41.

4. Ibid., 58.

5. Quoted in Gibbs, *Affectionately Yours, Fanny*, 129.

6. *Girlhood of Queen Victoria*, 1:128–29.

7. Ibid., 1:132.

8. H. Greville, *Leaves from the Diary of Henry Greville*, 1:61.

9. Smith, *Letters*, 2:620–21.

10. *My Conscience! Fanny Thimble Cutler's Journal*, 7–23.

11. Ibid., 9, 13, 23, 30.

12. Armstrong, *Five Generations*, 217.

13. Quoted in Furnas, *Fanny Kemble*, 144.

14. Kemble hated this play and thought it had no merit whatsoever. Nevertheless, she released it for publication since she was glad to be rid of it.

15. Kemble, *Records of Later Life*, 1:4.

16. Ibid., 1:29.

17. Letters Written by Frances Anne Kemble to Sarah Perkins Cleveland, the Berg Collection, New York Public Library.

18. Kemble, *Records of Later Life*, 1:41.

19. Jameson, *Letters and Friendships*, 160.

20. Kemble, *Records of Later Life*, 1:40.

21. Ibid., 1:34.

22. Ibid., 1:35.

23. Kemble, *Journal of a Residence*, 138.

24. Ibid., 66.

25. Kemble, *Records of Later Life*, 1:47.

26. Ibid., 1:68.

27. In the context of Pierce Butler's election as a delegate to the Pennsylvania Constitutional Convention, on November 2, 1836, the Philadelphia diarist Sidney George Fisher described him as having "a great deal of energy and character tho entirely without education. . . . He is immensely rich" (*Philadelphia Perspective*, 10).

28. Quoted in Blainey, *Fanny and Adelaide*, 100.

29. Quoted in ibid., 101.

30. Macready, *Journal*, 51.

31. Kemble, *Records of Later Life*, 1:74–75.

32. Carlyle, *I Too Am Here*, 98–99. In her memoirs, Kemble offers the following remarks about Jane Carlyle: "I do not know whether I am singular in not endorsing very heartily the enthusiastic admiration of his wife's genius bestowed upon her after her death by Carlyle. In my personal intercourse with her, she seemed to me a bright, clever, intelligent woman but as to any comparison between her mental powers and those of the two great geniuses of our day, George Sand and George Eliot, it was really absurdly inadmissable." Kemble concedes that when she visited the Carlyles, she was dressed in her habit and "necessarily" carrying her whip, "which I am not aware of ever practising (keeping my hand in the use of) with any creature but my horse" (*Further Records*, 81).

33. Kemble, *Records of Later Life*, 1:81.

34. Kemble, *Poems*, 169.

35. Kemble, *Records of Later Life*, 1:117.

36. Jameson, *Letters and Friendships*, 160.

37. Kemble, *Records of Later Life*, 1:137.

38. Hone, *Diary*, 1:340–41.

39. Kemble, *Records of Later Life*, 1:159.

40. F. Longfellow, *Selected Letters and Journals*, 53.

41. Ibid.

42. Channing, *Slavery*, 2:7; Channing, *Works*.

43. As Scott observes, Kemble had grown up at a time "when the movement for the abolition of slavery in the British Empire was advancing to a triumphant climax. Antislavery *mores*, by 1832, were an established fact among the British people, and it never occurred to Fanny that a self-respecting person could hold pro-slavery views" ("On the Authenticity of Fanny Kemble's *Journal of a Residence*," 234).

44. Kemble, *Records of Later Life*, 1:51.

45. Ibid., 1:155.

46. Quoted in Martineau, *Writings on Slavery and the American Civil War*, 43.

47. Kemble, *Records of Later Life*, 1:216.

48. Ibid., 1:177.

49. Ibid., 1:221.

Chapter 7. A Dreary Lesson of Human Suffering

Note to epigraph: Kemble, *Journal of a Residence*, 275.

1. Ibid., 64.

2. As Scott notes, the statistics of crop production on the Butler estates for this period are in the Day Book, 1844–1853, presently in private possession on St. Simons Island, and in the Butler Papers, 1771–1900, of the Historical Society of Pennsylvania ("On the Authenticity of Fanny Kemble's *Journal of a Residence*," 235).

3. In October 1840, Kemble wrote to Harriet St. Leger that her time in the South "was so crowded with daily and hourly occupations that, though I kept a regular journal, it was hastily written and received constant additional notes of things that occurred and that I wished to remember, inserted in a very irregular fashion in it" (*Records of Later Life*, 2:39).

4. Bell, *Major Butler's Legacy*, 376–78. The publication history of the Georgian *Journal* reflects the politics of American race. In 1961, Knopf published a reprint as part of a commemoration of the centennial of the Civil War; 1961 was also marked by the Freedom Rides and the beginning of the American civil rights movement. In 1975, a New American Library paperback appeared, but by the early 1980s the *Journal* was again out of print. In 1984, Scott's splendidly edited edition (with a very helpful introduction) brought the *Journal* back into print. When Scott was preparing his edition for publication, he was approached by Margaret Davis Cate with a plea to halt publication. Cate claimed that Kemble's *Journal* was riddled with errors and would exacerbate racial tension. Scott refused and in March 1960 Cate published an article entitled "Mistakes in Fanny Kemble's Georgia Journal."

5. Scott observes that the English edition "arrived on the scene after the tide of popular opinion had begun to run heavily in favor of the North, and in any event too late to affect the issue of war and peace" ("On the Authenticity of Fanny Kemble's *Journal of a Residence*," 239).

6. The time that Kemble spent on the plantations and the conflict between her abolitionist views and Pierce Butler's position have been central in two recent dramatic presentations, one vulgarly simplistic and the other intelligently affective. *Enslavement* (2000), a Jane Seymour television movie vehicle, shows, among other things, Kemble helping slaves escape from Georgia on the Underground Railroad and Kemble standing between a female slave about to be flogged and a whip-wielding Pierce. The film has her performing in America in the 1840s and inaccurately features Elizabeth Sedgwick, who lived and ran her school in Massachusetts, as a Philadelphia socialite. *Unbound: The Journals of Fanny Kemble*, conceived and directed by Davis McCallum and performed in New York in February 2005, skillfully weaves selections from the American and Georgian journals and presents a strong and sympathetic portrait of Kemble.

7. Kemble, *Journal of a Residence*, 216–17.

8. Booth, "From Miranda to Prospero," has been helpful to me in thinking about Kemble and *The Tempest*. Booth argues that Butler Island is a "negative pastoral or disenchanted Prospero's Island, in which the workers are brutalized, the country house is a worn cabin, the master a licentious monster, and the mistress herself a gothic captive" (238). I do have some reservations, however, regarding Booth's argument that Kemble asserts a "shared

enslavement" with Caliban. From the time Kemble arrives in Georgia to her departure, she possesses a good deal of agency and autonomy, despite her felt sense of confinement through marriage.

9. Ritchie, *Chapters from Some Memoirs*, 197.

10. Kemble, *Journal of a Residence*, 77.

11. Kemble, *Notes upon Some of Shakespeare's Plays*, 2:135.

12. Kemble, *Journal of a Residence*, 302; *The Tempest*, 2.2.18.

13. Kemble, *Journal of a Residence*, 67.

14. Ibid., 84.

15. Ibid., 342.

16. Hadley, *Melodramatic Tactics*, 3.

17. As Fox-Genovese points out in her study of life within the plantation household, tradition endowed the plantation mistress with the potential for maternal sympathy and benevolence: "The mistresses, alternating between impatience with and compassion for—their female slaves, were trapped at the center of a web of human relations in which both they and their slaves, however unequally, defined the responsibilities and imposed the burdens that constituted the role of mistress" (*Within the Plantation Household*, 132).

18. At times her descriptions of the Southern landscape anticipate (or perhaps echo) Dickens's conjuring of the spot at the junction of the Ohio and Mississippi rivers (the "dismal" Cairo) in *American Notes*: "The trees were stunted in their growth; the banks were low and flat; the settlements and log cabins fewer in number; and their inhabitants more wan and wretched than any we had encountered yet . . . a breeding-place of fever, ague, and death. . . . A dismal swamp" (171). Since Kemble revised her *Journal* over the years between the visit to Georgia in 1838–39 and the publication in 1863, it is possible that Dickens's *American Notes* (published in 1842) was known to her and even influenced her writing.

19. Kemble, *Journal of a Residence*, 140.

20. Ibid., 226.

21. Ibid., 6, 223, 241.

22. Butler, *Statement*, 20–21.

23. Kemble, *Journal of a Residence*, 10–11. An English visitor to America in the 1850s, Marianne Finch, imagines an idealistic future for mixed-race children: "These children, doubly-wronged, suffering from paternal, as well as national injustice, uniting the sternness, and love of independence of the Saxon—with the warm feelings, and strong animal nature of the African—will, when the hour of retribution arrives, be the leaders of their mother's race, and the avengers of its wrongs" (*An Englishwoman's Experience in America*, 322).

24. Kemble, *Journal of a Residence*, 70.

25. Ibid.

26. *Southern Agriculturalist*, December 1828.

27. In his useful study of Anglo-American nineteenth-century travel narratives, Mulvey sensibly observes that Kemble was "unusual in the force of her rejection of Southern claims to civilisation . . . but she was not unusual in her acceptance of certain attitudes, beliefs, and responses that would be identified as racist in the twentieth century" (*Transatlantic Manners*, 84–85).

28. Kemble, *Journal of a Residence*, 77.

29. Ibid., 260.

30. Dickens indicts slave owners as "cowards" who "notch the ears of men and women, cut pleasant posies in the shrinking flesh, learn to write with pens of red-hot iron on the human face, rack their poetic fancies for liveries of mutilation which their slaves shall wear for life and carry to the grave" (*American Notes*, 242–43).

31. Bird, *The Englishwoman in America*, 174.

32. Murray, *Letters from the United States, Cuba, and Canada.*

33. Thackeray, "A Mississippi Bubble," in *Letters and Private Papers*, 365–66.

34. A. Trollope, *North America*, 2:70, 351–52.

35. Today, visitors to Butler Island can see the brick ruins of one of the chimneys that fueled the rice-grinding mills. The island is completely flat and threaded with traces of the ditches dug to cultivate the rice, suggesting what it must have been like in 1838 with the fields full of slaves, the rice being transported to the grinding mills.

36. Kemble, *Record of a Girlhood*, 3:104.

37. Kemble, *Journal of a Residence*, 184.

38. Ibid., 26.

39. Ibid., 260.

40. Ibid., 261. Mulvey argues that as Kemble "continued to live among blacks and as she lost the superciliousness sometimes evident in her journal of 1832, she became aware of the negative racism of these men and women" (*Transatlantic Manners*, 91).

41. Kemble, *Journal of a Residence*, 295.

42. Ritchie, *Chapters from Some Memoirs*, 214.

43. Kemble, *Journal of a Residence*, 96.

44. Ibid., 114.

45. Ibid., 139.

46. Lydia Maria Child to Ellis Gray and Louisa Loring, December 5, 1838, in *Lydia Maria Child: Selected Correspondence*, 95–96; also quoted in Bell, *Major Butler's Legacy*, 266.

47. Kemble, *Journal of a Residence*, 160.

48. Ibid., 210.

49. Ibid., 214.

Chapter 8. "A Woful Ruin"

Note to epigraph: Kemble, *Poems*, 33.

1. Barlow, *On Man's Power*, 12, 13, 60–61. Although Kemble and Pierce were in London in early 1843, it would not have been possible for her to hear Barlow's lecture: the Butlers sailed from Liverpool for America on May 4, 1843.

2. Barlow, *On Man's Power*, 12, 13, 6–61.

3. Fisher, *Philadelphia Perspective*, 87.

4. Butler, *Statement*, 35.

5. Ibid., 26.

6. Kemble's willingness to leave her infant, her suicidal tendencies, and the volatility of her emotional condition should not be interpreted in any way as a sign of insanity. Certainly, as Elaine Showalter points out in her study of women, madness, and English culture between 1830 and 1980, the mid-nineteenth century was a period that saw an increasing number of unhappy and mentally disturbed women classified as "insane" and institutionalized. Showalter notes "that the domestication of insanity and its assimilation by the Victorian institution coincide with its feminization" (*The Female Malady*, 52). Despite Butler's insistence that Kemble's mind was "diseased" and evidence from contemporaries that describes her often strange, unpredictable behavior, there is nothing to suggest that she was clinically insane. In today's terms, she was neurotic and would probably be diagnosed with clinical depression.

7. Smith-Rosenberg, *Disorderly Conduct*, 198.

8. Ibid., 202.

9. Court of Common Pleas, Philadelphia, *Pierce Butler vs. Frances Anne Butler, Libel for Divorce with Answers and Exhibits*, 31, Van Pelt Rare Book and Mss. Furness Collection, Library of the University of Pennsylvania, Philadelphia.

10. Kemble, *Records of Later Life*, 3:259.

11. Butler, *Statement*, 33–39.

12. Ibid., 41.

13. Macready, *Journal*, 128–29.

14. Kemble, *An English Tragedy*, in *Plays*, 3:2.

15. When published, *An English Tragedy* was dismissed by the *Saturday Review* as nothing more than a melodrama about adultery: the blank verse was termed "reckless" and Kemble, overall, "deficient in that nicety of ear for the musical flow of sound without which it is hazardous for a writer to venture beyond the rules of the more rigid school of versifiers." In sum, the critic concludes, the play was "very well as a lady's exercise in dramatic composition; but it should have remained unprinted in Mrs. Kemble's desk." Reprinted in *Littell's Living Age* 14 (1864): 118–19.

16. Kemble, *Records of Later Life*, 2:38

17. Ibid., 2:40.

18. Macready, *Journal*, 170.

19. Kemble, *Records of Later Life*, 2:66.

20. Ibid., 2:62.

21. Charles Dickens to Wilkie Collins, January 19, 1856, in Dickens, *Letters*, 8:30.

22. Kemble, *Records of Later Life*, 2:73.

23. Ibid., 2:75.

24. Ibid.

25. Ibid., 2:125–26.

26. Kemble and Franz Liszt remained friends until the end of their respective lives. Kemble's grandson, the son of Sarah Butler and Owen Wister, a Philadelphia physician, was a talented pianist and in the late summer of 1881 was in Bayreuth to see *Parsifal*. Owen Wister, Jr., had brought with him to Europe a letter of introduction from his grandmother to the now seventy-two-year-old Liszt, whom he spotted sitting in Wagner's box at the

performance in Bayreuth. Owen reported to Fanny Kemble that Liszt was still strikingly handsome, with shoulder-length white hair. After listening to Owen play, Liszt wrote to Fanny that her grandson had "un talent prononcé" (Payne, *Owen Wister*, 3–5).

27. On December 23, 1842, Elizabeth Barrett wrote to Mary Russell Mitford that Edward Sartoris was said to be "presentable—which I suppose is about as much as the husband of a genius ought to be—and tonight is her last night at the theatre. I wonder what her real feeling upon this retiring *is, and will be. You* wonder perhaps at me for wondering—but consider! She has attained an Art. She has given to the attainment, years—studious years! . . . And now, to abandon all just when she embraces all—and to be evermore the Countess Sortaris (is *that* the name and spelling?) Instead of Adelaide Kemble!! Do you think the sacrifice is not felt?" (Browning and Browning, *The Brownings' Correspondence*, 6:235–36). Barrett's remarks testify to Adelaide's fame in 1842. Interestingly, Barrett has nothing to say about Fanny Kemble's "Art"; obviously, Barrett could not have seen Kemble perform but her praise of Adelaide suggests some foundation for Fanny's feelings that when she returned to London in 1841 her celebrity was eclipsed by that of her sister.

28. Dickens, *Letters*, 2:431. Kemble met Dickens for the first time just before he left for America on January 3, 1842. In April, she wrote to Theodore Sedgwick, "I admire and love the man exceedingly, for he has a deep warm heart, a noble sympathy with and respect for human nature, and great intellectual gifts wherewith to make these final moral ones fruitful for the delight and consolation and improvement of his fellow-beings" (*Records of Later Life*, 2:207).

29. Kemble, *Records of Later Life*, 2:119.

30. Ibid., 2:145.

31. Ruskin delivered his lecture "The Storm-Cloud of the Nineteenth Century" at the London Institution on February 4, 1884. He recalls a day in July 1871 when the sky was "covered with grey cloud;—not rain-cloud, but a dry black veil, which no ray of sunshine can pierce; partly diffused in mist, feeble mist, enough to make distant objects unintelligible, yet without any substance, or wreathing, or colour of its own" (Ruskin, *The Genius of John Ruskin*, 447).

32. Kemble, *Records of Later Life*, 2:146.

33. Quoted in F. Wister, *Fanny the American Kemble*, 178.

34. Ibid., 180.

35. Henry Crabb Robinson reports that at one of Samuel Rogers's famous breakfasts, "Rogers showed Tom Moore some manuscript verses, rather sentimental, but good of the kind by Mrs. Butler" (*Henry Crabb Robinson on Books and Their Writers*, 2:633).

36. C. Greville, *The Greville Memoirs*, 1:75.

37. Kemble, *Records of Later Life*, 2:281.

38. Butler, *Statement*, 77.

39. Kemble, *Records of Later Life*, 2:265.

40. Ibid., 2:257.

41. Elizabeth Barrett Browning to Mary Russell Mitford, December 12, 1842, in Browning and Browning, *The Brownings' Correspondence*, 6:235–36.

42. Browning and Browning, *The Brownings' Correspondence*, 4:308.

43. Court of Common Pleas, Philadelphia, *Pierce Butler vs. Frances Anne Butler*, 1–2.

44. Court of Common Pleas, Philadelphia, *Pierce Butler vs. Frances Anne Butler*, summary by counsel for Frances Anne Butler, 74.

45. Butler, *Statement*, 65–77.

46. Court of Common Pleas, Philadelphia, *Pierce Butler vs. Frances Anne Butler*, summary by counsel for Frances Anne Butler.

47. Butler, *Statement*, 176.

48. Kemble, *Records of Later Life*, 2:285.

Chapter 9. *The Havoc of a Single Life*

Note to epigraph: Kemble, *Poems*, 265.

1. Fanny Kemble to Sarah Perkins Cleveland, July 17, 1843, Berg Collection, New York Public Library.

2. Mathias, *The First Industrial Nation*, 236.

3. Fanny Kemble to Sarah Perkins Cleveland, July 1, 1842, Berg Collection, New York Public Library. Kemble confided her worst fears about losing her children to Cleveland. On November 15, 1844, for example, while she was still living in Philadelphia at the boardinghouse but clearly contemplating her departure from America, Kemble anticipated the separation that was to come: "Perhaps dear Sally in your foreign wanderings you will see my children; then you will not fail to remind them of their mother."

4. Kemble, *Records of Later Life*, 3:10.

5. Bell, *Major Butler's Legacy*, 298. Bell quotes from the diary of Thomas J. Cope, a Philadelphia merchant.

6. Letter from Kemble to Butler written on June 20, 1837, in Butler, *Statement*, 10.

7. Kemble, *Records of Later Life*, 3:38–39.

8. Ibid., 3:29.

9. Tennyson's *Poems* was published in 1842; the volume included "Ulysses," "Locksley Hall," and a poem whose melancholy tone may well have had a strong appeal for Kemble at this time, "Break, Break, Break": the last of the four stanzas reads, "Break, break, break, / At the foot of thy crags, O Sea! / But the tender grace of a day that is dead / Will never come back to me." I can find no evidence that Kemble ever submitted her review to the *Knickerbocker*.

10. Kemble, *Poems*, 19.

11. Macready, *Journal*, 204.

12. Ibid., 204–5.

13. Butler, *Statement*, 100–104.

14. Ibid., 104.

15. Ibid., 116.

16. Schott, *Statement*.

17. Fisher, *Philadelphia Perspective*, 161. The full story of this episode is in the Butler-Schott Duel Folder, box "Miscellaneous B," George Cadwalader Papers, Historical Society of Pennsylvania, Philadelphia.

18. Ibid., 168.

19. Butler, *A Year of Consolation*, 1:6–7.

20. Smith, *Letters*, 2:826.

21. Fanny Kemble to Sarah Perkins Cleveland, November 15, 1844, Berg Collection, New York Public Library.

22. Sumner, *Selected Letters*, 1:141.

23. Fanny Kemble to Anne Thackeray Ritchie, December 23, 1879, Eton College Library. Pierce Butler Leigh lived only twenty-four hours.

24. Quoted in F. Wister, *Fanny the American Kemble*, 194.

25. Kemble, *Poems*, 132–33.

26. Fisher, *Philadelphia Perspective*, 168.

27. Kemble, *Records of Later Life*, 3:81.

28. Ibid., 3:91.

29. Ibid., 3:101.

30. Ibid., 3:107.

31. Ibid., 3:422. Under the Married Women's Property Act of 1870, women were granted the right to possess and control the wages they earned after marriage, money invested in specified ways (including savings banks), and legacies of less than two hundred pounds. The Married Women's Property Act of 1882 gave a woman possession of all the property she held before and after marriage as her "separate estate." See Holcombe, *Wives and Property*.

32. Confirmation of Pierce Butler's determination to alienate Sarah and Fan Butler from their mother is in a letter written in October 1847 by Adelaide Sartoris to an unidentified correspondent: "The other day she got a letter written in secret by her eldest girl telling her that her own letters to them were suppressed by their father, who had forbidden *her* to write to her mother, while the other poor little child, who is too young to be trusted with her father's bad secrets, is allowed to write letter after letter (which letters are never sent) and getting no answer, to think that her poor-heart-broken mother has forgotten her" (quoted in Blainey, *Fanny and Adelaide*, 231).

33. Kemble, *Records of Later Life*, 3:113.

34. Ibid., 3:120.

35. The reviews from the *Spectator* and the *Examiner* are reprinted in *Littell's Living Age* 13 (1847): 471–72.

36. Butler, *A Year of Consolation*, 2:62.

37. Kemble, *Poems*, p. 265, ll. 70–73, 88–90.

38. Sartoris, *A Week in a French Country-House*, xxxvii; Ritchie, *Chapters from Some Memoirs*, 198.

39. Ritchie, *Chapters from Some Memoirs*, 199.

40. Butler, *A Year of Consolation*, 2:29.

41. Kemble, *Poems*, p. 269, ll. 47–52.

42. Fanny Kemble to Sarah Perkins Cleveland, January 16, 1847, Berg Collection, New York Public Library.

43. Kemble, *Records of Later Life*, 3:252.

44. Macready, *Journal*, 242.

45. Quoted in Pascoe, *The Dramatic List*, 210.

46. Coleman, *Fifty Years of an Actor's Life*, 2:414–16.

47. Kemble, *Records of Later Life*, 3:220.

48. Downer, "Players and Painted Stage," 522. Downer also notes that even while rebelling against the inherited conventions, Macready still relied on various "attitudes" to achieve theatrical effect: Downer quotes from a recollection in *Our Recent Actors* (1890) of Macready's performance in Byron's *Werner* as follows: "With a shrill of agony, as if mortally pierced by a dart, he bounded from his seat, and then, as if all strength had failed him, wavered and fluttered forward, so to speak, till he sank on one knee in front of the stage" (526).

49. Martin, *On Some of Shakespeare's Female Characters*, 49.

50. Kemble, *Records of Later Life*, 3:375–76.

51. William Hazlitt believed that Macready, at least early in his career, overdid details of what was termed "the domestic style of acting." Hazlitt complained that Macready indulged in commonplace gestures: "To express uneasiness and agitation, he composes his cravat, as he would in a drawing-room" (quoted in Downer, "Players and Painted Stage," 542).

52. Donohue, *Dramatic Character in the English Romantic Age*, 262–63.

53. Kemble, *Notes upon Some of Shakespeare's Plays*, 57–58.

54. Dickens, *Letters*, 5:245.

55. Kemble, *Records of Later Life*, 3:411. In this letter, Kemble goes on to say that in England "we have an extended right of suffrage, a smaller army, a cheaper government, reduced taxation, and some modification of the land tenure,—change, but no revolution."

56. Ibid., 3:259.

57. Ibid., 3:264–70.

58. Ibid., 3:317.

59. Botta, *Memoirs*, 319. In this letter, Kemble also says that the two years of labor she had "chalked out" for herself are weighing heavily upon her spirits; a holiday in Italy, she hopes, will be earned "by all that I have gone through of misery, of bitterness, of disquiet, of irksome labor and most unrecognized effort." As things turned out, Kemble did not go on holiday in Italy, or anywhere else: in the summer of 1848 she returned to Philadelphia to defend herself against Pierce's charges of desertion.

Chapter 10. Fanny's Master

Note to epigraph: Kemble, *Poems*, 60.

1. James, "Frances Anne Kemble," in *Henry James: Literary Criticism*, 1079.

2. Ibid., 1079.

3. Ibid., 1086.

4. The terrified little boy was a "little Mr. Maclean" and according to Edward FitzGerald, who related this incident to a friend, the boy was still recovering from the experience. See FitzGerald, *Letters of Edward FitzGerald*, 2:272.

5. Auerbach, *Private Theatricals*, 8.

6. Boaden, *Memoirs of Mrs. Siddons*, 66.

7. *Jezebel and Ahab, Met by Elijah* hangs in the Scarborough Art Gallery.

8. Charles Churchill, *The Rosciad* (1761), quoted in West, *The Image of the Actor*, 106.

9. Bate, *Shakespearean Constitutions*, 142–43.

10. Adam Badeau, "Mrs. Kemble," in *Actors and Actresses of Great Britain and the United States*, ed. Matthews and Hutton, 254–55.

11. Kemble, *Records of Later Life*, 3:414.

12. Ibid., 3:344.

13. Clapp, *Reminiscences of a Dramatic Critic*, 178.

14. In *Records of Later Life* (3:372), Kemble lists the following as the plays she "delivered": *King Lear, Macbeth, Cymbeline, King John, Richard II*, two parts of *Henry IV, Henry V, Richard III, Henry VIII, Coriolanus, Julius Caesar, Anthony* [*sic*] *and Cleopatra, Hamlet, Othello, Romeo and Juliet, The Merchant of Venice, The Winter's Tale, Measure for Measure, Much Ado About Nothing, As You Like It, A Midsummer Night's Dream, Merry Wives of Windsor*, and *The Tempest*.

15. Kemble, *Records of Later Life*, 3:339.

16. Ibid., 3:310.

17. Ibid., 3:410.

18. Macready, *Journal*, 249.

19. Quoted in F. Wister, *Fanny the American Kemble*, 201.

20. Fisher, *Philadelphia Perspective*, 210.

21. Gratz, *Letters*, 351–52.

22. For a transcript of the hearings, see Court of Common Pleas, Philadelphia, *Pierce Butler vs. Frances Anne Butler, Libel for Divorce with Answers and Exhibits*, Van Pelt Rare Book and Mss. Furness Collection, Library of the University of Pennsylvania, Philadelphia.

23. F. Wister, *Fanny the American Kemble*, 204.

24. Gratz, *Letters*, 356.

25. Grossberg, *Governing the Hearth*, 239.

26. Fanny Kemble to Sarah Cleveland, July 18, 1848, Berg Collection, New York Public Library.

27. In a letter written by George Dallas to Theodore Sedgwick dated June 28, 1849, Dallas notes his agreement to a clause in the final agreement between Pierce Butler and Fanny Kemble stating that it be restricted to the withdrawal of application for trial by jury. Dallas's letter suggests, therefore, that Pierce may have wanted to include other matters in the agreement and that Fanny and her lawyer wished it to be restricted to her withdrawal of the application for trial by jury. The letter is located in MSS 6987, Papers of Fanny Kemble, Special Collections, University of Virginia Library.

28. Butler, *Statement*, 91.

29. Quoted in Kahan, "Fanny Kemble Reads Shakespeare," 84.

30. F. Longfellow, *Selected Letters and Journals*, 220.

31. E. FitzGerald, *FitzGerald to His Friends*, 220. FitzGerald made this comment in December 1878, writing to a friend, Charles Merivale. Kemble first met FitzGerald when

her brother John Mitchell was at Cambridge, and they remained close and loyal friends until his death.

32. In her memoirs, writing in May 1876, Kemble recalls her friendship with Longfellow: to her, he was "one of the most amiable men I have ever known" (*Further Records*, 172).

33. Hone, *Diary*, 2:862–63.

34. Fisher, *Philadelphia Perspective*, 226–27.

35. In an undated letter to William Furness, but probably written in 1849 given the reference to New York, Kemble discusses her earnings from the time she made her debut in 1829. She notes that her sister Adelaide received a salary of £100 a week when she "came out" at Covent Garden, and that she herself had "received as much as one hundred and sixty in the provinces. For my readings, Mr. Mitchell never paid me more than eighty pounds a week when he farmed them tho' his profit on them must have been four or five times as much. When I read on my own account in New York I made five hundred pounds a week." The letter is located in the Miscellaneous Letters to and from Frances Anne Kemble, Van Pelt Rare Book and Mss. Furness Collection, Library of the University of Pennsylvania, Philadelphia.

36. Quoted in Kahan, "Fanny Kemble Reads Shakespeare," 94–95.

37. Macready, *Journal*, 260.

38. Quoted in Kahan, "Fanny Kemble Reads Shakespeare," 89. Rebecca Gratz was amazed by Fanny's ability to impersonate every character in the plays (*Letters*, 359).

39. Hawthorne, *Nathaniel Hawthorne and His Wife*, 1:362–63.

40. This passage from Melville's letter is quoted in Oliver, "Melville's Goneril and Fanny Kemble." With virtually no evidence, Oliver speculates that "the most savage caricature in all of Herman Melville's work is the briefly drawn study of Goneril in *The Confidence-Man*" (489). There is no question that Melville found Kemble, at the very least, unfeminine and that her supposedly indecorous behavior was an affront to many men (and women), but it is difficult to accept Oliver's argument since it is grounded solely in Melville's depiction of a woman who had dark hair and is physically robust and daring.

41. The newspaper cuttings from the *Cleveland Democrat*, the *Worcester Aegis*, and an unidentified Philadelphia newspaper are pasted into the back pages of a copy of the 1849 John Wiley edition of *A Year of Consolation* that I studied for this biography.

Amelia Bloomer deflated the rumors of Fanny Kemble and half the women of Lenox parading around in "coats, vests and pantaloons, and all the other paraphernalia of a gentleman's dress." Kemble was wearing nothing more radical, Bloomer asserted, "than a loose flowing dress falling a little below the knees, and loose panteletts of drawers confined to the ankle by a band or cord." Regardless of the precise nature of Kemble's dress, it scandalized various residents of Lenox and several newspapers (Bloomer, "Mrs. Kemble and Her New Costume."

42. FitzGerald, *Letters*, 2:461.

43. *International Magazine of Literature, Art, and Science* 1 (October 1, 1850): 310–11.

44. Ibid., 311.

45. See Faderman, *Surpassing the Love of Men*, 220.

46. Johnson, *American Actress*, 118. Coleman notes that Cushman's performance as Romeo was so authentically rich with "masculine proclivities" that the women in the company were shocked and the men provoked to satirical comment. See *Fifty Years of an Actor's Life*, 3:362–63.

47. Faderman notes that when Elizabeth Barrett Browning met Charlotte Cushman and one of her lovers, Matilda Hays, in Rome in 1852, she wrote "that the two women had a 'female marriage,' and that Charlotte and Matilda 'have made vows of celibacy and eternal attachment to each other—they live together, dress alike'" (*Surpassing the Love of Men*, 224). See also *Charlotte Cushman: Her Letters and Memories of Her Life*, ed. Emma Stebbins (1881).

48. Kemble, *Records of Later Life*, 3:277.

49. Lynn, *Realities*, 1:72.

50. Ibid., 1:75–76.

51. Linton, *Autobiography of Christopher Kirkland*, 2:181.

52. Ibid.

53. Linton, *Autobiography of Christopher Kirkland*, 2:182–83.

54. Kemble, *Poems* (1866), 52–54.

55. It is interesting that the *Atheneum*, in reviewing the volume of Kemble's poems published in 1844, declares, "There is a masculine strength and vigor in her verses, not a little remarkable in an age when men are proud to write effeminately . . . [the poems] are distinguished by an earnestness of purpose and energy of style." Reprinted in *Littell's Living Age* 2 (1849): 455. In her memoirs, Kemble records her belief that "all poets have a feminine element (good or bad) in them, but a feminine man is a species of being less fit, I think, than even an average woman to do battle with adverse circumstances and unfavorable situations" (*Records of Later Life*, 3:103).

56. Rogers, *Recollections*, 186.

Chapter 11. Mothers and Daughters

Note to epigraph: Fanny Kemble to Henry Lee, 1864, Harvard Theatre Collection, Harvard College Library.

1. In an undated letter to Katherine Minot included in *Fanny the American Kemble*, Kemble explains the omission from her memoirs of her pain in being separated from her daughters: "No such account of past misconduct and misery should be preserved to grieve the hearts of those who remain after us. I have so dreaded wounding my children's hearts by these painful revelations that I have effaced from the MSS of my memoirs that I made for Sarah every expression of my bitter heartsick yearning for her and her sister during my years of separation from them that when I am gone they may not grieve over my past agony" (206).

2. Kemble, *Records of Later Life*, 2:208.

3. Kemble, "On the Stage," *Notes upon Some of Shakespeare's Plays*, 9–10.

4. Kemble, *Further Records*, 312.

5. Kemble was delighted by her nephew's resemblance to his father and to his grandfather. See Kemble, *Further Records*, 225.

6. H. Greville, *Leaves from the Diary of Henry Greville*, 1:358; Ritchie, *Chapters from Some Memoirs*, 195.

7. FitzGerald, *Letters*, 2:68.

8. Ritchie, *Chapters from Some Memoirs*, 196.

9. Barrington, *The Life, Letters and Work of Frederic Leighton*, 1:184.

10. Browning, *Elizabeth Barrett Browning*, 202. In this letter, Barrett Browning relates that the "air was not quite mild enough to admit" of her going safely on the expedition.

11. James, *Henry James: Literary Criticism*, 1094.

12. Kemble, "Upon a Branch of Flowering Acacia," in *Poems* (1866), 262–64.

13. Ritchie, *Chapters from Some Memoirs*, xx–xxii.

14. This reading was witnessed by Henry Morley, who found "the great beauty of the readings" to lie in the "charm which Mrs. Kemble throws over the characters of Hermia and Helena." His praise of her interpretation of female characters provides an interesting balance to the accolades she received for her astonishing impersonations of Shakespeare's tragic and comic male figures. See Henry Morley, *Journal of a London Play-goer*, February 10, 1855, quoted in Matthews and Hutton, *Actors and Actresses of Great Britain and the United States*, 254.

15. Henry Crabb Robinson to Lady Byron, in Robinson, *Henry Crabb Robinson on Books and Their Writers*, 2:446.

16. When Kemble arrived back in America, she was also troubled by what she saw as the nation's almost suicidal deformation of the vigorous independence of mind and body that had spawned her separation from the mother country. Writing to Arthur Malkin from Syracuse where she was reading in April 1858, she recorded her distaste for an audience of seven hundred assembled schoolteachers: they were intelligent, conceited, eager-looking beings, but with sallow cheeks, large heads and foreheads, and narrow chests and shoulders. Somehow, they embodied her feelings about America: clever and conceited, aggressive and unappealing. See Kemble, *Further Records*, 321.

17. F. Wister, *Fanny the American Kemble*, 152.

18. Barrington, *The Life, Letters and Work of Frederic Leighton*, 1:264.

19. Quoted in Blainey, *Fanny and Adelaide*, 270.

20. Gratz, *Letters*, 400. It is also possible that during this difficult visit to Lenox with her mother in May 1856, Sarah Butler might have been preoccupied with a young woman named Jeannie Field Musgrove. According to Smith-Rosenberg, Sarah and Jeannie had a "deep and intimate friendship" that lasted until old age: quoting at length from their passionate correspondence, Smith-Rosenberg argues that "their affection remained unabated throughout their lives, underscored by their loneliness and their desire to be together" ("The Female World of Love and Ritual," 5).

21. Fanny Kemble to Arthur Malkin, November 29, 1857, in Kemble, *Further Records*, 319.

22. H. Greville, *Leaves from the Diary of Henry Greville*, 2:381.

23. Louisa May Alcott did not exactly meet the Prince of Wales in 1860, but she saw him "trot" over Boston Common: "A yellow-haired laddie very like his mother. Fanny W.

and I nodded and waved as he passed, and he openly winked his boyish eye at us. . . . We laughed, and thought that we had been more distinguished by the saucy wink than by a stately bow" (Alcott, *Louisa May Alcott*, 123).

24. Fisher, *Philadelphia Perspective*, 360.

25. F. Wister, "Sarah Butler's Civil War Diary," 275.

26. Fisher, *Philadelphia Perspective*, 277.

27. Doesticks [Mortimer Thomas], "What Became of the Slaves on a Georgia Plantation?" 5.

28. Ibid., 10.

29. Kemble, *Further Records*, 325.

30. H. Greville, *Leaves from the Diary of Henry Greville*, 3:265.

31. Fanny Kemble to Arthur Malkin, May 8, 1860, in Kemble, *Further Records*, 331.

32. H. Greville, *Leaves from the Diary of Henry Greville*, 3:332–33.

33. Ibid., 3:341.

34. Ibid., 3:373–74.

35. F. Wister, "Sarah Butler's Civil War Diary," 294.

36. Fisher, *Philadelphia Perspective*, 375.

37. Kemble, *Further Records*, 331.

38. Fisher, *Philadelphia Perspective*, 417.

39. H. Greville, *Leaves from the Diary of Henry Greville*, 4:40.

40. This letter to Charles Greville was appended to the first English edition of *Journal of a Residence on a Georgian Plantation in 1838–1839*, 422.

41. FitzGerald, *Letters*, 2:525.

42. In her memoirs Kemble notes that William Thackeray called the "Address" a "womanifesto" (*Further Records*, 190).

43. In response to receiving the "Address," Harriet Beecher Stowe promised to establish in America a similar committee to that which had collected the half a million signatures in Britain. The effort was unsuccessful, but following the outbreak of the Civil War, worried about the English dependence on American cotton, Stowe reminded the British of their own words condemning slavery nine years earlier. Her "Reply to the Affectionate and Christian Address of Many Thousand Women of Great Britain and Ireland to Their Sisters the Women of the United States of America" was dated November 27, 1862, and appeared in the *Atlantic Monthly*.

44. Kemble, *Journal of a Residence*, 390.

45. Fisher, *Philadelphia Perspective*, 456.

46. Ibid., 459.

47. Clinton, *Fanny Kemble's Civil Wars*, 178. Clinton's chapter on the Civil War, "Battle Cries for Freedom," provides a useful account of the different responses of Fanny Kemble and her daughters to the conflict. Equally useful is Clinton's detailed presentation of the relationship of Pierce Butler to Sarah and Fan, particularly during the war years (see the aforementioned chapter 7 and that which follows, "Lost Causes").

48. Frances Butler Leigh to Fanny Kemble, May 1, 1881, Wister Family Collection, Historical Society of Pennsylvania, Philadelphia.

49. Kemble, *Further Records*, 342.

50. Fisher, *Philadelphia Perspective*, 531.

Chapter 12. The Unfurling Sea

Note to epigraph: Fanny Kemble to Harriet St. Leger, *Further Records*, p. 287 (undated letter; almost certainly summer 1878).

1. Leigh, *Ten Years on a Georgia Plantation*, 12–13.

2. Ibid., 20.

3. Ibid., 237.

4. Kemble, *Further Records*, 52.

5. See Smith-Rosenberg, "The Female World of Love and Ritual," 4–5.

6. Kemble, *Further Records*, 1:294.

7. Barrington, *The Life, Letters and Works of Frederic Leighton*, 2:84.

8. Thomas Sully painted thirteen portraits of Fanny Kemble, three from an initial sitting that took place on March 10, 1833, shortly after Kemble's arrival in Philadelphia, and the others from memory. According to Clubbe, "Fanny obsessed Sully"; her favorite of the thirteen portraits, now hanging in the Pennsylvania Academy of Fine Arts, features her as Beatrice in *Much Ado About Nothing*. See Clubbe, *Byron, Sully, and the Power of Portraiture*, 117.

9. O. Wister, *Owen Wister Out West*, xii.

10. Ibid., 5.

11. Quoted in Payne, *Owen Wister*, 56.

12. Ibid., 56.

13. See Payne, *Owen Wister*, 57–59.

14. When Sarah Butler Wister died in 1913, S. Weir Mitchell, who had known her for many years and was a distant relation, wrote to a friend, "I have lost the brilliant kinswoman, Mrs. Sarah Wister; the gipsy Kemble cross on the Irish aristocratic Butlers created the most interesting woman I have known" (Burr, *Weir Mitchell*, 238). That the health of Sarah Butler Wister may have improved over the following years is indicated by a letter written to her by Frances Power Cobbe on May 24, 1893: Cobbe says, "It is a joy to know you are 'better than you have been for four or five years.'" Wister Family Papers, box 4, folder 1, Historical Society of Pennsylvania, Philadelphia.

15. Fisher, *Philadelphia Perspective*, 534.

16. Ibid., 535.

17. Alcott, *Louisa May Alcott*, 194–95.

18. Kemble, *Further Records*, 23.

19. Fanny Kemble to Horace Furness, January 17, 1874, Van Pelt Rare Book and Mss. Furness Collection, Library of the University of Pennsylvania, Philadelphia.

20. Kemble, *Further Records*, 113–14.

21. Ibid., 61.

22. Ibid., 12.

23. Ibid., 64.

24. Ibid.

25. Kemble, *Further Records*, 24.

26. Kemble had long intended to leave all her papers to Frances Power Cobbe and immediately on concluding her arrangements with Richard Bentley, she wrote to Cobbe, as she put it in a letter to Harriet St. Leger, "as in duty bound, as soon as I entered into this arrangement for printing any portion of the Memoir, because, before I availed myself of these Records, to stop the gap in my income, I had obtained her permission to leave all my papers to her, a charge which she had most kindly and considerately accepted, and which might have involved some trouble and responsibility" (*Further Records* 102).

27. Ibid., 121.

28. Ibid., 60.

29. Ibid., 150–51.

30. Ibid., 181.

31. Ibid., 215.

32. James, *Selected Letters*, 1:318. Some speculate that James might have been in love with Sarah Wister, but Follini persuasively argues that although Sarah may have "commanded James's respect and gratified his vanity" she never "captured his tenderness or answered his artistic needs. That role, it seems, was left to her mother" ("The Friendship of Fanny Kemble and Henry James," 234). Owen Wister, Jr.'s biographer, Darwin Payne, claims that the character of Mrs. Rushbrook in James's story "The Solution" is based on Sarah Butler Wister: the narrator of the story, a young officer in the English diplomatic corps in Rome, falls in love with Mrs. Rushbrook, a woman five years his senior, who has "chestnut hair of a shade" never seen before by the narrator, and who paints, studies Italian, and collects "the songs of the people" (*Owen Wister*, 673).

33. James, *Letters*, 2:352.

34. For example, the behavior of Fanny Kemble's brother Henry, who was engaged (unofficially) in 1842 to Mary Ann Thackeray, daughter of the provost of King's College Cambridge and not related to William Thackeray, resembles, somewhat, the behavior of Morris Townsend in *Washington Square*. Mary Thackeray's father threatened to disinherit her if she married Henry Kemble and eventually she abandoned him. Follini also notes that Kemble is credited in James's notebooks with "being the genesis of such tales as 'The Solution' and 'The Patagonia'" ("The Friendship of Fanny Kemble and Henry James," 240). The *Notebooks* also give details of a story told to James by Fanny Kemble, which she claims was told to Edward Sartoris, who, in his turn, heard it from his daughter-in-law, Nelly Grant Sartoris. It is the basis for a short story titled "Georgina's Reasons" that appeared in the *New York Sun* on August 3, 1884—the melodramatic tale of a girl in the far West who marries for love, has a child, and travels to Italy in the care of an older woman when her army officer husband fails to return home; the child is given to an Italian family, the young woman remarries, and her first husband returns. See James, *Complete Notebooks*, 26–27.

35. Fanny Kemble to Anne Thackeray Ritchie, from the Granville Hotel, Ramsgate [indecipherable date], Eton College Library.

36. Follini, "The Friendship of Fanny Kemble and Henry James," 235.

37. James, *Letters*, 2:148.

38. Kemble, *Further Records*, 137.

39. George Eliot notes in a letter dated February 27, 1878, addressed to Barbara Bodichon, that on the twentieth of that month, she and Lewes attended a "drum" at Hamilton Aidés—"at which Fanny Kemble and Lady Salisbury were the two to whom we mostly talked" (*The George Eliot Letters*, 9:219). Kemble's social connections were widespread: for example, she noted to Harriet St. Leger in 1877 that a daughter of Theodore Sedgwick was about to marry William Darwin, the son of Charles.

40. James, *Letters*, 2:241.

41. Fanny Kemble to Eliza Callahan Cleveland, February 19, 1880, Berg Collection, New York Public Library.

42. James, *Letters*, 2:233–34.

43. Ibid.

44. James, *Letters*, 2:340.

45. Ibid., 3:171. Little of James's correspondence with Kemble survives. There are fifteen letters from Kemble to James in the Houghton Library (bMS Am 1094, 288–302); they appear to be her only extant letters to James.

46. Frances Power Cobbe to Sarah Wister, March 31, 1880, Wister Family Papers, box 4, folder 6, Historical Society of Pennsylvania, Philadelphia.

47. Fanny Kemble to Horace Furness (1884?), Van Pelt Rare Book and Mss. Furness Collection, Library of the University of Pennsylvania, Philadelphia.

48. Fanny Kemble to Anne Thackeray Ritchie, August 5, 1888, Eton College Library.

49. Fanny Kemble to Anne Thackeray Ritchie, 1889, Eton College Library.

50. Kemble, *Poems*, 23.

51. Frances Cobbe to Sarah Wister, February 19, 1990, Wister Family Papers, box 4, folder 1, Historical Society of Pennsylvania, Philadelphia.

52. Ritchie, *Chapters from Some Memoirs*, 203–4.

53. James, "Frances Anne Kemble," in *Henry James: Literary Criticism*, 1076, 1096.

54. Henry James to Frances Power Cobbe, April 4, 1893, Cobbe Papers, box 1, Huntington Library.

55. James, *Selected Letters*, 213.

Bibliography

Published Works by Fanny Kemble

Kemble, Frances Anne. *Francis the First. A Tragedy in Five Acts. With Other Poetical Pieces, in Which Is Included an Original Memoir*. New York: Peabody, 1832.
Butler, Frances Anne. *The Journal of Frances Anne Butler*. 2 vols. London: John Murray, 1835.
———. *The Journal of Frances Anne Butler*. 2 vols. Philadelphia: Carey, Lea and Blanchard, 1835.
———. *The Star of Seville*. London: Saunders and Otley, 1835.
———. *Poems*. Philadelphia: John Pennington, 1844.
———. *A Year of Consolation*. 2 vols. New York: Wiley and Putnam, 1847.
Kemble, Frances Anne. *Answer of Frances Anne Butler to the Libel of Pierce Butler Praying for a Divorce*. October 9, 1848.
———. *Journal of a Residence on a Georgian Plantation in 1838–1839*. Ed. and intro. John A. Scott. Athens: University of Georgia Press, 1984. Reprint: Alfred A. Knopf, 1961 (1863).
———. *Plays*. London: Longman, Green, 1863.
———. *Poems*. London: Edward Moxon, 1866.
———. *Record of a Girlhood*. 3 vols. New York: Richard Bentley and Son, 1878.
———. *Records of Later Life*. 3 vols. London: Richard Bentley and Son, 1882.
———. *Notes upon Some of Shakespeare's Plays*. 2 vols. London: Richard Bentley, 1882.
———. *Far Away and Long Ago*. New York: Henry Holt, 1889.
———. *Further Records: 1848–1883. A Series of Letters*. 2 vols. New York: Henry Holt, 1891.
Fanny Kemble's Journals. Ed. and intro. Catherine Clinton. Cambridge: Harvard University Press, 2000.

Unpublished Material Relating to Fanny Kemble

Kemble, Fanny. Fragments from Autobiographical Mss. British Library Department of Manuscripts. Add. MS. 55048. Macmillan Archive.
Kemble, Fanny. Papers. Special Collections, University of Virginia Library, Charlottesville.
Kemble, Frances Anne. Papers. Huntington Library, San Marino, California.
Letters written by Frances Anne Kemble to Charles Sedgwick and his wife, 1848–1860. Special Collections. Columbia University Library, New York.
Miscellaneous Letters written by Frances Anne Kemble. Trinity College Library, Cambridge.
Miscellaneous Letters written by Frances Anne Kemble. Eton College Library, Windsor.

Miscellaneous Letters to and from Frances Anne Kemble. Van Pelt Rare Book and Mss. Furness Collection, Library of the University of Pennsylvania.

Letters written by Frances Anne Kemble to Sarah Perkins Cleveland. Berg Collection, New York Public Library.

Lawrence, Thomas. Correspondence. Royal Academy Library.

Original Letters of Dramatic Performers. Collected and Arranged by Charles Britiffe Smith. Garrick Club Library.

Wister Family Papers, Historical Society of Pennsylvania, Philadelphia.

Covent Garden Playbills. Special Collections, Van Pelt Rare Book Room and Mss. Furness Collection, the Library of the University of Pennsylvania.

Biographical Studies of Fanny Kemble

Armstrong, Margaret. *Fanny Kemble: A Passionate Victorian.* New York: Macmillan, 1939.

Blainey, Ann. *Fanny and Adelaide: The Lives of the Remarkable Kemble Sisters.* Chicago: Ivan R. Dee, 2001.

Bobbe, Dorothy De Bear. *Fanny Kemble.* London: Elkin Mathews and Marot, 1932.

Buckmaster, Henrietta. *Fire in the Heart.* New York: Harcourt, Brace and Company, 1948 (biographical fiction).

Clinton, Catherine. *Fanny Kemble's Civil Wars.* New York: Simon and Schuster, 2000.

Driver, Leota S. *Fanny Kemble.* Chapel Hill: University of North Carolina Press, 1933.

Furnas, J. C. *Fanny Kemble: Leading Lady of the Nineteenth-Century Stage.* New York: Dial Press, 1982.

Gibbs, Henry. *Affectionately Yours Fanny: Fanny Kemble and the Theatre.* London: Jarrolds, 1947.

Jenkins, Rebecca. *Fanny Kemble: Reluctant Celebrity.* London: Simon and Schuster, 2005.

Marshall, Dorothy. *Fanny Kemble.* London: Weidenfeld and Nicolson, 1977.

Stevenson, Janet. *The Ardent Years.* New York: Viking Press, 1960 (biographical fiction).

Wister, Fanny Kemble, ed. *Fanny, the American Kemble: Her Journals and Unpublished Letters.* Tallahassee, Fla.: South Pass Press, 1972.

Wright, Constance. *Fanny Kemble and the Lovely Land.* New York: Dodd, Mead, 1972.

Works Cited

Adams, John Quincy. *The Diary of John Quincy Adams, 1794–1845: American Diplomacy, and Political, Social, and Intellectual Life, from Washington to Polk.* Ed. Allan Nevins. New York: Frederick Unger, 1951.

Agate, James. *These Were Actors: Extracts from a Newspaper Cutting Book, 1811–1833.* Selected and annotated by James Agate. London: Hutchinson, 1943.

Alcott, Louisa May. *Louisa May Alcott: Her Life, Letters, and Journals.* Ed. Ednah D. Cheney. London: Sampson Low, Marston, Searle, and Rivington, 1889.

Altick, Richard D. *The Shows of London.* Cambridge: Harvard University Press, 1978.

Armstrong, Margaret. *Life and Letters of an American Family, 1750–1900.* New York: Harper, 1930.

Auerbach, Nina. *Private Theatricals: The Lives of the Victorians.* Cambridge: Harvard University Press, 1990.

Austen, Jane. *Mansfield Park.* London: Oxford University Press, 1970 (1814).

Baer, Marc. *Theatre and Disorder in Late Georgian London.* Oxford: Clarendon Press, 1992.

Baker, H. Barton. *The London Stage: Its History and Traditions from 1576 to 1888.* 2 vols. London: W. H. Allen, 1889.

Barbauld, Anna Laetitia Aikin. *Eighteen Hundred and Eleven: A Poem.* London: J. Johnson, 1812.

Barish, Jonas. *The Antitheatrical Prejudice.* Berkeley: University of California Press, 1981.

Barlow, John. *On Man's Power over Himself to Prevent or Control Insanity.* London: William Pickering, 1849.

Barrington, Mrs. Russell. *The Life, Letters and Work of Frederic Leighton.* 2 vols. London: George Allen, Ruskin House, 1906.

Bate, Jonathan. *Shakespearean Constitutions: Politics, Theatre, Criticism, 1730–1830.* Oxford: Clarendon Press, 1989.

Bell, Malcolm, Jr. *Major Butler's Legacy: Five Generations of a Slaveholding Family.* Athens: University of Georgia Press, 1987.

Bentley, Richard & Son. *Archives of Richard Bentley & Son, 1829–1898.* Cambridge, UK: Chadwyck Healey, 1976–77.

Bird, Isabella Lucy. *The Englishwoman in America.* Foreword and Notes by Andrew Hill Clark. Madison: University of Wisconsin Press, 1966 (1856).

Birkbeck, Morris. *Notes on a Journey in America: From the Coast of Virginia to the Territory of Illinois.* London: James Ridgway, 1818. Readex Microprint, 1966.

Bloomer, Amelia. "Mrs. Kemble and Her New Costume." *The Lily* 1 (1849). Seneca Falls, N.Y.: Committee of Ladies.

Boaden, James. *Memoirs of Mrs. Siddons, Interspersed with Anecdotes of Authors and Actors.* Philadelphia: H. C. Carey and I. Lea, and E. Littell, 1827.

Bodichon, Barbara Leigh Smith. *An American Diary, 1857–1858.* Ed. from the Manuscript by Joseph W. Reed, Jr. London: Routledge and Kegan Paul, 1972.

Booth, Alison. "From Miranda to Prospero: The Works of Fanny Kemble." *Victorian Studies* 38, no. 2 (1995): 227–54.

Boswell, James. *Boswell's London Journal, 1762–1763.* Ed. Frederick A. Pottle. New York: McGraw-Hill, 1950.

——. *Life of Johnson.* Ed. R. W. Chapman. Oxford: Oxford University Press, 1970.

Botta, Anne Lynch. *Memoirs of Anne C. L. Botta Written by Her Friends: With Selections from Her Correspondence and from Her Writings in Prose and Poetry.* Ed. Vincenzo Botta. New York: J. Selwin Tait, 1893.

Bratton, Jacky. "Working in the Margin: Women in Theatre History." *New Theatre Quarterly* 10, no. 38 (1994): 122–31.

——. *New Readings in Theatre History.* Cambridge, UK: Cambridge University Press, 2003.

Braudy, Leo. *The Frenzy of Renown: Fame and Its History.* New York: Oxford University Press, 1986.

Browning, Elizabeth Barrett. *Elizabeth Barrett Browning: Letters to Her Sister, 1846–1859.* Ed. Leonard Huxley. London: John Murray, 1931.

Browning, Elizabeth Barrett, and Robert Browning. *The Brownings' Correspondence.* Ed. Philip Kelley and Ronald Hudson. 6 vols. Winfield, Kans.: Wedgestone Press, 1984–.

Burke, Edmund. *Two Speeches on Conciliation with America and Two Letters on Irish Questions.* Intro. Henry Morley. London: George Routledge and Sons, 1886.

Burr, Anna Robeson. *Weir Mitchell: His Life and Letters.* New York: Duffield, 1929.

Burroughs, Catherine B. "'A Reasonable Woman's Desire': The Private Theatrical and Joanna Baillie's *The Tryal.*" *Texas Studies in Literature and Language* 38, nos. 3–4 (1996): 265–84.

———. "Introduction: Uncloseting Women in British Romantic Theatre." *Women in British Romantic Theatre: Drama, Performance, and Society, 1790–1840.* Cambridge, UK: Cambridge University Press, 2000.

Butler, Pierce. *Mr. Pierce Butler's Statement. Originally Prepared in Aid of His Professional Counsel. Butler vs. Butler.* Extract from the Opinion of the Court of Common Pleas, delivered by the Hon. Edward King, President Judge, January 20, 1849. Published 1850.

Byrne, Julia Clara Busk. *Gossip of the Century: Personal and Traditional Memories—Social Literary Artistic, Etc.* 2 vols. London: Ward and Downey, 1892.

Carlyle, Jane Welsh. *I Too Am Here: Selections from the Letters of Jane Welsh Carlyle.* Introduction and notes by Alan Simpson and Mary McQueen Simpson. Cambridge, UK: Cambridge University Press, 1977.

Cate, Margaret Davis. "Mistakes in Fanny Kemble's Georgia Journal." *Georgia Historical Quarterly* 44 (March 1960).

Channing, William Ellery. *The Works of William E. Channing D.D.* 2 vols. Boston: James Munroe, 1843.

Clapp, Henry Austin. *Reminiscences of a Dramatic Critic.* Boston: Houghton Mifflin, 1902.

Clark, G. Kitson. *The Making of Victorian England.* New York: Atheneum, 1971.

Clubbe, John. *Byron, Sully, and the Power of Portraiture.* Aldershot: Ashgate, 2005.

Cobbe, Frances Power. *Life of Frances Power Cobbe As Told by Herself.* With additions by the author and introduction by Blanche Atkinson. London: Swan Sonnenschein, 1904.

Cobbett, William. *A Year's Residence in the United States of America: Treating of the Face of the Country, the Climate, the Soil, the Products, the Mode of Cultivating the Land, the Prices of Land, of Labour, of Food, of Raiment; of the Expenses of Housekeeping, and of the Usual Manner of Living; of the Manners and Customs of the People; and of the Institutions of the Country, Civil, Political and Religious.* Carbondale: Southern Illinois University Press, 1964 (1819).

Cohran, Peter. "Edward John Trelawny." *Oxford Dictionary of National Biography.* Oxford: Oxford University Press, 2004–2005.

Cole, G. D. H., and Raymond Postgate. *The Common People, 1746–1946.* London: Methuen, 1961.

Coleman, John. "Fanny Kemble." *Theatre,* March 1893.

———. *Fifty Years of an Actor's Life.* 3 vols. London: Hutchinson, 1904.

Corbett, Mary Jean. *Representing Femininity: Middle-Class Subjectivity in Victorian and Edwardian Women's Autobiographies.* New York: Oxford University Press, 1992.

Courtney, Janet E. *The Adventurous Thirties: A Chapter in the Women's Movement*. London: Oxford University Press, 1933.

Cox, Jeffrey N. "Baillie, Siddons, Larpent: Gender, Power, and Politics in the Theatre of Romanticism." *Women in British Romantic Theatre: Drama, Performance, and Society, 1790–1840*. Cambridge, UK: Cambridge University Press, 2000.

Crane, David. *Lord Byron's Jackal: The Life of Edward John Trelawny*. London: Harper Collins, 1998.

Davis, Tracy C. *Actresses as Working Women: Their Social Identity in Victorian Culture*. London and New York: Routledge, 1991.

——. *The Economics of the British Stage, 1800–1914*. Cambridge, UK: Cambridge University Press, 2000.

Dickens, Charles. *The Life and Adventures of Nicholas Nickleby*. London: Oxford University Press, 1950 (1839).

——. *Martin Chuzzlewit*. London: Oxford University Press, 1951 (1844).

——. *American Notes and Pictures from Italy*. London: Oxford University Press, 1957 (1842, 1846).

——. *David Copperfield*. London: Oxford University Press, 1948 (1850).

——. *Bleak House*. London: Oxford University Press, 1948 (1853).

——. *The Letters of Charles Dickens*. Ed. Madeline House and Graham Storey. 12 vols. Oxford: Clarendon Press, 1965–.

Doesticks, Q. K. Philander [Mortimer Thomas]. "What Became of the Slaves on a Georgia Plantation? Great Auction Sale of Slaves, at Savannah, Georgia, March 2nd and 3rd 1859. A Sequel to Mrs. Kemble's Journal." *New York Tribune*, 1863. Historical Society of Pennsylvania.

Donohue, Joseph W., Jr. *Dramatic Character in the English Romantic Age*. Princeton: Princeton University Press, 1970.

Doran, F. S. A. *Annals of the English Stage from Thomas Betterton to Edmund Kean: Actors, Authors, Audiences*. 2 vols. London: Wm. H. Allen, 1864.

Downer, Alan S. "Players and Painted Stage: Nineteenth Century Acting." *PMLA* 61, no. 2 (June 1946): 522–76.

Dunlap, William. *History of the American Theatre*. New York: Burt Franklin, 1963 (1797).

Eliot, George. *The George Eliot Letters*. 9 vols. Ed. Gordon S. Haight. New Haven, Conn.: Yale University Press, 1954–1978.

Erickson, Charlotte. *Leaving England: Essays on British Emigration in the Nineteenth Century*. Ithaca: Cornell University Press, 1994.

Faderman, Lillian. *Surpassing the Love of Men: Romantic Friendship and Love Between Women from the Renaissance to the Present*. New York: William Morrow, 1981.

Fender, Stephen. *Sea Changes: British Emigration and American Literature*. Cambridge, UK: Cambridge University Press, 1992.

Ffrench, Yvonne. *Mrs. Siddons: Tragic Actress*. London: Cobden-Sanderson, 1936.

Finch, Marianne. *An Englishwoman's Experience in America*. New York: Negro Universities Press, 1969.

Fisher, Sidney George. *A Philadelphia Perspective: The Diary of Sidney George Fisher Covering the Years 1834–1871*. Ed. Nicholas B. Wainwright. Philadelphia: Historical Society of Pennsylvania, 1967.

FitzGerald, Edward. *FitzGerald to His Friends: Selected Letters of Edward FitzGerald*. Ed. Alethea Hayter. London: Scolar Press, 1979.

——. *The Letters of Edward FitzGerald*. Ed. Alfred McKinley Terhune and Annabelle Burdick Terhune. 2 vols. Princeton: Princeton University Press, 1980.

Fitzgerald, Percy. *The Kembles: An Account of the Kemble Family Including the Lives of Mrs. Siddons, and Her Brother John Philip Kemble*. 2 vols. London: Tinsley Brothers, 1871.

Follini, Tamara. "The Friendship of Fanny Kemble and Henry James." *Cambridge Quarterly* 19, no. 3 (1990): 230–42.

Foster, James. *The Married State, Its Obligations and Duties*. London: H. G. Clarke, 1844.

Fox-Genovese, Elizabeth. *Within the Plantation Household: Black and White Women of the Old South*. Chapel Hill: University of North Carolina Press, 1988.

France, Peter, and William St. Clair, eds. *Mapping Lives: The Uses of Biography*. Oxford: Oxford University Press, 2002.

The Girlhood of Queen Victoria: A Selection from Her Majesty's Diaries Between the Years 1832 and 1840. 2 vols. Ed. Viscount Esher. London: John Murray, 1912.

Gould, Warwick, and Thomas E. Staley, eds. *Writing the Lives of Writers*. Houndmills, Basingstoke: Macmillan, 1998.

Gratz, Rebecca. *The Letters of Rebecca Gratz*. Ed. and intro. David Phillipson. Philadelphia: Jewish Publication Society of America, 1929.

Greville, Charles C. F. *The Greville Memoirs: A Journal of the Reigns of King George IV and King William IV*. 3 vols. Ed. Henry Reeve. London: Longmans, Green, 1875.

Greville, Henry. *Leaves from the Diary of Henry Greville*. 4 vols. Ed. Viscountess Enfield. London: Smith Elder, 1883.

Grossberg, Michael. *Governing the Hearth: Law and the Family in Nineteenth-Century America*. Chapel Hill: University of North Carolina Press, 1985.

Hadley, Elaine. *Melodramatic Tactics: Theatricalized Dissent in the English Marketplace, 1800–1885*. Stanford: Stanford University Press, 1995.

Hall, Francis. *Travels in Canada and the United States in 1816 and 1817*. London: Longman, Hurst, Rees, Orme, and Brown, 1818.

Hallam, Arthur. *The Letters of Arthur Henry Hallam*. Ed. Jack Kolb. Columbus: Ohio State University Press, 1981.

Hamilton, Thomas. *Men and Manners in America*. Edinburgh: William Blackwood and Sons, 1843 (1833). New York: Johnson Reprint, 1968.

Hawthorne, Julian. *Nathaniel Hawthorne and His Wife*. 2 vols. New York: Houghton Mifflin, 1884.

Held Captive by Indians: Selected Narratives, 1642–1836. Ed. Richard Van Der Beets. Knoxville: University of Tennessee Press, 1973.

Highfill, Philip H., Jr., Kalman A. Burnim, and Edward A. Langhans. *A Biographical Dictionary of Actors, Actresses, Musicians, Dancers, Managers and Other Stage Personnel in London, 1660–1800*. 16 vols. Carbondale: Southern Illinois University Press, 1973–1993.

Holcombe, Lee. *Wives and Property: Reform of the Married Women's Property Law in Nineteenth-Century England.* Toronto: University of Toronto Press, 1983.

Hone, Philip. *The Diary of Philip Hone: 1828–1851.* 2 vols. Ed. Allan Nevins. New York: Dodd, Mead, 1927.

Howe, M. A. DeWolfe, ed. *The Articulate Sisters: Passages from Journals and Letters of the Daughters of President Josiah Quincy of Harvard University.* Cambridge: Harvard University Press, 1946.

Hunt, Leigh. *Autobiography: With Reminiscences of Friends and Contemporaries.* 2 vols. London: Smith, Elder, 1850.

———. *Dramatic Essays.* Ed. William Archer and Robert W. Lowe. London: W. Scott, 1894.

James, Henry. *Selected Letters of Henry James.* Ed. Leon Edel. London: Rupert Hart-Davis, 1956.

———. *The Letters of Henry James.* Vols. 2 and 3: 1875–1883. Ed. Leon Edel. London: Macmillan, 1978.

———. *Henry James: Literary Criticism; Essays on Literature, American Writers, English Writers.* New York: Library of America, 1984.

———. *The Complete Notebooks of Henry James.* Ed. Leon Edel and Lyall H. Powers. New York: Oxford University Press, 1987.

———. *Complete Stories, 1884–1891.* New York: Library of America, 1999.

Jameson, Anna. *Letters and Friendships, 1812–1860.* Ed. Mrs. Steuart Erskine. London: T. Fisher Unwin, 1915.

———. *Characteristics of Women, Moral, Poetical and Historical.* London: George Routledge and Sons, 1870.

Jelinek, Estelle C. *The Tradition of Women's Autobiography from Antiquity to the Present.* Boston: Twayne, 1986.

Johnson, Claudia. *American Actress: Perspective on the Nineteenth Century.* Chicago: Nelson-Hall, 1984.

Kahan, Gerald. "Fanny Kemble Reads Shakespeare: Her First American Tour, 1849–50." *Theatre Survey* 25, nos. 1–2 (1983):77–98.

Keach, William. "A Regency Prophecy and the End of Anna Barbauld's Career." *Studies in Romanticism* 33 (Winter 1994): 569–77.

Keats, John. *The Letters of John Keats, 1814–1821.* 2 vols. Cambridge: Harvard University Press, 1958.

Kelly, Linda. *The Kemble Era: John Philip Kemble, Sarah Siddons and the London Stage.* New York: Random House, 1980.

Kennard, Mrs. A. *Mrs. Siddons.* London: W. H. Allen, 1887.

King, R., Jr. "On the Management of the Butler Estate, and the Cultivation of the Sugar Cane; by R. King, jr. Addressed to William Washington, Esq." *Southern Agriculturalist,* December 1828. South Carolina Historical Society.

Kolb, Jack. "Arthur Hallam and Emily Tennyson." *Review of English Studies* 28, no. 109 (1977): 32–48.

Leigh, Frances Butler. *Ten Years on a Georgia Plantation Since the War.* London: Richard Bentley, 1883.

Linton, E. Lynn. *The Autobiography of Christopher Kirkland*. 3 vols. Victorian Women Writers Project: An Electronic Collection, Indiana University, 1998 (1885).

Longfellow, Fanny Appleton. *Selected Letters and Journals*. Ed. Edward Wagenknecht. New York: Longmans, Green, 1956.

Longfellow, Henry Wadsworth. *The Poetical Works of Longfellow*. London: C. Arthur Pearson, 1899.

Lynn, E. *Realities*. 3 vols. London: Saunders and Otley, 1851.

Macready, William Charles. *Macready's Reminiscences and Selections from His Diaries and Letters*. Ed. Sir Frederick Pollock. London: Harper and Sons, 1875.

——. *The Journal of William Charles Macready, 1832–1851*. Ed. J. C. Trewin. London: Longmans, Green, 1967.

Martin, Helena Faucit. *On Some of Shakespeare's Characters; Ophelia, Portia, Desdemona, Juliet, Imogen, Rosalind, Beatrice*. Edinburgh: Blackwood, 1885.

Martineau, Harriet. *Society in America*. 3 vols. London: Saunders and Otley, 1837.

——. *Autobiography*. 2 vols. London: Virago Press, 1983 (1877).

——. *Writings on Slavery and the American Civil War: Harriet Martineau*. Ed. Deborah Anna Logan. De Kalb: Northern Illinois University Press, 2002.

Mathias, Peter. *The First Industrial Nation: An Economic History of Britain, 1700–1914*. London: Methuen, 1969.

Matthews, Brander, and Laurence Hutton, eds. *Actors and Actresses of Great Britain and the United States: From the Days of David Garrick to the Present Time. Kean and Booth; and Their Contemporaries*. New York: Cassell, 1866.

Mesick, Jane Louise. *The English Traveller in America, 1785–1835*. New York: Columbia University Press, 1922.

Moore, Thomas. *The Poetical Works of Thomas Moore*. 5 vols. Leipzig: Bernhard Tauchnitz, 1841.

——. *The Journal of Thomas Moore*. Ed. Wilfred S. Dowden. 5 vols. Newark: University of Delaware Press, 1986.

Mowatt, Anna Cora. *Autobiography of an Actress, or Eight Years on the Stage*. Boston: Ticknor and Fields, 1853.

Mulvey, Christopher. *Transatlantic Manners: Social Patterns in Nineteenth-Century Anglo-American Travel Literature*. Cambridge, UK: Cambridge University Press, 1990.

Murray, Amelia. *Letters from the United States, Cuba, and Canada*. http://erc.lib.umn.edu:80/dynaweb/travel/murrlet (Letter XVII).

My Conscience! Fanny Thimble Cutler's Journal of a Residence in America Whilst Performing a Profitable Theatrical Engagement: Beating the Nonsensical Fanny Kemble Journal All Hollow. Philadelphia: Historical Society of Pennsylvania, 1835.

Nelson, Dana D., ed. *Principles and Privilege: Two Women's Lives on a Georgian Plantation: Frances A. Kemble and Frances A. Butler Leigh*. Ann Arbor: University of Michigan Press, 1995.

Odell, George. *Annals of the New York Stage*. 15 vols. New York: Columbia University Press, 1928–1949.

Oliver, Egbert S. "Melville's Goneril and Fanny Kemble." *New England Quarterly* 18, no. 4 (December 1945): 489–500.

Otto, Peter. "The Regeneration of the Body: Sex, Religion and the Sublime in James Graham's Temple of Health and Hymen." *Romanticism on the Net* 23 (2001), http://users.ox.ac.uk/~scat0385/23otto.html (accessed February 2, 2004).

Oxberry, William. *Dramatic Biography and Histrionic Anecdotes*. 6 vols. London: G. Virtue, 1825–1827.

Pascoe, Charles Eyre. *The Dramatic List: A Record of the Principal Performances of Living Actors and Actresses of the British Stage. With Criticisms from Contemporary Journals*. London: Hardwicke and Bogue, 1879.

Payne, Darwin. *Owen Wister: Chronicler of the West, Gentleman of the East*. Dallas: Southern Methodist University Press, 1985.

Poirier, Richard. *Trying It Out in America*. New York: Farrar, Straus and Giroux, 1999.

Pope-Hennessy, Una. *Three English Women in America*. London: Ernest Benn, 1929.

Porter, Roy. *London: A Social History*. Cambridge: Harvard University Press, 1998.

Postlewait, Thomas. "Autobiography and Theatre History." In *Interpreting the Theatrical Past: Essays in the Historiography of Performance*, ed. Thomas Postlewait and Bruce A. McConachie, 248–72. Iowa City: University of Iowa Press, 1989.

Puritans Among the Indians: Accounts of Captivity and Redemption, 1676–1724. Cambridge: Belknap Press of Harvard University Press, 1981.

Quarterly Review 54 (July and September 1835). London: John Murray, 1835.

Richards, Sandra. *The Rise of the English Actress*. London: Macmillan, 1993.

Ritchie, Anne Thackeray. *Chapters from Some Memoirs*. London: Macmillan, 1894.

Roberts, R. Ellis. *Samuel Rogers and His Circle*. London: Methuen, 1910.

Robinson, Henry Crabb. *Diary, Reminiscences, and Correspondence*. 2 vols. Ed. Thomas Sadler. Boston: Fields, Osgood, 1869.

——. *Henry Crabb Robinson on Books and Their Writers*. Ed. Edith J. Morley. 3 vols. London: J. M. Dent, 1938.

Rogers, Samuel. *Recollections of the Table-Talk of Samuel Rogers, to Which Is Added "Porsoniana."* New York: Appleton, 1856.

Ruskin, John. *The Genius of John Ruskin: Selections from His Writings*. Ed. John D. Rosenberg. Boston: Houghton Mifflin, 1963.

Sanders, Valerie. *The Private Lives of Victorian Women: Autobiography in Nineteenth-Century England*. Hemel Hempstead, UK: Harvester Wheatsheaf, 1989.

Sartoris, Adelaide. *A Week in a French Country-House*. Preface by Mrs. Richmond Ritchie. London: Smith Elder, 1902.

Schott, James, Jr. *Statement of July 29, 1844*. N.p, n.d.

Scott, John A. "On the Authenticity of Fanny Kemble's *Journal of a Residence on a Georgian Plantation in 1838–1839*." *Journal of Negro History* 46, no. 4 (1961): 233–42.

The Secret History of the Green Room: Containing Authentic and Entertaining Memoirs of the Actors and Actresses in the Three Theatres Royal. London: H. D. Symmonds, 1792.

Sedgwick, Catharine Maria. *The Power of Her Sympathy: The Autobiography and Journal of Catharine Maria Sedgwick*. Ed. and intro. Mary Kelley. Boston: Massachusetts Historical Society, 1993.

Sheppard, Francis. *London: A History*. Oxford: Oxford University Press, 2000.

Showalter, Elaine. *The Female Malady: Women, Madness, and English Culture, 1830–1980.* New York: Pantheon Books, 1985.

Siddons, Henry. *Practical Illustrations of Rhetorical Gesture and Action Adapted to the English Drama.* London: Richard Phillips, 1807.

Smith, Sydney. *The Letters of Sydney Smith.* Ed. Nowell C. Smith. 2 vols. Oxford: Clarendon Press, 1953.

Smith-Rosenberg, Carroll. "The Female World of Love and Ritual: Relations Between Women in Nineteenth-Century America." *Signs* 1, no. 1 (1975): 1–29.

——. *Disorderly Conduct: Visions of Gender in Victorian America.* Oxford: Oxford University Press, 1986.

Stebbins, Emma, ed. *Charlotte Cushman: Her Letters and Memories of Her Life.* Boston: Houghton Osgood, 1878.

Sumner, Charles. *The Selected Letters of Charles Sumner.* 2 vols. Ed. Beverly Wilson Palmer. Boston: Northeastern University Press, 1990.

Surtees, Virginia. *Jane Welsh Carlyle.* Salisbury: Michael Russell, 1986.

Tennyson, Alfred. *The Poems of Tennyson.* Ed. Christopher Ricks. London: Longmans, Green, 1969.

Thackeray, William Makepeace. *Vanity Fair.* Boston: Houghton Mifflin, 1963 (1848).

——. *The Letters and Private Papers of William Makepeace Thackeray.* Ed. Edgar F. Harden. New York: Garland, 1994.

Thompson, David W. "Early Actress-Readers: Mowatt, Kemble, and Cushman." In *Performance of Literature in Historical Perspectives,* ed. David W. Thompson. New York: University Press of America, 1983.

Tomalin, Claire. *Mrs. Jordan's Profession.* New York: Viking, 1994.

Trollope, Anthony. *North America.* 2 vols. London: Dawsons of Pall Mall, 1868 (1862).

——. *An Autobiography.* Harmondsworth: Penguin Books, 1993 (1883).

Trollope, Frances. *Domestic Manners of the Americans.* Ed., with a History of Mrs. Trollope's Adventures in America, by Donald Smalley. New York: Alfred A. Knopf, 1949 (1832).

——. *Domestic Manners of the Americans by Mrs. Trollope, Complete in One Volume.* London: Printed for Whittaker, Treacher, New York, reprinted for the booksellers, 1832. With "A Brief Inquiry Into the Real Name and Character of the Author of This Book, by the American Editor."

Vandenhoff, George. *Dramatic Reminiscences; or, Actors and Actresses in England and America.* London: Thomas W. Cooper, 1860.

Vicinus, Martha. *The Industrial Muse: A Study of Nineteenth-Century British Working-Class Literature.* London: Croom Helm, 1974.

Weld, Isaac. *Travels Through the States of North America.* 2 vols. Intro. Martin Roth. New York: Johnson Reprint, 1968 (1807).

West, Shearer. *The Image of the Actor: Verbal and Visual Representation in the Age of Garrick and Kemble.* London: Pinter Publishers, 1991.

Whitman, Walt. *Complete Poetry and Collected Prose.* New York: Library of America, 1892.

Williamson, Jane. *Charles Kemble: Man of the Theatre.* Lincoln: University of Nebraska Press, 1970.

Wister, Fanny Kemble. "Sarah Butler's Civil War Diary." *Pennsylvania Magazine of History and Biography* 102 (July 1978): 271–327.

Wister, Owen. *Owen Wister Out West: His Journals and Letters.* Ed. Fanny Kemble Wister. Chicago: University of Chicago Press, 1958.

Wister, Mrs. O. J., and Miss Agnes Irwin, eds. *Worthy Women of Our First Century.* Plainview, N.Y.: Essay Index Reprint Series, Books for Library Press, 1975 (1877).

Woodward, Judge, and Bishop Hopkins. *The Views of Judge Woodward and Bishop Hopkins on Negro Slavery at the South, Illustrated from the Journal of a Residence on a Georgian Plantation by Mrs. Frances Anne Kemble (late Butler).* N.p.: Judge George M. Stroud, 1863.

Wordsworth, William. *The Prelude. William Wordsworth: The Major Works.* Ed. Stephen Gill. Oxford: Oxford University Press, 2000.

Wu, Duncan. *Romanticism: An Anthology.* Oxford: Blackwell, 1994.

Index

Acknowledgments

Writing this book proved more difficult than I had anticipated. As a literary critic reasonably seasoned in the writing of books about Victorian literature and society, I imagined, foolishly, that biography merely required a switching of narrative voices, together, of course, with doing the substantial amount of long-term research that provides the meat for any respectable work of biographical investigation. Many colleagues and friends showed me where I was going wrong, and how I might get things right: they helped me discover my interpretive relationship to Fanny Kemble; they listened as I tried out various arrangements of the material; and, most important, they helped me find a fresh voice for doing a kind of writing that was new to me. Barry Qualls, to whom this book is dedicated with much affection, was the first to dissect some early chapters, alert me to uncertainties of approach and style, and agree that Fanny Kemble was the performer of her own life. I thank him for his incisive readings. Linda Bree, Kate Flint, Elaine Freedgood, Eileen Gillooly, Dan O'Hara, Helen Small, and Louise Yelin listened encouragingly and made many helpful suggestions; Sally Mitchell kindly shared with me her research on Frances Power Cobbe; and Nancy Fix Anderson steered me to Eliza Lynn Linton. I am very grateful to Rebecca Jenkins for her generosity in sharing her access to the unpublished manuscript of Robert Bernard Martin dealing with Fanny Kemble. I also thank the estate of Professor Martin for allowing me to quote from his work.

For invaluable help in archival research, I thank the following: the staff at the Rare Book and Manuscript Library, Columbia University; Daniel Traister, curator of research services at the Walter H. and Leonore Annenberg Rare Book and Manuscript Library, University of Pennsylvania; the staff in the Manuscripts and Rare Books Library, University of Virginia; the staff at the Henry W. and Albert A. Berg Collection of English and American Literature, New York Public Library; the staff at the Huntington Library; Mark Pomeroy at the Royal Academy of Arts Library; Francesca Odell at the National Portrait Gallery Library; Trinity College Library, Cambridge; Michael Meredith and Linda Fowler at the Eton College Library; Betty Beesley, Enid Foster, and Sir Donald Sinden at the Garrick Club Library; and, finally, many helpful people at the British Library. A study leave from Temple University facilitated my research, as did a grant from the Kline Foundation for research assistance.

I was fortunate to benefit from trying out ideas by giving lectures and participating in seminars: in particular, I thank the Department of English, University of New Mexico, Albuquerque; the British Women Writers' Conference held at the University of Tulsa; the Yale Center for British Art; the Department of English, University of Maryland, College Park; the Bread Loaf School of English, Santa Fe; the Department of English, University of Alabama, Tuscaloosa (especially Peter Logan); the Women's Studies Program at Auburn University; the Department of English Victorian Seminar at Keele University (particularly John Bowen and David Amigoni for their constructive questioning); the Victorian Seminar at Cambridge University organized by Heather Glenn; the Victorian Seminar at Oxford University organized by Jo McDonagh; and the Department of English at King's College, University of London (particularly Max Saunders).

Jerry Singerman has been a superb editor; I am grateful for his encouragement, efficiency, and sheer professional brilliance. Mariana Martinez did a terrific job in keeping track of all the bits and pieces that go into publication, as did the entire production staff at Penn Press. Throughout the writing of this book, my husband, John Richetti, was always willing to listen to ideas, help me clarify knotty arguments, and cheer me on. I thank him for this, and for all he has given me over our many years together.